Resources, Power, and Economic Interest Distribution in China

Based on an investigation of economic and resource allocation factors and their close relation to economic power, this book puts forward the power paradigm, a new economic research paradigm revealing the relationship among power, institutions, and resource allocation mechanisms, helping to establish a valid connection between macroeconomics and microeconomics and shedding light on real-world economic issues.

Drawing on classical, neoclassical, and institutional economics and how these schools of thought have impacted on economic development in China over the past century, the book sheds light on distribution processes and argues that enterprise contracts, market pricing, policies, laws and regulations can all be classified as interest distribution mechanisms informed by a variety of power games. The power paradigm suggests that to achieve full utility and an optimal allocation of resources to foster social welfare, power reciprocity needs to be shared among different economic agents at the same hierarchy level while making sure that power and responsibility are equivalent for each economic agent.

The book will appeal to research students and academics interested in heterodox economics, pluralist approaches, institutional economics, and game theory.

Zhang Yishan a senior professor in the Business School at Jilin University, has been engaging in the teaching and research of quantitative economics since 1980 and has fruitful achievements in the fields of distribution economics and institutional economics.

Yu Weisheng is Professor in the Business School at Jilin University. He specializes in mathematical economics, decision-making and modeling, economic game theory, and advanced operations research.

Wang Guangliang is Professor in the Business School at Jilin University. He specializes in the research of enterprise contract theory and application of game theory.

China Perspectives

The *China Perspectives* series focuses on translating and publishing works by leading Chinese scholars, writing about both global topics and China-related themes. It covers Humanities & Social Sciences, Education, Media and Psychology, as well as many interdisciplinary themes.

This is the first time any of these books have been published in English for international readers. The series aims to put forward a Chinese perspective, give insights into cutting-edge academic thinking in China, and inspire researchers globally.

To submit proposals, please contact the Taylor & Francis Publisher for China Publishing Programme, Lian Sun (Lian.Sun@informa.com)

Titles in economics partly include:

China's Economic Reform and Development during the 13th Five-Year Plan Period
Lin Gang, Wang Yiming, Ma Xiaohe, and Gao Debu

Cultural Economics
Li Yining

Technological Innovation and Economic Development in Modern Japan
Guan Quan

Resources, Power, and Economic Interest Distribution in China
Zhang Yishan, Yu Weisheng, and Wang Guangliang

Industrial Development in Modern China
A Quantitative Analysis
Guan Quan

For more information, please visit https://www.routledge.com/China-Perspectives/book-series/CPH

Resources, Power, and Economic Interest Distribution in China

Zhang Yishan, Yu Weisheng, and Wang Guangliang

LONDON AND NEW YORK

First published in English 2021
by Routledge
2 Park Square, Milton Park, Abingdon, Oxon OX14 4RN

and by Routledge
605 Third Avenue, New York, NY 10158

Routledge is an imprint of the Taylor & Francis Group, an informa business

British Library Cataloguing-in-Publication Data
A catalogue record for this book is available from the British Library

Library of Congress Cataloging-in-Publication Data
A catalog record has been requested for this book

ISBN: 978-0-367-65455-9 (hbk)
ISBN: 978-0-367-65469-6 (pbk)
ISBN: 978-1-003-12956-1 (ebk)

Typeset in Times New Roman
by codeMantra

Contents

Figures

Tables

Preface

This book, *Resources, Power, and Economic Interest Distribution in China*, has been a historical mission and focus for our research since the end of 2013. We believe that the relationships between resources, power, and the distribution of economic interests have both theoretical and practical implications.

First, and theoretically, for the four factors of economic activity—production, distribution, exchange, and consumption—we ask, what is central to economic development? Western classical economics believes that production is the most important factor. Say's Law reasons that in order to buy, a buyer must have produced something to sell, which implies that the source of demand is production. Keynesian economics states that consumption is the most important factor, and a lack of effective demand affects economic development. According to this view, the government should stimulate consumption during an economic recession. The perspective of new institutional economics places more emphasis on the role of exchange whereby transaction costs explain almost all economic problems; exchange requires the clarification of property rights, and the property rights system is the basis for economic activity. We believe that the most critical factor for economic activity is distribution because distribution determines exchange, consumption, and production. Only after distribution can property rights be clarified, and when property rights are exchanged, each party extracts what is necessary for consumption. Thus, the extent of distribution determines the extent of exchange, which, in turn, determines the extent of consumption. Whether or not the distribution of enterprises is equitable only determines the input amount of production factors although it also affects the efficiency of production factors.

How, then, are the distribution system and distribution results formed? An enterprise's contract, market prices, and government policies and regulations are all forms of interest distribution mechanisms, and any change in contract, price, or the introduction of policies and regulations are forms of interest redistribution. Looking at the institution, the essence of the institution is that of an interest distribution mechanism. Any institution is directly or indirectly related to interests. If an institution is not concerned with interest distribution, it arguably should not be considered an institution.

The formation of an interest distribution mechanism is the result of various power games. The type of interest distribution mechanism that exists will therefore be influenced by the kind of power system that exists. The power referred to here is influence and control over agents by others who are advantaged by the resources they possess, as is generally accepted in theoretical circles. Bargaining power, also termed negotiation power, is an external manifestation of influence in the negotiation process. The power of an agent in a certain game is determined by the importance, scarcity, and substitution of the resources that an agent holds; thus, the endowment of resources determines the endowment of power, which, in turn, determines the nature and structure of the institution. The fundamental reason for change in an institution is that the resource endowment structure has undergone a transformation, which has led to a major change in the power structure. The new powers require the redistribution of interests to reflect the new power structure. When the extent of this change reaches a certain level, a new institution emerges that reflects the latest distribution of interests.

Second, a general belief is that a market economy should avoid the intervention of power, but what type of power should the market avoid? Power can be categorized as political power, economic power, and social power, and political power is represented as administrative power in relevant government departments. Power is dispersed throughout society, and any organization or individual has a certain amount of power. As far as the field of economics is concerned, regardless of whether an enterprise, government, or consumer has the corresponding economic power, they wield some level of influence and control over other economic entities with the resources they have. For example, on the one hand, consumers have the power to sell labor by virtue of their physical strength and intelligence. On the other hand, consumers can choose whether to purchase certain goods and services with their income. Enterprises can use their means of production to decide what to produce and what not to produce. Similarly, the government can use tax revenues and fiscal budgets to determine the areas, objects, and quantities of their purchases and investments. It is precisely these economic powers held by economic agents that ensure that the market economy functions properly. Without economic powers, there would be no market economy. China's planned economy is an example of these mechanisms. The essence of a planned economy is the distortion and substitution of administrative power over economic power. Social power is reflected in various unofficial, non-profit social organizations, such as industry associations. Such associations are not mandatory, and whether economic entities accept and exercise such social power is entirely voluntary. Therefore, there is no need for the market to avoid the intervention of such power. From this point of view, the market should circumvent only administrative power, not all power.

Third, we ask whether the healthy and stable development of an economy requires government intervention. Market fundamentalism believes that the less a government intervenes in economic activities, the better. In a context where an economy is developing steadily, most companies would agree with this view. However, once a major economic crisis occurs, many companies will turn to the government seeking support. Of course, some scholars believe that an economic crisis is an inevitable product of economic cycle fluctuations caused by the problems of the economic structure itself. Thus, the best solution is to allow the crisis to correct itself in accordance with natural rules; otherwise, any intervention is palliative and would further worsen the crisis. Nevertheless, the companies and industries suffering through a crisis hinder economic development. Can these companies be eliminated in the long run? For example, the economic crisis that swept the world in late 2008 was caused by the US subprime mortgage crisis. Most financial institutions in the United States have problems and are unsustainable. If they are allowed to fail on their own, can the United States, or the entire world economy, afford such a failure? Whether some laws and rules of natural sciences are completely suitable for social sciences is still worthy of in-depth study.

There are three main aspects of market failure. One is externality. According to the theory of new institutional economics, as long as property rights are clearly defined and the transaction costs are less than the government regulation costs, property rights can be resolved through market transactions without government effort. But who can define property rights other than a third party, which is the government? In addition, when studying market transactions, the negotiating parties are always set up as two legal or natural persons. In fact, the majority of victims are often peripheral to the negotiating parties. Allowing the victims to form a unified opinion and speak with one voice is extremely difficult to do, and the organizational costs far exceed government regulations. The second aspect of market failure is monopoly. Theoretically, the greater the competition, the more beneficial it is to consumers and economic growth. However, all enterprises want to monopolize, and an artificially created monopoly is not controlled by the market mechanism and must be regulated by government policies and regulations. The third aspect is equity, which can be categorized as economic equity and social equity. Economic equity is equivalent exchange. When a certain factor of production is oversupplied, its reward may be less than its contribution. But the surplus is always related to ordinary labor, if the vital interests of labor are involved, can the government ignore this imbalance? The main concern of social equity is the right to subsistence and development; thus, social equity is the basic responsibility of the government. Enterprises and markets do not have responsibilities and functions in this regard. Therefore, the government's intervention in economic activities has both the objective of ensuring economic development and actively participation driven by economic benefits. Therefore, it is not a question of whether the government should intervene in economic activities, but when and to what extent.

China has accumulated substantial economic practical experience in the past 30 years from its reform and opening up, but interpretation of the reasons for its success has been mixed. Some consider China's success to be based on property rights reform while others consider it the result of competition from local governments. Some theorists credit China's success to a combination of micro-market competition and macro-central coordination. Although these views all illustrate a certain problem from a certain aspect, we believe that the essence of China's success is nothing more than decentralization and interest concessions. Taking agriculture as an example, China's economic reforms began in rural areas; that is, the household contract responsibility system was first implemented by farmers in Xiaogang Village, Anhui. This system was composed of two core directives: the decentralization of land use rights and management rights and to stay in the collective until there are sufficient resources for the country; then, the rest is your own. All gains belong to the collective has changed so that some of the benefits go to farmers under certain conditions. In summary, the system is one of decentralization and interest concessions. In practice, China's rural reforms have lifted rural populations out of poverty and provided them with much needed staples such as food and clothing. The reforms have transformed the Chinese economy from one characterized by shortage to one characterized by abundance, and have laid a solid foundation for sustainable economic advancement.

For industry and commerce, before the reform and opening up, China had factories and a retail sector but no enterprises. The essential characteristics of an enterprise are to have "independent management" and be "self-financing." In the planned economic era, what is produced and how much is produced is determined by the national plan. Thus, various means of production are allocated by the state, products are purchased and sold by the state, and factories and stores simply execute the plan. Regardless of autonomy, profit, or loss of employees, the remuneration is fixed. Initially, China's industrial and commercial reforms reflected the lessons learned from the rural reforms. These lessons influenced everything from contracting and leasing to the separation of government and enterprises, a process of decentralization and interest concessions, which gradually transformed factories and shops into self-managed and self-financing industrial and commercial enterprises. Of course, private enterprises naturally operate independently and bear their own profits and losses. Therefore, to develop the economy, the state encouraged and promoted the development of the private economy. At the same time, the state attracted foreign investors to invest in Chinese enterprises. The variety of dynamic enterprises has enabled China's economy to advance by leaps and bounds.

Finally, with respect to government, before the reform and opening up, the local governments were plan-executing agencies within the economy. Local governments had limited decision-making power over major economic issues. All income was turned over to the state, and expenditures were entirely funded by the central government. After the reform and opening up, local governments had sufficient power to promote economic development, and the development of local economy became a significant performance indicator of the cadre of local governments. In addition, through tax and fee reforms, local governments have the autonomy to collect and control local taxes and land transfer fees. It is the central government's delegating powers to local governments that provides local governments with the potential and enthusiasm for economic development, and has spurred fierce competition among local governments in terms of investment promotion, product promotion, and project application, resulting in the rapid development of China's economy.

Recalling the phenomenon of "Shenzhen Speed," how did Shenzhen speed come about? In the early stage of construction in Shenzhen, to level the land, the earth and rocks on the hills had to be transported to low-lying land. Many earth-moving trucks were sent creating snake-like truck transportation; but the snake was frozen. Regardless of how many cars and stones were pulled, the driver's income remained constant, so drivers had little incentive to visit the dusty environment loading soil and stones and they sat in the road instead. To complete the project on time, the construction headquarters was forced to adopt a method of compensating drivers per load of soil. With this new motivation, the transportation snake soon descended into chaos. However, the matter was reported to the central government who took control. Ultimately, Shenzhen actually profited because the central government was granted Shenzhen Special Administrative Region the power of special affairs, and the essence of this power was to link contributions to interests. Therefore, "Shenzhen Speed" was partly a result of decentralization and interest concessions.

While the significant achievements of China's reform and opening-up over the past 30 years are the result of decentralization and interest concessions, the current imbalance in the distribution of interests reveals that this decentralization has been inadequate, and this restricts the further rapid and healthy development of China's economy. This situation is reflected in three aspects. First, urban citizens and rural residents have unequal rights. As citizens of the People's Republic of China, farmers do not enjoy the same rights to education, free migration, and social security. Additionally, the means of production–that is, land–is expropriated without their consent under the contract period, but most of the transfer fees for use rights fall directly or indirectly into the hands of the government and developers at the same time. The large rural population and low average incomes have caused insufficient domestic demand, making exports the main force driving China's economic growth. Second, there is inequality among groups and civilians. Some unscrupulous businessmen and corrupt cadres have combined to form interest groups. These interest groups control a large amount of social wealth and have substantial influence over government decision making. Introducing policies and regulations that are conducive to improving people's livelihoods, curbing corruption, and preventing excessive profits is difficult. As a result, the civilian class failed to improve its income and welfare and has almost no voice. The Chinese People's Political Consultative Conference (CPPCC) and People's Congress at all levels, who originally intended to provide a platform for civilians to participate in politics and discussions, are barely visible. The power imbalance between interest groups and the civilian class, and the resulting imbalance in interests, are the main hindrances to reform, opening up, and economic development, widening the gap between the rich and the poor and undermining stability and unity. Third, there is inequality among large monopoly enterprises and small and medium-sized private enterprises (SMEs). Large enterprises, particularly large state-owned enterprises, rely on preferential access to public power and public resources to conduct overt or covert monopoly operations. However, SMEs do not enjoy the same treatment in terms of market access and resource acquisition, which makes it difficult for them to compete. SMEs are the main driver of economic development and employment. Therefore, if the rights imbalance between large monopoly enterprises and SMEs cannot be effectively solved, China's economic restructuring and growth in private wealth will suffer.

In summary, we believe that the fundamental purpose of economic activities is to pursue the maximization of interests, both material and spiritual. Because of the collective nature of economic activities, interests must be obtained through distribution. The formation of interest distribution mechanisms is the outcome of various power games. The pattern of power determines the pattern of distribution. The distribution system and the power system are isomorphic. The power structure is determined by the importance, scarcity, and substitutability of resources controlled by economic agents. To achieve optimal allocation and full utilization of resources so that social interests and welfare can be optimized, it is necessary to ensure power equivalence among different economic agents at the same hierarchy level. At the same time, power and responsibility must be symmetric for the same economic agent.

The completion of this book is the result of the joint efforts of our academic team. I am only a provider of ideas, a team organizer, and a participant in the work. In the research process, although we referenced academic literature worldwide, the basic ideas and theoretical framework described in this book are unique. Therefore, it is inevitable that there are inadequate considerations, omissions, and even errors. Readers are kindly requested to offer their criticisms and correction.

Professor Zhang, Jilin University Center for
Quantitative Economics Research

1   Introduction

Power plays a critical role in social economic development, and the subject of power is increasingly garnering the attention of society. In China, for the past century, economic change and development has reflected as structural change and economic and political power games. Economic development is a process of continuous adjustment and improvement in various powers, for power relations play a central role.

China's development from primitive capitalism to industrial capitalism during the late Qing Dynasty was believed hindered largely by underdeveloped science and technology and backward political institutions. In fact, the fundamental reason for the hindrance was the monopoly of the dynasty's imperial power. Politically, China's Qing Dynasty abolished the institutions conducive to the development of a decentralized system, which constricted the creativity of local authorities and people. Economically, the government monopolized all large-scale organized activities including the production of salt, iron, and matches. Free enterprise did not exist. The Westernization Movement during Qing Dynasty was characterized by government monopoly over big industries. The industries were partly business and partly government. Such a centralized feudal bureaucratic system impeded the emergence of industrial and commercial capitalists. Because bureaucrats controlled every aspect of society, there was no legal room for private activities. Any economic activity was surrendered to imperial powers and to bureaucratic control and pressure. It was impossible to have a fair and sound market order or to establish private firms. When state power sought the interests of the privileged class, and consequently, damaged public interests, China inevitably experienced economic stagnation.

In the period of the Republic of China, the economy was alternately controlled by military forces and foreign powers. On the one hand, warlord scuffles, anti-Japanese wars, civil wars, and social unrest frequently occurred. On the other hand, foreign concessions and privileges continued to infiltrate. In cities, only a few industrial firms had backward technology. Moreover, most were controlled by either the four most influential Chinese families or foreign capital. Therefore, the working class was enslaved by foreign and comprador capital. Even the national bourgeoisie did not obtain political and economic power and were pushed aside forced to live dependently on others. In rural areas, landlords and rich peasants, who accounted for less than 10% of the population, possessed over 90% of production materials and land. This wealth brought economic and political power to exploit and oppress the peasants. Moreover, foreign invaders plundered and pillaged. Chinese peasants lived in extreme poverty, suffering from hunger and cold for a long time. When there was no way to ensure rights to subsistence for the masses, the only solution was dictatorship of the proletariat and equal distribution of land through armed uprisings to seize economic and political power.

After the establishment of the People's Republic of China in 1949, land reforms expropriated the land of landlords and rich peasants through forceful political power, and the land was distributed to peasants. Due to natural resource shortages, such reforms gave most Chinese farmers the right to subsistence and development and resolved the power imbalance to some extent. Therefore, productive forces were liberated and the agricultural economy advanced. For urban industries, the new government confiscated comprador and foreign capital and emancipated national capital in the early days of the People's Republic of China, which gave all economic agents relatively equal economic power. As a result, every social class was highly motivated, and the industrial economy advanced rapidly. With agriculture and industry development, people's lives improved, as the most basic needs of the people were met. Unfortunately, the socialist transformation of capitalist industry and commerce around 1954, the Great Leap Forward Movement in 1958, and the People's Commune Movement in 1960 rendered all production materials publicly owned, including land, which led to highly centralized economic power and, consequently, a planned economy emerged. The planned economy allowed administrative power to penetrate every aspect of society from production, distribution, exchange, and consumption to politics and culture. Such distortion and expansion of administrative power caused consecutive political movements. These movements culminated in the Great Cultural Revolution and deeply affected Chinese economic development.

Chinese economic reform after 1978 was a complex process of power decentralization instituted by the central government. The reform was a process that comprehensively redefined the frontier of each power and cultivated market entities. Reforms returned power to individuals and firms by rearranging power structures to realize the economic incentives of micro-agents. On the one hand, China's gradual reform is a process of defining economic power that increases in complexity as it progresses. The structural changes in the process can be categorized into four phases.

The first stage is to define the right to use a product, the right to benefit, and the right to use labor and land. Such definitions significantly improved efficiency in production and exchange. The improvements were reflected in the household contract responsibility system in rural areas, the state-owned enterprise contracting system in urban areas, and the emergence of privately or individually owned business in the early 1980s. In the second phase, the right to transfer products and labor and the right to benefit from labor were defined. The rights were demonstrated in the transformation of state factories and shops into state-owned enterprises and in the separation of ownership from management. Meanwhile, private enterprises and township and village enterprises emerged and grew. The third phase defined financial assets and land transfer rights evidenced by the establishment of stock markets and the emergence of real estate business in coastal areas. The fourth phase defined ownership and recognized personal and corporate property rights. Particularly, the recognition of private property in the Constitution made the distribution of such rights more in accordance with the requirements of market orientation. As proof, the scope of state ownership reduced and its weight decreased. Moreover, the private sector became the main driver of economic growth. On the other hand, China's regional separation of power was consolidated by institutionalizing the financial relationship between the central and local governments. In the process of reform, the central government decentralized different administrative power among regions. In the 1980s, there were four Economic Special Zones. Then, 14 coastal open cities were established under direct planning by the state, municipalities with independent planning status under the national social and economic development, the development of the Pudong area, the development of the western region in China, the revitalization of the northeast regions, and the rise of the central China followed. Each round of power decentralization to local authorities motivated local development and provided experience and a driving force for the next round of reforms.

However, the power decentralization was excessively slow for rural reforms, and the peasant masses did not obtain the power they deserved. In the late 1970s, land use right in rural areas was assigned to the peasants. From 1984, they were allowed to transfer such rights partly. Such early form of household contract responsibility system did result in remarkable improvements in agricultural productivity, but the inchoate process of power decentralization and balancing reached a standoff in 1985. The focus shifted to city and industrial reforms, which rendered the newly improved countryside largely forgotten. The unreasonable power structure in the rural areas is reflected in the following aspects.

First, there is an absence of land ownership. The People's Commune Movement caused peasants to lose land ownership and the right to use it because governments could commandeer the land at any time in the name of public interest. Without long-term ownership of land and land use right, there is no incentive to build farmland capital construction. Therefore, agriculture lacks long-term, steady, and rapid development. Second, there is no right to education, and peasants have no access to higher education and vocational training. Even the nine-year compulsory education is not ensured. Without education, how can the rural population find opportunities for employment? How can they improve labor productivity and escape poverty? Third, the right to social security is also absent. Due to policy reasons, peasants face a range of discrimination. The rural population is deprived of a minimum wage, medical insurance, unemployment compensation, and living allowances including the cooperative medical service and free education that they were entitled to before the reforms. Fourth, the free migration right is absent. Although peasants are common civilians, they cannot relocate to cities to work, live, and study on an equal basis due to the household registration system. Of course, they are unable to enjoy the fruits of Economic Reform and Open Up and the opportunities of development. Fifth, the right to free speech is denied to peasants. Peasants are the most disadvantaged group among all of China's social classes. Because it is geographically scattered, the rural population lacks organization and knowledge concerning rights protection. It is safe to say that a lack of power is the root cause of the long-standing problems besetting China's agriculture sector, its rural areas, and its farmers. Therefore, the solution is to award peasants the same power as other social classes.

This context explains our motivation to investigate power and its effect on economic and social development, particularly with respect to resource allocation and the distribution of interests. Power has become a widespread social phenomenon since interpersonal dominance behavior emerged in civilized society. Power relationships exist among individuals, between individuals and groups, and between groups and other groups. Thus, the power relationship can be considered an objective need and the basis of the survival and development of society. Without certain power to maintain, adjust, or develop the basic order of society, society will collapse. Hence, society is a power entity composed of various power networks. Power is narrowly defined as political power, the control given to an individual over other individuals by a specific organization, and the broad definition of power refers to the ability of an individual or social group to influence the behavior of others from their own perspective. The definition of power in this book, as generally recognized by theoretical circles, is the influence and control of a behavioral subject on other subjects based on the resources owned by the controlling agent. Bargaining power, or negotiating power, is an external manifestation of power in the negotiation process. The power of the behavioral subject in a certain game is determined by the importance, scarcity, and substitutability of the resources it controls. "Right" is different from "power." "Right," a term we use in this book, as Coase notes, is the entrepreneur's authority to manage and conduct the allocation of resources. To some extent, it is the equivalent of the power of control, or property rights (Coase, 1995).

Research questions

The essence of neoclassical economics is a free market competition mechanism that yields prices whose fluctuations provide signals between demand and supply. According to these signals, the distribution of social wealth and the allocation of social resources readjust. In this process, commodity prices are determined by the market as are wages, interests, and land rents. There is no room for power in this economic process; power of all types subdues non-personified market effects. All decisions are the response to market orders. The limitation of neoclassical economics lies in its excessively idealistic presumptions and conclusions.

After Keynes, the neoclassical synthesis incorporates social economic reality. However, there is irreconcilable contradiction between market clearing and unemployment under this framework. Macroeconomics pays attention only to aggregate demand adjustment, while microeconomics is only concerned with the emergence of costs and prices. Macroeconomics and microeconomics are not necessarily connected, leading to a lack of individual rational choice based on macroeconomics, while microeconomics cannot explain macroscopic reality sufficiently. One cause of this phenomenon is an overemphasis on the formalization of economic theories. From Ricardo's abstract deduction (1891) to Marshall's economic modeling (1961), when economics became a science, the curse of formalism was entrenched. As neoclassical studies highlight the pure economic factors of social phenomena in the models, the relationship between individuals transforms into relationships between individuals and things, even between one thing and another thing, based on the rational choice of economic subjects in a market environment. The economic agent was completely materialized; there is no difference in labor, but the subjective initiative is ignored. As a result, economics has lost its vigor and become blackboard economics.

The formalization of economics has another deleterious consequence; economic research is completely separate from politics. Since Keynes, government intervention in the economy has always been the center of the argument. Neoclassical economics believes that the market mechanism will automatically lead to optimization of resource allocation, and government intervention will only bring deadweight loss to the economic system since the government has no better information than the market. The opposite opinion is that the economy cannot reach optimal levels through market mechanisms; even if it does have such capability, the adjustment will be long and painful. In fact, economy and politics were not initially separated, and economics was born out of politics. The purpose of classical economics is to formulate relative national policies based on economic research results to promote social development, which is the logical order according to old institutional economics. Galbraith (1992), the institutional economist, states that the attempt to separate the economy from politics and political intentions is completely meaningless; it obscures true economic power and its intention. This attempt to separate the two is also the main reason for economic decision errors and misjudgment. Pure economic theory that does not integrate the political environment and institutions will inevitably ignore the effects of political intentions on the economy. Such ignorance usually has serious consequences. In fact, there is no economic process that leaves behind the socio-political system or a pure political process that does not pursue benefits. The economy and politics are always co-mingled, and the relationship between them is not as simple as one of influencer and the influenced. Economic theories can provide politics with a decision framework, but they also do more. Government procurement and investment are economic acts in themselves. The government does not have to be the third party in the process of institutional change. Friedman (2009) believes that the economy and politics cannot be separated, and the political arrangement cannot be integrated with the economic arrangement all the time. Friedman argues that there are limited ways to integrate the economy with political arrangements.

Unlike neoclassical economics, new institutional economics emerges from the concept of the market mechanism and believes that transaction costs exist in the market. Therefore, there are other organization forms, such as firms that complete transactions, which completed the transformation by studying the relations between individuals and things with the relations between individuals. The starting point is Coase's attempts to open the black box—firms. In his research, Coase raises the significance level of firms to that of the market and no longer treats firms as simply the supply side of products or the demand side of market production factors (Coase, 1995). We are still unable to define the nature of the firm because economists have not reached a consensus on this subject, transaction costs, or the relations between firms and markets after Coase.

Alchian and Demsets (1972) believe that the market is more universal than firms as firms are nothing but a complex set of market contracts. Production technology may require team production in some sense; however, for such a production process, the residual claims of firms can solve the monitoring and pricing problems of different production factors. Unlike the theory espoused in these studies, Williamson (1975) regards the hierarchy as the main feature that differentiates firms from the market and notes that it is obvious that the employment relationship differs from the equal transaction relationship in the market. The hierarchy weakens opportunism through an authority relationship. In other words, due to high market transaction costs, the firm mechanism can replace the market mechanism to solve resource allocation problems.

Later, Grossman and Hart (1986) suggested the residual control model based on Williamson's work. One of the core viewpoints of both principal-agent theory and corporate governance theory is that operators possess residual control and private information after ownership and management rights are separated. Therefore, principals must select or design optimal contracts to overcome the agency problem. The principle of contract design and selection is that the arrangement of corporate power should unify residual claims and control (Grossman & Hart, 1986). Still, the reality is less ideal than people expect. In modern firms, residual control belongs to managers or human capital. Residual claims not only include the contribution of production factors but also risk. Human capital obtains residual control but cannot fully bear the risks. When operation losses threaten firms, those losses can only be made up by material capital even though human capital also bears the risk of future income loss. However, firm residuals cannot be naturally divided into two categories; that is, residuals for material assets that bear risks and those that correspond to residual control. It is safe to say that it is never possible for modern firms to have residual control unified with residual claims on a certain production factor. The reason for this lies in the concepts of residual claims and control. The concepts developed through a comparison of traditional and modern corporate systems can explain the evolution of corporate systems although they cannot solve the problems faced by modern firms.

In fact, although new institutional economics has begun to pay attention to the cooperation for mutual interests and the distribution process as economic subjects, the theory has indirectly explained the relationship between people through the relationship between people and things (Property right system and Corporate system). When institutions become the research object and, hence, endogenized, a more fundamental institutional system is required because only under this framework can the choice constraint be spelled out for economic agents. The secondary institutional change depends on the institutional environment, and fundamental institutional change is attributed to ideology and morale (North, 1990). New institutional economics only recognizes the importance of both institutions and their innovations in social economic development and has not satisfactorily answered the questions of how institutions originate and how they change.

The theory of institutional economics represented by Commons suggests that the determinant of resource allocation is not the market but the power structure under social institutions (Commons, 1934). Galbraith (1983) even states that economics is meaningless and unrealistic if the role of power is not considered. He notes that the economic behavior of modern individuals should be described as the pursuit of wealth as well as the pursuit of power. Consequently, economic theories that ignore social institutional structure cannot explain the reality of capitalism. According to different means of power operation, Galbraith (1983) classified three types of power: condign power, compensatory power, and conditioned power. The corresponding[1] sources of power are personality, property, and organizations. In modern industrial society, organization, adjustment, and control are the main sources and means of exercising power. The allocation of resources, to a great extent, depends on a producer's power that stems from the possession of production means.

In this respect, Galbraith and Marx have similar views. According to Marx (1911), there is never pure economics nor pure political science; the allocation of resources can only be carried out under given power relationships, and the basis of this power can be summarized as a means of production. Another similarity between Galbraith and Marx is that they both adopted the method of contradiction analysis instead of equilibrium analysis.

Marx (1911) claims that the contradiction and conflicts between productive forces and relations of production promote social development. Galbraith (1983) considers that the power imbalance between a planned economy and a market system thwarts a capitalistic society.

Both Galbraith and Marx conduct power analysis based on class, which is one of the main reasons they are not accepted by mainstream economics. Studies on the concept of power are limited to a narrow and specific scope, and their implications and significance have not been recognized practically (Acemoglu & Robinson, 2000, 2001; Palermo, 2000; Young, 2000). The situation has changed fundamentally only recently. Acemoglu[2] (2005) believes that economic institutions are affected by other factors, such as political power, and depicts a complete framework of economic institutional change within which the major factor for institutional choice is the power possessed by every group involved. The source of such power comes from the form of political power as well as the actual political power. The former is endowed by political systems, and the latter is the power that can affect political decisions derived from economic resource distribution, essentially, economic power. The form of political power and actual economic power in the current period determine the political systems in the next period while the political systems determine the allocation of resources in the next period of economic development. This theory clearly notes that power plays a critical role in institutional change. It is the distribution of power that determines economic institutions, resource allocation, and economic growth.

Ren (2000) suggests the concept of power economics. He argues that western economics is reflected by the privately owned economic system and market competition, but the basis for the survival of western economics was destroyed by China's unitary system of property rights and imperial ownership. Therefore, western economics cannot explain such a special economic institution. Ren believes that the analytical framework of power economics might help and hopes to establish an economic theory that is entirely different from western economics under the premise of a unitary property rights system and capable of explaining the history and reality in China. What Ren expounds is merely an economic explanation of power rather than a power theory of economics. This book argues that power plays the determining role for the existence of and change in institutions. Only when the significance of power is again recognized in social affairs can history be explained correctly (Russell, 2004).

Economic research is concerned with the interest relations among people. Whether a concept discusses market competition or transaction cost, such concepts cannot fully capture the relations. However, this is not the case with the concept of power. Power relations are mutual, and the exercise and realization of power depends on the choice of objects by power. The concepts of contracts, property rights, and institutions describe the interest relations between people, but they assume the existence of priori-super rationality or mandatory regimes, which weakens the explanatory ability of the concepts. Particularly, these concepts cannot explain where the institutions come from and how institutions change. Based on the above ideas, we suggest a power paradigm of economic studies based on a re-thinking of both the neoclassical and old as well as new institutional economics. The paradigm is defined as an analysis of some problems according to a certain type of logic under certain assumptions and premises. The power paradigm of economic studies re-expounds economics from the perspective of power to provide a complete framework for studying economic reality. Such a paradigm reveals, in depth, the essential elements of economic activities and solves problems naturally, such as the fracture between macroeconomics and microeconomics and the relationship between economics and politics.

The power paradigm presented in this book focuses on the study of the concept of power and analyzes it in the context of three power games: the market, firms, and government. Such an analysis reveals the relations among power, institutions, and resource allocation mechanisms.

Exploration of the research questions

Human economic activities are expressed mainly through material changes that occur as a result of production, distribution, exchange, and consumption. These changes are not the same as natural or seasonal material transformations such as spring blossoms or an autumn harvest. Human economic activities are artificial and collective. A purely personal activity, even if productive, is only a survival activity and not an economic activity. The fundamental objective of economic activities is to maximize interests. For each individual, this idea can be expressed as utility maximization. For firms, maximizing interests implies maximizing profits while, for governments, interest maximization implies maximizing social welfare. Under the premise that each economic agent seeks an individual's own interests, the group and social nature of economic activities manifests as interest distribution among people. Such distribution includes the division of production cooperation, distribution of cooperative income, and transactions between economic agents. Distribution is the most important of the four factors of economic activities: production, distribution, exchange, and consumption. Distribution determines exchange, consumption, and production. For a firm, whether distribution is reasonable will affect the inputs of every production factor and fully display their efficiency. Therefore, the equity of interest distribution is the necessary condition for maximizing interests. Distribution plays a central role in economic activities whereby it determines whether the related activities can be conducted and affects the outcomes. Among economic agents, the structure of interest distribution relies on the structure of power. Following is a discussion on the formation of distribution systems and methods from three aspects: firms, the market, and government.

Firms

According to interpretations of new institutional economics, a firm is an economic organization composed of a series of contracts. A firm offers a way to transact that is characterized by collaborative production and common benefit. Consequently, business contracts represent the interest distribution structure for various production factors. All types of contracts are directly or indirectly related to interests; if a contract is not concerned with interests, it arguably should not be considered a contract. Moreover, the formation of enterprise contracts is the result of long-term games among all factors. The bargaining chips include the demand-supply relation in factor markets, the specific properties of each factor, and the significance of factors in terms of collaborative production. During contract negotiation, individuals who control scarce resources have market influence and power. Thus, these individuals dominate negotiations and ultimately benefit from the terms of the contract. Since the contest among factors determines the distribution and ownership of residual claims and control, for the non-Pareto state, there always exists the situation where one side initiates adjustments to the contract to further their interests. All parties have no consensus about the decision-making rights that are ambiguous or not addressed; thus, the parties engage in continuous negotiations for their own interests. Improper control and claim allocations are adjusted until the structure of power matches that of the interests. Of course, there are no absolute criteria for what is reasonable. The process is reasonable so long as every agent participating in the economic activity accepts it, and the accepted production relation and distribution structure becomes institutional. If the power structure changes between factors, new institutions will replace the old, and the interest distribution structure will change accordingly. That is, because the change in the power structure of the production factors requires corresponding adjustment in the interest distribution structure, the enterprise contract will change, and the driving force behind the contract change comes from the change in the power structure. The latest development in modern corporate theories emphasizes the idea that firms are not only a combination of contracts of free transactions but also a set of power relations (Cui, 2004).

The market

Traditional market economic theory states that price, the invisible hand, adjusts all economic activities continuously, which eventually optimally allocates resources. Price itself reflects one type of interest distribution relation. What determines such distribution, or, effectively, the equilibrium price? Some consider the answer to be the demand-supply relationship of goods. However, is this really so? In a perfect monopolistic market, the demand-supply relationship is only a tool to calculate the possible relative quantities of demand at different price levels. The price depends on the level that will embody the company's strategic goals or maximize firm values. Therefore, in such a market structure, price is not determined by demand-supply relations but by monopolistic power over the market, which is the economic power that an entity possesses. In an oligopolistic market, price is not determined by the demand-supply relationship either. All tangible and intangible strategic alliances and price agreements, such as Cartels or Konzern, are the result of games between oligopolists using their economic power. The greater the control over the market, the more likely the oligopolists are to set favorable prices. In a monopolistic-competitive market, the reason that firms strive to weed out old and bring in new products and technologies is to gain a monopoly over a certain function of similar goods through product differentiation and then win initiatives in pricing so that profits or values are maximized. Therefore, in a monopolistic competitive market, it is not supply and demand that determines prices, it is manufacturer's control over certain functional characteristics of goods. In a perfect competitive market, due to the quantity of demand and supply between individual buyers and sellers only account for a small part of the market share. Particularly, all commodities of similar products have no difference in quality, and each individual firm can only be the market price taker without any control over the price. Only in this case can price be determined by the market demand-supply relation. This does not mean that the economic power of agents has no role in setting prices, only that the influence of their power is reciprocal.

Market mechanisms are not merely the equilibrium between demand and supply. Market mechanisms embody the relationship of interest distribution either on the demand or supply side or between the two sides regarding the transaction surplus. Changes in market price are the focus of both demand and supply in the fight for interests, which represent the contest of power. Power is determined by whether the maximum amount of obedience can be obtained at minimum cost. If buyers have strong demand but no alternatives, firms can obtain more obedience at minimal cost, which, in turn, controls consumers. Market competition eases the expansion of firm's power, and consumers resist this power by establishing cooperatives or purchasing associations. If the initial state between producers and consumers is given; that is, either consumer's information is passed on to producers through price, or producers induce consumers through commercial advertisements, the interest distribution structure between demand and supply—price—will be determined to a large extent by the struggle for consumers among producers. Contests between firms are everywhere—price wars, brand wars, function and technology innovations, management and production efficiencies, negotiations for alliances, and breakdowns in negotiations. The strength of an enterprise in the market relative to other enterprises depends on economic power; it is not the case that the relationship between supply and demand determines an enterprise's market share and return. The power relation is the most obvious in oligopolistic markets. Any oligopolist's action will result in another's reaction. The inter-dependence of oligopolists' strategies is the interactive relation between oligopolists. Such relations determine the structure of market share. It must be true that market distribution structure conforms with the power structure among oligopolists; otherwise, agreements would not be implemented. Even in a monopolistic industry, firms must expend some rents to contest against potential rivals. Such rents include costs to maintain advanced technology, patents on innovation, and rents to persuade government to support monopolistic behavior and to accept or consent tacitly to the monopolistic price. The aim of such expenditures is to maintain monopolistic position and to prevent new firms from entering the market. Of course, monopolist power is reflected in the monopolist's complete control over the industry and forced acceptance by consumers and workers. Marx (1911) once predicted that human labor would not generate fortunes in a direct way after technology is extensively applied to production; therefore, the function of working time is no longer a measurement of the values of fortune. Since there is no single objective criterion to measure the contributions of production factors, naturally, prices, wages, and interest rates lose the objective of market fairness and become the outcome of power relations. Therefore, the market is not really operated by price, the invisible hand, but by power, a hand sometimes visible or invisible. Full competition can control economic power although any economic agent hopes to restrict or avoid competition.

Government

The main economic function of government is to achieve social equity and maximize social welfare through a series of fiscal and financial policies and the implementation of related legislations and regulations, which is also the redistribution of interests. How are such policies and rules made? For example, what categories of taxes should be designed; what tax rates should be set; on whom are the limited fiscal revenues to be spent; and how much should be spent? Such questions are resolved directly by administrative power. However, the decision-making process should consider ways to help maximize social wealth and welfare, how economic entities will react, and the actions they might take. It is clear that the outcome results from games between the administrative and economic powers. As another example, anti-trust and pollution prevention laws are made by government to respond to market failure, the essence of which is an economic power that is out of control. To prevent the power from losing control, government intervention and coercion is necessary. However, it is inevitable that government adjustment and control will be influenced by different interest groups. This influence allows advantaged groups, who possess strong economic and political power due to substantial public resources, to influence government decisions directly and indirectly and make policies and regulations that benefit their own interests. In contrast, disadvantaged groups under long-term containment do not have representatives to fight for their interests in law making, regulation, and policy creation. It is a general belief that the process toward market-orientation and liberalization will bring improvements in efficiency and economic development while administrative regulatory behavior mitigates the distribution disparity among different income levels. These two dynamics are complementary. However, market liberalization does not necessarily promote economic development. On the other hand, centralized monopoly of power may result in unequal income distribution. Both administrative regulation and market competition are institutional forms of production and the distribution of social wealth. In the economic transition process, individuals reject market penalties and often resort to government for protection. Government is more willing to act as the savior. Consequently, government monopoly in institutional design is increasingly common. It is necessary for the rulers and the ruled to reach agreement on power and responsibility or agreement of rights and obligations. Such contracts stipulate what the government must do and the power to which it is entitled. In the meantime, it is more important to stipulate what government must not do and what rights cannot be taken away from the ruled. Such contract arrangements define constitutionalism. Under constitutional principles, unconditional power is illegitimate. People have the right to effectively restrain and supervise power.

To summarize, because economic activities are collective, interests are obtained through distribution. The emergence of interest distribution mechanisms is, in turn, the result of power games. The distribution and the power systems are identical, and the pattern of power determines the pattern of distribution while the power structure is determined by the scarcity, importance, and substitutability of resources that economic agents control. To attain full utilization and optimal resource allocation to maximize social interests and welfare, it is fundamental to realize power reciprocity among different economic agents at the same hierarchy level and the ensure symmetry between power and responsibility for the same economic agent.

Traditional economic theory has sufficiently shown that perfect competition is the ideal state for realizing optimal allocation of resources even though it is not realistic. The essence of a perfect competitive market is power equality among economic agents, which means each individual economic agent has no dominant role in market transactions. Keynesian theory has illustrated that the necessary and sufficient condition for full employment and full utilization of resources is that goods markets, labor markets, and monetary markets are simultaneously in equilibrium. The essence of such equilibrium is that the overall influence and effects are equal for all input factors. Once the control and influence power of an economic agent or a group of agents has changed substantially, the initial equilibrium will be broken causing disequilibrium and gradual attainment of a new equilibrium. Only when power reciprocity is realized, which means general equilibrium under perfect competition, can full utilization and the optimal allocation of resources be achieved simultaneously. Although such reciprocity and balance are almost impossible, the objective is perpetually pursued.

The optimization of social benefits and welfare requires a certain mechanism to induce resource movement and allocation. For economic agents, only when power is reciprocal and power and responsibility are symmetrical can social wealth be guaranteed to continuously increase and to be distributed fairly. The essence of the principal-agent problem is not the asymmetry between agent's power and interests, it is agents' absolute power over firms' management and no explicit obligation of success or failure of business management, which represents asymmetry between power and responsibility. For the same economic agent, its power and responsibility must be clarified. In other words, the economic agent must understand in advance what they can and cannot do and the corresponding rewards and punishment. If there is only power and no corresponding responsibility, that power will be unrestricted power, or infinite power. If there is only responsibility and no power, then responsibilities cannot be guaranteed and bear results. Therefore, the micro-foundation of enhancing corporate value and realizing full utilization and optimal resource allocation is that an economic agent has symmetry between power and responsibility.

The social justice problem that people have been pursuing is, in essence, the pursuit of a power mode with two-way effects; in other words, the equity problem. This is so because in the mode of one-way effects, one party's claims on interests cannot be expressed or even mentioned if they are to be realized. For example, the arable land in China's rural areas was wantonly occupied, and the peasants did not receive a reasonable subsidy. This is not a market problem since the marginal returns after changing the purpose of arable land are much higher than retaining the land for agricultural usage even after deducting rent-seeking returns for administrative agencies. It is neither a land property rights problem, since the Constitution clearly stipulates that land is owned by the state or the collective (peasants who contract the land are entitled after 50 years of farming the land), nor a principal-agent problem since agents in the grass-roots cadres are not elected by peasants. The source of the problem lies in a hidden power imbalance. The property rights institution without protection from power means nothing. The latent rules in a society become the basis of decisions by economic agents even if they are not documented in written regulations or recognized by laws due to the support of power. In land transactions, the real owners, and the individual who creates benefits, have virtually no opportunity to express opinions. They have neither the power nor the ability to influence the allocation of land. Therefore, the transactions are, inevitably, a one-way process of transferring interests, which is a transfer from the disadvantaged to the advantaged.

The structure of this book is as follows. Chapter 2 defines power and the historical basis of the economic power paradigm. Chapter 3 analyzes how control rights are distributed among members of a firm and the sources of these rights based on economic power. Chapter 4 discusses the formation of price under the power game among market subjects. In Chapters 5–7, we investigate transaction prices in goods markets, financial markets, and labor markets. Chapters 8 and 9 focus on government intervention and the optimal allocation of production factors, respectively. Chapter 10 presents the nature of institutions and the dynamic mechanisms of institutional change from the perspective of power. The final chapter addresses some limitations that we encountered and suggests directions for future research on economic power.

Notes

1 There is a certain correlation between a particular means to exert power and the source of a particular power but it's not exclusive. For example, organizations can exert the conditioned power externally but the condign power internally. A nation as an organization can use all of the three kinds of power. The means of the exertion and the source of the power exerted are interlaced.

2 D. Acemoglu is professor in the economics department of M.I.T. He's made valuable contributions in various areas. Especially, his work in institutional and political economics has been innovative and influential in the related areas. He was awarded in 2005 the John Bates Clark for his work. The medal is often called the junior Nobel Prize.

2 Power and economic power paradigm

The history of the development of any discipline is characterized by the continuous alternation of various paradigms. In the history of Western Economics, from the late 19th century to the early 20th century, the classical economics paradigm experienced a serious crisis and transitioned from classical economics to the paradigm of neoclassical economics. The new paradigm offered a broader space for the development of neoclassical economics and, after World War II, facilitated the remarkable era modern economics. The school of institutional economics developed rapidly in the late 20th century. Unlike neoclassical economics, a unified and perfect scientific system for institutional economics was not established, but a basic analytical paradigm emerged.

The characteristics of this new paradigm are embodied in the following two aspects. First, experts hold different views on aspects such as the formation of institutions and the specific impacts of institutions on economic behavior. Nevertheless, the role and status of institutions with respect to economic performance are recognized and accepted by a growing number of economists. Second, Coase (1995) was the first to achieve a breakthrough in classical economic thought and coined the term "transaction costs" which laid down a fundamental concept that became the basis of new institutional economics. The concept of transaction costs has become a basic tool in new institutional economics. The economic paradigms that existed in a certain historical period had substantial significance for the stable development of economic theory and facilitated economic practice. The transition of paradigms represents not only an objective requirement of social practice for the development of economic theory, but also an inevitable result of the development of economic theory itself.

It is widely accepted that power is a common and significant phenomenon in society and exists in the fields of politics and economics. Although power relationships are a critical phenomenon in economic activity, neither the mainstream school of economics in the West nor Chinese academia in economic fields pays enough attention to power dynamics. However, practice has proven that the market itself cannot achieve Pareto optimality and free competition automatically while monopolies, price signal distortions, the production failure of public goods, the existence of externality, and information asymmetry have become normal states. Because there is power, or "an invisible force," behind market mechanisms, power is always at work.

The concept of power

Power became a widespread social phenomenon with the emergence of interpersonal dominance behavior in civilized society. Power relationships exist between individuals but also between individuals and groups and between groups and other groups. The power relationship can be considered an objective need and the basis of the survival and development of human society. Without certain power to maintain, adjust, or form the basic order of society, a society will collapse. Hence, human society is a power society interwoven by various power relationship networks.

The meaning of power

Definition of power

Power can be defined in both a broad and narrow sense. Power in the narrow sense refers to the political power and the ability of an individual entrusted by a specific organization to control other individuals. German sociologist Weber (2009) defined power as the ability for an individual or individuals in a social relationship to achieve their will even in the face of opposition from others. Power is the ability or potential of individuals with certain social statues under certain social systems to specify conditions, make decisions, and take action on a series of life-threatening problems related to the survival of others.

While power in the broad sense removes the mandatory constraints of power, generally, it is the ability of an individual or a social group to affect the behavior of others from their own perspective. Power essentially refers to the ability to do something, or the capacity to generate certain results. Hobbes (1998) argues that the power of a man is his present means to obtain some future apparent good. Wrong (1979) holds that power is the capacity of some persons to initiate intended and foreseen effects on others. Any individual or group that enables others to change their own will is considered to be in a position of power. To conclude, power in the broad sense is the influence and control over others with the resources behavioral subjects have. Power is influenced and restricted by various factors such as force, wealth, knowledge and information, image and reputation, the form and size of organizations, and charisma. Based on the above analysis, power can be expressed by the mathematical symbols $\tau = a \times R$ where

$$a = (a_1, a_2, \cdots, a_n), R = (R_1, R_2, \cdots, R_n)^T$$

In the above expression, R_i denotes the i-th resource controlled by the behavioral subjects, and a_i denotes the power coefficient of the i-th resource (i = 1, 2, ..., n).

The attributes of power

RELATION

The power phenomenon in social activities emerges only if dominant behavior occurs between the subjects of power and the objects of power. If we put the relationship between subjects and objects aside, we are unable to determine which party has power over the other party. There are numerous individuals involved in societal activities, not every individual has power over others. To explain power from the perspective of a relationship is a dynamic view that emphasizes that power is only a potential state under the static state.

ASYMMETRY

Only when the influence of power subjects is greater than the influence of power objects can power emerge, so power's outward manifestation is asymmetry. When the influence of the subjects of power is equivalent to that of the objects of power, power is implicit.

SELF-REINFORCEMENT

From the perspective of the operation of power, once power is formed, it has a self-reinforcing property. Although people are always trying to change this trend, we see from the history of social development that it is extremely difficult to restrain the self-reinforcing property of power and quite costly to do so. If there are no constraints, the boundaries of power will continue to expand until they meet constraints.

The structure of power

At the macroscopic level, the power structure is reflected by types and quantities of power object and subject as well as their interactions. The power structure of a certain society is formed by interrelated and interacted power roles. A certain power role tends to interact with different other power roles. A power role may be the subject under a certain power relationship, while the object under another, whether it is the subject or object depends on the angle of observation. Every power role interacts with others under various power relationships and forms the power structures in society. The power structure is the basic framework of societal activities.

At the microscopic level, any type of power has four elements: (1) the subjects of power—that is, the specific affiliation of power, in other words, who will exercise the power; (2) the objects of power—that is, the objects controlled and dominated by power; (3) the contents of power—that is, the concrete forms of power, such as ownership, the right to use, management rights, and the right to lease; (4) the scope of power—that is, the permissions or boundaries of power including the scope of power in terms of space and time and organizational and institutional limitations.

The classification of power

Different types of resources determine the different nature of power and form different subjects of power. Power in modern society can be classi-fied into the following three categories: political power, social power, and economic power. Political power is manifested as administrative power in government.

Political power is the ability of a political subject, in order to achieve cer-tain fundamental interests, to dominate and control the political objects relying on their political resources. In a certain society, there are three types of political subjects: citizens, political organizations, and government. The three types of subjects are concerned with the interests of the social system as a whole or the interests of certain big interest groups. The subjects create and distribute these values or interests, or affect the creation and distribu-tion of social values by various types of resources. Political power has the following characteristics: (1) public nature—political power, particularly government power, is imposed on social and public affairs; (2) legally man-datory nature—an important feature of political power, which differs from the other powers, is its mandatory nature, that is, national political power is based on violence (the apparatus of violence includes armies, police, courts, and prisons); (3) expansionary nature—the expansionary nature of political power means that political power breaks through its own scope and penetrates other areas. (The penetration ability of political power has been strengthened in modern society and is deeply embedded in the fields of economics, culture, and ideology.)

Administrative power is the exhibition and execution of political power in the management of daily affairs. The subjects of administrative power are government departments and all levels of government hierarchy. In daily economic activities, it is the administrative power that both interacts with and has influence over economic power. In a market economy, the adminis-trative power of government is manifested as the supply of public goods, the construction of the market system, and the enactment and implementation of policies and regulations.

Social power can be defined as the ability of a social subject, in order to achieve specific purposes, to dominate and influence social objects through their social resources. Social power always emerges in non-official and non-profit organizations, such as religions, families, and trade associations, and is generally not mandatory. The religious power of society was once in a socially dominant position in history. For certain purposes, religious subjects dominated and influenced believers, heretics, and non-believers through religious rules. Religious power is complex and extensive and includes the power relationship within the organization and the influence and domination of secular society. This type of religious hierarchy became integrated with social hierarchy in some countries. Theocratic forms of rule existed for a long time in ancient Egypt, ancient Rome, and ancient India. In medieval Europe, after fierce struggles between the magisterium and the throne, the magisterium finally established its higher position and assumed supreme authority. Theocratic forms of rule still exist today in some countries in Africa and West Asia. Social power also has some influence over economic activities, such as providing a guiding role. In modern market economies, compared with political power and economic power, social power is typically weak—entities can decide whether to accept or exercise social power.

Economic power can be defined as the ability of economic subjects, in order to achieve their own purposes, to influence others (including economic objects) using economic resources at hand. The resources here refer to everything necessary for economic activities, which include physical resources such as plants, equipment, materials, funds, and organizations, and intangible resources such as physical strength, intelligence, information, and reputation. The power of economic entities to influence certain economic activities is determined by the importance, scarcity, and substitutability of the resources at their disposal. The owner's influence on and control over other economic subjects in the bargaining process will be stronger if the resources are more important, scarce, and substitutable; hence, resource endowments determine power endowments.

In the field of economics, firms, government, and consumers all have economic power; that is, they can rely on the resources at their disposal to gain some type of influence and control over other economic subjects. For example, on the one hand, consumers have the right to determine whether or not to sell their labor by virtue of their own physical strength and intelligence. On the other hand, consumers can determine whether or not to buy goods and services depending on their gains. Firms can determine what to produce depending on the means of production at their proposal while the government can determine the areas, objects, and quantities of procurement and investment by virtue of tax revenue and budget.

The sources of power

Resources are the foundation of power. Different scholars have their own interpretations of the resources of power. Etzioni (1974) argues that mandatory assets, utilitarian assets, and normative assets correspond to the symbol of military force, material rewards, and legitimacy, respectively. Moreover, power was the social expression of this symbol. Gamson (1969) proposes a similar trichotomy: mandatory resources, induced resources, and persuasive resources. Wrong (1979) holds that the basis of power is individuals who control resources and organizations composed of individuals. He did not classify resources but refers to all the resources that can be dominated by individuals as the basis of personal power while organizations are the synthesis and tendentious use of personal resources. Analyzed from the viewpoint of the state of power in the process of social development, power resources include meta-resources, that is, the resources with which an economic agent is naturally equipped. Power resources also include derivative resources; that is, the resources that combine with meta-resources and generate power based on meta-resources.

Meta-resources are the resources owned by the human agent under normal conditions that the agent cannot be deprived of unless harmed biologically, for example, deteriorating fitness or intelligence. Meta-resources include natural endowments and the related contents obtained in the process of individual growth. They include the capacity to behave and to think, or an influential relationship. Any existing individual has a certain amount of meta-resources, but the quality and quantity of the meta-resources they own differ. Meta-resources are the guarantee of survival given to individuals by nature. Any deprivation of meta-resources might be a violation of the laws of nature. Although this concept includes certain philosophical ideas, it also contains a deeper meaning of economics. On the one hand, the agent can obtain other resources to ensure their survival in the market via the exchange of meta-resources, for example, earning a wage through labor. On the other hand, meta-resources are the baseline from which other economic agents to impose power. In a totally free competitive market, based on the concept of fairness, any deprivation of meta-resources is strictly prohibited.

Derivative resources are the resources that can affect others when combined with meta-resources and under certain forms. They include organizations, capital, and information and so on.

Organization is defined in either the broad or narrow sense. In the narrow sense, organization refers to a collective or a group that relies heavily on collaboration between people to achieve certain goals, whereas organization in the broad sense is the system that integrates elements in a certain manner. Weber (2009) argues that any organization should be based on some form of power. Moreover, organizations of all types should have a hierarchical structure, and the behavioral consistency in members, the essence hidden behind this hierarchy structure and consistency is power. In his argument, power is the essential characteristic of organization. The superior and subordinate hierarchical relationships of organizational structure contain the corresponding power relationships. There is segmentation at the same level of power hierarchy among the horizontal divisions in the organization structure. Members rely on the constraints and influence of power in this system to maintain consistency in behavior and purpose. The integration of resources by an organization is achieved by the contract on which the establishment of the organization is based. Organizations use contractual constraints to ensure that individual behavior choices are in accordance with the unified goal of the organization, which reduces the power conflicts between members. Hence, it is often believed that the behavior of individuals within the organization has consistency in goals.

The existence of organizations depends on personal resources while it is also possible to integrate personal resources tendentiously and expand personal power. The individuals and an organization are a community of interests. The greater the power of the organization, the more interests obtained from external organizations, and the more individuals will benefit from the organization. Economic individuals establish or participate in certain organizations based on rational considerations and follow the organization's rules of conduct. Therefore, the formation of economic organizations is not to reduce the transaction costs as Coase's theory states. The establishment of organizations reflects individual motives for the pursuit of power. Considerations of transaction costs are attempts by individuals to improve their profitability from internal resources from the perspective of thrift while the pursuit of organizational power is a type of behavioral performance by individuals in an attempt to obtain external resources.

Capital (mainly material capital) as a valuable production input is scarce. While a necessary factor of production in the production process, capital has clear attributes of property rights and certain risks inherent in its investment. The traditional economic theory of capital is based on materials, such as currency and production materials, which is consistent with social productivity of the time. In addition, existing capital theories are concerned with capital's right to distribute the surplus value and analyze how to gain revenue by means of capital while other manifestations of capital ownership are ignored. The clear attributes of capital property rights are manifested as the claim on investment returns and the decisions before investment; that is, owners of capital have the right to determine the direction and scale of capital investment. This decision-making power directly affects the supply-demand relationship and has the capacity to adjust the equilibrium quantity; it is also an effective strategy of owners of capital to fine-tune the market. If supply and demand reflects price determination, to control and affect supply and demand by means of capital ownership is the real underlying content.

Information is the state of motion and the process of things. Information is also the knowledge regarding these states and processes or the formalized relationship perceived by subjects of behavior regarding states and patterns of the motion of things. The function of information is to strengthen the degree of certainty of things. Due to the spatiotemporal differences in the real world, the cost of information collection and transfer is relatively high; hence, information becomes a valuable scarce resource and leads to divergences between the information owned by different subjects. Information asymmetry has become the normal state of markets. The quantity of information affects the accuracy of individual decision making and the outcome of games. The party who has more information can reduce mistakes due to an information advantage and leverage market competition resulting in more benefits. The theory of information economics has proven that in market exchange, if there is information asymmetry, the outcome of a transaction is that the interest distribution is always biased toward the party with information advantage while prices become the legitimate means to obtain benefits.

Historical basis of the economic power paradigm

Power is a common and critical phenomenon in economic operations. Power is the most important factor in resource allocation; power allocates market resources. We analyze this concept from a historical perspective.

Primitive society: the gradual formation of power relations

Power has become a widespread social phenomenon with the emergence of civilized society and interpersonal domination. Primitive society was a society without rules and a natural state without any restrictions. In such a state, to survive according to the requirements of intrinsic human nature, individuals had to adapt to nature and transform using their own capabilities. Initially, there were no affiliations and constraints among people because mandatory rules did not exist. Territorial interpersonal conflicts occurred gradually. Individuals with inherent advantages benefited from the conflicts or even seized property. A mechanism was required that could protect an individual's property accumulated through labor. Moreover, communities needed to organize and assume command. The distribution of food demanded institutional rules, and the disputes within a group called for a just verdict. Objectively, an organization was necessary to protect interests in the form of a contract. Thus, tribe members handed over certain rights to the tribal clan in the form of a contract to reduce inequality by the power of the tribal clan. Chiefs and heads emerged. These leaders made decisions on the allocation of food and commanded the actions of the group. At this time, there was no authentic exchange relationship among people even if there was accidental exchange of goods. Therefore, the concept of power in society was relatively simple; the power structure was not an institution in the modern sense but manifested as rules under kinship.

Slave society: an absolute unbalanced power structure

During conflicts between primitive tribes, some prisoners were forced to become slaves. In some cases, the inability to repay heavy debts forced people into servitude. Gradually, society became unequal society—slave society. The differences in power structure between slaves and slave owners are the greatest compared with other societal power structures. Slave society's absolute unequal power structure resulted in the highest possible reward for any investment made by a slave owner since slaves were forced to provide maximum labor. The absolute power structure determined that slaves were only an asset without legal rights. Slaves were not entitled to property. They could not control their labor and were forced to comply with their slave owner's demands. Slaves had no qualifications with which to bargain with slave owners, and slave owners suppressed any rebellions. However, the costs of doing so were small compared with the wealth they amassed from slaves. Therefore, the absolute solidified power structure of slave society determined the social institution, which was an inflexible institution. Slave society opposed the adoption of new production methods to improve efficiency and prevented institutional change to reduce costs. When slaves, the assets of slave owners, became an unbearable cost, the slave trade emerged. As rebellions and uprisings by long-oppressed slaves increased in frequency, the violence shocked the foundation of slavery. As a result of this absolutely imbalanced power structure, armed uprisings were one way to change the institution.

Agricultural society: a relatively closed and unbalanced power structure

The establishment of the agricultural social institution was based on the centralization of power and monopoly of land-based property rights. Historically, the power performance of different agricultural societies was very different. In China, the emperor was the supreme ruler, and all land belonged to the emperor. The emperor owned everything, while peasants depended strongly on the land owner. The behavior of peasants was the most basic economic relation. Agricultural tax constituted the core of a nation's wealth, but business and trade were underdeveloped and suppressed. In the agricultural societies of Europe, state power was mastered by the aristocracy, constantly changing, and its basic unit of economy was the manor. Agricultural society is often referred to as feudal society. The concept of the feudal system has two implications from the perspective of economics: it is the natural form of a small-scale peasant economy based on self-sufficiency and is the basis of a vassal system.

From the perspective of power, agricultural society includes two levels of power relationships. One is the power relationship between the monarch and the vassal, and the other is the power relationship between the vassal and the peasants. Monarchs enabled vassals to be the owners of land and peasants by granting them an official rank or authorization. The vassals paid a certain percentage of tax to the royal family. The monarch's power was supreme, but the vast territory meant that the monarch needed a group of officials to share political power. The distribution of political power between the members of this group was uneven. The vassals only exercised the power delegated to them by the monarch while the monarch supervised the performance of subordinates endowed with the power and could reclaim the power at any time. There were no strict legal procedures for power reclamation.

Due to the constraints of geography and the household registration system, peasants had economic relations only with their vassals. Peasants cultivated land and had partial operating rights, but ownership belonged to the landowners. The main way for vassals and landowners to obtain interest was to grant the land directly to peasants while the peasants had the obligation and responsibility to pay for the land rents with materials or currency. The relationship between monarch and ministers, and the relationship between landlords and peasants, in many cases, were clarified by a series of contracts. These contracts benefited the dominant party, the monarch and landlords. Because the monarch and the landlords had the power to change the contract, particularly in harvest years, and changes in market demand raised grain prices, landowners would add new lease rents to the contracts. In the natural economy, peasants would make full use of the land to increase production efficiency. Compared with slave society, the institution in agricultural society provided technological incentives, and the advancement of productive forces was beneficial for both landlords and peasants. However, the rate of technological change was slow, and peasants were bounded in their production units; that is, fixed and closed land. Nevertheless, as long as population migration occurred, the efficiency of societal labor improved.

In the pre-industrial era, peasants and slaves had no private property rights with independent economic attributes. The possession of production materials (mainly the land) of each private owner must be realized with the help of ultra-economic political or social power (such as the power of church in medieval Europe). Property rights were connected with theocracy and sovereignty, and there were varying degrees of personal dependence relations. This ultra-economic nature of the power structure originated from the institutional arrangement whereby political power is over ownership and the widespread impact of such an arrangement on ideology. This unbalanced power structure was not conducive to the development of productive forces and market transactions. The market-centered power structure and the capital system established by this structure promoted the formation of modern industrial civilization.

Early industrial society: from single-element to a multi-element power structure

In the 1760s, the British industrial revolution saw the factory system characterized by machines replace manual workshops. The industrial revolution first sparked a wave of technological innovation where machines produced cotton in the UK's textile industry, and the systems spread to France, Germany, the United States, and other countries. The industrial revolution was the solid material base of industrial society: mechanized industry. The machine was just a factor of production and could not establish the relations of production and the economic institutions of industrial society. The relations of production in industrial society became dominant in two ways. The first was the bourgeois revolution. For example, the French bourgeois revolution in 1789 ended the monarchy in France through armed violence. French society had been based on a feudal small-scale peasant economy and had lasted nearly one thousand years. The second way that production relations gained dominance was through peace negotiations. For example, in Britain, the capital-oriented social and economic institution was established by noble bourgeoisie, feudal landlords, and the monarch through power games.

Although the industrial revolution was due to the invention of the steam engine, it mainly depended on the corporate system with discretionary property rights. In the natural economy of the hand-tool workshop, there was no space for large-scale machines, but machine production required many production factors to be used in the same space in a centralized and cooperative manner. Machine production, organized in accordance with the principle of dominant capital power, demanded huge amounts of initial capital. Machine production also required wage labor attached to the power of capital and hoped for maximum profit. The organizational structure that can accommodate a variety of factors of productivity is the corporate system. For example, to promote greater development of the company system enterprises, capital owners understood the defects of the unlimited liability companies system. Capital groups promoted the legal protection of the rights and interests of investors using their economic and political power. Hence, the limited liability companies system became a widely debated topic in the United Kingdom. British parliament finally confirmed that registered companies had only limited compensation liabilities for debts and enacted the first limited liability company legislation in 1855. Thus, the basic framework of a corporate system in industrial society was set, and the companies, whether large or small, emerged. The success of the industrial revolution in the United Kingdom depended on the invention of the steam engine but also the formation of a modern enterprise system promoted by economic power. This was the fundamental cause of rapid economic growth during the British industrial revolution that lasted more than 100 years and UK's lead in economic advancement.

The power relations and structure of industrial society in the 19th century had the following characteristics. First is the asymmetric power structure in market demand and supply. Since productive creativity as a whole was not sufficient, supply was in a state of relative scarcity. The formation of market equilibrium price depends largely on the power of supply. The supply, the wealth producer who controls resources, determines the demand for society; in other words, the seller dominates the market demand and supply relations. Thus, production costs including capital, labor, and natural elements, had significant impact on market value. Second, economic relationships at that time manifested as classical property ownership; that is, 100% or over 50% of property rights were absolutely controlled by individuals or families. The institution of private property rights in the industrial age which replaced the private ownership of feudal society, characterized by the concentration of capital in the hands of a few people, promoted productivity dramatically. However, this ownership with absolute power of control exhibited its limitations when confronted with mass machinery production and became an impediment to the development of social productivity. Third, the power relationship in some businesses retained the typical traits of agricultural society. In terms of scale, enterprises in the 19th century were small, and individual proprietorship and partnerships were the main form of enterprises. Property rights were concentrated among a few individual families or their relatives and friends, with blood ties and geopolitics shadowing the economy of a natural division of labor. Therefore, the main ownership structure was a relatively closed one, while the management and ownership of businesses were not separated but highly centralized within firms.

Compared with feudal agricultural society, the economic power structure of early industrial society was decentralized, open, and relatively diverse. It was the historic changes in power structure that caused market economy civilization to integrate with the private ownership of industrial society. The economic institution corresponding to these historic changes in power structure is a state with a high level of free competition. The property ownership of economic subjects in a market economy is the most critical and basic rule and incentive mechanism in transactions. The nature of transactions between economic subjects is the transfer of ownership from one economic subject to another. The property rights structure in a business is not a simple natural economy of labor division nor a family organization, but a socialized economic organization. The company system enterprises, having replaced the classical business system, introduced an alternation of production organization patterns and an innovation of the property system. The extreme asymmetry between the power of capital and that of labor in the 19th century was particularly reflected in capital's exploitation and occupation of labor under primitive capital accumulation. With respect to political power, the government acted as a night watchman and adopted a laissez-faire economic operation policy. Political power had little intervention in economic power.

The power structure of 20th century industrial society

The power structure of 20th century industrial society had the following new characteristics:

1   Weakened capital ownership
    With the development of company system enterprises, the size of enterprises required extensive use of technology and complicated the

management process. The shareholding system expanded businesses while changing the nature of the firm; that is, businesses transformed from natural businesses to legal entities. The life cycle of a business lengthened because it was no longer restricted by the life cycle of individuals. The separation of ownership from management occurred naturally as the shareholding system transformed the natural business into a legal entity. The separation of ownership from management created professional managers, and management became a new factor in the production and management process. The "manager revolution" advanced the division of labor in industrial society; that is, the division of labor between capitalists and managers brought by the separation of ownership from management. As managers became professional executives, capitalists became professional investors. Because manager's income is linked to the profitability and growth of businesses, as Schumpeter (1939) states, the mission of managers is to continuously explore potential profit and turn that potential into actual profits by means of diverse innovations. Non-capital owners can participate more in capital management, and the control of capital by capital owners weakens. The emergence of managers renders businesses the investment objects of capital owners, and the privacy of the usufruct of capital presents extensive social search by means of social income distribution and redistribution.

2   The economic power structure is characterized by the monopolization of goods and concentrated control over resources

In current industrial society, the development of a shareholding system is moving toward a more concentrated form of organizational capital. That is, shareholding system replaces the individual ownership in industrial society, and the subject of shareholding has shifted from private persons to legal entities. The traditional shareholding system of private capital is replaced by the shareholding system of corporate capital. The corporate capital (including corporate and institutional entities) has replaced private capital with the largest shareholder. Therefore, companies are larger, and the representatives of legal entities closely supervise managers, which has ensured company's long-term development. In the 20th century, particularly after World War II, marketization, further advancements in the division of labor, and fierce competition worldwide placed limitations on the private share capital ownership system. Limited ability to raise funds and the personalized shareholding system led to short-term business operations. The ownership of corporate body capital has gradually replaced private share capital ownership system and seized a dominant position.

Compared with private share capital ownership system, corporate capital ownership system has the following characteristics. First, legal entity shareholdings strengthen the links between legal entities and companies, which overcome short-term corporate behavior. Modern enterprise is no longer controlled by certain capitalists but managed by professional managers with higher management skills. Second, corporate bodies have replaced individuals and become the main body of shareholders, which broadens the financing channel of the stock corporation, boosts production, and further concentrates capital. After World War II, in addition to commercial banks and investment banks, non-banking financial institutions, such as funds and insurance companies, flourished due to access to huge amounts of monetary capital. Such institutions entered the capital market and became shareholders of large corporations. Because most of these institutional corporate bodies are public utility organizations, such as pension funds and health insurance funds, the power structure of capital has gradually formed an open system of property rights and absorbed different sectors of the economy. Hence, different subjects of property rights coexist in the same economic organization. This corporate system has increased partnership-type business's ability to raise funds and has opened the structure of property rights. Property rights are more diversified and socialized. The power structure in the 20th century is reflected in the diversification of capital sources, the decentralization of property rights, and the securitization and marketization of capital. The power of capital is concentrated on the surface but is actually dispersed, which has led to an increase in the welfare of society as a whole. The "people's industrial society" has emerged.

3   The state increasingly intervenes in economic activities

The most notable change in the 20th century's industrial economy is state power intervention. After World War II, Western industrial society, except the United States, had to be rebuilt, which provided objective conditions for political power to intervene in the economy. From the perspective of economic equilibrium, Keynes (1937) argues that the fundamental role of state intervention is to affect social aggregate demand and aggregate supply through the adjustment of resource allocation to achieve the goal of full employment. Particularly, government spending including direct investment, transfer payments, and government procurement could increase demand in the whole society. The nationalization movement in developed Western economies enabled the state to operate the production of large public goods such as postal services, railways, petroleum, and electricity and infrastructure construction directly. The nationalization guaranteed the scale supply effect of public goods and important commodities, which, to some extent, guaranteed the effective operation of a market economy. The primary causes of government intervention in the economy were the following. First, organized private interest groups can leverage state power to increase their own income. Second, intervention is the result of the expansion of political power and the needs of group interests. Third, due to the growing electoral power among low-income classes, higher educational level of laborers and increasingly powerful unions, people demanded social protection from losses caused by economic instability such as unemployment and disease by means of government intervention.

4   Capital power allocates resources globally with the aid of national political power.

If the enhancement of state power intervention in economies has made the socialization of private capital a state feature, the development of multinational corporations has strengthened the internationalization features of capital power. Both the General Agreement on Tariffs and Trade (GATT), signed into effect in 1948, and the World Trade Organization (WTO) with multilateral trade negotiations at core, established in 1995, have played an important role in the development of economic power globalization in industrial society in the 20th century. With the aid of state power, economic power institutionalized the world market and the resource-sharing system. With the progress of industrial society, the globalization of economic power is a prominent driver. First, in the process of economic globalization, many economic activities used the world as a platform to overcome different natural and social barriers, particularly transportation barriers, communication barriers, and market barriers. Second, the primary vehicle of economic globalization has been multinational companies. According to the World Investment Report 2017, the world has more than 100,000 multinational parent companies and more than 860,000 affiliated companies and subsidiaries. These companies control the world market through their own advantages in funds, technology, brands, and sales networks. They also control one-third of production, two-thirds of international trade, 70% of technology patents, and 90% of foreign direct investment globally. The nature of economic globalization is a process whereby multinational companies organize production and circulation worldwide. From the perspective of power relations, the expansion of multinational companies can be viewed as games played by a variety of global economic powers through which these companies profit from economic growth. In reality, multinational companies expanded their activities in locations with low costs, favorable market conditions, and economic potential. In the 20th century, multinational companies are the primary driving force of economic globalization as well as transnational special economic power groups: the business empire. Third, regional economic cooperation (i.e., regional economic integration) has become a form of economic globalization. Regional economic cooperation is a major trend in world economic development. Moreover, it is central to economic globalization. There are approximately 140 economic cooperation organizations worldwide, but only three occupy a large share of the market and play a decisive role in economic cooperation—the EU, the North American free trade area and the emerging East Asia free trade area. The rise and fall of the world economy is closely related to these three major regional economic blocks. After five rounds of expansion, the EU has become the world's most integrated regional union. The EU has adopted a single currency and established the euro zone.

In essence, regional economic cooperation as the most critical form of economic globalization reflects that economic power establishes a sphere of influence. This influence expands the market and income through state power forming a relatively stable system. In fact, the result occurs due to games played by a variety of global political and economic powers. Due to its position in industrial society, particularly due to its advantages in capital and intellectual property (technology), economic power has benefited greatly from the global market and resource sharing.

In summary, compared to the slave and agricultural societies, the power structure in industrial society is more decentralized and relatively equal. Since the 20th century, power in society has become more centralized on the surface but actually more dispersed. Its open system of property rights enables the power in society to assimilate in different sectors of the economy, and allows multiple subjects of property rights to coexist in the same economic organization, which has formed a complicated, scattered, and unique system of property rights. In today's society, due to the knowledge economy, information technology, and the diversity of resources and hierarchy of interests, different types of economic power frequently change. However, the power of different economic subjects at the same level has shown a growing trend of equalization.

The logic behind the emergence of an economic power paradigm

Economics requires basic assumptions that are linked to basic methodology. In other words, basic assumptions can best reflect the philosophy and methodology of economics, which is the logical starting point or theoretical premise that an economic system relies on. The assumption of economic man is a fundamental assumption in economic theory and the basis of the Western market economy framework. Without this assumption, there would be no market economy theory and market economy system.

Any type of economic analysis should be based on the behavior of subjects of economic activities. The design and arrangement of an economic system rely on assumptions about the nature of these subjects. Therefore, according to the assumption that economic power is everywhere in the economy, we propose the notion of "power economic man," based on the assumption of economic man, to reflect economic activities in the real

world. Human economic activities are relational activities among different economic subjects. The pursuit of profit maximization is achieved only
through production, exchanges, consumption, and distribution. The pursuit
of profit maximization is a claim on nature but also a claim on distribution.
We believe that economic power is the ability of an economic subject to
affect others to achieve their goals under the condition of having sufficient
productive resources at their command. The concept of economic power
is a relational concept. An individual has no power alone. Only in the exchange process can the mutual influence of power be reflected. The premises
of human economic activities are exchange and labor division. The need
to work with others, as well as the influence of an individual's power over
others, emerges in the process of exchange and labor division. In the following sections, we discuss the content and rationality of power economic man
from the perspective of the development and logical path of economic man
assumptions.

Classic assumptions of economic man

The economic man assumption was first introduced by Adam Smith (1950),
a famous political economist, as follows. Subjects of market economy were
postulated under the premise of the assumption of economic man.

> As every individual, therefore, endeavors as much as he can both to
> employ his capital in the support of domestic industries, and so to di-
> rect these industry that its produce may be of the greatest value; every
> individual necessarily labors to render the annual revenue of the society
> as great as he can. He generally, indeed, neither intends to promote the
> public interest, nor knows how much he is promoting it. By preferring
> the support of domestic to that of foreign industry, he intends only his
> own security; and by directing that industry in such a manner as its
> produce may be of the greatest value, he intends only his own gain, and
> he is in this, as in many other cases, led by an invisible hand to promote
> an end which was no part of his intention. Nor is it always the worse
> for the society that it was not part of it. By pursuing his own interest he
> frequently promotes that of the society more effectually than when he
> really intends to promote it.

In "The Theory of Moral Sentiments," Adam Smith (1822) emphasized
that:

> Every man is, no doubt, by nature, first and principally recommended
> to his own care; and as he is fitter to take care of himself than of any
> other person, it is fit and right that it should be so. Every man, therefore,
> is much more deeply interested in whatever immediately concerns him-
> self, than in what concerns any other man.

The economic man assumption had a profound impact on the understanding of human relationships and the link between man and society. Everyone seeks their own gain at the expense of other's interests, but people should work with each other. This type of cooperation is brought by exchange and the division of labor. Due to self-interest, people exchange goods, which can also bring about the division of labor. Smith (1822) even believes that the awareness of exchange is an enduring feature of human nature.

> But man has almost constant occasion for the help of his brethren, and it is in vain for him to expect it from their benevolence only. He will be more likely to prevail if he can interest their self-love in his favor, and show them that it is for their own advantage to do for him what he requires of them.

Regarding the relationship between individuals and society, Smith even argues that the common nature of all human beings is a love of order, orderliness, art, and creation, which creates a willingness to promote the social system. Smith (1822) said:

> It is thus that man, who can subsist only in society, was fitted by nature to that situation for which he was made. All the members of human society stand in need of each other's assistance, and are likewise exposed to mutual injuries......and though no man in it should owe any obligation, or be bound in gratitude to any other, it can still be maintained on the basis of a consistent valuation by focusing entirely on profitable reciprocity.

The term economic man has the following characteristics in economic activities. First, the self-interestedness of economic man is economic man's universal motive. Second, the self-interestedness of economic man is not the same as selfishness. Economic man is not equivalent to the selfish person. To acquire needed products, economic man will exchange the surplus goods that come from hard work rather than do something that will benefit them at the expense of others. Third, economic man is a person who acts rationally. Economic man can compare the gains from interests with the losses and grasp alternative ways and means of behavior and the consequences of such behavior. The assumption of economic man analyzes the pros and cons of various types of labor division, the gains and losses of exchange, and the amount of investment earnings. These analyses are stamped with the characteristics of rational analysis.

As the outstanding advocate and father of classical economics, Adam Smith expounded on how the pursuit of maximizing self-interest could lead to the maximization of social welfare based on the assumption of economic man. Smith proposed and initially discussed the principle of "the invisible hand," which established a basic framework for Western market economy theory.

Perfectly rational economic man in neoclassical economics

In neoclassical economics, economic man is supposed to have completely ordered preferences, complete information, and impeccable computing capability. Economic man is a person who always weighs marginal cost and marginal revenue. The cost-benefit analysis of behavior is the foundation on which economic man becomes a rational person, which is also prerequisites and main basis for effective analysis of economics.

To be more specific, first, a set of alternative choices exists. Second, each of the plans corresponds to a certain expected net income and some progress toward a goal. Third, economic man will always choose the plan that will ensure maximum expected net income. The rational assumption implies that a rational person has access to all the information about the target, can analyze the target, and make judgments on the basis of the information obtained within a reasonable period of time. Such judgments and the actions based on these judgments are not affected by psychological factors. Complying with theoretical assumptions, such as self-interest and complete rationality of economic man, neoclassical economics formulated the theory of marginal utility and general equilibrium to explore perfect markets in classical economics. The trend of applying mathematics to economics has particularly dehumanized economic man, which has caused economists to deviate from individual market behaviors and focus only on the logical choices of purpose or tools. The market is a standardized and programmatic mechanical structure.

From early classical economics to modern neoclassical economics, after continuous abstraction, economic man's rationality has deviated from the scope of economic man's rationality defined by Smith. Rational behavior is considered an act of choice to find the best solution, which should comply with a series of rational axioms. Particularly for the theory of general equilibrium and the theory of subjective expected utilities, where a wide range of mathematical techniques are applied, economic man has acquired deity-like rationality. Simon, who first coined the term "bounded rationality," called such a man "super- economic man."

The assumption of bounded rational economic man

Simon was a leading critic of the concept of complete rationality of economic man. In 1949, Simon and other political scientists, economists, engineers, and psychologists conducted joint research on organizations and management. Simon (1997) argued that the premises of the rational model were to postulate that the decision maker knew all the possible plans and outcomes. However, this is impossible in reality. He proposed five limiting factors of the rational choice model: (1) incomplete and imperfect information; (2) the complexity of the decision problem itself; (3) the limitations on the human ability to solve problems; (4) decisions being made within a period of time;

and (5) an individual's understanding of the objectives of the organization being always inconsistent and controversial. Simon called these factors the limits of rationality and stated that decisions in reality were made with bounded rationality. Simon's theory of bounded rationality implies that a person with bounded rationality will always try to maximize the utility function but with limited ability to gather and process information. This limited ability leads to the inevitable presence of private information. When one subject attempts to acquire information another already has, it is highly possible that the costs will come to outweigh the benefits. Even if an individual tries to disclose such information to another, the information may not be confirmed by the recipient. The introduction of information asymmetry has created new branches of microeconomics. The theoretic achievements of these branches are known as the incentive theory, contract theory, and agent theory. We can now modify Smith's economic man to economic man with bounded rationality.

From transaction economic man to the contract economic man

As the father of institutional economics, Veblen initially incorporated institutions into the analytical framework of the relationship between the struggle for existence and human behavior. Veblen (1934) holds that the nature of institution was individual's or society's habit of considering relations and effects that were closely related to them. He believes that basic instincts establish the ultimate goals of human behavior and push human beings to achieve these goals through their efforts. Both personal and social actions are guided and dominated by instincts. These actions gradually form thoughts and habits and eventually form institutions. After the emergence of institutions, human behavior was restricted by those institutions. Institutions varied with environmental changes. The changing environment required people to change their thinking habits in response to environmental changes. The change in human behavior was an elimination process, the purpose of which was to adapt to the environment. Commons (1936) was the first to introduce economic activities of economic man from production to exchanges. In Commons's work on institutional economics, transaction corresponds to production, a generalized concept in orthodox economics. According to Commons's classification, the activity of production is a human activity of nature while the activity of transaction is a relation pattern between human beings. The production activity together with the transaction activity is composed of all human economic activities and ways of production. Commons holds that the basic unit of institutional economics is transaction, and the operation of institution is completed by numerous transactions. Commons classified transactions into three basic types: (1) bargaining transactions—the major form of activities of institutions in the market economy; (2) managing transactions—the relationship between orders and obedience; and (3) rationing transactions—the relationship between individuals and government. Commons argues that the three types of transactions covered all interpersonal activities, and different economic institutions could be viewed as different combinations of these basic types of transactions. Commons used transaction as the basic unit of institution to establish his framework of institutional economics. From the relationship of transactions among economic men, the institutional structure is at the heart of the activities of economic man. The behavior of any economic man is founded on voluntary exchanges and reciprocity, and transactions naturally become the object of institutional design and institutional change. At this time, the economic man described by Commons became the "transaction economic man."

The difference between institutional economics and new institutional economics lies in the existence of transaction costs. Commons (1936) conducted a thorough analysis on transactions, but transactions occurred almost instantaneously and did not require any costs. The term "transaction costs," coined by Coase (1995), is a central concept in new institutional economics. Transaction costs are an effective theoretical tool when analyzing all types of organizations and social activities. Transaction costs include the costs of collecting market information and implementing the contract and the costs of measuring, defining, and certifying property rights, the costs of finding both the objects of transactions and the transaction prices, the bargaining costs, the costs of signing contracts, the costs of enforcing and monitoring contracts, and the costs of maintaining transaction order. Transaction cost economics, represented by Williamson (1975), categorized transaction costs in both the broad and the narrow sense. Transaction costs in the narrow sense refer to the relative expenses incurred in the transfer and exchange process of property rights, which are outside the narrowly defined production process, whereas transaction costs in the broad sense refer to the operating costs associated with institutional changes. Hence, transaction costs have a general definition and become the costs of running an economic system. We can say that transaction costs are the source of institutions.

Therefore, unlike economic man, the postulated person in neoclassical economics, human behavior is not based on perfect information or complete rationality to maximize profit. Instead, the pattern of human behavior is based on motivations and the understanding of the environment. In terms of motivation, individuals pursue the maximization of wealth on the one hand, but, on the other hand, they will sacrifice some short-term benefits to achieve the goals of societal value such as reputation, faith, and altruism. In terms of their understanding of environment, individuals are always subject to imperfect information; therefore, their rationality is bounded, and their optimal decisions are unattainable. Under the condition of imperfect information, it is impossible for a person dominated by different motivations to live without friction as described by neoclassical economics. Transaction costs are similar to friction. New institutionalism introduces economics to a world with friction from a frictionless world. Different organizations and institutional arrangements used for reducing transaction costs only appear in transaction cost economics. Transaction economic man, coined by Commons, has become transaction economic man with transaction costs. Economic man is now called "contractual economic man" or "institutional economic man." Contractual economic man is, in an economic activity, under the premises of bounded rationality, a person who seeks transaction cost minimization to reduce the risk of opportunism and guarantee the enforcement of contracts.

The assumption of "power economic man"

The Coase theorem holds that the completeness of property rights depends on whether the owner of property rights has the exclusive use rights, the exclusive right to income, and the right of free transfer. After the property right is well defined, persons involved in an economic activity will negotiate with each other spontaneously to internalize an externality and to enhance resource distribution efficiency. In other words, as long as the property right is clearly defined, regardless of who owns it, private costs will not deviate from social costs. Theoretically speaking, private property rights and public ownership are not mutually exclusive. Private property rights require only that public ownership is voluntary rather than coercive. A "voluntarily consulted" contract, signed through market transactions, can lead to the best allocation of resources. The word "voluntary" is significant.

The emergence of contracts originates from labor division and transactions. The division of labor is a process whereby workers are assigned to particular professions. Transaction is the transfer of goods or services through different markets. People in different professions allocate their products by means of mutually beneficial exchanges to ensure labor division through the transaction and to attain the maximization of social welfare. Then, how is a contract formed? New institutional economics holds that the conclusion and arrangement of contracts are completed through two basic ways: one is voluntary, and one is coercive (usually the contract formed and controlled by government is coercive). The voluntary contractual arrangement is a cooperative arrangement made by individuals who have reached an agreement, and any individual can withdraw legally. This situation implies that consensus among decision makers is required. The costs to accept this decision are lower than the transaction cost of giving up the contract. While the coercive contractual arrangement does not provide the option of withdrawal, consensus is not required in an action, but decision rules should be respected and followed. New institutional economics emphasizes that a voluntary trading contract between economic subjects is carried out in accordance with the participant's will. However, completely voluntary and completely coercive are two extremes. There may be many possible semi-coercive and semi-voluntary structures between these two extremes. What factors might be the basis for the choice between personal voluntary cooperation and governmental arrangement? To realize what choice economic subjects are willing to embrace depends on the domination of scarce resources. Similarly, the imposition of a coercive contract on others should be based on the domination of resources to which others become dependent; otherwise no one would accept coercion.

To illustrate various possibilities of willingness between voluntary trades and coercive trades, we define the term "willingness to trade." In short, willingness to trade is the willingness of both economic subjects and economic objects to carry out a transaction. To be specific, willingness to trade refers to an economic subject's spectrum of options concerning whether to trade with an economic object, under what range of conditions the trade will occur, and how to trade with the object based on the advantages of their economic resources. As the willingness to trade between the two parties increases, the likelihood of signing the contract and completing the transaction increases. The willingness to trade is inversely proportional to the transaction costs, which implies that the lower the transaction costs, the higher the willingness to trade. Conversely, the higher the transaction costs, the lower the willingness to trade. The intensity of willingness to trade depends on the influence of the subject on the transaction object; that is, the economic power. The size of the economic power of an economic subject determines the willingness to trade, the willingness to trade of two or more parties determines the amount of transaction costs, and the amount of transaction costs, in turn, determines the conclusion of contracts or institutions; that is, closing the deal.

Now, we propose the "power economic man" assumption. Power economic man refers to an agent who use economic power to affect the fulfillment and implementation of contracts in an economic activity to achieve maximum benefit under the premises of bounded rationality. Economic power refers to the economic subject's ability to influence economic objects and to reach personal goals using their dominant resources. In this case, the extent of economic power is determined by the quantity and quality of resources controlled by economic subjects. The quality refers to the importance, scarcity, and substitutability of resources. The following chart illustrates the logical relationship of the formation of power economic man.

The economic man assumption is a historical concept, which has different connotations in different stages. Since Adam Smith, economists have made a series of assumptions concerning economic man: from pursuing maximum benefits to pursuing maximum utility; from complete rationality to bounded rationality; from complete self-interest to altruism. The power economic man proposed here is a theoretical discussion. Undoubtedly,

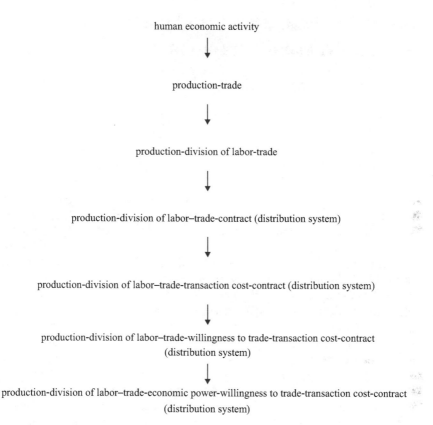

Figure 2.1 Logical relationship of the formation of power economic man.

reinterpreting economic man has become a new trend in the development of economic frontiers. As economists deepen their understanding of human behavior, the assumptions concerning human nature will continue to evolve, and the scope of economic research will widen. With such a trend, assumptions concerning economic man will become increasingly realistic.

3 Economic power and corporate contractual arrangements

Since Coase (1991) drew attention to the "black box," a reference to the firm, there has been rapid development of firm contract theory. In neoclassical economics, the firm is considered a micro-organization of production. Enterprise behavior is geared toward the pursuit of profit maximization, the distribution of production resources inside the firm, and the allocation of the firm's income among its members can be resolved by the competition in the factor market. In reality, firms face additional challenges. For example, the organizational and capital structure of firms varies according to the industry. Additionally, it is entirely possible that the manager's behavior is not geared toward the pursuit of profit within a firm. The manager theory argues that for their own interests, managers may be inclined to pursue market share, sales targets, or autonomy. The development of modern enterprise contract theory provides a better explanation for the behavior of internal firm members and the structure of the firm in the following three aspects.

First, we consider the contractual nature of the firm. We explain the nature of the firm from the perspective of the contract and at a level where the firm can be unified with the market. This is different from traditional theory. Traditional theory holds that the market and government are two methods of resource allocation. Both firms and residents are two economic subjects in the resource allocation process, but enterprise contract theory argues that the firm is another conduit for resource allocation in addition to the market and the government; the firm is not only an economic subject in the market but also an organizer of different production resources. The varied organizational structure of firms reveals different allocation efficiency of resources, and transaction cost is an indicator of the efficiency of the two methods of resource allocation, which are bureaucracy and market competition. Second, we consider the enterprise target. The firm is composed of economic subjects pursuing different goals. The behavior of the internal members of the firm have strong externalities on the organizational level of the firm; therefore, the internal property rights arrangements and the income distribution of the firm significantly affect the behavior of firm members and firm performance, which reflect on the different efficiency of corporate governance. Third, we consider property rights transaction and institutional change. The concept of transaction costs and the tradability of property rights provide a platform for institutional research. The firm, as an institutional form, is a result of economic entities pursuing economic efficiency and profit. Therefore, the endogenous theory of institutional change and the evolution of the firm's organizational form developed.

In this chapter, we develop the enterprise contract theory based on the concept of economic power. We hold that the power structure among economic subjects affects the property rights arrangement, income distribution, and the firm's efficiency in the contracting process of the firm's contract. The firm's performance appears to be determined by different corporate governance structure, but we show in this chapter that it is the distribution of economic power among different economic subjects that plays the decisive role in a firm's performance. Either the governance structure or the income distribution structure and even the performance of the firm are endogenous variables.

This chapter can be divided into three parts. First, we address the formation and allocation of the corporate right of internal control. Second, we discuss the distribution of the firm's revenue among its different members, including the nature of corporate governance, residual claim, and firm pricing. Third, we present a model on the power structure and firm performance before concluding the chapter. The content of this chapter is progressive. The distribution of the right of control among different members is the basis of a firm's organizational structure and serves as a basic indicator to distinguish the different corporate governance structures. In summary, the pursuit of the right of control is the same as the pursuit of profit. Hence, the allocation of a firm's profit determines the productivity and shirking behavior of the internal members of the firm. On the contrary, the behavior of firm members determines a firm's performance.

The formation and allocation of the corporate right of internal control

The nature of the firm's contract

Coase (1995) suggests the concept of transaction costs explicitly and at a level of significance equal to production cost. Coase also elevates the firm to the market level. He holds that the coordination mechanism of organizational division has two basic forms: one is to coordinate and organize the allocation of production resources through the entrepreneur's authority while the other is the price competition mechanism oriented toward liquidity of assets in the market. These two patterns of organizational division are substitutes. Compared with market transaction costs, when management and coordination costs are high, the market price mechanism is more effective. If the management and coordination cost is lower than market transaction cost, coordination by the firm is more effective. When management and coordination costs are equal to market transaction costs, the two mechanisms have the same coordination effect. Hence, the boundary of the firm is determined. Based on transaction costs,[1] research on the theory of the firm develops extensively and rapidly.

As the research advances, there are two different points of view concerning the nature of the firm. Some believe that both the firm and the market are contracts, but they are different in nature—the market transaction is based on equal exchange while the firm is based on the authority of the entrepreneurs and bureaucracy. Coase (1995) puts the firm and the market at the same level and places the firm and the market on two opposing sides. Then, the author determines the enterprise boundaries by the amount of the transaction costs. While others maintain that both the firm and the market are contractual in nature, the differences lie in the content, time, and binding of the contract. Zhang (1996) suggests that there are no differences between the firm and the market in nature; the firm is the factor contract substitute for the commodity contract. In economic reality, the definition of the boundaries of firm and market is vague. Particularly with the evolution of the organizational structure of the firm, the corporate alliance structure emerges with regular chains, franchise chains, and voluntary chains. The relationship between the enterprise scale and the market scale is not as theory predicts: one aspect wanes while the other waxes. In the process of market expansion, large-scale expansion of the organization of the firm occurs frequently in different periods while the organization of the firm sometimes shrinks. However, it is more likely that both the market and the organization of the firm expand synchronously. Such a phenomenon is most likely influenced by technological advancement and government regulation.

The dispute raised by the concept of transaction costs is also reflected in the different interpretations of the Coase theorem. The Coase theorem holds that as long as property rights are well defined under zero transaction cost, how property rights are defined does not affect the operating efficiency of economic institutions. In other words, when the transaction cost is non-zero, different property rights arrangements have a substantial impact on economic efficiency.

Since the Coase theorem was introduced to China, Chinese scholars have suggested different interpretations; the focus of Chinese scholars can be divided into three categories. First, because the transaction cost is non-zero, and different property rights arrangements have substantial impact on economic efficiency, Chinese scholars consider how to better define property rights to improve economic efficiency. The theory of vertical and lateral integration (GHM theory) is a canonical example of such a perspective. This theory takes a firm's performance as the objective and considers whether the firm should allow the upstream or downstream sections to assume residual control in the integration process. The criteria for evaluation are concerned with the trade-offs associated with the motivation of some specific investment and with the distortion affecting the side that relinquishes residual control.

Second, if the transaction costs are small enough, then clear definitions of property rights can contribute to the enhancement of economic efficiency. Therefore, defining property rights is clearly a key factor in improving economic efficiency. The reform of the state-owned enterprise in China has been pursuing such a principle and considers the definition of property a central objective of the reform. The reformers want to encourage the economic subjects to chase residual income through a clear definition of property rights and, ultimately, to enhance the performance of the state-owned enterprise.

Third, transaction costs originate from the definition of property rights; hence, the need to define property rights is determined by the amount of transaction costs or the comparison of the costs and benefits according to the definition of property rights. The difference between the first one and the third one is that the first understanding emphasizes the comparison of the different ways to define property rights while the third one is to define property rights or not. Zhang (1996) holds that contract adoption of the market and the firm should be determined by the transaction costs of the two mechanisms. Yang (1998) notes that the degree of clarity of property rights is determined by the comparison between transaction costs and the profit of labor division.

The root of the problem is that in describing the ideal state, Coase theorem ignores the relationship between transaction costs and property rights. The theorem only emphasizes the importance of transaction costs from the perspective of general social welfare. Moreover, Coase theorem fails to consider the allocation of profit among different economic subjects during the process of defining property rights. Using the prisoner's dilemma as an example, the contradictions between personal interest maximization and Pareto optimality originate from the inconsistency between production cooperation of interests and the allocation of interests among different subjects. Assuming that we place the prisoner's dilemma within a fully competitive market with perfect information where subsequent punishment can be imposed, active cooperation among individuals is unnecessary as all economic subjects are facing the same problem: selecting their own optimal behavior under a given economic structure. Even if there is no clear definition of property rights, individual optimal choice inevitably results in social Pareto optimal choices. When the perfect market assumption is relaxed and factors such as information asymmetry and the uncertainty of future expectations are taken into account, conflicts will occur as subjects cooperate with each other. Alternatively, during the allocation of cooperation gains, high transaction costs lead to market trade failure. If property rights are clearly defined, the range of a player's choice of strategy and their expectations with respect to others are given, which is conducive to conflict settlement. However, the problem is that the definition of property rights affects the amount of cooperation gains but also the results of interest distribution. Hence, how to define property rights is far more important than solving the problem of resource allocation.

In fact, the two different views on the nature of contracts are not irreconcilable; the analysis in this chapter is an effort in this direction. To address the problem of how to define property rights, we must begin with the transaction costs but use the concept of transaction costs alone to analyze the definition of the firm's internal property rights and revenue distribution is not enough; we need to introduce the concept of economic power. We hold that the nature of the contract is interest distribution. In the process of the social division of labor, cooperation between economic entities increases their income while the organizational cost is included; that is, the transaction costs include the external cost caused by the production behavior and shirking behavior of different members, the bargaining costs in firm's interest distribution, the cost of signing the contract, and the cost of supervising the implementation of the firm's contract.

The fundamental nature of the firm's contractual arrangement is the relationship of co-production and interest distribution reached by the firm members in the negotiating process. The accompanying contexts of the firm's contract include the control right allocation and corporate governance mechanisms. The difference between the firm's contract and the market contract is not the internal authority of the firm and the bureaucracy but the method of allocating the benefit of cooperation, in other words, the difference between the method of pricing and revenue distribution based on market exchange. The similarity of the firm's contract and the market contract is that these two different methods of resource allocation are realized at the same time as both sides of the transactions strive for revenue. It seems that the performance of the firm is determined by the contractual arrangement of the firm and corporate governance, but it can be ultimately determined by the power structure of the firm member.

The view of power vs. the view of efficiency

For modern enterprise theory, economic power is not a new concept. In essence, property rights and the right of control are the embodiment of certain economic powers. The authority of entrepreneurs is always simply understood as the implementation of power. But corporate contract theory itself rarely uses the concept of power to study the allocation of internal corporate control rights and the distribution of revenue. Williamson (1985) distinguished the view of power and the view of efficiency in research on the firm's contract. The view of efficiency holds that the enterprise mechanism can be used as a substitute for the market mechanism because of the reduction in transaction costs. With the goal of the pursuit of efficiency, the firm's contract determines the allocation of rights among the different firm members. The view of power holds that the power structure of different subjects determines the firm's contract. Mainstream firm theory, including transaction cost economics and the enterprise contract theory, takes efficiency as the goal of a firm's internal allocation of rights under the frame of "efficiency vs. power." "Right" is different from "power." A term that we mention in this book, the right, as Coase (1995)notes, is the entrepreneur's authority to manage and conduct the allocation of resources. To some extent, right is equivalent to the right of control or property rights. Transaction cost economics argues that the allocation of rights should minimize the sum of ex ante transaction costs and ex post transaction costs. GHM theory holds that the allocation of rights must stimulate specific investment while right originates from the ownership of material capital.

Rajan and Zingales (1998) develop the GHM theory and raise the issue of power within a firm. The authors hold that the right of control protects the rent of specific investment from being violated but also guarantees the owner's control rights to enjoy the firm's rent without specific investments. If critical resources are used as a substitute for material capital and access rights replace property rights, privileged access to critical resources is a more efficient way to provide incentives for specific investments than the right of control. The combination of specific investment and critical resources is the main difference between the author's theory and GHM theory. Another difference is that Rajan and Zingales' theory holds that the bargaining power of the subjects will increase as a result of investments while GHM theory holds that specific investments increase the risk of rent deprivation; hence, the power of negotiation weakens. However, the theory does not surmount the "efficiency vs. right" framework. A similar analysis exists in the research on the theory of endogenous institutions. Acemoglu (2003) regards this view of efficiency evolution as a political version of the Coase theorem.

We believe that power exists prior to the firm and contractual rights; it originates from the ownership of visible material resources and from the control rights and ownership of intangible resources such as information, ability, and credit. Right is the influence and control economic subjects entrusted by the institutionalized contract. Comparatively, the extension of right, property right and the right of control is less than the extension of power, right and the right of control depend on the firm's contract, an institutionalized carrier. The problem itself is not a conceptual distinction but a decision as to whether or not to admit the bargaining power of economic subjects who input factors of production. More specifically, the difference between the framework of efficiency vs. right and the framework of power vs. efficiency is whether priority is given to efficiency or power.

The mainstream theory of the firm treats efficiency as its primary criterion and analyzes the character of different factors of production, such as the inseparability of human capital, the material capital's capacity to be mortgaged, scarcity, information resources, and the power of negotiation. The firm's contract can be reached during the bargaining process among various members of production. The contract provides the position of firm members within the firm's structure, the right within a firm, and the distribution of a firm's profit. If we accept that the firm's contract can be reached after the bargaining process among various members of the firm, compared with the view of efficiency, the view of power is more realistic. The reason is that the firm is a collective composed of different firm members. Collective interests exist clearly and prior to the distribution of personal interests, but in the process of signing the firm's contract, the presence of the economic subject in charge of collective interests is not required. In the signing of the contract, each economic subject is concerned with their personal interests. In other words, in the bargaining process, different economic subjects do not value the ultimate efficiency of the firm, but they attach importance to the distribution of the firm's profit, particularly the level of personal interest. The analytical framework where efficiency is a primary objective implies a premise; that is, altruism. This premise contradicts the economic hypotheses of the firm members. Palermo (2000) holds that the efficiency principle is not suitable to explain the existence of institutional change and institutional arrangements.

The viewpoint of power priority has gradually been seriously considered with respect to firm's behavioral theory and stakeholder theory. Cyert and March (1963) argue that the firm is a common wealth of economic subjects with different and even conflicting interests. The members of the common wealth have permanent differences in values, faith, information, interests, and reality concepts. The power within a firm is considered a means and tool for the power's main body or group to pursue personal interests, and it is not a product of a designer who pursues efficiency as the target. The decision within a firm and the results of a decision's implementation are the result of negotiation and compromise. The most powerful members of the firm will reap the greatest rewards from the firm (Pfeffer, 1981). Stakeholder theory accepts the personal interests of different firm members, but not in the same way as the logic of firm's behavioral theory. Stakeholder theory begins with the profit motive of different economic subjects and their impact on the firm's decisions. This theory holds that the firm's decision makers should behave in a morally responsible manner and in the interests of the shareholders and the numerous stakeholders.

The residual value and firm's right of control

There are a number of variables in the firm's contract that can be identified by the contracting parties but cannot be identified by a third party (the court and the labor arbitration body). These unidentifiable variables include the level of worker effort, the supervisor's level of supervision, and the autonomous behavior of the manager. For profit distribution, the firm contract only identifies a few variables and cannot exhaust all possible future outcomes. For example, wage rates and labor hours are usually clearly identified in the contract's contents while many non-wage contents, such as pension, promotion opportunities, training opportunities, and employment security, are not included in the firm's contract in detail. For those contents not clearly identified in the firm's contract, disagreements may occur in the future; the definition of property rights in the residual value is typically considered to be the allocation of the right of control.

GHM theory holds that the residual value led to the problem of allocating the residual control rights. However, from the perspective of economic power, the residual represents only the premise of the right of control. Although the right of control is reflected in the incompleteness of the contract, the residual of the contract does not necessarily generate the right of control; the real source of the right of control is the comparison of power before the two parties signed the contract. Judging from the concept of the right of control, although the residual right of control is not defined in the contract compared with the general right of control, its attribution is clear; the right of control does not exist without attribution. If the residual exists within the contract, the residual certainly does not belong to the right of control. This part of the residual is the residual of future status as described in the contract. The residual of the contract involves the following two situations.

First, although the contract does not clarify some future states, there exists acquiescence or even agreements among contracting parties that one party has the right to make decisions by discretion regarding future states; this decision-making power mentioned is the right of control. The members who have the right of control have the right to make decisions based on an ambiguous and randomly continuous future state according to personal preferences. Such judgments are arbitrary and self-serving in nature, but the remaining contracting parties can expect the impact of the decisions made by the party with decision-making rights on the firm's total income and income distribution. The party who owns the right to make decisions by discretion does not have obvious decision-making rules and processing rules on such a series of future states. On the contrary, the behavior of the remaining contracting parties is clear. The contract does not detail the provisions on the uncertainty states within the scope of right of the party who has decision-making right. It is entirely possible that the cost of defining the contracting parties' property rights is greater than the benefits. From this perspective, while the content of the contract is incomplete, the function of the contract is complete. Although the firm's contract has the residual, the rights to be defined in the contract are fully allocated. For example, the rights of the parties are stipulated in a company's articles of association. For any circumstances in the future of the firm, parties will make their own decisions within their scope of rights. The general right of control and the residual right of control belong to this type of right.

Second, the future state that leads to inconsistent understanding among different contracting parties due to the ambiguity is simply not mentioned in the contract. All the contracting parties do not have a clear understanding of their own disposal rules within this state; hence, all contracting parties have a certain type of decision-making power. Final decision-making results depend on the joint decision of all relevant members, and any separate party does not have full responsibility to manage these affairs. If the state that is not defined in the contract emerges in the future, the contracting parties will compete with each other for their own personal interests. Such competition is reflected in the re-negotiation of the firm's contract, and such negotiations will persist. Of course, after lengthy negotiations, the terms of the contract will be settled in the contract, or even the right of control under the first case, as long as the contracting parties reach consensus on the problem or write it explicitly into the contract.

Concerning the distribution of the firm's right of control among its members, the majority of current views believe that the nature of the factor is mortgageable. The ability to take risks and the asset specificity, for example, are key factors of rights allocation. The exogenous differences of capital determine the statutes of the various forms of capital within the firm. Mainstream economics argues that before a contract is signed, the relationship between firm members is one of fair market exchange. Even after the contract is signed, the relationship between the two parties is still a fair contractual relationship. However, the doctrine we have explained is not enough to explain the formation of authority within a firm. From the perspective of the costs of defining property rights, it is unnecessary and impossible for the contract to define all possible future states, and this does not mean that the transaction cost is a sufficient condition for controlling the formation of control rights. The authority of different factors can be reflected as the right of autonomous control over the production process, and the incompleteness of the contract is due to bargaining power's claims on future earnings. Figure 3.1 illustrates that the incompleteness of the contract originates from the consideration of transaction costs.

Suppose two people play a game, and the rules of the game are unambiguous, but only one party, namely party A, fully understands the rules of the game, while the other party, namely party B, is in a novice status. Before the game starts, A will tell B the rules of the game and B just roughly

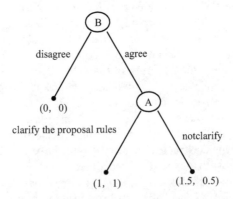

Figure 3.1 Ambiguity of rules and the right of control.

learned the rules of the game due to the complexity of the rules, but B is able to compete with A. Such a state may appear in the game. Before the game starts, A did not tell B such a special state will appear; hence, B and A's understandings on such a special state is contradictory. At this time B is in a disadvantaged status of the game because A does not clarify all the rules of the game (including the rules of any possible future state) and hence, A has the control right. If the future state is beneficial to A, A will tell B the original rules of such special state clearly; if the future state is beneficial to B, either B does not know such a state is beneficial to him or A will hide the normal rules.

If the two parties do not want to participate in the game, then the income of both sides is 0. If the two parties participate in the game and all the rules of the game are clear, then the income of both sides is 1; if A, the instructor of the rules of the game, hides a special rule of the game, then A's income is 1.5 and B's income is 0.5. By reverse induction, we know that the sub-game perfect Nash equilibrium of this game is B choose to participate in the game while A chose not to clarify the rules of the game regarding the special case—the final income of the two parties is (1.5, 0.5). From this game we know that if one party does not clarify the proposal rules of a certain possible future state while the other party has insufficient understandings on that state, then the party who does not clarify the disposal rules has the random decision-making right of control, while the other party's behavior under all states is unambiguous and is controlled by the party who does not clarify the disposal rules. It can be seen clearly that the so-called right of control is the right of random decision-making within the individual choice set under the situation that the other party's disposal rule is clear.

Economic power and allocation of the control right

We use a game model to illustrate how to determine the signing of contract and the distribution of the right of control through the power structure among firm members. Suppose on whether to write certain kind of uncertainty event in the future into the contract, the choice of the two parties, X and Y, can be either definitude (dented as D) or ambiguous (denoted as A). If the two parties both choose A, the contract cannot be reached because neither X nor Y chooses to define the future state clearly and the income of both sides is 0 due to rent consumption. If the two parties reach an agreement, and both choose D, then the benefit of cooperation is 1.[2] According to the structure of negotiation power of different factors, we set the distribution ratio of the benefit of cooperation as b $(0 < b < 1)$.[3] Suppose in the contract signed by the two parties, the probability of the occurrence of this relative future state is p $(0 < p < 1)$, and the payoff matrix of the game is given as illustrated in Table 3.1. If party X chooses D, party Y chooses A, and under the circumstance that the relevant future states does not appear, the benefit of cooperation is still allocated according to the ratio of b; when

Table 3.1 The payoff matrix of the game model on the firm's contract

	Party Y chooses D	*Party Y chooses A*
Party X chooses D	$b, 1-b$	$b(1-p), p+(1-b)(1-p)-c(b)$
Party X chooses A	$p+b(1-p)-c(1-b), (1-b)(1-p)$	$0,0$

the relevant future states occur, party Y, who does not clearly express his own views, will commit unethical behavior afterwards. The payoff received by party X who expresses his own views clearly is 0, while party Y will receive all the corporation benefits, which is 1. But party Y might lose part of the benefit due to party X's resistance. The loss of party Y, denoted by $c(b)$, can be regarded as a function of party X's power b, we assume that $c'(b) > 0, c''(b) > 0, c(0) = 0, c(1) = 1$. When party Y cannot persuade party X, party Y cannot receive extra profit due to the ambiguity of rules. On the contrary, if party X chooses A, party Y chooses D, and under the circumstance that the relevant future state appears, then the profits received by party Y is 0, while party X will receive all the corporation benefits, but the loss caused by party Y's resistance, which equals to $c(1-b)$, should be subtracted. The Nash equilibrium of this game consists of four cases.

When $c(b) > bp$, $c(1-b) > (1-b)p$, $c(b)$ denotes the loss of party Y due to the resistance to party X, bp denotes the possible gain of party Y as party Y choose not to define the contract clearly. $c(1-b)$ denotes the loss of party X due to party Y's resistance, $(1-b)p$ denotes the possible gain of party X as party X chooses not to clarify the contract. If this condition holds, it implies that the gain of not clarifying the proposal rules regarding the relevant future states is less than the loss of trying to obtain this benefit, hence two parties both choose to sign the contract clearly. It is obvious that the Nash equilibrium (D, D) emerges, and two parties choose to define their own rules of decision-making clearly with regard to relevant future states in the contract.

When $c(b) > bp$, $c(1-b) < (1-b)p$, it implies that as party Y tries to get extra benefits through the ambiguity of the rules, the loss is larger than the extra benefits generated as a result of the resistance of party X. On the contrary, when party X chooses not to clarify the rules, party X's loss due to the resistance of party Y is smaller than the extra benefits. Hence only party X is able to choose not to clarify the proposal rules on relevant future states while party Y has to clarify. Here the Nash equilibrium is (A, D), where party X chooses not to clarify the proposal rules while party Y chooses to clarify. When $c(b) \langle bp$, $c(1-b) \rangle (1-b)p$, the condition is just the opposite; that is, the Nash equilibrium is (D, A).

When $c(b) < bp$, $c(1-b) < (1-b)p$, it means that both parties can receive extra benefits through the vague future decision-making rules. In addition to the two pure strategy Nash equilibriums (A, D) and (D, A), we have a mixed strategy Nash equilibrium. This equilibrium strategy is that party X chooses D with probability r, chooses A with probability $1-r$, and party Y chooses D with probability s, chooses A with probability $1-s$, where

$$r = \frac{(1-p)(1-b)}{pb+(1-p)(1-b)-c(b)}, \quad s = \frac{b(1-p)}{p(1-b)+b(1-p)-c(1-b)}$$

Under the condition that $c(b)<bp$, $c(1-b)<(1-b)p$, differentiating b with respect to r and s, and combining this with the properties of the function $c(b)$, we have

$$\frac{dr}{db} = \frac{(p-1)\left[p-c(b)-(1-b)c'(b)\right]}{\left[pb+(1-p)(1-b)-c(b)\right]^2} < 0$$

$$\frac{ds}{db} = \frac{(1-p)\left[p-c(1-b)-bc'(1-b)\right]}{\left[p(1-b)+b(1-p)-c(1-b)\right]^2} > 0$$

This implies that, as the power structure changes, the more powerful party is more likely to choose not to clarify the rules, while the less powerful one is more likely to choose to clarify the rules.

In order to show the dependency relationship between the allocation of control right and power structure, and further the analysis on the conditions of above four cases, we combine the loss function of the two sides due to their counterpart's resistance in a way similar to Edgeworth box (illustrated in Figures 3.2 and 3.3). Where $c(b)$ is party Y's loss function due to party X's resistance, correspondingly, $c(1-b)$ is party X's loss function due to party Y's resistance, pb and $p(1-b)$ are lines with slope p. By the symmetric and monotonic property of function $c(b)$, there exists a unique b^*, which satisfies $c(b)=bp$, $c(1-b)=(1-b)p$.

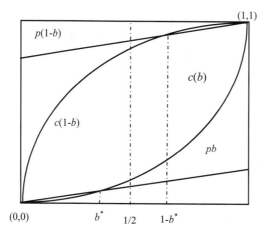

Figure 3.2 Power resistance Edgeworth box (p small).

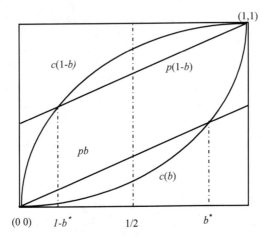

Figure 3.3 Power resistance Edgeworth box (*p* large).

If $p(>0)$ is sufficiently small, then $b^* < \frac{1}{2}$. When the power structure satisfies $0 < b < b^*$, the Nash equilibrium is (D, A), party Y has unilateral right of control; when the power structure satisfies $1 - b^* < b < 1$, the Nash equilibrium is (A, D), party X has unilateral right of control; when the power structure satisfies $b^* < b < 1 - b^*$, the Nash equilibrium is (D, D), the contract clearly defines the proposal rules of future states, neither party X nor party Y has the residual control right.

If $p(>0)$ is sufficiently large, then $b^* > \frac{1}{2}$. When the power structure satisfies $0 < b < 1 - b^*$, the Nash equilibrium is (D, A); when the power structure satisfies $b^* < b < 1$, the Nash equilibrium is (A, D); when the power structure satisfies $1 - b^* < b < b^*$, the three Nash equilibriums are (A, D), (D, A) and mixture strategy. Hence under a relatively symmetrical power structure, the allocation of control right depends on other potentially relevant factors, such as the will power of certain party or compromises, etc.

The most special case is, if the probability of relevant future events *p* makes $b^* = \frac{1}{2}$. When $0 < b < b^*$, the Nash equilibrium is (D, A); when $b^* < b < 1$, the Nash equilibrium is (A, D); when $b = b^* = \frac{1}{2}$, there are four Nash equilibriums (A, D), (D, A), (D, D) and mixed strategy Nash equilibrium, respectively. Obviously, (D, D) is Pareto optimal equilibrium.

Based on the above discussion, we reach the following conclusions. When the degree of power structure asymmetry is sufficiently large, the contract favors the more powerful party in terms of the right of control while the less powerful party is forced to clarify their own behavior. When the power

structure is relatively symmetric, for some uncertainty events, if the probability of the uncertainty event is relatively small, two parties will choose to
sign a contract. If the probability of the uncertainty event is relatively large,
neither party wants to clarify their own behavior and allow their counterpart the right of control. Thus, they negotiate with their counterpart on this
phenomenon in the future.

In addition, we observe the process of signing enterprise contract, in
other words, the formation of the firm's organization. Before the contract is
signed, the bargaining process of different factors of production is a contest
of economic power. The contest is characterized by persuading and inducing. After the contract is signed, the relationship between the firm members
can be considered the implementation of corporate authority expressed as
command and obedience within a firm. The similarity between the enterprise contract and the market contract is that they are both self-enforced
contracts; any transaction party can choose to enter and exit freely. The difference is that enterprise contract has contractual rights compared with the
market contract. Hence, both the firm and the market are means of resource
allocation; enterprise organization formation is the transformation of different definitions of property rights and is the process of economic rights
(market competition) transformed into corporate authority (organization
structure). Alternatively, the formation of enterprise organization can be
considered the formalization and institutionalization of the power structure
of different production factor owners.

The firm's pricing mechanism and interest distribution

The firm's residual income

Market firms have long faced an uncertain environment. The owners of
different production factors sign a contract and participate in production activities together, but the price of the produced product is uncertain. In other
words, the firm's income is a random variable. Therefore, it is impossible for
all the factors to realize stable rewards. If the outcome of negotiation is that
some members are willing to receive a fixed income, the firm's residual is
the balance after deducing all fixed income. At this stage, the residual claim
enjoys the firm's profits while also undertaking the risk of failure. There
is no doubt that even if none of the members are willing to receive a fixed
income, the firm's residual still exists. The fundamental motivation of firm
members is to obtain profits (to compensate for the cost and to receive net
income), both material capital and human capital have residual claim, and
the distribution ratio depends on multi-party negotiations.

In fact, the complete contract theory endowed firm's residual income
with a more important theoretical significance. Alchian and Demsetz's
team production theory holds that the nature of the firm can be considered
team production. The reason production teams evolved into firms is that

the high efficiency of production brought by team production generates the free ride problem (Alchian & Demsetz, 1972). The characteristic of the firm is not authority, which is different from the market, but the firm's ability to supervise the opportunism within a firm and measure the productivity of factors and remuneration prior to the market mechanism. Hence, transaction costs are reduced. The effective operation of team production organization requires supervisor to observe and measure the contributions of other members in the firm. To motivate the supervisor, the residual claim of the firm should be given to the supervisor. The basic characteristic of the firm is that the supervisor of team members is also the residual claim owner. The enterprise owner as investor is also the supervisor who has the right of ownership, possession, use, disposition, and income from assets while other members produce under the supervision of the supervisor and receive the corresponding gains.

The residual income of a firm plays an important role in principal agent theory. Principal agent theory is one of the most significant breakthroughs in contract theory. Principal agent theory studies how principals design the optimal contract to encourage their subject as the principal addresses conflicts of interest and information asymmetry. On the firm level, the principal is the owner of the firm; that is, the shareholder is a firm's operator or manager. Suppose all the economic subjects are rational; that is, the pursuit of maximizing personal income and the manager's behavior is not solely the pursuit of maximizing the firm's income but the pursuit of the scale of production, market share, and personal power. If the manager's behavior can be predicted by the shareholders, the shareholder should design an effective way of income distribution while signing the principal-agent contract with the manager. Hence, the manager is motivated to behave in the interests of the shareholder's pursuit of maximum revenue. In other words, the distribution of a firm's residual income directly determines the firm's production results.

Principal agent theory holds that the agent's fixed income can reach the Pareto optimal level when there is no uncertainty in a firm's external market. Even if uncertainty exists, as long as the manager's behavior can be supervised, fixed income and supervision can still enable the manager to achieve the Pareto optimal level of effort. If uncertainty exists and the firm's revenue is irrelevant to the manager's level of effort, Pareto efficiency can still be achieved; that is, the person who is risk neutral bears the risk of uncertainty while the risk averter obtains fixed income. If there is uncertainty in future income, the information on the supervision of the manager's behavior is incomplete, and the manager's behavior affects the firm's revenue directly to motivate the agent's level of effort, the agent should bear the risk. If the agent is risk neutral, the principal obtains the fixed income while the agent bears all the risk, and the Pareto optimal level of effort can be achieved. If the agent is a risk averter, a trade-off between the risk and the motivation is required, and the Pareto optimal level of effort cannot be achieved.

The impacts of the residual distribution of a firm on the Pareto optimal level of a firm's production show that the residual claim is both an incentive and a risk for the agents. On a theoretical level, we place more emphasis on risk, but we place more emphasis on incentives in reality. Theoretically speaking, the agent can share the residual claim of a firm because the firm's revenue is related to the manager's effort level. In extreme cases, the agent should fully enjoy the residual claim. Taking the agent's risk aversion into account, the owner and the manager of a firm should share the firm's residual claim, which is a sub-optimal contract on the distribution of a firm's revenue. This finding implies an upper limit on the subject's proportion of residual claim. In reality, the manager's behavior is stimulated to meet the pursuit of maximum firm revenue. Therefore, we should partly link the manager's income with the firm's income.

Principal agent theory has presented a dilemma since its inception, the reference object of which is the traditional enterprise system. The analysis of the concept compares the modern enterprise system and the classical enterprise system, such as shareholder primacy or the residual claim. Therefore, such a theory only reveals the problems faced by modern firms and does not solve these problems. The most perfect and thorough solution is to eliminate the modern enterprise system and restore the unification of ownership and management rights. The scientific nature and the applicability of the incentive theory established on this basis are also doubtful. Theoretically, the allocation criteria of the benefits of firm cooperation depend on the contributions of the factors of production. However, due to the difficulties in measuring these contributions,[4] the problem of income distribution is not a pure problem of economics but a problem of power and ethics. Marx's labor theory of value is strong evidence that capital exploits labor, whereas modern corporate governance theory holds that the manager encroaches on the interests of asset owners (Marx, 1911).

Economic power and corporate governance

From the perspective of governance mechanisms, corporate governance can be divided into two categories: shareholder primacy theory and stakeholder theory. Shareholder primacy theory holds that according to principal-agent theory, the autonomous control rights of the firm manager trigger moral hazard behavior against the interests of the investor. When the incentive mechanism is not an effective way to eliminate such behavior, alternative supervision mechanisms are required. Corporate governance forces the manager's behavior to meet the shareholder's interest; hence, an organizational arrangement is required whereby the firm's operations are guaranteed to be in the interests of investors. Stakeholder theory holds that in addition to the interests of shareholders, the manager of a firm should consider the interests of stakeholders including bondholders, employees, suppliers, and communities.

Corporate governance that practices shareholder primacy is based on principal-agent theory. From the perspective of the evolution of the enterprise system and the role of human capital in the production processes of a firm, the theory appears somewhat one-sided. Comparatively speaking, stakeholder theory's concerns of business goals and revenue distribution are more comprehensive, but this theory is proposed as a direct response to shareholder primacy theory. Stakeholder's theory is based on the concept that firm managers should care about stakeholders, except the shareholder at a moral level due to the increasingly important role of team production and human capital within a firm. This concept differs from the behavioral theory of the firm that practices the viewpoint of power logically and operates primarily based on the decision-making behavior of a firm. A manager operates a firm under the constraints of a number of economic subjects. The decision-making process of a firm naturally takes into account the interests of stakeholders while it is not the manager's initiative to balance the distribution of benefits. The power structure determines that the viewpoint of corporate governance provides a solid theoretical basis for stakeholder theory. The relationship between the economic power structure of the members of a firm and corporate governance can be described by the following game model.

The set of players is $N = \{1, 2, \cdots, i, \cdots, n\}$. The players of corporate governance include stakeholders such as firm managers, shareholders, employees, and suppliers. In contrast to stakeholder theory, the players mentioned here are not all economic subjects relevant to the interests of the firm but economic subjects who have economic power over the behavior and outcome of the firm. For example, the public interest organization that relies heavily on firms. Although firms provide these public interest organizations economic support, it is not conceivable that these organizations affect the behavior of the firm.

We use the notation $S_i = \{s_{i1}, s_{i2}, \cdots, s_{im}\}$ to denote the strategy set of player i. The strategy set is a set of behaviors available for the player, and this is the embodiment of the player's economic power including the selection of other counterparties, the opportunistic behavior in the transaction process and autonomy. According to the different stages of the game, the strategy set can be divided into ex-ante strategy set S_{ix}, in-between strategy set S_i, and ex-post strategy set S_{ip}. Before the game starts, economic power is manifested as participation in the formulation of transaction rules, in other words, the right of free transaction in signing the contract. The transaction parties can enter or exit the contract freely depending on the scope of the counterparties. In the game process, economic power is manifested as the ambiguity of transaction rules; that is, the autonomous right of control within the transaction rules of the transaction parties depends on the characteristics of the factors of production provided by the members of the firm in the firm's production process. From the last section, we know that as a result of economic power, this right of control is manifested as different forms of influence and control. After the game, economic power manifests itself as the right to modify transaction rules. This type of economic power and the economic power before the game starts are essentially the same. However, over time, the resource endowments and production capacity of firm members will change. Hence, the choice set will also change. Therefore, the corresponding economic power strengthens as more rivals emerge, more opportunism states become available in the transaction process, and the scope of autonomy widens. We do not discuss re-negotiations after the game in this chapter. The game process is divided into the following two stages.

1   All the economic subjects select appropriate counterparties from their own strategy set and draft mutually satisfactory transaction rules; that is, the corporate governance structure G established by the contracting parties. The governance structure includes the allocation of control rights discussed in the last section and the method and quantity of a firm's residual income distribution among different members. The arrangements of the corporate governance structure determine who will control the firm among numerous stakeholders and how to control the firm.

2   According to the requirements of the corporate governance structure, all players choose their own production behavior and autonomous behavior s_i from the in-between strategy set, and the behavior of the firm is formed by these behaviors altogether. Finally, the outcome of the game is the allocation of a firm's income among different players $P = (p_1, p_2, \cdots, p_n)$, which is determined by the arrangements of the governance structure and the autonomous behavior.

On the surface, corporate governance structure determines the behavior of different members and the enterprise target; that is, in the second stage, under the given corporate governance structure, the maximized profit of player i determines the behavioral choices in the game process. Suppose $(s_1, s_2, \cdots, s_n) = L(G)$, but the actual game process is such that the behavior of the second stage is predicted in the first stage. We choose the maximized profit of ex-ante behavior, namely p_i, and the notation $(s_{1x}, s_{2x}, \cdots, s_{nx}) = F(s_1, s_2, \cdots, s_n)$ to denote ex-ante behavior. Thus, the governance structure is $G = G(s_{1x}, s_{2x}, \cdots, s_{nx})$. In other words, the strategy choice set of players; that is, the economic power structure and production function together determines the governance structure. Under the assumption that all economic subjects are rational, before signing the contract, every firm member already knows all possible personal behaviors in the economic process and the results on the final income distribution of a firm. Therefore, the firm's revenue distribution is an outcome that can be predicted before signing the contract, and every member of the firm is willing to accept the outcome. This represents the best result that the economic subjects can select from the available strategy set. The result is the scope of the strategy set, or the economic power determines the revenue distribution of a firm. For example, a worker knows that according to certain economic criterion, their contribution to the firm and the wage obtained does not match, but the only choice the worker can make is to refuse employment from this firm and accept employment from another firm instead. It is entirely possible that this choice cannot increase the worker's income.

The firm's pricing function and distributional effects

In market transactions, suppose that the initial resource endowments are given. According to the principle of free exchange, a transaction will economically benefit at least one party without making any other party worse off. This dynamic is the Pareto efficiency criterion. The market transaction price is determined by factors such as the relationship between supply and demand. For the enterprise organization, the outcome of a corporate transaction[5] is the allocation of the firm's common output while the common output is considered public goods for firm members, and the contract between the members of the firm is incomplete; that is, information asymmetry. Therefore, the firm is a pricing mechanism that is fundamentally different from the market (we have already discussed the nature of the firm and the market in previous sections). This view is evident in mainstream firm theory. The team production theory holds that a supervisor's duty is to supervise the members' behavior and evaluate their contributions to the firm (Alchian & Demsetz, 1972). Therefore, the residual claim is the pricing of the supervisor. GHM theory holds that control rights are helpful to guarantee that the specific investment before the game begins receives its deserved later investment gains (Grossman & Hart, 1986). Yang (1998) notes that the firm is an indirect pricing mechanism of human capital. Unfortunately, the pricing function of the firm is often ignored, and this is reflected by the suspicions concerning a firm's income distribution. The Edgeworth box, illustrated in Figure 3.4, explains the differences between the firm's pricing and the market's pricing.

Suppose there are two subjects A and B respectively in a certain market transaction, the two goods, X and Y are exchanged between the two subjects in the course of trade, and the initial resource endowment is at point E. Obviously, for the two subjects if goods Y shifts from A to B, while goods X shifts from B to A, then the two subject's utility will be increased. When the shifted price is within a certain range, it will be satisfactory for the two people. The upper and lower limits of the transaction price are determined by the location of the initial point and the marginal rate of substitution of the two indifference curves. If the transaction is reached between the upper and lower limits of the price range, the distribution of goods will go along either A's indifference curve M or B's indifference curve N. More likely the prices will be in the middle, namely in region II, illustrated in Figure 3.4. According to neoclassical economics, transaction price is determined by the relationship of supply and demand.

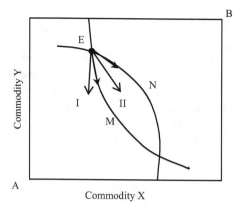

Figure 3.4 Enterprise pricing and market pricing.

We analyze the firms' transactions. If the efficiency principle is abandoned (we have already analyzed the viewpoints of power first and efficiency first in the previous section), it is possible that the actual transaction price may exceed the acceptable transaction price in the market, such as the prices in region I in Figure 3.4. In fact, whether market pricing or corporate pricing, the degree of the voluntary nature of transactions determines whether the transaction is an efficient evolution. If the transaction is not voluntary but forced, the transaction may not be an efficient evolution. Such an involuntary transaction originates from the limited choice set of individual behavior. Under the economic institution of the social division of labor, it is natural that an individual will accept the monopoly price voluntarily. The signing of the transaction contract of the market and the firm depends on the free will of the two subjects. While the power formed by social division of labor and resource endowment will treat the choice of different economic subjects differently, it will also determine the distribution ratio of different economic subjects in corporate earnings.

For the firm, if the contributions of the factors are technically undividable, as a resource allocation and pricing mechanism, the firm requires a self-enforcing contract to define the distribution of revenue among the firm members. Therefore the firm's total revenue is maximized. However, the signing of the firm's contract is not necessarily a Pareto optimization process. The role of efficiency is to accelerate or hinder the adjustment of the firm's contract only. If the contract of the firm changes the boundaries of interest while possessing Pareto efficiency improvements, the adjustment of the contract will be smoothly advanced. If the function of the firm contract is to shift the boundary of interests from one side to another, the contract's adjustment process will encounter resistance from the party that suffered loss; the source of this resistance is economic power. In the analytical framework of the viewpoint of power rather than the viewpoint of efficiency, the emphasis on managers' invasion and occupation of the shareholders' benefits and capital's exploitation of labor are ethical problems rather than economic problems.

For senior executive compensation, the accusation of managers' invasion and occupation of shareholder benefits from the perspective of revenue allocation outcomes is based on unsound economic evidence. If we admit that the resource allocation mechanism of the firm is more effective than the market, and the firm is able to substitute the pricing of the factor market, the accusation concerning the outcomes of a firm's income distribution is illogical. Under irregular market transactions and irregular firm institutions, senior executive compensation should be vulnerable to economic constraints and moral condemnation. If the income gap between senior executives and ordinary employees causes the income distribution of society as a whole to deteriorate, it is the government's duty to set up a benefit compensation system via redistribution and to regulate the market structure.

Doubts on the rationality of a firm's income distribution originate from the confusion that the role of market pricing in the income allocation of a firm is only subsidiary. If we admit that the firm is a resource allocation mechanism that differs from the market, the firm should be a pricing mechanism that differs from the market. The revenue distribution of a firm is a pricing mechanism with unique characteristics. Once the pricing mechanism is mentioned, the role of the market is exaggerated. Traditional firm theory holds this viewpoint, and the significance of factor markets is also emphasized by contractual firm theory. Zhang (1996) holds that the firm can be considered the replacement of a product market by a factor market because the transaction costs of a factor market are lower than the pricing cost of a product market. The theory of corporate governance emphasizes the product market's restrictions on manager's behavior while also emphasizing the control of the autonomous rights of the managers by the manager market and the market of the right of control.

Although the theory of the contract places the firm and the market at the same level as the resource allocation mechanism, the market is indispensable for a firm's pricing function. This is particularly the case for a firm's factors of production. If a certain factor market is perfectly competitive, managers do not need to supervise or measure the input of the factor owners. In extreme cases, if all the factor markets are perfectly competitive, the total output is allocated exactly by all the team members, which reverts to the general equilibrium of neo-classical economics. Such an ideal state cannot be achieved due to transaction costs, attitudes towards risk, division of labor, and the very nature of factors of production. However, we admit that in all other markets, factors of production have achieved equilibrium, and that changes in certain factor markets will inevitably affect the marginal productivity of such elements and its power of negotiation within a firm, and result in reallocation of power within a firm. Therefore, the analysis on a firm's institutions should not be limited to within the firm. External market mechanisms, and the contracts within the firm altogether, form the corporate governance mechanism. Yang's insight into this viewpoint states that the transactions of the firm should be a trade-off between the cost of potential transaction parties and the cost of current transaction parties (Yang, 1998). This indicates that the enterprise mechanism is based on the market mechanism. However, the firm as a resource allocation mechanism is different from the market, and its pricing function is different from the pricing functions of the market. The distribution of firm revenue is the external reflection of the power structure between the factors of production.

Economic power and firm performance

Cooperation between human capital and material capital

Wealth creation is the main topic of economic and social development. At the beginning of the establishment of economic science, economists focused on the problem of creating social welfare. However, the crux of the problem is that the allocation of social income underlies the research on social income creation. Since it is reasonable that income should be distributed among the class who created it, the main problem that challenges economic research is the inconsistency between wealth creation and income distribution. In the development of economic history, mercantilism first proposed the concept that wealth is created from circulation, which meets the need of business capital ideology. Physiocrats hold that wealth is created from agriculture, while landlords, handicraftsmen, and the aristocracy do not create any type of wealth. From William Petty to Adam Smith, as economics gradually formed a scientific system, the labor theory of value prevailed, emphasizing that effort created wealth during the production process. Until the emergence of subjective price theory, the concept of value and wealth creation acquiesced to market and price. Factors, such as land, labor, and capital used in the production process, are contributing factors in wealth creation. The firm's income should be distributed among the owners of these factors. Unfortunately, prevailing neoclassical economic theory did not find consensus on price theory and distribution theory among economists.

For capitalist classical firms, Marx (1911) holds that the capitalist exploits the worker's surplus value. For modern firms, the theory of corporate governance argues that as a result of information asymmetry between the manager and the shareholder, the capital owner's profit will be encroached upon as the manager tries to maximize their own profit, which is the fundamental problem of the firm. The corporate governance structure is designed to protect monetary capital profit from erosion. To encourage manager's behavior not to veer too far from the shareholders' interests, some extra profit that traditionally belonged to monetary capital should be given to the manager. The question is: Why has the investor's status changed so dramatically from exploiter to victim? In the traditional theory of economics, capital is a factor that enjoys the firm's residual claim at the cost of assuming managerial risk. Capital's exclusive control on profit is guaranteed by the capital owner's power. According to Galbraith's (1983) theory of power distribution, in any society, power is always combined with the most irreplaceable factor of production, and the agent who supplies such factors will enjoy the firm's residual income. In feudal society, land is the most important factor of production. The landlord is the supplier of this factor of production; thus, the landlord benefits from the rent. In a capitalist economy, capital takes the place of land, becomes the most important factor of production, and the residual claim of the firm transfers to the capitalist. In the present era of information knowledge, due to industry and technology advancements, there is an increasing demand for knowledge. Specialized knowledge is more complex and has become a main factor of production in promoting economic growth and enhancing productivity. Spontaneously, workers who possess such knowledge and skills enjoy power corresponding to their knowledge and skills. Capitalized human resources enjoy the firm's residual claim as a result of the changes in capital structure.

We hold that material capital lost its dominance because of the changes in power structure related to material capital and human capital. Power structure is a state of interaction while profit is the driving source of interaction. If the structure of benefit distribution meets the power structure, a steady state is reached among economic subjects. Changes in power structure, as a result of changes in the resource endowments structure, incur modulations in bilateral behavior. Thus, benefit adjustment is reached, and new resource distribution and cooperation structures emerge under the motive of pursuing maximum profit. These efforts, in turn, influence the power structure until the new steady state is reached.

For classical firms, disparity in income status between material capital and human capital reflects the market bargaining power of both parties. The workers choose to sell cheap labor for two reasons: the social environment at the time and the prevailing mode of production at the time require primitive and pure labor that is abundant. If advanced production technology is so complicated that high-quality labor is required, the cooperation process between both parties will focus on wage negotiation and include residual claims.

It is impossible for material capital to maintain the exclusive advantages of profits without the use of advanced modes of production. Ricardo (1891) notes that accompanying economic growth, the share of rent will become increasingly large. Malthus, Winch and James (1992) predict that the wage of labors can only maintain their standard of living. A fact of modern economic growth is that rent as a proportion of revenue decreases while the economy grows rapidly; wage rates and labor income increase as the economy grows. When the power of material capital is strong enough that workers have little strength to resist, competition among material capital intensifies, and the result is that capital continues to adopt new technology to raise productivity. Mincer (1974) argues that accumulation of material capital will enhance the marginal products of human capital. It is a powerful stimulus for ordinary workers to realize the high income of the managerial class and the highly skilled, and workers will continually invest in themselves in terms of knowledge, intelligence, and skills. During this process, capital utilization and output will improve at the same time.

Compared with material capital, human capital characteristics differ from those of property rights. The advancement of human capital's status in the firm results in the re-distribution of the corporate right of control between them. The most important feature of human capital is that it is inseparable from the owner. Because of its inseparability, human capital is weak in terms of information display capability and cannot be mortgaged or transferred. The wide diversity of human capital implies its heterogeneity and the ease with which it can be hidden, which leads to monopolization of human capital. Thus, human capital is difficult to measure. When human capital and material capital cooperate with each other, the failure of the firm means the owner of human capital will lose their property gains but will not lose the property itself. Hence the promise of material capital is reliable while human capital can easily avoid the risk of business failure. Under the property rights system, with limited liability, the owner of material capital transfers its right of management and administration while reserving the right of supervision in the use of capital. Some scholars argue that the trend of human capital investment leverages specialization and the team dynamic (Fang, 1997). Therefore, human capital can be mortgaged and considered a stakeholder.

The differences between the two described views originate from the difference between two concepts in firm theory:[6] the specificity and exclusiveness of assets. The specificity of assets implies that the rent of assets may be possessed in future cooperation; that is the risk of being trapped. The exclusive nature of assets reflects bargaining power and increases the bargaining chips for future cooperation. However, this is not the case in reality. For human capital with an exclusive nature, the threat of leaving the firm is unbelievable threat because human capital has specificity in nature at the same time. Intrinsically, the monopoly of transaction exists in the specificity and exclusively of assets to varying degrees. The discussion on the specificity and exclusively of human capital adds vagueness to the characteristics of human capital. From the results, the two points of views are different because they have a different understanding of risk. If the risk compensates for the fixed payment resulting from a lack of ex-post income, in an economic society where currency is the ultimate means of payment, material capital is the ultimate risk unless a credible promise can be made using human capital, for example, power license; the loss of reputation becomes significant. If the risk is understood as the uncertainty of future earnings, both material capital and human capital cannot achieve the goal of risk aversion. Material capital can exit more easily due to the monetization and securitization of the material capital, while human capital cannot easily do so because of its nature of specificity.

Human capital's property rights characteristics and the changes of supply and demand in the market led to the transformation of the classical capitalist firm to a modern firm. This likely indicates that the property structure and the contract of modern firms are more effective. In reality, proprietorship and modern firms co-exist, which implies that the owner of material capital accepts the new property structure and the new interest distribution structure based on the weighing of the pros and cons. In other words, the formation of power of different components based on a relatively stable power structure is a result of the negotiation on both parties. The firm's residual income is a mixture of risk compensation brought by the external market circumstances and the return of management functions caused by capital mobility. There are no clear-cut and reasonable standards to evaluate the contributions and the income of both sides. If you do have to find such a standard, the factor markets that provide a reference for both sides to sign a contract after negotiation are a good example; marginal revenue reflects the contribution of the production factors, the amount of which determines the remuneration of factors of production.

Similar to our analysis on the firm's pricing mechanism in the previous section, there are two problems in the method to determine the firm member's income according to market prices. The first problem is that the market is not perfectly competitive. Coase (1995) argues that because a higher market transaction cost is required to judge the performance of different parties' products, firms use transaction contracts. Second, the total amount to be allocated between both parties is greater than the sum of the contribution of all the factors (otherwise, there would be no cooperation), and there is no way to prove that the benefits of cooperation equal the marginal product of one side when there are no other opportunities for cooperation. A price higher than the market price can only be used as a participation constraint. In fact, the enterprise system is considered to be the chief culprit of the imbalance in interest distribution because, subjectively speaking, the price in the market is never satisfactory. From the point of view of supply and demand, when the potential supply of human capital exceeds the potential supply of material capital, human capital's negotiation strength is insufficient because its weakening scarcities results in diminishing income distribution. On the contrary, as the supply of material capital increases, the relative scarcity of the firm's human capital becomes increasingly obvious, and human capital has the ability to ask for more return. Thus, the distribution structure of the firm's residual income changes naturally.

The power structure and the distribution of firm's revenue

The firm's income will ultimately be distributed among its participants, including the investors, the management, and the employees. According to neoclassical economics firm theory, the income of the factors of production is determined by their marginal productivity. The total income created by the firm is distributed among all factors of production. If there is excessive profit or loss, the equilibrium distribution under perfect competition is guaranteed by the entry and exit of new firms. This is what market-deciding theory tells us. If the firm is considered a different resource allocation mechanism compared with the market, the firm has its own income distribution mechanism for the factors of production, which is different from market price. We assume that the firm's distribution criteria are settled as the firm's contract is signed. A majority of the managers and employees must obey the stipulations of the contract if they want to participate in certain business activity. The premise of such obedience is that the economic power of these individuals is much weaker than that of the firm's owners.

Within a firm, economic power is related to the key resources that the participants of the firm hold. If an individual possesses the resources necessary for the firm's development, the more important and irreplaceable these resources, the greater the negotiating power of an individual. The result of the game is a larger share of the income distribution. According to enterprise contract theory, the firm's contract is determined by bargaining among participants before the contract is signed. The income distribution among these contractors depends on their negotiating power. Such examples in real life are not hard to find, particularly in North America and Europe where the market economy is more mature. Successful CEOs always ask the board for a relative high salary. The reason why these CEOs have such negotiating power is that they control the key resources that are vital for the firm's development. The negotiation power is the external expression of economic power during the contract negotiation process. Conversely, why are migrant workers' wages so low and often defaulted on by their employer? The main reason is that migrant workers lack organizations such as unions. Thus, an individual migrant worker has no capability to negotiate with the capitalist leading to unfair distribution of income between migrant workers and the capitalist. Recently, under the state's intervention, migrant worker's residual claim has increased along with their negotiating power.

In a Nash bargaining model, the power of negotiation is actually the participant's economic power formed by the amount of capital owned, the criticality of that capital, the leadership of the business organization, and the ability to obtain non-public information. These factors determine the influence and control of different players during the bargaining process. It reveals the influence and control of different players during the bargaining process. We denote the negotiation power of one-side as τ, where $0 < \tau < 1$. Generally speaking, as one-side's negotiation power increases, the other side's negotiation power decreases, and the conditions that one side's negotiation power is infinity or zero may not exist. We assume that τ is a function of resources vectors necessary for the firm, $\tau = f(p_1, p_2, \cdots, p_n)$, where $p_1, p_2, \cdots, p_n$ denote resource vectors. Though an implicit form of τ is not given, there is no doubt that negotiation power increases as different components of power rises, so we assume τ is an increasing function of p_i.

Assume both parties have a starting point, namely $d = (\mu^0, v^0)$, it indicates that when the two parties cannot reach an agreement, one party can receive payoff μ^0, while the other party can receive payoff v^0, which are the two player's retained earnings. Let S be the set of all possible payoff vectors (μ, v) reached by negotiation or bargaining between two parties, $(\mu^0, v^0) \in S$, and we have the following two assumptions.

Assumption 1: Pareto-efficient frontier of the bargaining result S, is a concave curve h defined on a closed interval $\left[\underline{\mu}, \overline{\mu}\right]$, and there exists $\mu \in \left[\underline{\mu}, \overline{\mu}\right]$ with $\mu > \mu^0$, $v = h(\mu) > v^0$. This assumption indicates that the participants' utility can be increased by negotiation.

Assumption 2: The set of all weak Pareto-efficient payoff (μ, v) is closed.

The pair (S, d) which satisfies assumption 1 and assumption 2 is defined as a Nash bargaining problem. Following the two assumptions above and the axiomatic assumptions of Nash bargaining problem, for every $\tau \in (0,1)$, the solution to Nash bargaining problem is a unique solution of the following optimization problem.

$$\begin{cases} \max f = (\mu - \mu^0)^\tau (v - v^0)^{1-\tau} \\ s.t. \mu \geq \mu^0, \ v \geq v^0, \ v = h(\mu) \end{cases} \tag{3.1}$$

Suppose each party's negotiation power is represented by τ_1 and τ_2 respectively, and $\tau_1 + \tau_2 = 1$. We denote the firm's output, under the cooperation of players as $\varphi(\varphi > 0)$, $\varphi = \mu + v$. If participants fail to cooperate with each other, then the retained income is $\phi(\phi > 0)$, $\phi = \mu^0 + v^0$. If the two parties choose to cooperate with each other, the ultimate distribution ratio of income must satisfy the solution to Nash bargaining problem. Differentiating $f = \left(\mu - \mu^0\right)^\tau \left(v - v^0\right)^{1-\tau}$ with respect to μ, we obtain an expression of μ and τ.

$$\frac{\partial f}{\partial \mu} = \tau_1 \left(\mu - \mu^0\right)^{\tau_1 - 1} \left(v - v^0\right)^{\tau_2} - \tau_2 \left(\mu - \mu^0\right)^{\tau_1} \left(v - v^0\right)^{\tau_2 - 1} \tag{3.2}$$

By the first order condition $\dfrac{\partial f}{\partial \mu} = 0$ above, we obtain

$$\frac{v - v^0}{\mu - \mu^0} = \frac{\tau_2}{\tau_1} \tag{3.3}$$

This shows that two parties' ratio of gross income is equal to the ratio of their negotiation power. In other words, power as represented by the negotiation power determines income distribution.

Income distribution and the firm's performance

The distribution of a firm's income affects its productivity. In this chapter, we use the modified Acemoglu's model to analyze the relationship between productivity and the distribution of a firm's income among its participants (Acemoglu, 2005). Let t be the firm's operating circle. We assume the participants of a firm as a whole can be divided into two groups:[7] a set of investors and a set of managers. For convenience, we normalize the amount of investors and the amount of managers to one; that is, we treat different parties of the game as a group.

We use c_{t+j} to denote the proprietor's income, and e_{t+j} is the effort (labor or investment) paid by the proprietor to obtain the income. At every period, the manager's utility equals income minus cost. Taking inter-temporal income discount into account, we assume that both the manager and the investor discount the future with the same discount factor δ. Then, the manager's utility function has the following form.

$$u_t = \sum_{j=0}^{\infty} \delta^j \left[c_{t+j} - e_{t+j} \right]$$

Assume the firm has access to the following Cobb-Douglas production technology;[8] that is,

$$y_t = K_t^a e_t^\beta \tag{3.4}$$

where K_t denotes the capital invested at time t, and e_t denotes the effort made by the manager at time t where $\alpha + \beta < 1$. One important point captured by (3.4) is that the firm's output will increase if the investor invests more capital and the manager exerts more effort. However, due to information asymmetry, the power between the investor and the manager is not equal, and we assume the manager will hide a fraction ω_t of output during the production process. It is entirely possible that the investor is able to predict this. Because hiding output is costly, we suppose that a fraction $\lambda \in [0,1]$ of the hidden output is the manager's cost of hiding the output. Apparently, λ is related to the amount of private information the investor has. The scarcity and alternative of managerial resources is the embodiment of the investor's economic power and can also represent the manager's economic power in that $1-\lambda$ reflects the manager's economic power. Suppose the investor's distribution ratio is ζ_t, the income received by the manager is,

$$c_t = \left[(1 - \zeta_t)(1 - \omega_t) + (1 - \lambda)\omega_t \right] y_t \tag{3.5}$$

Expression (3.5) implies that the manager's income can be divided into two parts: the income after deducting the hidden output and the hidden output. Then, the investor's income is

$$W_t = \zeta_t (1 - \omega_t) y_t \tag{3.6}$$

At each period of the game, the investor should decide how much capital I_t to invest in the next period. Such investment generates the next period's capital $K_{t+1} = I_t$. Generally, at time $t (t = 0, 1, 2 \cdots)$, the player's decision-making order is given as illustrated in Figure 3.5. To be more specific, we have:

1   The firm inherits K_t units of physical capital from time $t-1$, which is the result of the investor's decision I_{t-1} at time $t-1$ (the initial K_0 is a given exogenous variable).
2   The manager chooses the level of effort e_t, and the corresponding output at time t is $y_t = K_t^a e_t^\beta$.
3   The investor chooses the income distribution ratio ζ_t and how much to invest in the next period (period $t+1$) I_t; that is, the next period's physical capital K_{t+1}.
4   The manager chooses the proportion of output to hide ω_t.

The game process is a typical Markov process; when the player chooses the size of decision variables according to the game structure, he can just maximize the discounted sum of utility from the current period, and this is equal to maximum discounted sum of utility from time $t = 0$. Markov perfect equilibrium (MPE) is a set of strategies $(e_t, \zeta_t, I_t, \omega_t)$; at time t, the choice of these strategies only depends on the current state, the strategy set $\{e(K_t), \zeta(K_t), I(K_t), \omega(K_t)\}$ corresponding to K_t. The feature of MPE is the equilibrium distribution, and choice of strategies of the current period is determined by the previous period's production and investment. We can put the solution procedure at any given period. In such a period, taking K_t

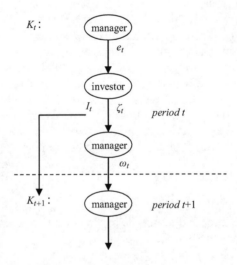

Figure 3.5 Decision-making order of period t.

as given, we can determine $e_t - (\zeta_t, I_t) - \omega$ respectively by backward substitution. First of all, let us start with the choice of ω_t.

Due to the moral hazard incurred by information asymmetry, the manager will hide a proportion of the output, ω_t, for his own profit. At time t, the manager takes K_t, e_t, ζ_t, I_t as given variables and maximizes his own utility function by choosing a proper ω_t.

$$u_t = \sum_{j=0}^{\infty} \delta^j \left[c_{t+j} - e_{t+j} \right]$$
$$= (c_t - e_t) + \delta(c_{t+1} - e_{t+1}) + \delta^2 (c_{t+2} - e_{t+2}) + \cdots$$
$$= \left[(1-\zeta_t) + (\zeta_t - \lambda)\omega_t \right] y_t - e_t + \delta \left\{ \left[(1-\zeta_{t+1}) + (\zeta_{t+1} - \lambda)\omega_{t+1} \right] y_{t+1} - e_{t+1} \right\} + \cdots$$

In the expression above, ω_t only appears in the term specifying the utility of current period, i.e., $(1-\zeta_t) + (\zeta_t - \lambda)\omega_t \rfloor y_t - e_t$; this indicates that we can maximize u_t by choosing a proper ω_t that maximizes current period's utility. Therefore strategies for the manager to decide how much output to hide are:

$$\omega_t = \begin{cases} 1 \ (\zeta_t > \lambda) \\ [0,1] \ (\zeta_t = \lambda) \\ 0 \ (\zeta_t < \lambda) \end{cases}$$

According to different income distribution ratios and the cost hiding output, the proportion of output hidden by the manager may vary greatly. If the investor's proportion of earnings ζ is greater than loss $\lambda, \zeta > \lambda$, then the manager tends to hide all outputs; if the investor's proportion of earnings ζ is equal to the loss $\lambda, \zeta = \lambda$, then the manager tends to hide a proportion of output; if the investor's proportion of earnings ζ is less than the loss $\lambda, \zeta < \lambda$, then the manager will not hide any output at all. Investor is able to anticipate the strategy of choosing ω_t deployed by manager; as investor chooses the distribution ratio, the investor maximizes his utility of the current period by choosing a proper ζ_t . Same as the reason for choosing ω_t, one can maximize the aggregate utility from the current period, simply by maximizing the utility of the current period. The investor's current period utility is $W_t - I_t = \zeta_t(1-\omega_t) y_t - I_t$. On the one hand, the investor's current period utility increases as long as ζ_t increases, but on the other hand, the proportion of output hidden by the manager increases, as ζ_t increases; hence, the investor has to make his utility as large as possible while set $\omega_t = 0$. In such a game, the optimal strategy for the investor is to choose an income distribution ratio that equals to the cost of hiding output λ.

$$\zeta_t = \lambda \tag{3.7}$$

If $\zeta_t = \lambda$, whether manager's proportion to hide is 0 or 1, their final utilities are the same, then a smart manager will not take a risk to cheat the investor while the investor's income is maximized at the same time, and the equilibrium of the game is obtained.

As the manager expects that $\zeta_t = \lambda$, $\omega_t = 0$ and chooses proper e_t to maximize current period's utility, and u_t is maximized at the same time.

$$c_t - e_t = (1 - \lambda) K_t^\alpha e_t^\beta - e_t$$

Differentiating the expression above with respect to e_t gives

$$e_t = \left[\beta (1 - \lambda) K_t^\alpha \right]^{\frac{1}{1-\beta}} \tag{3.8}$$

The expression above indicates that, the level of effort maximizing manager's utility is an increasing function of the capital invested in the current period, and it is a decreasing function of the investor's proportions of earnings. Since $I_t = K_{t+1}$, for convenience, we solve K_{t+1} rather than I_t. Let $V(K_t)$ be the investor's overall optimal utility from time t, by the Bellman's equation, we have

$$V(K_t) = \max_{K_{t+1}} \left[W_t - K_{t+1} + \delta \cdot V(K_{t+1}) \right]$$

where $V(K_{t+1})$ denotes the overall optimal utility from time $t+1$. Because the investor is able to anticipate that $\zeta_t = \lambda$, $\omega_t = 0$, the Bellman's equation above can be rewritten as

$$V(K_t) = \max_{K_{t+1}} \left[\lambda \cdot K_t^\alpha e_t^\beta - K_{t+1} + \delta \cdot V(K_{t+1}) \right] \tag{3.9}$$

Suppose that K_{t+1} maximizes $V(K_t)$, by the first-order condition, differentiating the objective function in (3.9) with respect to K_{t+1}, we get

$$\delta \cdot V'(K_{t+1}) = 1 \tag{3.10}$$

Take K_t as the parameter of the optimization problem, applying the envelope theorem to (3.9) and the following expression yields,

$$V'(K_t) = \lambda \left[\alpha K_t^{\alpha-1} e_t^\beta + K_t^\alpha \beta e_t^{\beta-1} \frac{\partial e_t}{\partial K_t} \right]$$

Similarly, at time $t+1$, it follows,

$$V'(K_{t+1}) = \lambda \left[\alpha K_{t+1}^{\alpha-1} e_{t+1}^\beta + K_{t+1}^\alpha \beta e_{t+1}^{\beta-1} \frac{\partial e_{t+1}}{\partial K_{t+1}} \right] \tag{3.11}$$

By (3.8), it follows,

$$\frac{\partial e_{t+1}}{\partial K_{t+1}} = [\beta(1-\lambda)]^{\frac{1}{1-\beta}} \frac{\alpha}{1-\beta} K_{t+1}^{\frac{\alpha+\beta-1}{1-\beta}} \tag{3.12}$$

Substituting (3.12) into (3.11), together with (3.10), the following expression yields,

$$K_{t+1} = \left(\frac{\delta\alpha\lambda}{1-\beta}\right)^{\frac{1-\beta}{1-\alpha-\beta}}[\beta(1-\lambda)]^{\frac{1}{1-\alpha-\beta}} = K(\lambda) \tag{3.13}$$

The above expression (3.13) shows that K is not depending on time t, the firm's operation is in a stable condition from time $t=1$ given K_0 at time $t=0$. The investor's investment strategy is to guarantee that the level of physical capital in use at each period, from the first period, is maintained at the level determined by (3.13).

Table 3.2 illustrates the state variable K, the four variables determined by players of the game and the corresponding output y at period 0, 1, and t. The firm is in a stable state at time $t=1$, at the very beginning of each period, the physical capital used for production is $K(\lambda)$, the corresponding effort made by the manager is e_t, the output is y_t, the investor take a proportion λ of the output as his own and takes out $K(\lambda)$ to invest at time $t+1$. Under this allocation plan, the manager will not hide any proportion of output. Substituting the results in Table 3.2 into (3.5) and (3.6), we obtain the aggregate utility of the investor and the manager, u_t^* and $V^*(K_t)$ respectively.

$$u_1^* = \sum_{t=1}^{\infty}\delta^t\left[c_t^* - e_t^*\right] = \frac{\delta(1-\lambda)(1-\beta)}{1-\delta}\left(\frac{\delta\alpha\lambda}{1-\beta}\right)^{\frac{\alpha}{1-\alpha-\beta}}[\beta(1-\lambda)]^{\frac{\beta}{1-\alpha-\beta}} \tag{3.14}$$

$$V^*(K_t) = \sum_{t=1}^{\infty}\beta^t\left[W_t^* - I_t^*\right] = \frac{\delta\lambda(1-\delta\alpha-\beta)}{(1-\delta)(1-\beta)}\left(\frac{\delta\alpha\lambda}{1-\beta}\right)^{\frac{\alpha}{1-\alpha-\beta}}[\beta(1-\lambda)]^{\frac{\beta}{1-\alpha-\beta}} \tag{3.15}$$

Table 3.2 Equilibrium solution in different periods

variable	at time 0	at time 1	at time t
K_t	K_0	$K(\lambda)$	$K(\lambda)$
e_t	$\left[\beta(1-\lambda)K_0^\alpha\right]^{\frac{1}{1-\beta}}$	$\left[\beta(1-\lambda)K^\alpha(\lambda)\right]^{\frac{1}{1-\beta}}$	$\left[\beta(1-\lambda)K^\alpha(\lambda)\right]^{\frac{1}{1-\beta}}$
ζ_t	λ	λ	λ
I_t	$\left(\frac{\delta\alpha\lambda}{1-\beta}\right)^{\frac{\alpha}{1-\alpha-\beta}}[\beta(1-\lambda)]^{\frac{\beta}{1-\alpha-\beta}} = K(\lambda)$	$K(\lambda)$	$K(\lambda)$
ω_t	0	0	0
y_t	$[\beta(1-\lambda)]^{\frac{\beta}{1-\beta}}K_0^{\frac{\alpha}{1-\beta}}$	$\left(\frac{\delta\alpha\lambda}{1-\beta}\right)^{\frac{\alpha}{1-\alpha-\beta}}[\beta(1-\lambda)]^{\frac{\beta}{1-\alpha-\beta}}$	$\left(\frac{\delta\alpha\lambda}{1-\beta}\right)^{\frac{\alpha}{1-\alpha-\beta}}[\beta(1-\lambda)]^{\frac{\beta}{1-\alpha-\beta}}$

Under given game structure, u_t^*, $V^*(K_1)$ and the stable output of each period $y_t^*\,(t \geq 1)$ is a result of decision interaction between investors and managers all aiming at maximizing their own profit. The first and the second indicator characterize the player's profit under given game structure. The third indicator characterizes the firm's performance. These indicators are jointly determined by the importance of factors of production α, β, the discount factor δ, and the power indicator λ. (We have proved in the previous section, the power structure and the distribution structure is isomorphic.) An important question is, what kind of power structure can maximize the firm's equilibrium output $y_t^*\,(t \geq 1)$? What kind of power structure λ can maximize the investor's equilibrium utility $V^*(K_1)$? What kind of power structure λ can maximize the manager's equilibrium utility u_1^*? In other words, the firm's performance is related to power structure.

1   The power structure maximizes the investor's utility. Solving the optimization problem $Max_\lambda V^*(K_1)$, we obtain the power structure that maximizes the investor's utility,

$$\lambda_V = 1 - \beta \tag{3.16}$$

2   The power structure maximizes the manager's utility. Solving the optimization problem $Max_\lambda u_1^*$, we obtain the power structure that maximizes the manager's utility,

$$\lambda_u = \alpha \tag{3.17}$$

3   The power structure maximizes the firm's output $y_t^*\,(t \geq 1)$. Solving the optimization problem $Max_\lambda y_t^*$, we obtain the power structure that maximizes the firm's output,

$$\lambda_y = \frac{\alpha}{\alpha + \beta} \tag{3.18}$$

Under the equilibrium of the game, the share received by the investor is equal to his power λ; hence, (3.18) implies that when the balance of power enables owners of factor of production receive the share equal to their contribution to the output, the firm gets its maximum output—in other words, the firm is the most efficient.

Because $\alpha + \beta < 1$, comparing λ_y, λ_V, λ_u, we have $\lambda_u < \lambda_y < \lambda_V$. This result implies that, among the three power structures, λ related with maximizing the investor's utility is the biggest, while λ related with maximizing the manager's utility is the smallest, and λ related with maximizing the firm's output lies in the middle, which is a relatively balanced power structure. The distribution ratio of the firm's income depends on the stakeholder's bargaining power; that is, the power endowed by the firm's key resources under stakeholder control. A certain power structure determines the corresponding distribution structure, and a different income distribution structure determines the firm's efficiency. The model presented above also proves that the profit distribution ratio maximizes the firm's output when it lies between the profit distribution ratio that maximizes the investor's profit and the profit distribution ratio that maximizes the manager's profit. Therefore, if we only pursue the profit distribution ratio that maximizes the utility of the investor or the manager, the firm's maximum output under the given input cannot be guaranteed. This implies that during the firm's operation, maximum output cannot be achieved without friction using capital and labor. Therefore, the ideal firm under Walrasian equilibrium does not exist. The investor, the manager, and the ordinary employees will maximize their own profit using their power during the production process. The emergence of the rational behavior of pursuing profit is related to the limitations of individuals, and the firm will not reach an expected output under a given input. Similar to the market, sometimes the firm fails because of the bounded rationality of individuals. It is necessary to focus on the influence of the firm's power structure on its productivity to enhance the productivity of the firm. The power structure of the firm's participants should be reformulated. Focusing on the relationship between income distribution and the firm's performance, there is no self-implemented contract that guarantees that the firm will achieve profit maximization automatically.

More importantly, considering the role of power in the signing of a firm's contract, the efficiency of the enterprise system is not always evolutionary.[9] Considering the free contract signing and withdraw, we cannot reach the conclusion that the efficiency of the firm is evolutionary. Under an economic institution of social division of labor, it is natural that the price of the factor of production is monopolistic. When Pareto efficiency is neither sufficient nor necessary for institutional change, a suitable concept between power and contractual change is not efficiency but equilibrium. The relationship between power and institution is dynamical and interactive. On the one hand, the institutional framework endows economic power to different classes. On the other hand, institutional changes rely on the interaction of power among different economic subjects, but so does the relationship between the firm's contract and the power of factors of production. The contract surplus allows room for adjustment to the contract. In the long-lasting transaction procedure, changes in power structure require the contract, as a symbol of income distribution, an adjustment to satisfy the need of the new strongmen. However, a minor change in power structure will not result in the signing of a new contract and will not affect the firm's institution. One significant character of the firm's contract is its stability. The function of the contract is that it offers an action frame and an information conduit for the participants. Hence, the contract should be stable to some extent, but it is less stable than the institution. Although a minor change in power structure will not immediately reflect on the contract, it can trigger contract re-negotiation. When changes in the power structure are cumulated to some extent, changes in the firm's contract or the institution occur.

We rewire the enterprise contract theory from the perspective of economic power, including the influence of economic power on the control right allocation, the firm's income distribution, and the firm's performance. We hold that the formation of a firm's contract is a result of the transformation of economic power among owners of different factors of production. Unbalanced market power transforms into an unfair hierarchy system. The more powerful party tends to control the firm. The pricing function of the firm is different from the market, and the income distribution of the firm is an outward expression of the economic power structure of participants. More importantly, only pursuing the profit of one participant will not maximize the firm's output; an equal power structure will be helpful in enhancing the firm's performance.

Notes

1 Modern contract theories of the firm emphasize the dominant role that transaction costs play in defining internal property rights in a firm; however, the definition of transaction costs varies. Coase emphasizes the implementation fees in the management and co-ordination process while Cheung extends the concept of transaction costs to the social relationship involving more than one person. The team production theory by Alchian and Demsetz (1972) holds that transaction costs are the unobservable shirking behavior of employees in the firm and the measurement of their contributions to the firm. The theory of vertical and lateral integration by Grossman and Hart (1986, GHM theory in short) argues that transaction costs refer to the inadequate specific investments caused by the occupation of returns on investment. Williamson (1975) stresses on the ex-post adaptation costs. The ambiguity of the transaction cost concept results in the difference, even the obvious divergence, in understanding.
2 In our opinion, in addition to the reasons for transaction costs, the existence of enterprise organization forms must first have the existence of cooperation benefits. Simply comparing the costs of different transaction organization forms ignores the benefits of different transaction forms. Alchian and Demsetz (1972) pointed out that the essential characteristic of an enterprise is that the enterprise is a central contractor with residual claim rights. Yang Xiaokai and Huang Youguang (1999) define the enterprise as a residual right among trading partners. Structure, Yang Ruilong and Yang Qijing (2001) believe that the essence of an enterprise is the creation and distribution of organizational rents. A viable enterprise or organizational system is that the normal state of this organization is that the total revenue it creates pays the reservations of all organizational members. There is a surplus after the income, that is, the organization rent.
3 The determination of the distribution ratio here is the power of negotiation between the two parties, such as market pricing, group size and other factors. Since the retained earnings of both parties are set to the same 0 unit, it is believed that the cooperative earnings are not evenly distributed.
4 The problem of measuring income distribution does not exist in neoclassical economics, because the equilibrium of factor market prices inevitably distributes enterprise income precisely. Especially for homogeneous production functions,

Euler's theorem guarantees that the production factors get exactly the marginal income.

5 In the new institutional economics, the concept of trading has been expanded to the greatest extent. The production attributes of the enterprise are simplified and the exchange of property rights of different production factors is ignored.

6 In fact, in the final analysis, the status of production factors in the organization of enterprises is attributed to the bargaining power of production factors based on such concepts as bargaining power, scarcity, specificity, exclusiveness, substitutability, etc. In this chapter it is also impossible to use the concept of economic power to comprehensively represent the influence and control of the owner of the factor of production.

7 The average business worker is seen here as an invariant, or reduced to a labor-to-labor side. Of course, the relationship between ordinary workers and other members of the enterprise can also be considered separately. The analysis process and conclusions are the same.

8 The model in this chapter is different from the model of Asenoglu. First, the production function in the original model is the scale benefit unchanged, and the model in this chapter is the scale benefit is decreasing, because the period t in the model is indefinite, in the case of depreciation rate is not 1 the scale of production can be expanded indefinitely, so the scale yield is set to decrease. Second, in the production function of this chapter, in order to derive the process and analyze the problem simplicity, the technical coefficient is set to 1. However, this does not affect the final result; the technical coefficient can always be united by unit transformation. Third, the investment function of the original model is nonlinear, and the cost function of the operator is linear, and the cost function of the investor and the operator is set to linear.

9 Of course, if viewed from the long-term or overall trend, social progress and institutional evolution are efficient. But a certain or short-term institutional change is not necessarily efficient. For example, my country's transition from a semi-market economy to a fully planned economy is a good example.

4 Theory of transaction price based on the power paradigm

Price plays an increasingly important role in society, but what is the nature of price? How is price formed? Economics has yet to provide a satisfactory and definitive answer. Throughout the history of economics, scholars have proposed a variety of theoretical views on pricing. The concept of an equal and mutual beneficial price theory by Plato and Aristotle reflects the non-economic ethical thinking of the time (Barker, 2012). The theory of fair pricing proposed by Aquinas in the 13th century weakens the ethics of price theory while including religious and moral components and examines the issue of pricing from the perspective of ordered social development (Aquinas, 1997). The system of natural liberty theory, proposed by Smith in the 18th century, considers value as the basis of price and argues that rational economic man is guided by the "invisible hand" to conduct market transactions. Moreover, price formation reflects equilibrium thinking, and price is the monetary reflection of the equilibrium between market demand and supply (Smith, 1950).

However, as a consequence of excessively restrictive assumptions, equilibrium theory is a theory of "what ought to be" rather than "what really is." In addition, this theory assumes the scientific form and does not reflect social reality. Therefore, it is separated from reality and has become increasingly unrealistic. In fact, price should be at least divided into equilibrium price and transaction price (or trading price), but there is no clear distinction between the two prices in analyses of existing economic theories. The equilibrium price is the price at the intersection of the demand and supply curves of any good at a particular point. Because the demand and supply curves are unique and exist objectively, the equilibrium price is unique and objective. Due to the complexity of reality, people cannot obtain accurate demand and supply data for the entire market; hence, the corresponding demand and supply curves cannot be accurately determined. Then, it is natural that the equilibrium price becomes indefinite. Corresponding to the equilibrium price, the basis of transaction price is the marginal utility that the goods can bring to the subjects involved in the transactions. Utility is a subjective feeling, which exhibits heterogeneity due to environmental and individual differences. Therefore, the transaction price reflects the subjective judgment of trading subjects, and it may vary from subject to subject. Therefore, the transaction price is discrete with multi-values. However, the transaction price is clear for both parties involved in the transaction and is one type of available information on the market. Hence, it is definite.

It is these vague explanations of price by the existing theories that results in major theoretical differences yielding different theoretical perspectives. Only by clearly defining the price that is studied can we appreciate the significance of the study, assess the research methodology, and reveal the inherent nature of price formation.

Review of price theories

Price theories have evolved along with economic development. From classical economics to today's various schools of economic theories, theoretical research has moved from simple descriptions to applications of geometric and mathematical tools and has gradually established modern price theory, which is based on equilibrium analysis as the main methodology. The core content of the theories has evolved starting with Marshall's partial equilibrium, moving to Walrasian general equilibrium, and culminating with disequilibrium theory.

Equilibrium vs. disequilibrium price theory

Marshall (2009) was the first to link the equilibrium approach of classical economics to utility and cost theories establishing the theoretical foundation for neoclassical economics. The core of Marshall's partial equilibrium theory is equilibrium price theory. When analyzing the demand and supply relations and the price of any commodity, equilibrium price theory abstracts out the effects of other commodity prices as well as the demand and supply relations on the commodity in question. Moreover, equilibrium price theory argues that changes in any single commodity's demand and supply are only determined by the change in that commodity's price. Total market demand is the sum of all demand of every participant; thus, it is the total market supply. When market demand equals market supply, each consumer and producer attains their desired demand and supply, and the price is the equilibrium price. If demand or supply changes, the market mechanism of demand and supply will automatically adjust the price to restore the equilibrium. Marshall's partial equilibrium theory is a pioneering research on the price mechanism and establishes an analytical framework for the perfect competitive market. The theory incorporates demand and supply functions, production costs, and marginal utility theory. In addition, the theory analyzes the impacts of effective demand, effective supply, and money on price. In particular, by introducing the concepts of elasticity and utility, mathematical methods can analyze price changes. However, partial equilibrium is a particular market case. The theory abstracts out the interactions and inter-dependency among different markets and among different products in the analysis, but society is an integrated system with inter-dependent elements. Therefore, the theory has flaws and limitations.

The Walrasian general equilibrium theory is an improvement. General equilibrium theory assumes that demand, supply, and the prices of all goods are interdependent and interactive in a society. The theory is based on marginal utility and investigates the issue of price determination from the perspective of the behavior of microeconomic subjects when the demand and supply of goods reaches equilibrium. The theory also adheres to the necessary conditions for a set of equilibrium prices. Although the Walrasian general equilibrium is, in theory, a complete and full exposition, its solution for the equilibrium is under the conditions that equations are linear, independent, and unconstrained. When the equations are non-linear, or the system has additional constraints, there is no guarantee of a single solution. Moreover, in general equilibrium theory, all consumers and producers are price takers; moreover, demand and supply are infinitely elastic under a given market price. In other words, the market is perfect competitive. However, the reality is that demand and supply are rarely equal. The disequilibrium between demand and supply is a regular state in reality. Therefore, since the 1960, Patinkin (1984) and others have suggested the disequilibrium theory based on dynamic analysis.

The disequilibrium theory analyzes the problem of involuntary unemployment. The theory argues that involuntary unemployment is a disequilibrium phenomenon resulting from insufficient effective demand that puts quantity constraints on business production. Thus, the market supply is not controlled by price but by quantity. Clower (1986) analyzes household behavior under disequilibrium and notes the difference between demand and supply in theory and in reality. When households cannot supply labor according to their own wishes, the reduction in household income constrains their demand budget. Thus, it is not price but the excess supply in the labor market that leads to excess supply in the goods market.

Disequilibrium theory changes the binary analysis in the general equilibrium and has some unique features. First, disequilibrium discusses economic uncertainty and argues that the future is unknown, and the information that economic subjects can obtain is limited. Second, market resources are not fully utilized, and the market is not always in equilibrium. Third, in demand functions, price is no longer the only variable that affects purchase; income is an influencing factor. Fourth, in price analysis, the theory considers the interactions among the money market, labor market, and goods market as well as their effects, rather than analyzing only the goods market. Disequilibrium theory introduces the concepts of effective demand and effective supply; that is, the total trading volume of each commodity equals the minimum value in a pair of total demand and total supply. Therefore, it is not possible to make infinite exchanges at the market price. Every subject will perceive the quantity constraints on the maximum level of purchase or sales that they can achieve. If there is market scarcity, the formation of the equilibrium price will no longer be determined by demand and supply. There will be price makers and price takers in the market. The former will estimate the impact of their pricing decisions on sales (or purchase) through a perceived demand (or supply) curve. Of course, the actual parameters of the demand curve depend both on consumer behavior and on the pricing strategy of the price makers' opponents. However, the price makers do not have full information, so their assessment of the opponents has uncertainty. Therefore, if the market demand and supply are in disequilibrium, in the short run, the actual transaction price will not be the same as the price under a full Walrasian equilibrium.

The price theory of new institutional economics

Traditionally, economic research on price either assumed that institutions are given exogenously and do not affect economic performance or that institutions can operate at no cost. Consequently, the exposition on price theory does not analyze the impact on institutions. As the representative of the school of new institutions, Coase (1995) expounds on the market from the perspective of property rights. The market is viewed as an organizational platform for participants to trade property rights in accordance with contracts. Market transactions are represented by tangible goods but, in essence, they are the exchange of private property rights. Coase (1995) argues that market transactions are completed through contracts. Once property rights are clearly defined, both parties in a transaction will use the market mechanism to find a contract arrangement via signing contracts that minimizes the loss of their interests. Even in a perfect competitive market, the market mechanism will play its role only when property rights are clearly defined. The two parties will find low-cost institutional arrangements through a contract if there is a transaction cost. Coase is not the first to recognize the relationship of rights underpinning transactions, but the marginal analysis and concepts of marginal transaction costs presented by the author make it possible to conduct extensive research on the origin, nature, evolution, and functions of specific institutions based on an accurate empirical analysis of individuals.

From reality, it is clear that the premise for the possession of certain goods is to obtain the related property right or certain constraints on the power. Commodity transactions are the first of all property rights exchanges. Therefore, Demsetz clearly considers price as the value of rights. If two items of goods are the same in form but have different property rights attached, they are different goods with different market prices. Alchian also believes that the issue of how price is determined is essentially the issue of how to define property rights and how they should be exchanged (Alchian & Demsetz, 1972). The price analysis based on property rights loosens the restraints on traditional economic thinking, which considers only the commodity in the analysis. Such a price analysis explores the formation of price from the attributes of a commodity and incorporates factors such as institutions, information, strategy, and organization, all of which have important effects on price in the analysis of the pricing mechanism. As a result, the property rights-based analysis goes beyond traditional economics, which regards price as a superficial concept of product quantity relative ratio.

Moreover, from the inherent value of rights and property price, the property rights-based analysis both offers a new explanation and establishes the connotations of economics. Although it makes use of equilibrium analysis, the equilibrium is no longer just the equilibrium of quantity but an equilibrium in a general sense. Therefore, some scholars, based on Coase's property rights theory, define price as follows: price is the equilibrium solution to trading property rights games between players according to contracts under the constraints of institutions and information (Wang & Wu, 2004). Such a definition converts price from the ratio of product exchange as a market indicator to the ratio of property right costs and converts the determination of price from demand and supply to transactions. Price determination is no longer frictionless marginal equilibrium but the equilibrium of transaction games under the constraints of institutions and information. The formation mechanism of price is no longer the concept about a point but the whole transaction process. The formation is determined by multiple factors. Therefore, institutional economics pioneers the analysis on price mechanisms from the power perspective and no longer regards price only as a dependent variable determined by demand and supply.

Price theory of information economics

Information economics mainly discusses information values, the risk of uncertainty, and price formation under different modes of transaction, such as bargaining. The founder of information economics, Hayek (1945), introduces the concept of private information and argues that one function of the price mechanism is to convey private information effectively. If the purpose is to understand the true functions of price, the price system must be considered a mechanism of information exchange. Hayek notes that the price system is more a way for society to use economic information than a way to allocate scarce productive resources. If we have all the information on available resources, what remains is a pure logic issue. The crux of this issue, however, is that although it is an economic calculation, the solution is a vital step in solving socio-economic problems. All of the social information required for the calculation has never been provided to an individual who truly understands and is capable of solving it.

Stigler (1961) studies the phenomenon of price dispersion, which is ignored by conventional economists, and argues that the lack of information on trading opportunities is a significant cause of price dispersion. Price dispersion indicates that the transaction participants are ignorant about the market, and they must pay the cost to obtain market information.

For consumers, searching information becomes an economic issue that requires decisions. The optimal number concerning the search for information is that the searching cost equals the marginal revenue. Therefore, consumers will search within a limited range and select the optimal price to achieve transactions within the range. Hence, the transaction price will differ and lead to the existence of a dispersed price. In addition, because of the uncertainty of information, there are risks associated with transactions. To make decisions under uncertainty, transaction participants must consider, on the one hand, the probability distribution of the risk and, on the other hand, the decision depends on the decision-maker's attitude toward risk. These two aspects have a significant impact on the formation of transaction price.

Stigler also studies the impact of transaction modes on market outcomes. The existence of transaction costs in the real market means that the choice of transaction mode affects the transaction price and volume. How to transact and what mode to use become indispensable objects of economic analysis. According to information economics, there are two possibilities in the market to determine price. First, both parties of the transaction reach a transaction price through consultation and negotiation, which is under the basic assumption that the parties share a common opinion on the fairness of interest distribution. Second, the parties only consider their own interests in price decisions and must bargain to reach a transaction price. However, the acceptance or rejection of the price is still voluntary. Regardless of the transaction method, the formation of price is dependent on market factors rather than the natural equilibrium result between demand and supply.

Limitations of existing price theories

So far, price theories have established a sophisticated theoretical system by the extensive application of mathematical knowledge, but there are some limitations due to the intense pursuit of a perfect theory. There are too many assumptions that contradict reality in the general equilibrium theory; free competition is an example. In real economic society, due to inequality in the possession of resources, transaction behavior is far from perfect competition. At most, people have the freedom of behavioral choice as opposed to the freedom of transaction choice. As a result, in competitive equilibrium under the freedom of behavioral choice, some participants can exert power, which yields profits. The distribution of interests is not fair if it results from a transaction price based on free trading since it cannot truly reflect the willingness to exchange of the weaker parties in transactions. There is no fair auctioneer who can make effective adjustments to such situations in the real market. Participants in transactions cannot have complete market information; moreover, economic subjects respond to price signals and the quantity signal of demand or supply of other participants.

Information economics explains the impact of uncertainty on the formation of price, but it does not state clearly who ultimately determines the price, that is, the essential elements of price formation. In institutional economics, if the transaction mechanism is an endogenous variable and dependent on the asymmetric information in accordance with the framework of institutional economics, the other three factors—technology, preferences, and resource endowments—are difficult to maintain as exogenous variables. Thus, we lose the basis of theoretical analysis. At the same time, the analysis of the price mechanism from property rights is limited to the commodity itself in institutional economics, which ignores the role of property rights. Existing price theories cannot explain some market phenomena: there is no such corresponding relationship as described in theory between price and sales; some products do not sell better when prices fall but do so when prices rise. In particular, the government, as an administrator rather than a participant, regulates market price directly and participates in price formation in terms of neither demand nor supply factors, including the price formulation of special goods and domestic currencies that are beyond the scope of equilibrium theory.

Commodity exchange and the commodity economy are forms of economic connection among social members, which is the natural outcome when society develops to a certain level. The basic characteristics of commodity economy are that the relationships between people in economic activities are established via the relation between commodities and that social connection with respect to material productions must be realized via commodity exchange. The mission that should be accomplished by price theories is to explain the real reason of exchange at a certain ratio of quantity via currency, reveal the nature of individuals' social and economic relations behind the commodity exchange, and ultimately establish the socio-economic relations that suit social development through price. This concept of price theory is consistent with Schumpeter and Hayek's ideas, which state that economics must explain human behaviors.

Price as the carrier of interest distribution is a key factor in interest distribution adjustment. The right to determine price usually belongs to firms. Driven by the rationality of interest maximization, firms will set a price favorable to themselves using their rights to control price; therefore, in the study of market price, if we ignore the analysis of corporate power, the corresponding conclusions cannot be correct. Hay, D. Morris, and D. J. Morris (1991) note that,

> rich evidence on corporate power and the right of free decisions is sufficient to confirm the correctness of this theory, which is, a firm is an entity having market power; to some extent, its performance is independent on the overall performance of the industry.

Chakib Khelil, former President of OPEC and Minister of Algerian Energy and Mines, publicly states that the main reason for high oil prices is not demand and supply but the result of manipulation by large enterprises and some countries based on their power. Of course, consumers have the right to decide whether to buy and under what conditions they decide to buy. This shows that by relying on resources that they hold, economic subjects retain the power to set the market transaction price. The power determines subject's economic behavior, and the behavior determines market demand and supply. Finally, transactions are completed and the transaction price emerges.

In the process, demand and supply are just the surface phenomenon. The transaction price, in essence, is not determined by demand and supply, although they may be the most important factors affecting price. Price, however, does not fully reflect demand and supply; it is a market reflection of the power held by economic subjects. To analyze the price formation mechanism from the perspective of power makes the price determination by commodity exchange transfer to a process determined by economic man. This treatment avoids the dual structure of demand and supply in the analysis of price and provides a theoretical basis for price formation in reality where there is disequilibrium between demand and supply. In addition, analyzing price from the perspective of power effectively explains the influence of government and other factors that are not included in demand or supply, which establishes a valid link between the macroeconomy and the microeconomy.

Market power and its formation

Market power and its characteristics

From the perspective of economics, power is always associated with social resources, different resources generate different power, and the discrepancy of resources leads to power discrepancy. The two most common forms of power in the market economy are economic and political power.

Economic power is the ability of economic subjects to dominate or influence others via the control of economic resources. Through economic power, economic subjects directly participate in market activities including production, exchange, distribution, and consumption. Economic power includes the property rights of individuals and corporations and manager's organization power, which is a significant form of corporate economic power. Galbraith argues that both industrial and corporate power represent economic power. Economic power exists at all levels of economy and society and has an asymmetric power relation. This is reflected in two aspects. First, the institutional framework assigns economic power to economic subjects from different classes, which creates the difference in power across subjects through the unequal allocation of resources. For example, the contract signed by a firm and its employees appears to be the result of voluntary actions under free choice, but there is a relationship of dominance and obedience between the two sides. Such job contracts depend on power asymmetry. Second, economic power has a dynamic adjustment feature. Although voluntary, the constraints on individual behavior change in the social transaction process, that is, institutional improvement whereby economic power is reflected in the evolution of a system in which individuals are constrained. This dynamic shows that economic power's influence is cumulative in institutional evolution; adjustments to actions based on economic purpose lead to institutional changes from the quantitative to the qualitative stage and, eventually, to the rearrangement of the interest distribution mechanism.

Political power refers to the influence that state administrative agencies and bodies derive from the rules and contracts of social management. This influence is referred to administrative power, which is the product of irreconcilable contradictions in interests between social classes. The influence's effectiveness is the power ensured by state machinery with coercive features. Easton (1965) notes that administrative power is an authoritative process of social value distribution. Therefore, power and the economy are inseparable. In modern society, administrative power is extended to various aspects of the economy, and the form of its role becomes more direct. The influence of economic power on price lies in the power's capability to change the state of goods scarcity and replace natural scarcity with artificial scarcity. Administrative power allocates resources by adjusting the differences in power among the various subjects and, consequently, adjusting the structure of the interest distribution among economic subjects. In general, the existence of administrative power ensures the balance of power between subjects to prevent imbalance in the distribution of social interests.

Li (1996) argues that administrative power is a vector whose effects clearly indicate the direction and trajectory; moreover, if the power is exerted in the wrong direction, it will aggravate the imbalance of power between subjects. Usually, as long as a political group does not give up its rights, the political group that has administrative power will not commit to not using power for self-interests. Hence, expanding own political power becomes the inevitable choice of political groups as rational subjects. The possibility of market failure always exists in a market due to excessive intervention by the holders of administrative power, which renders administrative power the main force in allocating market resources. Consequently, administrative power is a convenient way for political groups to obtain more benefits. Therefore, defining reasonable boundaries and the directions of administrative and economic power are conducive to smooth market operations.

The subjects of power and market behavior

Supply and demand are the only subjects in the supply-demand price theory. Price, as a revealed signal, reflects the outcome of games between the two subjects. Although, in theory, the equilibrium price can be derived, it reflects only the static power structure between supply and demand at one moment and does not reflect the fairness of the price. If the power is not equal between subjects, the flow of market resources under the market mechanism will cause changes to the power structure. Under seeming economic equity, the long-run result of the market operation will be the polarization of the interest structure. When the polarization reaches a certain level, it will affect the effective flow of market funds and ultimately affect market operation. In this case, government, as the third party of interest adjustment, often participates in the market and adjusts the economic power structure between the transaction subjects using its administrative power. Therefore, considering the competitive relationship and the role of power, the subjects in the market include the producers, consumers, and the government.

Producers

A producer is an individual or organization with a certain amount of resources that provides products or services to gain profits. The sufficient condition for a producer's existence is production capacity. In modern societies, producers take the form of firms in most cases. The emergence of firms is the result of the evolution of the producer status from the process of social development. When the development of society and the upgrading of production require the division of labor and knowledge as well as associated cooperation, while the effects of this cooperation cannot be achieved through market mechanisms, the emergence of firms becomes necessary.

Neoclassical microeconomics does not extensively analyze the form, nature, and interest distribution structure of firms. Neoclassical microeconomics only takes firms as a production set that consumes a variety of production factors to maximize their own interests under the premise of rationality. Modern property rights theory argues that a firm is a connection of a series of factor transaction contracts and is a way of transacting personal property rights. Firms and markets jointly play the role of effectively allocating resources. In this process, firms differ from the market only in the sense that they use management and coordination while the market uses price mechanisms. Although new institutional economics argues that the reason for the existence of firms is that the cost of management and coordination is less than the market transaction costs, which is an alternative to the market price mechanism, this view ignores the firm's basic production functions.

As a form of organization, the fundamental purpose of a firm is to create wealth. The complexity of modern social production requires the accumulation of resources. Productive resources include necessary physical materials for production, core technology, personnel, customers, reputation, and brands. However, the quantity of resources is limited for each individual and, hence, unable to satisfy the requirements of production and competition. Therefore, it is necessary to pool and share resources through cooperation. Cooperation has become a prerequisite for modern production so that individuals within a firm have effective labor division and collaboration. Members of a firm place their own resources at the disposal of the firm to reduce transaction costs, and more importantly, create wealth through resource cooperation. In other words, only through the preferred integration of individual resources can their common goals be achieved. Hodgson (1999) notes that firms are not just places where various inputs are purchased based on the known level of productivity, nor the carriers of a series of contracts. Firms are, fundamentally, a collective that accumulates capabilities. Therefore, there are cost factors in the formation of firms, but the formation is not entirely determined by costs and expenses. Formation is also determined by the scope and quantity of resources exploited through cooperation, which, in turn, increases the power of individuals within the organization.

Producers have a certain amount of resources; hence, they have certain power. A producer should not just be viewed as an industrial unit who passively accepts the constraints and decisions on performance according to market structure. On the contrary, producers have subjective dominations over the utilization of resources, are decision makers over their own behavior, and can conduct a range of activities in a given market structure, for example, pricing, engaging in innovation, research, and promotion. These activities yield the effects of power and affect other subjects in the market, which places the producer in a dominant position in complex market relations. Consequently, the producer gains a large share of the distribution in the exchange. With the ability to obtain more resources, or power, than individuals, firms in modern society are gaining increasing power compared to the simple production of individuals. Under general circumstances, large enterprises have greater influence on consumers and occupy a dominant competitive position; thus, their profitability is relatively strong.

The greater the quantity of resources, the greater the power; moreover, power and interests are isomorphic. Business executives often give priority to growing their firm. Coase argues that the boundary of a firm depends on the ratio of its administration expenses to the transaction costs. Administration expenses increase as the firm's size grows. When the expenses equal the transaction costs, firms no longer have the incentive to expand. However, this view is increasingly questioned. In general, production has scale effects. Growth in administration expenses does not mean the expansion is unprofitable. Meanwhile, the transaction cost is, as a variable, difficult to determine from statistical data. Various firms, market environments, and periods have different transaction costs. Transaction costs include all types of cost involved in market transactions; hence, their magnitude is difficult to gauge. Therefore, it is difficult to have any effect by comparing costs with expenses. In fact, the size of a firm is more likely to depend on the necessary production resources and the quantity of resources available. If the transaction costs fall, it is easy for the firm to obtain the necessary resources, and the products will have better trading opportunities in the market. Firms realize more benefits and, as a result, the firm grows. This is the fundamental reason why the size of a firm often grows with the market. If there is a possibility of becoming a monopoly, the firm will not miss such an opportunity, which implies high market transaction costs. Even so, the firm will still obtain high monopoly profits.

Consumers

Consumers are members of society who purchase or use goods and services. They are the end-users of the products or services. Each consumer is a subject of conduct with certain resources, including primary and other resources. The power generated by these resources is protected by law or institutions; that is, consumers have the right to use their own resources and to exchange them for other substances necessary for survival through the market. Under normal circumstances, consumers use money or other wealth resources for market transactions. Consumers who lack resources use other primary means, such as selling or using labor as a direct exchange for goods. Consumption is the premise for the existence of markets. As Smith states, consumption is the sole purpose of all production. Only when the interests of consumers are promoted should the interests of producers become a concern. In today's market economy, consumers have a significant impact on commodity prices, which is reflected by the consumer's right to choose goods. Whether to consume a commodity is up to the consumer, which is power that impacts the formation and evolution of commodity prices. Moreover, power is the basis for valid equilibrium analysis.

The effect of the consumer's right to choose on price formation is not direct. That is, the effect of consumer's "voting with their feet" provides feedback that adjusts the existing market price. This influence on price is a market effect when consumer behavior is considered as a whole. The effect of such adjustments depends on the magnitude of the power to choose products and on the degree of organization among individual consumers. The consumer's right to choose is related to the consumer's purchasing power, the substitutability of goods, information, and the size of consumer organization. The purchasing power of consumers depends on their exchangeable resources. The greater the amount of exchangeable resources, the greater the consumer's purchasing power. Moreover, the broader the scope of choice, the more searching costs the consumer can afford, consequently, the greater the right to choose. The substitutability of goods is related to market supply, and its influence is the weakening of corporate power caused by competition between firms. This weakening corresponds to an indirect increase in consumer power. This dynamic is the inevitable result of technology advances and improvements in production capacity. The stronger the goods' substitutability, the greater the power of consumer choice. At the same time, consumers expand their own power through various forms. Consumer organizations improve the power of individual consumers who enhance their effect on resources through the organizations and increase their individual impact on the market. As their own power grows, consumers' market position strengthens, which increases their concern for the objective of firms. When deciding pricing strategies, firms pay more attention to consumer demand and sentiment. On the other hand, consumers are also the providers of production factors; they decide the price of production materials as labor. The price of labor has a direct impact on the cost of production, and the cost is the basis for commodity prices. Therefore, consumers, as sources of labor, have a certain impact on price formation in the production process.

Government

The government is the executive body of state power. Government actions reflect the will of the state. In addition to basic functions, such as protecting national security, citizens' livelihoods, property, and maximizing social welfare, the government as an organization has a dual identity in the market. First, the government plays the role of market administrator with executive power and owns the rights to set transaction rules and to monitor and administrate such rules. Second, the government acts as a market participant with economic power. Government conducts transactions in markets using resources and, thus, is directly involved in economic activities such as the government procurement and national investments. It is this dual identity that provides government with a wide scope of responsibility. As a market administrator, government responsibility is to ensure economic equity, that is, to ensure that the process and results of transactions between subjects are fair, which is achieved by the government's executive power.

Due to its source and nature, administrative power is structurally endogenous and is a type of transformation of rights. Power comes from citizens' basic human rights. To better protect their fundamental rights, citizens transfer some of their rights to the government, which is representative of public opinion. The rights transferred from citizens become the ultimate source of executive power. Executive power is often considered a coercive force. It is not necessary to resort to this force. However, the punitive threat of force is a manifestation of power; therefore, the force has the effect of power. Executive power has institutional constraints. Government can only exercise the power given by the citizens through laws and cannot exercise the power that is not explicitly stipulated in laws. As a market participant, the government is a rational economic subject with a certain degree of economic power. Constrained by the rules of market behavior, the government uses its economic resources to participate in market competition and to maximize its self-interest under the concept of economic equity. The government's dual identity causes some degree of contradiction between its economic behavior and executive responsibility. On the one hand, it has to ensure economic equity; on the other hand, it pursues economic interests. In the market of non-equal distribution of social resources, it is difficult to have both goals achieved simultaneously. Therefore, the government must find a balance between ensuring market equity and achieving its own interests.

What is the role of the government as an administrator in a market economy? What is the relationship between the government and the market? The understanding of these questions varies significantly in existing economic theories. If markets are efficient, the government should not intervene using its executive power, and the market retains the ability to attain equilibrium automatically as market fundamentalists argue. The theory of market failure gives the government broader scope of actions. According to the theory, even if market competition is relatively effective in solving the problem of resource allocation, the distribution pattern that follows is not necessarily fair. Then, the question becomes how to determine which type of allocation is in most conformity with the socially acceptable principles of equal distribution. Obviously, the market cannot make this choice because it does not have the function to make ethical and value judgments. Imperfect competition and information asymmetry are the nature of the market, which are determined by the complexity and variability of the market. Relying solely on the market cannot be an effective solution. To solve the problem requires resorting to the government. Market failure theory argues that, in general cases, the allocation of resources by the market is efficient while market failure is only the exception.

However, Greenwald and Stiglitz (1986), based on thorough discussions, assert that the market is efficient only in exceptional cases, and market failure is the norm. If the market fails in most cases to varying degrees, then management by government becomes necessary. In other words, the purpose of state intervention is to address market failure and to ensure the fairness of market transactions, which are embodied in the formulation and implementation of economic institutions. Economic institutions determine the initial distribution of resources and the adjustment mechanism of resources in market operations. Different institutions produce different market structures and market operation mechanisms. Regardless of a society's structure, it will be a mixture of a market mechanism with government regulation. The two are indispensable for the effective functioning of an economy. At least until now, the executive functions of government cannot be replaced by the market mechanism. Economics has proven that the Nash equilibrium resulting solely from the competition between demand and supply does not reflect fairness; moreover, achieving social equity conditional on efficiency is the responsibility of the government. Thus, Stiglitz advocates a new economic development strategy that enhances government control in a market economy. Government must ensure both the effectiveness and fairness of market transactions. If government power is introduced to competition to fix the limitations of the mechanisms that allocate resources and oversee the fairness of transactions in cases of power asymmetry, the optimal distribution of social resources is possible, and economic goals will be achieved. This cannot occur through a market mechanism alone.

The government's economic role as a participant is attracting increasing attention. On the one hand, the government has substantial economic resources and controls a number of large enterprises that have monopoly power in the market. As a seller, the government is in a strong position; thus, ordinary consumers lack the economic power to effectively negotiate prices. On the other hand, as a buyer, the size of government purchases is growing. Moreover, the government has outstanding economic strength and market credibility. Hence, the government is the ideal consumer for the majority of firms. Because of the substantial resources to hand, whether as a buyer or seller, the government is in a strong position transaction wise. More critically, the government has the power to make rules concerning market behavior. If there is a need for constraints, the transaction rules that government imposes driven by its interests cannot be guaranteed to be fair. In other words, the government may also malfunction.

Power games and price formation

Re-defining economic rationality

There are differences in the natural endowments of individuals and organizations; therefore, there is inequality in the power ascribed to different subjects. Power inequality is an original state of society. The magnitude of power depends on relative scarcity or the difficulty to substitute in factor markets for the key resources owned by an economic subject. At the same time, resources are also mobile and constantly transferred in market competition. Correspondingly, the magnitude of power that any individual or organization obtains from controlling resources will naturally change with the transfer of resources. Therefore, power is adjustable.

In neo-classical economic theory, each individual will search for the best way to achieve goals through explicit or subconscious cost-benefit analysis under specific and changing constraints. Moreover, each individual will attain the most desirable outcome in the most desirable way in terms of economic advantage. The individual rationality of economic subjects is an axiom that requires no proof. Individual rationality states that consumers are maximizing individual utility while firms are maximizing profit for investment. However, for firms, profit is only one of the conditions ensuring stability and growth. Therefore, Galbraith (2001) refutes the rational belief in conventional economics on profit maximization, introduces the analysis of power into the exposition of economic rationality, and suggests the concepts of consumer and producer's sovereignty which means consumers and producers have their own sovereignty and pursue the power to control others in transactions.

Moreover, the magnitude of both the power of demand and supply determines the competitive structure of the market. Galbraith (2007) notes out that at the early stages of industrial development, consumer sovereignty dominates, and the relative simplicity of technology allows consumers to have a full understanding of what they want. Such subjective demand information is passed on to the market, which guides firm's production. However, with the development of human technology, producer sovereignty gradually assumes the consumer's sovereignty position as the key factor controlling the market. In the era of producer sovereignty, firms guide individual consumption by improving technologies and producing new designs, new products, and advertising. Thus, producer sovereignty expands. In competition, the side that has greater power gains more benefits from the market by setting up more favorable prices, which, in turn, expands that side's own power. The pursuit of market control and ensuring each individual's long-term survival in the market is the best choice for any rational subject. Maximizing benefits in the current period is only a means for a firm to achieve an individual's rational goal given the market conditions. As Galbraith (1983) states, the economic behavior of today's individual is not the pursuit of wealth, but also that of power.

The power games among market players and price equilibrium

Whether the exchange rate between countries, the market prices of ordinary goods, or the wages in labor markets, all are settled through negotiations among the subjects of power involved in different trading conditions. Bargaining power determines each party's benefits.

With respect to exchange rates, the basic exchange rate is always determined by a government according to its own interests. Even in a country where currencies are free to exchange, the government will closely watch the fluctuations in the exchange rate and directly intervene with foreign reserves when fluctuations are excessive. This shows that the exchange rate, the price in the exchange of different currencies, is closely related to national interests in international trade. The government will always set exchange rates in their favor. However, whether currency prices are accepted depends on the government's international status or the government's power when it interacts with other countries. Changes in the Japanese Yen in the last century clarify this point. Under the strong pressure of United States' economic sanctions, the Japanese government was forced to let the yen appreciate, which caused the Japanese economy to enter a downturn that persisted for nearly ten years. In the process of China's reforms and opening up, the RMB exchange rate has also been adjusted several times, and each adjustment accelerates the development of China's export-oriented economy. In recent years, the United States has repeatedly requested adjustments to the RMB exchange rate. The exchange rate has become a focus of an economic game between the two countries in recent years. Facing pressure from the US government, the Chinese government has sufficient bargaining power to contend with the US government and retain the right to determine the exchange rate.

For prices of ordinary goods, traditional economic theories posit that a free competition mechanism in the market forms prices. Price fluctuations pass some signals between the demand and the supply, which adjust the allocation of social resources and the distribution of social wealth. All prices are determined by the market and all decisions are the response to market orders. When demand and supply reach equilibrium, the price based on market exchange is a reasonable equilibrium price. Although they analyze the impact of differences in goods on the price, these theories continue to take price as an object and ignore the influence that other resources of the goods owner may have on price formation. Kaldor's research shows that in most cases, producers are price makers and quantity takers rather than price takers and quantity makers, as the Walrasian equilibrium theory notes. This finding shows that prices are mainly determined by producers; moreover, demand has some impact on prices but is not the dominant factor in price formation. Price, as the information on exchanges, reflects the quantitative relationship among objects and the relationship between people and objects and between people. The exchange of goods is actually the disposal of private property rights. Price formation is actually determined by individuals. Transactions occur under the premise that goods have clearly defined property rights, and the property rights are assigned to different subjects. Clarity of rights, particularly the privatization of property rights, is the basis of price formation (Kaldor, 1985).

Therefore, since Coase (1995) proposed property rights theory, incorporating power into the theoretical analysis has become the direction of price theory. The power paradigm of economic research has drawn increasing attention. The inevitability of power's influence lies in the considerations of *ex post* distribution and is contained in *ex ante* control over strategic development (Dietrich, 1994). Therefore, economics with no consideration of economic power is meaningless and unrealistic. Moreover, price theory without power analysis cannot account for the real process of pricing mechanisms in goods markets. Analysis on market issues from the perspective of power injects new content to traditional price theory: the market is, first of all, the market of power, that is, a power field. The circulation of things is realized by the exercise of power. The premise for any subject's disposal of goods is the possession of full property rights or a bundle of these rights. Thus, the transaction of goods is above all the exchange of property rights and is the transaction of things based on property rights. The price, or volume ratio of objects traded, is essentially the cost ratio of power value in the process of transferring ownership.

Price determination is essentially the issue of how property rights are defined and exchanged as well as the issue of which pattern is chosen in the exchange. The exchange value of any goods depends on the property rights contained in the transaction (Alchian & Demsetz, 1972; Furubotn & Pejovich, 1972). Therefore, some scholars define price as the equilibrium solution to the game of exchanging property rights between traders. However, this definition does not reveal how resources exert impact on prices. Property rights are only one type of power that affects market prices. Price formation is also affected by other factors in the market including information on institutions, consumer organizations, and strategies. Using institutions as an example, although they are not a direct production factor, the effectiveness of institutions is the guarantee of effective market operations. Power is the core form through which institutions and other resources have an effect.

Traditional price theories assume voluntary transactions between demand and supply sides as the premise for price analysis in market mechanisms. If the formation and evolution of institutions are the outcome of the power game between economic subjects, and institutional change is due to non-equilibrium between an economic subject's power and interests, then the formation of prices has involuntary components since power has the ability to impose costs with coercion on others (Samuels & Schmid, 1997). Nye (1995) believes that there is no reason to treat power differently from other goods. From a normative point of view, as long as one transaction party is not entirely voluntary, non-reciprocal transactions occur. Therefore, in a market with power in non-equilibrium, even if demand and supply reach a deal and attain equilibrium quantity, the distribution of interests is not in equilibrium.

Assuming there are only two game players, A and B, competing for market interests, τ_a and τ_b stand for the power of A and B, respectively, relying on the possession of resources. According to the relationship between power and interests, the equilibrium outcome of the distribution of market interests is: A gets $\tau_a / (\tau_a + \tau_b)$ while B gets $\tau_b / (\tau_a + \tau_b)$. If $\tau_a = \tau_b$, market interests are evenly distributed between A and B. If the power between them is not equal, the party that has more power will gain more benefits. Thus, in a market where parties in the transaction have non-reciprocal power, although transactions can be reached at a certain price level, such transactions are at the expense of the disadvantaged party's market interests. The larger the difference in the resources that generate power, the greater the inequality of interest distribution. If resources are allocated according to market mechanisms for a long time, the final result will be polarization of the interest structure. Market data illustrate this point. Collins and Preston (1969) conclude a positive correlation between corporate profits and market concentration based on market statistics. In addition, this correlation is more obvious among large firms that have cost and technical advantages. Martin (1988) studies the profit issue for firms using firm level data on capital rental costs, market share, and capital intensity. Martin argues that when a company is characterized by constant returns to scale, corporate profits are positively correlated with market share, rental costs of capital, and capital intensity. This argument shows that the more resources a party has, and the scarcer the resources, then one party in the competition is more competitive and will obtain more revenues than its competitors.

From the perspective of consumption, the existence of competition causes the highest bidder to obtain the trading opportunity; moreover, the highest bidder controls the most resources. Schmid (2003) argues that resource allocation led by market mechanisms has become the power expansion of economic subjects. Those who already possess resources will obtain much more. The real implications of "let the market decide" is that market interests will be allocated to those who already possess economic power. Therefore, price reflects more the will of the stronger side and allows the stronger side to use this information of exchange to obtain greater benefits. The market mechanism covers such unfairness in the allocation of interests. Only the market equilibrium that is based on the equal distribution of power resources can ensure equality in the distribution of interests. The price formed under this condition is the equilibrium price referred to in traditional economic theory.

In labor markets, compared to enterprises, ordinary workers have fewer resources. Consequently, workers are often in a weak position when negotiating. Government often uses administrative power to protect ordinary workers' reasonable income. The Law of Worker Protection, minimum incomes, trade unions, and other relevant laws and regulations compensate for the weak power position of the ordinary worker. For senior managers, the government sometimes sets a maximum level on their salary to prevent them from claiming a larger share of the profits. In periods of economic crisis, the government sets a maximum wage standard for business executives, which is a constraint on the executives who have significant power in business management. Through government adjustments to power on both sides, the basic equilibrium of interest distribution is achieved. The Initial allocation of power resources is unequal; moreover, power inequality is a normal market state. This inequality is the result of unequal personal qualities and ability and a reflection of social institutions and their legitimate operation. The flow of resources causes the power of each subject to change. When the power structure is not sufficient to support the current mode of interest distribution, the equilibrium breaks. The market reaction to this is price volatility.

If the market fails, the competition mechanism that relies solely on demand and supply will lead to more serious failure and cannot effectively adjust to the failure. Therefore, the market has never been free from government intervention. Even the most laissez-faire traditional economies since Adam Smith have recognized the fundamental role that government plays in establishing necessary rules and institutions to facilitate market operation. The coercive nature of government's administrative power ensures the effectiveness of government participation in the market.

First, such coercion is the premise for the existence of property rights. It does not make sense to discuss property rights in a society without coercion (Nye, 1995). Second, the government is expected to ensure that each economic subject has the necessary conditions to survive, that is, to ensure that the disadvantaged will not be totally deprived of their resources by the privileged. If the pricing mechanism causes resources to be allocated unequally, the government has the ability to develop an appropriate system to adjust the allocation of social resources coercively, such as taxation and social welfare. At some time, or in specific markets, the government is directly involved in formulation. For example, by setting a minimum wage, the government ensures reasonable returns to the workers who lack resources. By setting price ceilings for the products essential for daily life, the government prevents rapid increases in prices due to merchants bidding up prices, which cause the living standards of the disadvantaged to plummet. This phenomenon goes beyond equilibrium price theory and can only be explained from the perspective of power. That is, at any time, the government does not lose control over price.

However, whether the government is involved in price setting depends on the situation of transaction parties, manager awareness, and the benefits that the government can possibly obtain. In most transactions, although the two sides have significant differences in power, the difference has minimal influence on the market in the short term. Therefore, the government typically does not participate in specific transaction actions but only adjusts the macroscopic state of the market as a whole. At the same time, as a subject of action, the government has the incentive to seek economic interests. Moreover, the coercion of executive power places the government in a favorable position when competing for economic interests. The government is an organization composed of people, so there is no absolutely ideal decision-making process. Fortunately, the development of society minimizes the possibility of distortions. The government's power comes from the authorization of a number of economic subjects. Holding power, or power tools, does not entitle any ruler to unlimited power. In other words, government has coercive power but also assumes great social responsibility. The existence of government is to ensure social equity; hence, the government cannot deprive citizens of their primary resources for no reason. A government that renders one side worse-off through coercive means for their own economic interests risks survival. Such a government will be peacefully replaced in a democratic society and violently overthrown in a non-democratic society. Therefore, fair market participation is the optimal choice for government. Effective functioning of market mechanisms is the consequence of a power equilibrium under mutual constraints on the three parties: producers, consumers, and the government.

Fluctuating international oil prices are the best example of the power of all parties to participate in market behavior. As an indispensable production resource in the development of industrial countries, petroleum has always been the focus of competition among countries. Prior to the 1960s, western developed countries, led by the United States, leveraged their oil transnational corporations to control the entire international oil market and signed colonial "concession agreements" with major Middle Eastern oil-producing countries. Buying Middle Eastern oil at a price of $3 a barrel, the US garnered a substantial amount of residual value in the oil industry chain. To change the current situation of unequal transactions, in September 1960, small and medium-sized oil-producing countries jointly established the Organization of Petroleum Exporting Countries (OPEC) to coordinate and unify the oil policies of member states, master oil production and pricing rights, and maintain international oil accessibility. Market prices stabilized ensuring that oil-producing countries received a steady income from the oil industry. After struggles with Western oil companies, the oil-producing countries have gained greater rights to set rates for production and pricing and more benefits in the oil industry chain.

However, with the development of petroleum exploration technology, other countries in the world successively discovered large-scale oil reserves, and OPEC's production ratio to the world's total oil production began to decline. For OPEC members, it became increasingly difficult to maintain world oil prices unilaterally, particularly in the 1970s. Stable oil prices brought huge foreign exchange gains to the Soviet Union, and the United States is a major consumer of petroleum products. US spends $200 billion on Middle East oil every year. In particular, the Soviet Union's invasion of Afghanistan gave Saudi Arabia, a major oil producer in the Middle East, serious cause for concern. For the sake of common interests, the United States and Saudi Arabia cooperated to manipulate world oil prices. Saudi Arabia's output accounted for 40% of the world's total output. Because of the regional geological structure and the superiority of its geographical location, oil extraction is easy, and Saudi Arabia can quickly expand its production capacity in a short time. If oil prices could be reduced by increasing production, the American consumer would benefit and the increased production would weigh heavily on the Soviet economy. If the price of oil fell from $34 a barrel at the time to $20, US international expenditure would be reduced by $70 billion. Nationals would receive a 1% dividend from the US gross domestic product while the Soviet Union would lose billions of dollars. The decrease in oil prices also reduced the income of other oil-producing countries in the Middle East. Many of these countries were buyers of Soviet arms. The decrease in income had a significant effect on the sales of Soviet arms. As a result, Saudi Arabia increased crude oil production in the early 1980s, and world crude oil prices plummeted. While the United States profited, the Soviet Union lost huge profits causing economic collapse and the disintegration of the country.

Supply and demand are not the determinants of prices. What really determines price formation is power. Kissinger has a sharper statement: "If you control oil, you control all countries; if you control food, you control all people; if you control currency, you control the entire world." It is the United States and Saudi Arabia's manipulation of the oil market through government power that led to huge fluctuations in oil prices and the redistribution of the benefits of the oil industry, which is described in more detail by Frederick William Engdahl's (2004) "A Century of War." Therefore, rather than saying that price is a game equilibrium solution for traders to trade property rights under contractual conditions such as constraints, it is better to say that price is a game equilibrium solution for traders' respective market powers under a system, information, and other constraints.

5   Price determination in goods market

The market equilibrium price defined by new classical economics may exist. However, in reality, people cannot possess accurate knowledge about the equilibrium price of any good. In real transactions, demand and supply are dynamic, and the price is changing. Therefore, people's perceptions and concerns are reflected in the transaction price. This chapter explains that the transaction price emerges under a specific trading mode and a type of interest distribution. Bargains are the core component of specific trading modes. Bargaining ability—economic power in market transactions—determines the transaction price.

Price dispersion in the e-commerce market

Under the assumption of complete information, there should only be one transaction price for the same commodity at the same time. The e-commerce market is considered a transaction scenario close to complete information in the real world. However, the spatial dispersion of commodity prices in the e-commerce market is no less that of the traditional offline market. Zhao (2005) conducts a systematic investigation of this subject.

The sample used in this study is composed of nine categories of 536 products sold by 93 e-commerce retailers (B to C) registered in Beijing. To ensure the comparability of prices, the researchers strictly limited the identification conditions of the same product. For example, we used the ISBN number to define the style of books or audiovisual products,[1] and we used the manufacturer's brand and model to define other types of products. The price data are from the sales prices shown on 93 home appliance store websites from 5 July to 8 July, 2004. Because e-commerce retail in China usually adopts the method of trading at a marked price, we assume that these marked prices represent the actual transaction price.

From the researchers' reports, we obtain several insights. First, there is widespread price dispersion in the e-commerce market, and the degree of dispersion is not significantly lower than the traditional market. In May 1992, the coefficient of price variation of COSINA cameras in the Guangzhou offline market was 13.66% and, according to the research conducted on April 10, 2003, the coefficients of price variations of several Sony DSC digital cameras were 11.03% and 5.14%, 5.34% and 12.91%; the maximum value is almost equal to the offline market. The Internet has substantially reduced the search costs of consumers, and the price gap of the same product should converge significantly. However, the above results do not seem to prove this convergence, and there must be other factors that lead to price dispersion.

Second, Zhao (2005) analyzes the drivers of price dispersion in terms of merchant characteristics, commodity categories, and market structure of the same commodity. In terms of merchant characteristics, the dispersion of service level variables, such as delivery and payment and logistics queries, affects the price dispersion of the same product at a significance level of 0.1 to 0.01. If you consider the merchant service as an extension of the quality of goods, these findings are understandable for the same commodity; merchants who provide quality services will charge a higher price. However, the researchers' further regression analysis of price levels and merchant service levels (not dispersion level) shows that for most commodities, merchants with robust delivery and payment services will instead list lower commodity prices (such as Table 5.1, row 3, except for digital cameras), which may imply the impact of merchants' competitive strategies.

Different types of commodity prices and merchant characteristics show different relationship styles. For example, for video cameras and digital cameras, merchants that provide more detailed product information will charge a higher price, while for gifts and cosmetics there is no significant correlation between product information and price. This may be because cameras and digital cameras are technically complex products, and consumers are willing to pay higher prices to obtain detailed product information. As another example, consumers of gifts and cosmetics are particularly concerned with the issue of returns; therefore, merchants who provide more detailed return instructions will charge higher prices for goods. In general, books, audiovisual products, gifts, cosmetics, video cameras, and digital cameras form three groups, and the product prices in the group show the same relationship with merchant characteristics. Books and audiovisual products, camcorders and digital cameras are all rationally purchased products, but the information of books and audiovisual products is relatively simple; consumers of gifts and cosmetics are more inclined to make decisions based on feelings. Consumers of the three groups of commodities pay attention to different core interests. Thus, a diversified potential contrast with the merchants that provide corresponding services to different degrees shows price dispersion.

The more sellers there are of the same product, the closer the product market is to a completely competitive market, and the more likely it is that price will converge to the same level. Surprisingly, Zhao's (2005) research found that price dispersion increases at a significance level of 0.01 with an increase in the number of merchants distributing the same product. This is the result

Table 5.1 Results of regression analysis of commodity prices on merchant characteristics

Product type	Books	Audiovisual	Notebook	Gift	Cosmetic	MP3	Video camera	Digital camera	Cell phone
Merchant type (pure online vs. mixed)	-0.22 ***	-0.09	0.09	-0.29 ***	-0.22***	-0.17 ***	-0.10 **	-0.23 ***	-0.04
Delivery and payment	-0.05	-0.16 *	-0.30 ***	-0.20***	-0.02	-0.26***	0.08	0.15 ***	0.07
Shopping convenience (evaluation and search)	-0.15***	-0.17***	0.02	0.15***	-0.07*	0.10**	0.05	-0.01	-0.38***
Transaction reliability (logistics inquiry)	0.09***	0.01	0.36*	0.39***	0.05	-0.01	-0.13**	-0.20***	0.02
Website speed	0.04	0.17***	-0.32**	-0.01	-0.03	0.04	0.07	-0.07	0.06
How detail commodity's information provided	0.12***	0.17***	0.12	0.02	0.01	0.04	0.13 ***	0.23***	-0.05
How detail are return instructions	-0.21***	0.00	0.08	0.11***	0.08***	0.06	0.07	-0.02	0.00
Time to market	-0.19***	-0.17**	0.09	-0.10***	0.05	-0.12***	-0.07	-0.12***	-0.22***
Third-party certification	0.06*	-0.01	-0.06	0.14***	0.12***	0.00	0.09	-0.28***	-0.17
Number of website links	-0.01	-0.07	0.09	0.35***	0.10***	-0.07	0.12**	0.12***	0.40***
Number of samples	1,172	469	242	760	1,022	713	508	648	779
Adjusted R²	0.30	0.15	0.18	0.12	0.07	0.12	0.05	0.15	0.22

Note: Significance level *** $p < 0.01$, ** $p < 0.05$, * $p < 0.1$

regardless of the type of product used or whether it is adopted. Whatever method of measuring price dispersion is steadily established, the importance of search costs is significant. When there is a search cost, it is impossible for consumers to search all businesses exhaustively. Each business has its own consumer group or its own sphere of influence. The smaller the sphere of influence overlap, the lower the merchant's pricing competition brings constraints.

The explanation of the above phenomena is, fundamentally, the subjective speculation of the author of this book, which is limited to the data provided by the original researchers. We cannot prove the accuracy of these speculations, but these phenomena are sufficient to illustrate that the factors affecting the price of commodities are various. Many factors come into play by changing the balance of power between buyers and sellers. The following uses this idea to build a theoretical model.

Commodity pricing properties

Equilibrium price vs. transaction price

The influence of new classical price theory is so profound that to explain price changes, economists immediately resort to the change in demand and supply. However, the transaction price varies across trading partners and for the same commodity even at the same moment, which is common for price dispersion. We can explain dispersion as a random distribution with the equilibrium price as its expected value. However, we question whether the deviation of price from the associated equilibrium level is really random. To answer the question, we must distinguish between equilibrium and transaction price.

The equilibrium price theory established by new classical economics shows the effects of demand and supply on price formation. The logic strictly depends on the assumption of a perfect competitive market. When the price is investigated for a particular transaction, the transaction price is not necessarily the equilibrium price because the market is not perfect competitive, or even if the market is perfect competitive, it is influenced by other factors such as the urgency to purchase and regional market distribution. Obviously, new classical price theory ignores some factors that are more akin to the determination of transaction prices.

Stigler (1961) is the first to deal with the phenomenon of price dispersion. Stigler notes that transaction prices exhibit dispersion in different markets at the same time for the same car brand or for the same quality of coal. He attributes the reason to the difference in search costs of the economic market agents. Undoubtedly, incomplete information is a realistic reason, but not all. Using the coal market again as an example, the buyers include both an ordinary town resident whose annual consumption of coal is only several tons and a thermal power plant whose usage is in the tens of thousands of tons every month. Clearly, the two buyers would not be expected to purchase the coal at the same price. Such a situation is described as market power in industrial organization theory. Considering the ticket pricing policies of airlines, it is difficult for a traveler to buy a discount ticket close to the departure date because the airline can exploit the fact that the traveler is anxious to travel and will be willing to pay more for a ticket.

As we mentioned, the group structure of buyers and sellers, complete market information, and some characteristics of a particular trading party will lead to different transaction prices even for the same good. Such dispersion is not an accidental deviation from market equilibrium price; rather, it is the effect of certain idiosyncrasies of both parties on the transaction results and a reflection of market laws that are ignored by new classical theory. To understand the nature of goods markets, we must begin with the transaction price and also explore the equilibrium price theory of new classical economics.

The other reason that our analysis must begin with the transaction price is that the equilibrium price theory of new classical economics lacks operability. In fact, regardless of what type of goods market, it is difficult to determine whether the observed transaction price is the equilibrium price or fluctuates around the equilibrium price. This is the case even for the often quoted agricultural product market. Moreover, due to the openness of the market system, demand and supply in every market are affected by many factors and, consequently, continue to change. Before arriving at the market equilibrium price described by new classical theory, there are always some factors that cause the transaction price to deviate from the original locus of change and then converge toward the market equilibrium price. Such factors are the equilibrium path depicted in the cobweb model in perfect competitive market and the equilibrium path depicted in the dynamic matching model (Gale, 2000). The method used to study the transaction price does not have such ambiguity because we only need to show the reason why the transaction price between A and B is higher than the transaction price between A and C. Or, we can say that the object of our research is observable. The task for researchers is to explain the observed price and understand its determining factors. Such understanding is vital to theoretical researchers and the participants of economic activities because price is the signal that directs resource allocation and a mechanism that distributes economic interests under any market structure.

The distribution function of price

For allocating resources to work, the premise regarding price is that all markets, including goods and factor markets, must be fully competitive. This is obviously an extreme assumption. If this assumption is not satisfied, it is pointless to discuss resource allocation. In a fully competitive market, what role does price play, and why do all the trading parties consider price to be the primary factor of concern?

Setting aside the disputes and quarrels over concepts and theories, economic activities are actually quite basic. They can be summarized as efforts to seize resources, produce all types of products and services, and then to enjoy the achievements. Because everyone's needs are diversified, self-sufficiency hinders the creation of wealth and economic development; therefore, labor division emerges. The division improves productivity, but it makes the exchange of products necessary. Consequently, prices emerge. A high price is favorable to sellers while a low price is favorable to buyers; therefore, price is essentially a type of interest distribution mechanism. Any change in price is a redistribution of interests. For example, in a simple two-person economy, A and B produce in their specialized areas, respectively. A produces 10 units of clothing and B does 10 units of food. We use an Edgeworth box to describe the relationship between them (as showed in Figure 5.1). In the figure, the horizontal axis represents the quantity of clothing while the vertical axis represents the quantity of food. O_A is the coordinate origin of A. Any point to the right or above this origin indicates that A has more of both clothing and food. O_B is the coordinate origin of B, and any point to the left or below this origin implies that B has more of both clothes and food. W represents the initial endowment of both parties when they first enter the market, which states that the initial endowment of A is 10 units of clothing and 0 unit of food while the initial endowment of B include 0 unit of clothing and 10 units of food. If the unit price is 1 yuan for both clothing and food, then the bundle of goods after the exchange will move along the line of WP_1. If the unit price is 1 yuan for clothing but 2 yuan for food, then the bundle will move along line WP_2. For any quantity that A is willing to give up (such as A is willing to give up 6 units of clothing), the bundle that resulted in the second price (clothing = 10−6 = 4 while food = 6 × 1/2 = 3) will be definitely inferior to that in the first price (clothing = 10−6 = 4, food = 6 × 1/1 = 6) — although it is always possible find a point on line WP_2 that maximizes A's utility. Putting aside the elusive concept of utility, the bundle under the second price reduces A's benefits in the economic cooperation and labor division.

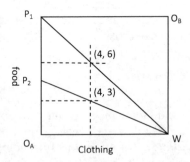

Figure 5.1 Commodity exchange relationship at different prices.

A change in price will affect the interest distribution between buyers and sellers and the interest distribution among a group of buyers and among a group of sellers. For example, when a manufacturer changes the price, it affects other manufacturers' sales and prices, which leads to a redistribution of the whole industry's benefits among the manufacturers. As another example, when a buyer raises the overall price level in the market due to high demand, the benefits of other buyers will inevitably be affected.

Because transaction price is a type of interest distribution mechanism, it is not difficult to understand why all trading parties seek to influence it. The remainder of this chapter focuses on how transaction price is determined.

Transaction mode and the bargaining process

Because we are concerned with the transaction price in reality, not the equilibrium price in theory, we begin with the transaction mode in the real economy when investigating the determinants of the transaction price.

Table 5.2 lists the main transaction modes in the real economy. Although they differ in detail, the modes have a common characteristic; that is, every transaction mode is composed of two processes—matching and bargaining. The bargaining process directly generates the transaction price, and the impact of the matching process on the price is embodied in the bargaining process.

Negotiation

Negotiation is a trading mode that does not require a regular marketplace and finds the transaction price through bargaining once a party identifies by searching the trading partner. As long as both parties form the pair through a search process, bargaining starts. If the price is agreed, the transaction is completed. If, however, the price cannot be agreed, both parties will enter the market and search for partners.

Table 5.2 Transaction modes in real economy

Transaction modes	Example	Quantities in the transaction	Mode of matching (seller vs. buyer)	First bidder	No. of bargaining rounds in every matching
Auction	Cultural relics	Fixed	One vs. many	Buyer	One round
Sellers quote price	Shop sales	No limits or high upper limits	One vs. many	Seller (counter price)	Usually one round; several rounds in a few cases
Negotiation	Iron ore trading	No limits or high upper limits	One vs. one	Uncertain	Multiple rounds
Buyers quote price	Agricultural products	No limits or high upper limits	Many vs. one	Buyer	Usually one round; several rounds in a few cases
Call for bids	Government procurement	Fixed	Many vs. one	seller	One round

Without loss of generality, we turn the bargaining process into an abstract form as follows. At the beginning of the negotiation, one party (such as A, who may be the seller or the buyer) proposes a price, P_{A1}. The other party (such as B, who may be the buyer or the seller) has three options: accept the price, reject the price and propose a new price, P_{B2}, or reject the price and exit the negotiation to search for new trading partners. When B chooses to bargain with A, the benchmark model for bidding negotiation will continue. In this case, A has three similar options. Both parties will bid alternately until one party accepts the other's offer or chooses to leave.

In a typical negotiation, the bargaining process is composed of multiple rounds. Figure 5.2 presents a general model that is applicable to most common trading modes. Of course, if we consider the pricing process of other trading modes in the real economy as bargaining, this feature of multiple rounds will be less typical; however, this does not affect the central role of bargaining in the transactions.

Auction

The most common type of trading mode is the English auction. Once the auction begins, the auctioneer (on behalf of the seller) announces a suggested opening bid,[2] also referred to as the reserve price, and then accepts increasingly higher bids from the bidders on the floor. When a bidder calls out a price, the auctioneer does not immediately reject or accept the price; instead, the auctioneer continues to ask for higher bids. The auctioneer does not place their hammer down until no one is willing to make further bids within a given timeframe.

The whole auction can be decomposed into two fundamental processes—matching and bargaining. Unlike the typical negotiation, the bargaining

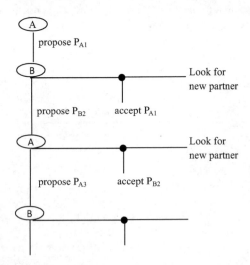

Figure 5.2 Benchmark model for bidding.

process has only one round at auction. After the first bid, the auctioneer does not offer any price; instead, the auctioneer asks whether anyone is willing to give a higher price. The action shows that the auctioneer chooses to temporarily reject the bidder to look for new trading partners. The transaction moves rapidly from the bargaining to the matching process. When a new bidder calls out a (higher) price, a new pair is formed, and the new party offers a suggested price. If the auctioneer continues to ask for higher prices, the auctioneer temporarily rejects the second bidder and starts to look for new trading partners. Once the auctioneer's hammer drops, the transaction is confirmed because it indicates that the auctioneer accepts the last bid.

Price quotation by sellers

This is a sales mode whereby sellers announce publicly the price in shop or net sales. After a buyer observes the price, if they accept the price, the buyer pays, and the bargain ends in one round. If the buyer does not accept the price, the buyer leaves, which is the equivalent of the search for new partners in the benchmark model, and the bargain also finishes in one round.

Price quotation by buyers

Microeconomic theory pays too much attention to the seller's initiative in the exchange of goods while neglecting the fact that a large number of transactions are organized actively by buyers. For example, the purchase of agricultural products, the recycling of waste and used materials, and the trading of handmade crafts are all transactions with many sellers but few buyers and where the price quotation comes from buyers. The bargaining process has the same structure in this mode as in price quotation by sellers; the only difference is that the buyer offers the price first.

Call for bids

An explanation of public tendering from the bargaining perspective is as follows: when an organization requesting tenders opens the first bidding document, the equivalent is an initiative quotation from the bidder. The organization temporarily rejects the quotation and searches for a new trading partner when it opens the second bidding document. After reading the second quotation, the organization continues to reject quotations. This process repeats until the organization rejects all bidders; then, the organization will look for the bidder who offers the lowest quotation and accept this quotation.

Comparing the above trading modes, regardless of the mode, the transaction can always be explained based on the matching and bargaining model. The transaction price emerges from the bargaining process, but the matching mode is also necessary. For example, at auction, the reason why the bidders continue to anxiously call out higher prices is that they know the trading matching scenario is one (seller) to many (buyers). The auctioneer can easily find a trading partner. Alternatively, the influence of matching modes on transaction price is indirect and is realized through the bargaining process. The bargaining process is the core of all trading modes. Therefore, in the following analysis, we first analyze a conceptual bargaining model where the parameters determining the transaction price (see section "Transaction mode and the bargaining process") are isolated. Then, the power behind these parameters is discussed in section "The bargaining model and transaction price," including the matching mechanism mentioned at the beginning of this section.

The bargaining model and transaction price

Assumptions

For the bargaining problem with alternating price bids, the most cited model is proposed by Rubinstein (1982). This model assumes that players in games have perfect computational abilities; hence, at the outset of bargaining, the player who offers the first bid suggests a price that the other player will immediately accept. According to this equilibrium solution, the actual bargaining is a two-step process—to bid and to accept—although the model claims that the bargaining can continue infinitely. Obviously, the assumption of perfect computational ability puts an excessive requirement on the rationality of the players. More importantly, bargaining is a process of constant information transmission between the parties involved in transactions. After several rounds of bargaining, both parties fully understand each other's reserve price and the extent of the concession. At this point, considering negotiation and searching costs, the players can decide whether it is worthwhile to increase the price or leave the negotiation table to find a new partner. Based on this idea, we use the process descriptive method (Balakrishnan & Eliashberg, 1995) to construct a bargaining model, as shown in Figure 5.3.

At the beginning of the negotiation ($t = 0$), the seller, S, offers the price X_0 first, then the buyer, B, gives the counter offer of price Y_0. Both parties obtain a preliminary understanding of the difference between them. In the following negotiations, it is in fact the process that both parties make up the difference through concessions. But since both parties have different positions, the extent of concessions may be different.

After the first period ($t = 1$), facing the B's proposed price Y_0, S has three options, namely to: (a) accept Y_0; (b) offer a new price X_1; and (c) stop the negotiation with B and search for new trading partners. For S, if he accepts B's proposed price, the transaction price is Y_0. If he rejects the price and gives his proposed price X_1 ($X_1 > Y_0$), then the resulted maximum benefit is $X_1 - Y_0$. If this benefit is greater than the single period negotiation cost of S, c_S, then bargaining is profitable and he should bargain. However, if

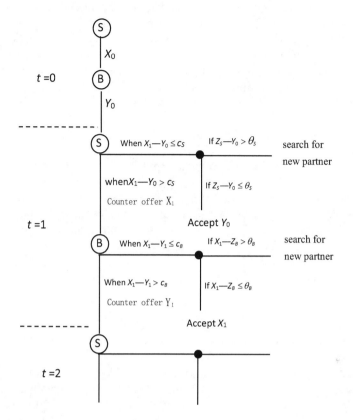

Figure 5.3 Bargaining model.

the benefit is less than or equal to the single period negotiation costs, that is, $X_1 - Y_0 \leq c_S$, then bargaining is meaningless and he should consider to receive Y_0 or look for new partners, which involves the cost and benefit of searching new partners. Assume that the searching cost of S for every new trading partner is θ_S ($\theta_S > 0$), and that except B, a second search may attain the expected maximum price of Z_S. If $Z_S - Y_0 > \theta_S$, he should search for new partner. If $Z_S - Y_0 > \theta_S$, then the searching can't bring any net benefit; hence, he should accept Y_0.

Assume that S gives a counter—offer, X_1, now it is B's turn to make a decision out of the three options. The corresponding decision conditions have been listed in Figure 5.3. c_B is the negotiation cost of B in each period. θ_B is the searching costs for every new transaction partner for B. Z_B is the expected minimum price that can be possibly attained through an additional search besides S.

In the second period ($t = 2$) and after, the bargaining sequence is same as that in the first period. If the negotiation cost is zero for both parties, according to the assumptions in Figure 5.3, both parties will choose to give a counter-offer price throughout and the bargaining will infinitely go on. But in fact, the negotiation cost is never zero. With the bids of both parties getting closer, benefits from further bargains will become fewer and fewer. There will be a period in which one party feels that benefits of further bargains are insufficient to compensate the negotiation costs; consequently, he needs to choose either to accept the price or to leave, and the negotiation ends.

Solution to the model

Solving the model involves two parts. First, let us assume that the negotiation cost is zero, ($c_S = 0$, and $c_B = 0$), that is, both parties will not accept the other's quotation nor look for new transaction partner, instead, they always bid and bargain. In this scenario, we can get the price quotation sequence for both parties. Then, take into account that the negotiation cost is not zero and solve for the condition that one party accepts the other's offer (transaction completed) and the condition that this party looks for a new transaction partner (breakup).

The quotation sequence when the negotiation cost is zero

Under the above-assumed conditions, the negotiation process can be simplified as the situation shown in Figure 5.4.

Since in every period the only decision that both parties must make is to give quotation of price, the analysis of bargaining process is actually to study how each party decides X or Y. Assuming that in period t, the quotations of S and B are X_t and Y_t, respectively; then in period $t + 1$, if S quotes the price first, how should S decide X_{t+1}? Obviously, S will reason as follows: first, the quotation of S in period t (X_t) has been rejected by B (because B gives the counter offer, Y_t); in order to make the transaction happen, the quotation of S should not be higher than X_t; second, although B quotes the price Y_t in period t, it is not necessary for S to offer a price lower than Y_t. Then, the quotation of S should be somewhere between X_t and Y_t. For its

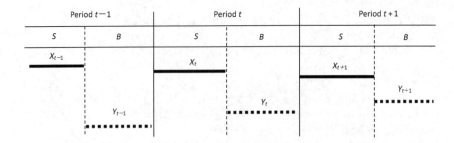

Figure 5.4 The bargaining model with zero negotiation cost.

own interests, S certainly will be better off if X_{t+1} is closer to X_t. But this action has the risk[3] that the transaction will fail. Here, we need to introduce an index of toughness, ρ_S, to describe whether S is worried about B's rejection and leaving. The greater the ρ_S, S will be less worried about B's leaving. In other words, the tougher the attitude S takes, the price, X_{t+1}, he offers will be closer to X_t. The mathematical expression is:

$$X_{t+1} = \rho_S X_t + (1 - \rho_S) Y_t \qquad (0 \le \rho_s \le 1) \qquad (5.1)$$

Applying the same logic to analyze B's decision on Y_{t+1}, we can get:

$$Y_{t+1} = \rho_B Y_t + (1 - \rho_B) X_{t+1} \qquad (0 \le \rho_s \le 1) \qquad (5.2)$$

where ρ_B is the B's index of toughness. The greater the ρ_B is, B is less worried about S's leaving.

Equations (5.1) and (5.2) constitute a second-order difference equation system, and solving the system gives:

$$X_t = \frac{X_1 - \rho_S \rho_B X_0}{1 - \rho_S \rho_B} + \frac{X_0 - X_1}{1 - \rho_S \rho_B} (\rho_S \rho_B)^t \qquad (5.3)$$

$$Y_t = \frac{Y_1 - \rho_S \rho_B Y_0}{1 - \rho_S \rho_B} + \frac{Y_0 - Y_1}{1 - \rho_S \rho_B} (\rho_S \rho_B)^t \qquad (5.4)$$

Notice that $X_1 = \rho_S X_0 + (1 - \rho_S) Y_0$ and $Y_1 = \rho_B Y_0 + (1 - \rho_B) X_1$; then (5.3) and (5.4) can be transformed into:

$$X_t = \frac{\rho_S (1 - \rho_B) X_0 + (1 - \rho_S) Y_0}{1 - \rho_S \rho_B} + \frac{(1 - \rho_S)(X_0 - Y_0)}{1 - \rho_S \rho_B} (\rho_S \rho_B)^t \qquad (5.5)$$

$$Y_t = \frac{\rho_S (1 - \rho_B) X_0 + (1 - \rho_S) Y_0}{1 - \rho_S \rho_B} - \frac{\rho_S (1 - \rho_B)(X_0 - Y_0)}{1 - \rho_S \rho_B} (\rho_S \rho_B)^t \qquad (5.6)$$

Equations (5.5) and (5.6) are the sequence of bidding—counter-offer when negotiation costs are zero for both parties. The equations show that if the negotiation costs nothing, and the negotiation has infinite rounds $\left(t \to \infty, (\rho_S \rho_B)^t \to 0 \right)$, the bids of both parties tend to converge at

$$X_\infty = Y_\infty = \frac{\rho_S (1 - \rho_B) X_0 + (1 - \rho_S) Y_0}{1 - \rho_S \rho_B} = P_\infty \qquad (5.7)$$

Taking derivatives of (5.7) with respect to ρ_S and ρ_B yields the following expressions:

$$\frac{\partial P_\infty}{\partial \rho_S} = \frac{(X_0 - Y_0)(1 - \rho_S)}{(1 - \rho_S \rho_B)^2} \ge 0, \quad \frac{\partial P_\infty}{\partial \rho_B} = -\frac{(X_0 - Y_0)(1 - \rho_S)\rho_S}{(1 - \rho_S \rho_B)^2} \le 0$$

They show that the tougher S is (the greater the ρ_S is), the higher the price is at the limit: the tougher B is (the greater the ρ_B is), the lower the price is at the limit.

The transaction price with non-zero negotiation costs

When the negotiation cost is non-zero, as the prices offered by both parties are getting closer, there always exists such a moment as t that one party perceives that the benefit isn't enough to cover the cost if he continues to bargain, facing other party's latest price offer. Thus he has to decide whether to accept the opponent's offer or to leave the negotiation table and look for another partner.

WHEN BUYER B FEELS THAT LOSSES WILL OUTWEIGH GAINS

Assume that X_t is the price quoted by S in period t, if B accepts this price, then the transaction price is X_t. If B rejects it, he will quote a new price, Y_t, following the quotation sequence (see equation 5.6), and the expected benefit is $X_t - Y_t$. Whether B should bargain is determined by whether the benefit is greater than the cost of negotiation, c_B. When $X_t - Y_t \leq c_B$, B will not bargain. He will either accept X_t, or leave the negotiation table and look for another partner. So the first condition that X_t becomes the transaction price is:

$$X_t - Y_t \leq c_B \tag{5.8}$$

Of course, the fact that B stops bargaining doesn't mean he will accept X_t. There is another possible outcome, that is, he leaves the negotiation table and looks for another partner. Only when the expected return from leaving is less than or equal to the cost of leaving behavior (finding another trading partner) will B surely accept X_t. So, the second condition for X_t to be the transaction price is:

$$X_t - Z_B \leq \theta_B \tag{5.9}$$

where Z_B is the minimum expected price that B can find in an additional search for new partner after he leaves the current negotiation. θ_B is the cost of the additional search.

Because at this stage the goal of analysis is to explore what level the transaction price is when both parties reach a deal, we assume that B will accept X_t and not look for another partner when he feels that losses will outweigh gains if he continues to bargain. This means that when the values of Z_B and θ_B satisfy equation (5.8), (5.9) must hold. The loss caused by such an assumption is to give up analyzing the effects of Z_B and θ_B on the price. This influence will be demonstrated in section "Solution to the model." Now, we focus on analyzing equation (5.8).

Taking (5.5) and (5.6) into (5.8) gives:

$$t \geq \frac{\ln c_B - \ln(X_0 - Y_0)}{\ln(\rho_S \rho_B)} \tag{5.10}$$

This is the time range that B accepts S's proposed price when the negotiation cost c_B is given. Because when t satisfies (5.10) at the first time, B will accept S's price and will not delay for several periods, the actual time that B accepts S's price is:

$$t_B^* = \frac{lnc_B - ln(X_0 - Y_0)}{ln(\rho_S\rho_B)} \tag{5.11}$$

Taking (5.11) into (5.5) yields the transaction price that emerges because B accepts S's quotation, which is,

$$X^* = \frac{\rho_S(1-\rho_B)X_0 + (1-\rho_S)Y_0}{1-\rho_S\rho_B} + \frac{(1-\rho_S)c_B}{1-\rho_S\rho_B} = P_\infty + \frac{(1-\rho_S)c_B}{1-\rho_S\rho_B} \tag{5.12}$$

Equation (5.12) shows that the higher the buyer's negotiation cost, the higher the transaction price will be.

WHEN THE SELLER FEELS THAT LOSSES OUTWEIGH GAINS

Assume that B's proposed price is Y_t in period t, and S has to decide whether to bargain or not in period $t + 1$. If S accepts the price, then the transaction price is Y_t. If he doesn't accept it, he will offer X_{t+1}, based on the quotation sequence (see 5.5), which will bring him the expected benefits of $X_{t+1} - Y_t$. Whether S should bargain depends on whether the benefit is greater than the negotiation cost, c_s. When $X_{t+1} - Y_t \leq c_s$, S will not bargain and will either accept Y_t or leave the negotiation table and look for other partners. So the first condition for Y_t to be the transaction price is,

$$X_{t+1} - Y_t \leq c_S \tag{5.13}$$

Similarly, S doesn't bargain doesn't imply that he must accept price Y_t. He can also choose to leave. Only when the expected return to leaving is less than or equal to the cost of leaving (finding other trading partners) will S surely accept the current price, Y_t. So the second condition for Y_t to be the transaction price is,

$$Z_S - Y_t \leq \theta_S \tag{5.14}$$

Z_S is the highest expected price that S can attain when he makes an additional search before leaving the current negotiation table. θ_S is the searching cost. Assume that if (5.13) holds, (5.14) also holds. Now we focus on analyzing (5.13). Taking (5.5) and (5.6) into (5.13), the solution is,

$$t \geq \frac{lnc_S - ln[\rho_S(X_0 - Y_0)]}{ln(\rho_S\rho_B)} \tag{5.15}$$

This is the time range that S accepts B's proposed price when the negotiation cost cs is given. Because when t satisfies (5.15) at the first time, S will accept B's proposed price and will not delay for several periods. The actual time that S accepts B's quotation is,

$$t_S^* = \frac{\ln c_S - \ln\left[\rho_S(X_0 - Y_0)\right]}{\ln(\rho_S \rho_B)} \tag{5.16}$$

Taking (5.16) into (5.6), then, yields the transaction price that emerges because S accepts B's quotation, which is,

$$Y^* = \frac{\rho_S(1-\rho_B)X_0 + (1-\rho_S)Y_0}{1-\rho_S\rho_B} - \frac{(1-\rho_B)c_S}{1-\rho_S\rho_B} = P_\infty - \frac{(1-\rho_B)c_S}{1-\rho_S\rho_B} \tag{5.17}$$

Equation (5.17) shows that the higher the seller's negotiation cost is, the lower the transaction price will be.

From the above analysis, two transaction prices can be obtained, that is, X^*, the transaction price comes from B's acceptance of S's quotation and Y^*, the transaction price comes from S's acceptance of B's quotation. For a given pair of trading partners, which is the actual transaction price depends on whether B accepts S's quotation first or S accepts B's quotation first. Once one party accepts the other's quotation, the negotiation will terminate. So there is only one transaction price. When $t_B^* \leq t_S^*$ (from (5.11) and (5.12), it follows that $c_B \geq c_S/\rho_S$.), B accepts S's quotation first; then, X^* will be the transaction price. However, when $t_S^* < t_B^*$ ($c_B < c_S/\rho_S$), S accepts B's quotation first; then Y^* will be the transaction price. The result states that the party with relatively higher bargaining cost might be the first to accept the other's price proposal.

Preliminary analysis of the transaction price

From the analysis in the above section, it is easy to see clearly the characteristics of transaction price. In the scenario of zero negotiation cost, when the bargaining goes on infinitely, there is a limit of P_∞ that the quotation of both parties tends to converge to. The level of this price at the limit is affected by the initial quotations X_0 and Y_0. The higher the initial quotation is, the higher the limit price will be. The limit price is also affected by the both parties' toughness. The tougher the seller is (that is, the greater the ρ_S is), the higher the P_∞ will be. The tougher the buyer is (that is, the greater the ρ_B is), the lower the P_∞ will be.

When taking into account the negotiation cost as in (5.12) and (5.17), the transaction price (X^* or Y^*) is the result of upward or downward adjustment to the limit price, P_∞, based on the cost factor. If the transaction results from B's acceptance of S' quotation ($c_B > c_S/\rho_S$, the cost of buyer is higher than that of seller), then the transaction price, X^*, is adjusted upward on the basis of P_∞. The magnitude of adjustment depends on buyer's negotiation cost, c_B. The larger the c_B is, the larger the upward adjustment will be. If the transaction results from S accepting B's quotation ($c_B < c_S/\rho_S$, the cost of buyer is lower than that of seller), then the transaction price, Y^*, is adjusted downward on the basis of P_∞. The magnitude of adjustment depends on seller's negotiation cost, c_S, and the larger the c_S is, the larger the downward adjustment will be. The results show that the party with a high negotiation cost is at a disadvantage in the negotiation; moreover, the reason for accepting the other party's quotation is that the party with a high negotiation cost senses that they cannot afford the delay. For example, in iron ore negotiations between China and Australia, China is often at a disadvantage. In addition to the monopoly market, a more significant reason is that the loss incurred from shutting down Chinese iron and steel production is too heavy.

To systematically explain the effect of various factors on the transaction price, Table 5.2 presents the calculated partial derivatives of two types of transaction prices with respect to all factors involved along with the corresponding economic interpretations.

Table 5.3 Factors that affect transaction price

Price	Line number	Partial derivative	Sign of partial derivative	Economic interpretation
X^*	1	$\dfrac{\partial X^*}{\partial \rho_S} = \dfrac{(1-\rho_B)(X_0-Y_0-c_B)}{(1-\rho_S\rho_B)^2}$	Positive	The tougher the seller is, the higher the price will be
	2	$\dfrac{\partial X^*}{\partial \rho_B} = -\dfrac{\rho_S(1-\rho_S)(X_0-Y_0-c_B)}{(1-\rho_S\rho_B)^2}$	Negative	The tougher the buyer is, the lower the price will be
	3	$\dfrac{\partial X^*}{\partial X_0} = \dfrac{\rho_S(1-\rho_B)}{1-\rho_S\rho_B}$	Positive	The higher the seller's initial price is, the higher the price will be
	4	$\dfrac{\partial X^*}{\partial Y_0} = \dfrac{1-\rho_S}{1-\rho_S\rho_B}$	Positive	The higher the buyer's initial price is, the higher the price will be
	5	$\dfrac{\partial X^*}{\partial c_B} = \dfrac{1-\rho_S}{1-\rho_S\rho_B}$	Positive	The higher the buyer's negotiation cost is, the higher the price will be
Y^*	6	$\dfrac{\partial Y^*}{\partial \rho_S} = \dfrac{(1-\rho_B)(X_0-Y_0-\rho_Bc_S)}{(1-\rho_S\rho_B)^2}$	Positive	The tougher the seller is, the higher the price will be
	7	$\dfrac{\partial Y^*}{\partial \rho_B} = -\dfrac{\rho_S(1-\rho_S)(X_0-Y_0-c_S/\rho_s)}{(1-\rho_S\rho_B)^2}$	Negative	The tougher the buyer is, the lower the price will be
	8	$\dfrac{\partial Y^*}{\partial X_0} = \dfrac{\rho_S(1-\rho_B)}{1-\rho_S\rho_B}$	Positive	The higher the seller's initial price is, the higher the price is
	9	$\dfrac{\partial Y^*}{\partial Y_0} = \dfrac{1-\rho_S}{1-\rho_S\rho_B}$	Positive	The higher the buyer's initial price is, the higher the price will be
	10	$\dfrac{\partial Y^*}{\partial c_S} = -\dfrac{1-\rho_B}{1-\rho_S\rho_B}$	Negative	The higher the seller's negotiation cost is, the lower the price will be

Note: The underlying parameter assumptions used for judging the signs of the partial derivatives in the table include $0\leq\rho S\leq1$, $0\leq\rho B\leq1$, $X0\geq Y0$, $X0-Y0\geq cS$, $X0-Y0\geq cB$; when the transaction price is Y^*, $cB>cS/\rho S$.

Source of bargaining power

From the above analysis, it is clear that initial price offers from both parties, the degree of toughness in the bargaining process, and negotiation costs are the key factors affecting the transaction price and ultimately determining the price. As in the bargaining models discussed previously, we refer to the above factors of each party as bargaining power, specifically, economic power. Bargaining power determines the transaction price, which is not new knowledge. What we are most interested in is what determines bargaining power. Why do both parties quote a particular number as the initial price and not another number at the beginning? What are the reasons behind the toughness or willingness to compromise that both parties exhibit in negotiations? What is the real meaning of negotiation cost? In this section, we analyze these factors that compose bargaining power.

To facilitate the analysis, we place both seller (S) and buyer (B) in one market. We assume that there are M sellers in the market with S as one of the sellers, and there are N buyers with B as one of the buyers. Moreover, before S meets B, each has contacted some negotiation objects separately. After S negotiates with B, if willing, both can search for new trading partners.

Initial quotation

Initial quotation of S, X_0

Based on our observations of bargaining behavior in reality, we conclude that the seller does not expect that the initial quotation will be the transaction price. The initial quotation is just the starting point, and there will be gradual compromises in later stages. The higher the initial quotation, the greater the leeway. Then, the final transaction price is more favorable to the seller. This has been proved in Table 5.2 (lines 3 and 8). Thus, why does the seller not quote an exorbitant price at the beginning of the negotiation? The reason is that if the seller's quotation significantly deviates from the buyer's anticipated price, the buyer will exit the negotiation. Then, how does the seller know what price the buyer is anticipating? This knowledge is obtained from previous contacts with other buyers.

In this $M \times N$ market, assume that the N buyers' price expectation of the product of S follows a $\left[0, \hat{P}_s\right]$ uniform distribution, whose probability density function is, $f(p) = \frac{1}{\hat{P}_S} I_{\left[0, \hat{P}_S\right]}(p)$, where $\hat{P}_S$ is the highest expected price. $I_{\left[0, \hat{P}_S\right]}(p)$ is an indicator function. That is when p is between 0 and $\hat{P}_S$, the function value is 1; otherwise, the value is 0. $\hat{P}_S$ can be viewed as the reflection of goods value of S product. The more valuable the good is to consumers, the greater the $\hat{P}_S$ will be.

Furthermore, assume that, before S meets B, he has contacted n buyers and observes a set of their anticipated prices, $(p_1, p_2, \cdots p_n)$. The maximum, p_{max}, has important effects on the initial price quotation when S meets B. Although we don't know the exact form of the relationship between X_0 and p_{max}, $X_0 = x(p_{max})$, we are certain that X_0 is an increasing function of p_{max}. Of course, since the n searches of S are random sampling behavior, we can't know exactly the value of p_{max}. Fortunately, we can calculate the mathematical expectation of p_{max}, $\bar{p}_{max}$, with the help of statistical knowledge. The calculation process is as follows.

Among n anticipated prices, $(p_1, p_2, \cdots p_n)$, the probability (density) for a particular price, p, being the highest is,[4]

$$f_{max}(p) = n\left[F(p)\right]^{n-1} F'(p)$$
$$= \frac{n}{\hat{P}_S^n} p^{n-1}$$

After n random searches, the expected highest anticipated price is,

$$\bar{p}_{max} = \int_0^{\hat{P}_S} f_{max}(p)p\,dp$$

p_{max} is substituted by $\bar{p}_{max}$, which yields,

$$= \frac{\hat{P}_S}{1+1/n}$$

$$X_0 = x(\bar{p}_{max}) = x\left(\frac{\hat{P}_S}{1+1/n}\right) \tag{5.18}$$

Equation (5.18) shows that the initial quotation X_0, when S meets B, is an increasing function of $\hat{P}_S$ and n. Indeed, $\hat{P}_S$ and n describe characteristics and quantities of two kinds of resource owned by S. $\hat{P}_S$ represents the value of goods for the buyers while n represents the information S possesses before meeting B. Therefore, the initial quotation, X_0, as one of the negotiation power indicators, is based on resources of both goods and information that S holds.

Initial quotation of B — Y_0

Similar to the above analysis about X_0, the initial quotation of B will not be arbitrarily low. It is based on the previous market information held by B.

Assume that the expected values of goods follow a $[Q_l, Q_h]$ uniform distribution for the M sellers with the probability density function being $g(q) = \frac{1}{(Q_h - Q_l)} I_{[Q_l, Q_h]}(q)$. Furthermore, assume that B contacts m buyers before he meets S; hence, he understands their anticipated values of the good, that is, $(q_1, q_2, \cdots q_m)$. The minimum q_{min} has important effects on the initial quotation, Y_0, when B meets S. Although we do not know the exact function form of $Y_0 = y(q_{min})$, which describes the relation between Y_0 and q_{min}, we are certain that Y_0 is an increasing function of q_{min}. Of course, since the m searches of B are random sampling behavior, we can't know exactly the value of q_{min} but we can calculate the mathematical expectation of q_{min}, $\bar{q}_{min}$. The calculation process is as follows.

Among m anticipated values $(q_1, q_2, \cdots q_m)$, the probability (density)[5] for some particular price q to be the lowest is,

$$g_{min}(q) = m \left[1 - G(q)\right]^{m-1} G'(q)$$
$$= \frac{m}{(Q_h - Q_l)^m} (Q_h - q)^{m-1}$$

After m random searches, the expected lowest anticipated price is,

$$\bar{q}_{min} = \int_{Q_l}^{Q_h} g_{min}(q) q dq$$
$$= \frac{Q_h + mQ_l}{1+m}$$

Using $\bar{q}_{min}$ to substitute q_{min} gives,

$$Y_0 = y(\bar{q}_{mim}) = y\left(\frac{Q_h + mQ_l}{1+m}\right) \tag{5.19}$$

Equation (5.19) shows that Y_0 is an increasing function of Q_l and Q_h but a decreasing function of m[6]. For all the sellers that B have contacted, the lower each seller's anticipated price is, the lower the initial quotation will be when B meets S. The more adequate the search B makes before meeting S, the lower the initial quotation after the meets will be. Moreover, it should be worth particular notice that the effect of Q_l on Y_0 is greater than that of Q_h, that is to say, the excessive low anticipated price of individual manufacturers for their own products will encourage greatly the squeezing down action on price of the buyer when he meets S later; moreover, this effect is much larger than that of excessive high anticipated price of individual manufacturers.

Toughness index

The relationship between transaction price and the toughness index shows that the tougher the trading party, the more favorable the transaction price will be for that party. However, toughness could also lead to a dangerous consequence; that is, the other party may leave the negotiations. Therefore, every trading party attempts to maintain a delicate balance between two conflict goals—being as tough as possible and keeping the other opponent in the negotiation. Against such a mechanism, a trading party should consider the benefit that the opponent will obtain from leaving the negotiation table a significant factor.

First, we consider the logic for S. We assume that there are substitute goods (whether directly competitive products or indirect substitutes). In other words, S's product has minimal substitutability. Then, if B leaves the negotiation table, the opportunity for B to gain benefits is narrow. In this scenario, S will assume a tough attitude. Sometimes, although there are many substitutes in the market, because their geographic locations are far from B, the transaction costs, including logistic and searching costs, are too high for B to locate those sellers and to purchase their products. In this case, the S's product is not geographically substitutable. With this understanding, S will adopt a tough attitude to negotiation.

Next, we examine the logic for B. For S, the value of B is its purchasing power. If the potential buyers in the market who need S's product are few, S will find it difficult to find other buyers if B leaves the negotiation table. Then, in this scenario, B's attitude will be tough. Or, although there are many potential buyers, B is the largest buyer. In this case, B's attitude will also be tough. Sometimes, although there are many potential buyers in the market and because their geographic locations are far from S, the transaction costs are too high for S to locate those buyers and trade with them. In this case, we consider that the buyer's purchasing power is not geographically substitutable. With such understanding, B will adopt a tough negotiating attitude.

We can refer to the non-substitutability of product functions and geographical location as seller's resource attributes, and refer to the number of potential buyers, the quantity that particular buyers purchase, and the non-substitutability of geographical location as a buyer's resource attributes. It is these resource attributes that determine both parties' toughness in the negotiation process.

Negotiation costs

In our models, for every cycle extended for bargaining, the parties involved will have to pay the corresponding costs, c_S (for the seller) or c_B (for the buyer). Although these costs can be interpreted as time, labor, and physical costs as decision parameters, they reflect more of a subjective assessment by the parties on the negotiation process. So, the negotiation cost reflects the urgency with which the parties want to complete the transaction. This urgency can be reflected in the negotiation process and constitutes the bargaining power of the parties, that is, the economic power.

The urgency to complete a transaction may be related to personal inclination, as is the case with risk preference. However, in most cases, the degree of urgency can be explained by the level of resources of the party in question.

Consider a producer with a current stock of circulating capital available for reproduction of w. To maintain regular production, the producer must inject c amount of cash in each operation cycle (here, the operation cycle equals the bargaining cycle). If there is no income from sales, the available cash in stock can provide the necessary capital to maintain production for w/c periods. Assume that the producer's normal profit in each period is π. Then, when the bargaining takes a total of t periods, the bargaining cost can be expressed as:

$$C(t) = \begin{cases} 0 & \text{when } t < \dfrac{w}{c} \\[2mm] \left(t - \dfrac{w}{c}\right)\pi & \text{when } t \geq \dfrac{w}{c} \end{cases}$$

So, when t exceeds w/c, the average negotiation cost for every period is $c_S = \left(1 - \dfrac{w}{ct}\right)\pi$. In this example, the producer's bargaining cost, c_S, is negatively related to the cash available. The more the available cash, the lower the bargaining cost in every period and the stronger the bargaining power.

For the buyer, the subject matter of transactions may be raw materials needed for production (purchased by industries) or materials for living (purchased as final consumer goods). Regardless of the category, the pressure on the buyer to complete the transaction is determined by the quantity of resources held by the buyer that can replace the subject matter. Moreover, this quantity forms the buyer's negotiating power in the bargaining process.

Summary analysis

In summary, under the standard bargaining trading mode, the transaction price is determined by the bargaining power of the parties in question, that is, their economic power. Bargaining power, as the extrinsic form of economic power, comes from the resources owned by the parties. The difference between standard and non-standard bargaining transactions is mainly reflected in the matching mode. In auctions, the matching pattern is one seller to several buyers. This pattern helps the seller to find new trading partners with little searching costs (θ_S); hence, auctions put pressure on the buyers to make bidding decisions.

However, in a tender system, the buyer will find new partners at little cost θ_B, which puts pressure on the sellers. Of course, the low cost here is under the premise that the expense to organize transactions (such as the charges involved in hiring discount banks or the fees paid for bidding companies) has become a sunk cost. If we consider the expense of organizing transactions, then we cannot say that the cost of searching for new trading partners by the organizer is low. Still, this does not matter because bargaining often occurs under the condition that the organization cost has occurred. Once the organizer spends the sunk cost, the expenditure is converted to economic power in the next step of bargaining, and the sunk cost obtains excess compensation in the bargaining. Each party has the ability to be the organizer because each trading mode requires a sufficient quantity of initial investment to begin operations.

From the resource condition, only the party that can afford the initial investment will have the opportunity to become the organizer and design legitimately matching methods that are favorable to their own interests. The choice of matching method is still subject to the precondition of the resources owned by the trading parties. Although we admit that the choice of trading mode has an ingenious function of saving expenditures (Williamson, 1985), which party will eventually receive benefits from the saving cannot be shown by the transaction cost paradigm itself.

Economic power and market efficiency

The preceding sections have shown that the power structure in the commodity market determines the price and, consequently, the distribution of benefits. Then, under what power structure can a particular price combination be reached, and does this combination lead to Pareto optimal utility for the participants?

Consumer choice theory shows that given the price, a consumer can always choose a consumption bundle to realize maximum utility under budget constraints. This logic ignores the fact that consumers are not always passive price takers. Consumers are at least able to affect the price in certain commodity markets. Consumers have different degrees of influence on different commodities. In commodity markets, it is more common to have unequal power and dispersed prices than one price. Under the premise that consumers have unequal power, if the allocation of power changes among consumers, the price also changes, which, in turn, results in a new consumption bundle. Will this change lead to Pareto improvement in the allocation of utility?

When an economic agent influences price formation, instead of choosing a consumption bundle directly, the agent will attempt to affect the price determination first and then select the bundle after the price is determined. To change the price is actually to change budget constraints. The greater the economic power, the stronger the ability to influence the price; then, the budget line will be shifted more toward the right-hand side. Hence, the individual utility level corresponding to the optimal consumption bundle will be higher. Meanwhile, the same consumer will experience changes in power in different markets, which will affect the slope of the budget line. Consequently, the agent's consumption structure is going to change. This implies the possibility of improvement; that is, every consumer's utility will be raised by adjusting the allocation of power in all markets for all consumers. Such adjustments continue until there is no room for further improvement given a particular power structure. Such a structure will be the most efficient one in a commodity market. We illustrate this point with the following example.

Suppose there are m goods, and n consumers in the market.

Consumer i ($i = 1,2...,n$) has the economic power of R_{ik} in commodity market k ($k = 1,2,...,m$), where the price he pays for the commodity is $P_{ik} = P_k(R_{ik})$. Following the analysis in the preceding sections of this chapter, $P_k(R_{ik})$ is monotonically decreasing. This means, the more power consumer i has in commodity market k, the lower the price he pays for commodity k. Consumer i's problem is how to maximize his utility U_i through choosing different consumption bundles $(x_1, x_2,..., x_m)$ given the income constraint I_i

$$\begin{cases} \max U_i(x_1, x_2,..., x_m) \\ s.t. \sum_{k=1}^{m} P_k(R_{i,k}) x_k \le I_i \end{cases} \tag{5.20}$$

The Lagrangian function for the above optimization problem is as follows,

$$L_i = U_i(x_1, x_2,..., x_m) + \lambda_i \left(I_i - \sum_{k=1}^{m} P_k(R_{ik}) x_k \right) \tag{5.21}$$

where λ is the Lagrangian multiplier. If bundle x^* maximizes consumer i's utility, given the budget constraint, then it follows from the first-order conditions that,

$$\frac{\partial U_i}{\partial x_1} = \lambda_i P_1(R_{i1}),...,\frac{\partial U_i}{\partial x_k} = \lambda_i P_k(R_{ik}), \frac{\partial U_i}{\partial x_l} = \lambda_i P_l(R_{il}),...,\frac{\partial U_i}{\partial x_m} = \lambda_i P_m(R_{im}),$$

That is, for any two goods, k and l, the following equation holds,

$$\frac{\dfrac{\partial U_i}{\partial x_k}}{\dfrac{\partial U_i}{\partial x_l}} = \frac{P_k(R_{ik})}{P_l(R_{il})} \tag{5.22}$$

Equation (5.22) states that consumer i always chooses the bundle that maximizes his utility, which makes the marginal rate of substation between the two goods equal to the price ratio.

Following the same logic, consumer j will choose the bundle y^* that makes

$$\frac{\dfrac{\partial U_j}{\partial x_k}}{\dfrac{\partial U_j}{\partial x_l}} = \frac{P_k(R_{jk})}{P_l(R_{jl})} \tag{5.23}$$

If consumer i and j have equal power, that is, $R_{ik} = R_{jk}$ and $R_{il} = R_{jl}$, then it follows that $P_k(R_{ik}) = P_k(R_{jk})$ and $P_l(R_{il}) = P_l(R_{jl})$. It can be derived from (5.22) and (5.23) that

$$\frac{\partial U_i}{\partial x_k} \Big/ \frac{\partial U_i}{\partial x_l} = \frac{\partial U_j}{\partial x_k} \Big/ \frac{\partial U_j}{\partial x_l} \tag{5.24}$$

Equation (5.24) states that if consumers i and j have equal power in every market, the allocation of commodities will reach Pareto optimality under the guidance of maximizing their own utility. On the contrary, if the consumers have unequal power in a certain market, the marginal rates of substitution will not be equal. Hence, there will be one possible result; that is, they will take x^* and y^* as initial endowments to make further exchanges, which will raise the utility of at least one side. In this case, Pareto improvement is attained. Therefore, equal power among consumers i and j in every market is the necessary and sufficient condition for Pareto optimality.

Notes

1 Chinese books and audiovisual products usually have only a single printed specification.
2 It should be noted that the auction price given by the auctioneer does not represent a price offer. Its one-dimensional function is to remind bidders to start bidding above this auction price. The truly binding bidding behavior starts with the bidder's bidding.
3 Because when the negotiation cost isn't zero, there is always a moment that one party either accepts or rejects and leaves. The tougher the attitude of S, the greater the probability that B leaves the table will be.
4 Obtained via the maximum distribution formula of multi-dimensional random variable.
5 Based on the maximum distribution formula of multi-dimensional random variable.
6 The partial derivative of Y_0 with respect to m: $\dfrac{\partial Y_0}{\partial m} = -\dfrac{Q_h - Q_l}{(1+m)^2} < 0$.

6　Price determination in financial market

Financial markets can be classified by different ways. According to the transaction subject, financial markets are classified as: foreign exchange, money, and securities markets. Many articles on financial theories have expounded in detail on the characteristics, functions, and trading techniques of various markets. The theoretical starting point of this chapter is to explore how an economic subject, relying on an economic power, affects trading prices to realize interest distribution in their own favor. In this chapter, we first analyze the microstructure of financial markets, the nature of the market trading price, and the influencing factors. We then build mathematical models for the determination of trading prices for major financial products. In this process, we reveal that trading prices are determined by power games, and we study the mechanisms in action regarding economic power and the influencing factors.

The microstructure of financial markets

In this section, we analyze the microstructure of foreign exchange markets, money markets, and securities markets. That is, we discuss market participants, participant resources, economic power, and the behavior and consequent impacts on trading price as an ideological foundation for analyzing the nature of the trading price in financial markets and building mathematical models.

Foreign exchange markets

Foreign exchange markets (forex market) are markets connected by intermediary agencies or telecommunications systems through which currencies of different countries are traded. The market can be tangible, as in foreign exchange trading locations, or intangible, such as inter-bank forex transactions via telecommunication systems. Participants in forex markets include import and export companies and multinational corporations because their business activities require foreign currency transactions. Central banks participate in forex markets because exchange rates are a primary economic variable that is prioritized by governments in their economic administration. Participants in forex markets include investor capital held by financial institutions and international fluid capital—funds controlled by investors who actively seek short-term returns.

The amount of resources held by each market participant differs depending on the extent of its economic power. Moreover, there are various channels through which economic power is reflected in the interactions between participants. For example, from an international perspective, a country's power is embodied by the dependence of other countries on that country. Such dependence may stem from many sources including technology, politics, natural resources, or military resources. Relying on the degree of mutual dependence–that is, the magnitude of economic power–countries will bargain to determine exchange rate trends in the long and medium-run. From a domestic perspective, games exist on the exchange rate between interest groups and the government. The government hopes to achieve economic growth by supporting associated industries with favorable exchange rates. For example, in the 2008 financial crisis, the US government used various means to stimulate appreciation in the RMB—the Chinese currency. The US government wanted to promote US exports and stimulate its manufacturing industry to prevent a recession. For the same reason, domestic interest groups lobbied policy makers for exchange-rate arrangements favorable to them. For instance, export businesses looked forward to depreciation to boost exports while import businesses welcomed appreciation to reduce costs.

Games also exist between international fluid capital and central banks in the forex markets. For example, the 1997 Asian economic crisis was sparked by an attack from international speculators on Southeast Asia's financial markets. The speculators sold out the currencies of these countries and bought US dollars, which led to a drastic fall in the exchange rates of these currencies and generated huge profits for the speculators. The governments of Indonesia, Malaysia, Thailand, and other countries as well as the central banks in these countries introduced various measures to stable their own currencies, such as increasing transaction costs and interest rates and even purchasing domestic currencies with their forex reserves. International fluid capital resources include huge amounts of cash, valuable information, and skillful speculative techniques. At the same time, International fluid capital took advantage of the disorder of the forex institutions and the slack regulations in these countries. However, the governments in these countries responded to the attack politically and economically. The 1997 economic crisis illustrates the game whereby the agents of interest affect exchange rates via the resources they have on hand to realize their own interests. Therefore, using game theory, the studies on the determination of exchange rates can objectively reflect economic reality.

Money markets

The economic agents in market economies can be characterized objectively as agents with capital surplus and agents with a capital deficit. The driving force behind the emergence and development of money markets arises from the desire to maintain capital liquidity. Money markets satisfy capital demand and provide capital suppliers with profitable opportunities by linking demand and supply with a variety of financial tools. At the micro level, money markets offer flexible administration to banks and enterprises. Money markets provide channels through which monetary policies conducted by central banks control and regulate economies. Additionally, money markets facilitate the development of financial markets.

The interest rate mechanisms of money markets are sensitive to the demand and supply of social capital. Hence, interest rates are an indicator of the position of capital in markets and a measure of the returns on financial products. Because it has the characteristic of price, the interest rate reflects the profitability of the parties involved in transactions. We believe that the interest distribution mechanism is formed as a result of power games and that the interest rate must also be formed on the basis of borrowers and lender negotiations.

For example, since a nation's central bank is empowered to make and conduct monetary policy and control and manage macroeconomic operations, central banks set basic interest rates on behalf of the government. This fiscal role of central banks affects market interest rates by adjusting the money supply under market conditions to achieve goals such as currency value stabilization and economic intervention. Deposits and loans are the bread and butter of commercial banks and the key functions affecting their profits. The competition between commercial banks for deposits is affected by factors such as the central bank's benchmark interest rate and the demand for credit macro-level firms.

At the micro level, these factors include the quality of service, network construction, and the marketing efforts of commercial banks. The micro-level factors are subject to the resources controlled by the banks, the bank's ability to set up extensive outlets to absorb more savings, and the competence of bank employees in attracting additional deposits. With respect to lending operations, commercial banks often provide differentiated financial products to realize profits under market conditions. In this process, banks must understand the operations of similar businesses served by their competitors, investigate borrower's qualifications as well as the expected returns to projects considering the risk, and engage in loan negotiations. How banks perform in these respects is closely related to the resources controlled by the banks.

Borrowers assume risky investments using bank loans to realize the associated returns. Facing differentiated financial bank products, firms often carefully consider their own qualifications, the prospects for returns on risky projects, and the degree of competition in the banking sector. Based on this information, borrowing firms bargain with commercial banks to secure low-cost loans. In the above process, firms can influence interest rates using their resources and gain favorable results. Hence, these companies garner benefits by influencing the determination of market interest rates.

Securities markets

Securities are issued and traded in the securities markets. These markets reflect and regulate the flow of capital; moreover, they impact overall economic performance. Superficially, securities markets are a trading mechanism that determines securities prices according to the relationship between demand and supply through competition. However, the returns to investors come largely from trading in this market. If some investors can affect the demand and supply, the price of securities will be indirectly affected, even determined. For example, manipulative behavior is common in this market. Relying on capital, information, and technical advantages, manipulators influence investor expectations through market and non-market behavior. This influence is, in turn, transmitted to prices through the demand and supply relationship. The purpose of manipulation is to obtain greater profits. In this process, the fundamental reason manipulators can influence market prices is that they control more resources, such as substantial capital, non-public information, and a professional investment team while market demand and supply simply serve as the means to manipulation and the pursuit of profits. The relationship between demand and supply under free competition cannot conceal the logic that resources provide power, and power is manifested in the transaction price, that is, interest distribution.

Participants in the securities market mainly refer to securities exchanges, securities issuers, securities firms, securities investors, service agencies, regulatory bodies, and trade associations. Since our focus is securities market prices, we analyze behavior patterns, desired interest levels, and the resources of securities investors. Investors are capital suppliers as well as buyers of financial products.

Investors can be classified into two categories: individual and institutional investors. Institutional investors include all types of enterprises, commercial banks, and non-bank financial institutions (such as pension funds, insurance funds, and securities investment funds). Institutional investors' investment directions, objectives, and sources of capital may differ, but this group typically has some market features in common such as plenty of capital, remarkable capacity to collect and analyze information, the capability to spread investment risks with effective portfolios, and a strong influence on the market. Some institutional investors can affect the market price and trading volume through resource advantages and may even create fictions in the market to induce other participants to trade in securities either to profit or transfer risks. In this process, institutional investors are the main price setters in the market. Market manipulation has a long history of various strategies. Section "Capital, information, and the determination of securities pricing" provides a detailed discussion on manipulation. Individual investors are the majority of investors in the securities markets, and their main goals are to insure and increase the value of capital. Compared with institutional investors, individual investors possess less capital, rely on lagged information, have little effect on the transaction price, and are price takers in the market.

The essence of financial goods pricing determination

Price determination is at the core of the majority of economic theories[1] because distribution is the most important of the four factors of economic activities: production, distribution, exchange, and consumption. Distribution determines exchange, consumption, and social reproduction. In the market, distribution is embodied by the possession of trading surplus[2] by the parties involved. In essence, the surplus depends on the transaction price of goods. Different prices reflect different relationships in trading surplus distribution among the parties involved in transactions, which must be considered when studying the market. Alchian and Demsetz (1972) emphasize that what price determines is more important than what determines the price. Only when the role of transaction price is clearly and fully understood can we properly analyze the factors that determine price, which is the focus of this section.

The duality nature of financial goods pricing

In theory, price is a monetary expression of value. Thus, price first functions as a unit of account. However, the price may deviate from the value of commodities due to the effects of a number of factors; moreover, any deviation implies a redistribution of economic interests between both sides of a transaction. Because of its duality, price is both a measure of value and economic leverage. In practice, price functions more as economic leverage, that is, price adjusts and regulates economic activities. For example, governments use price as a tool to stimulate or restrain production, to adjust production structures, or to allocate social resources to various enterprises, regions, and sectors so that the national economy realizes balanced development. Governments can also use the price as a tool to adjust the distribution of national income among regions and social groups to achieve social harmony. For other economic agents, price is a means for demand and supply sides to compete, to some extent, for the trading surplus; moreover, different prices reflect different ways of how the trading surplus is distributed. While the basic purpose of economic activities is to maximize individuals' interests while economic agents typically have unequal power, in reality, market prices cannot reflect the value of commodities due to power constraints. Therefore, the classical economic concepts that attempt to identify price by determining value have the flaw of not having the ability to find the value and a lack of theoretical logic.

For example, exchange rates are ratios between currencies, but they are also tools with which governments manage a national economy and realize national interests. Ma (2016) notes in his book "The Influence of Sea Power upon History" that self-interest is a sensible and fundamental driver of national policies, and there is no need to conceal this in hypocrisy. In an open economic environment, international anarchy causes countries to contend for interests and power following "the law of the jungle."[3] Under state interests, the exchange rate is a scale of currencies and a weapon in the fight for international interests among governments. Sun and Deng (2005) argues that when deciding the quantity of money supply, central banks should consider economic development, the social demand for money, economic stability, and that modern exchange rates have a duality nature or, in other words, a double function. Thus, we argue that classical theories cannot fully explain the determination of exchange rates because they either ignore or are unable to reflect state goals.

Interest rates also have a dual nature; that is, they are both the price of capital and the instrument of monetary policy. As the price of capital, interest rates are determined by the market while controlled by monetary authorities as a policy instrument. Therefore, the determination of interest rates should be discussed at two levels: both the market and the state level. State control of the interest rate is evident in benchmark interest rate adjustments by central banks, which affects the market rate and regulates the economy. Such action protects the national interests of the whole country. For example, the Federal Reserve (Fed) affects the capital costs of business banks in the United States through the federal funds rate. Moreover, in doing so, the Fed passes money shortage or surplus information from the inter-bank market to firms. Thus, the Fed regulates consumption, investment, and the national economy. The determination of market interest rates embodies the pursuit of economic interests by agents in financial transactions and reflects the degree of advantage that each side gains in the transaction. To summarize the analysis on both the state and the market, the interest rate can be considered an instrument of economic agents in pursuing their own interests and not simply an extrinsic form of monetary value.

The value of financial security products is based on asset ownership and claims on the surplus of the returns. A problem arises because when buying security products, traders do not intend to claim the remaining returns or the right of bankruptcy liquidation. Instead, traders only want to take the price margins. Meanwhile, it is difficult for traders to accurately measure asset values and the remaining returns. Therefore, in a sense, the price of securities is an instrument of big traders[4] to pursue profits because the market price directly determines the profits of all parties in the trades, and big traders make excess profits via the price.

Resources, power, and the price of financial products: logic and theory

Sociology finds that power is expressed in the interactions between subjects. Keohane and Nye (1973) emphasize that power is derived from asymmetric reliance while Strange (1995) notes in "Political economy and international relations" that the most effective factors in the economy are structures and relationships; that is, who is more dependent on others and why. More specifically, in the market, the power of agents to set prices comes from the extent of mutual dependence between the demand and the supply side. The emergence of either a buyer's or seller's market may be the result of one side being less dependent on the other and, hence, having more power in setting prices. Why should one side be more dependent? The answer is resources. That is, economic agents with more resources tend to be less dependent on others in market transactions.

Regarding exchange rates, when a country is strong economically and its people are relatively wealthy, other countries are more dependent on that country when trading because of its ability to export more products. Such dependence may result from investment and technology or even national security and military concerns. The same is true for the interest rate. The dependence between borrowers and creditors is affected by a number of factors, such as expected returns, deadlines, degree of emergency, market structures, and risks. The market power—that is, economic power—of both debtors and creditors will be affected. For the price of securities, big traders, due to their abundance of resources, will objectively influence the behavior of other investors and the price regardless of their intentions. For example, Warren Buffet purchased the stock of BYD Company, Ltd. in September, 2008, and the stock showed minimal price fluctuation during the financial crisis of 2008, a once-in-a-century financial tsunami.

We believe that the market price is essentially determined by the pricing power of each trading party based on the amount of resources they own. That is, relying on the influence of resources they have to hand in the market, some traders can affect their opponent's behavior choice and even manipulate the market to affect demand and supply. Consequently, the transaction price is affected or determined by some investors. Bowles and Gintis (1994) states that differences in wealth are reflected in the differences between feasible contract sets and individual contract choices. The author also notes that contract arrangements include authority structure;[5] that is, one party in the transaction has power over the other, and the fact that all parties trade voluntarily cannot stop the exercising of power. Moreover, the agent that exercises power is the agent with more wealth.

In the case of exchange rates, a country can force others to accept exchange rate arrangements in favor of its own interests through trades, investment, technology, and even political and military means. This dynamic is illustrated by the Plaza Accord signed by Japan and the United States in the 1980s. In the case of securities prices, big traders can influence the investment activities of other investors by affecting investors' expectations concerning maximum interests, which lead to prices favorable to the big traders. On this point, Schwartz (1987) comments that stock value is rooted in the equity's power involvement in the distribution of surplus and its returns but constrained by certain property rights systems and power structures. Any equity value determines the price of shares through investors' buying and selling activities and the market equilibrium between demand and supply. Therefore, stock price and power present an inherent symbiosis equilibrium system. Schwartz' comments are the same as ours by nature; that is, in essence, power structure determines the price of securities while market demand and supply are simply the means for realization. In the case of interest rates, both borrowers and creditors make behavior choices based on factors such as the abundance of capital in the market and the urgency of capital demand, which is essentially a game of power to determine market interest rates.

From the above analysis, financial market economic agents develop pricing power by relying on their resources; moreover, power determines agent behavior, and the behavior influences demand and supply. Ultimately, transactions are completed via interactions between demand and supply, and the market price emerges. In this process, demand and supply are only superficial factors and price, in essence, is not determined by demand and supply but by power games.

Power games and exchange rate determination

Exchange rate and national interests

Exchange rates affect financing and a country's economic and political stability. Therefore, discussions on exchange rate determination mechanisms are ongoing. Theories such as purchasing power parity (PPP), interest rate parity (IRP), overshoot theory, and equilibrium exchange rate theory are mechanisms of exchange rate determination from their own standpoints. Wang (2007) notes that although scholars have worked painstakingly and raised a variety of unusual but interesting concepts in a hope to discover the mechanism, these ideas merely reflect certain aspects of the exchange rate determination process. Considering equilibrium exchange rate theory, for example, its core idea is equilibrium both internally and externally. That is, under the equilibrium exchange rate, an economy can attain full employment with low inflation internally while maintaining balanced international payments and capital flows at desired levels externally. However, the real goal of any country is to attain national interests when the government uses exchange rates as an instrument to manage the economy and not simply to maintain mathematical balance. In other words, if disequilibrium can realize more interests, why should the state still select the balance as its goal? Starting from this point, the determination of exchange rates fits well into the duality nature of exchange rates; that is, the exchange rate is a ratio between currencies but also a government instrument to control the economy. Joseph Nye (2004), the well-known theorist of national relationships, notes that the state will act according to national interests regardless of the type of government.

Therefore, our view on the determination of exchange rate is as follows. As a significant variable and factor of international economic activities, the exchange rate directly affects both trades between countries and employment and capital markets in all countries. Hence, in seeking national interests, competition, cooperation, and contradiction among countries will determine the emergence of real exchange rates. Therefore, we assume that the maximization of national interests is the goal of all countries and adopt the perspective of game theory to reveal a real and complete exchange rate determination process by combining both the aspect of market influence and the aspect of state intervention.

Game theory is widely used to study the choice of international exchange rate systems and the determination of exchange rates. Taylor (1995) argues that changes in exchange rates mainly result from basic determinants and the intervention of central banks. Yue (2005) notes that a country will select an exchange rate system based on cost-benefit analysis and combine, to some extent, the fixed with the floating exchange rate. Wei (2004) notes that if denominated in euros, GDP and the total volume of trade in the euro zone would be roughly equal to the GDP and the total volume of trade of the United States. Therefore, the position of the US dollar has been challenged since the start of the euro zone. Wei also analyzes the exchange rate strategies of US and the euro zone. Above-mentioned studies note that exchange rate determination is affected by state factors. Specifically, the choices of states and mutual games play a critical role in determining real exchange rates.

In addition, the specific arrangements of exchange rate systems inevitably influence the interests of all parties involved. Broz and Frieden (2001) discuss the selection of exchange rate systems and the influence of movements in exchange rates on domestic income distribution. Li (2003) analyzes the exchange rate system and notes that a change in an exchange rate would cause an income redistribution effect, the related interest groups would bargain, and the government should respond. Consequently, a process of games results. Other scholars present similar views; that is, exchange rate determination is actually games among governments as they seek for national interests and analyze issues related to exchange rates based on these views (He & Li, 2002; Li & Dong, 2005). In the research on the selection of exchange rate systems among East Asian economies, Chen (2007) finds that appropriate exchange rate arrangements could improve a country's welfare. Jiang and Liu (2007) and An (2007) analyze how to attain national interests under appreciation pressure for RMB. These studies show that exchange rate determination is, in fact, a game among countries in the pursuit of national interests.

Modeling based on the desirable zone of exchange rate

Wang and Zhao (2005) study the RMB exchange rate against the US dollar from the perspective of the balance of trade between China and the United States. The authors established a game model for the two countries to show the best choice for the exchange rate in the context of the scale of the balance of trade. However, for exchange rate determination, trade is not the only factor that affects national interests. Therefore, we reconstruct the utility functions of both sides in the game and expand the analytical perspective so that the interest competition between countries is incorporated in the determination of exchange rate fluctuations. Wang and Zhao (2005) do not mention the factors that affect the game strategy on either side. Therefore, we introduce the economic power variable as the main analytical instrument; that is, economic power determines the equilibrium strategy and, consequently, determines the zone of real exchange rate fluctuations[6] and completes the distribution of interests among countries.

For the logic underlying the above analysis, Acemoglu (2005) states the following. Relying on the resources including the value of physical and human capital and resource scarcity, investors send out strong, believable signals to obtain an advantageous position before contracts are signed. By further enhancing their economic positions in negotiations, investors sign contracts that are the distribution structures of surplus distribution based on resource endowment. Goodhart (1998) notes that if money means power, governments would seek policies that are favorable to their domestic currency; moreover, large countries, particularly those with different ideologies, do not give up their control of exchange rates. Instead, governments take measures to consolidate their own currencies. Therefore, it is national power and politics that determine exchange rate relationships.

We suggest that countries have their own desirable exchange rate zones[7] to obtain specific economic interests. Specifically, there are two possibilities. First, if there is an intersection of sets of all exchange rate desirable zones, the actual exchange rate must be in the intersection. The reason is that when the exchange rate falls into this range, national interests are relatively satisfied for all countries; that is, all countries can tolerate the current situation, such as the balance of trade and domestic unemployment. In this scenario, the actual exchange rate depends on market demand and supply because national interests are embodied in the exchange rate once it falls into this area. Second, there is no such intersection. Thus, no matter where the actual exchange rate falls, it must be disadvantageous to some countries. These countries will attempt to shift the actual exchange rate into their desirable zone using their economic power. Given this idea, we re-examine the fluctuations in the exchange rates of the Japanese yen and Deutsche Marks in the 1980s and discuss changes in the RMB exchange rate in recent years. By constructing an exchange rate game model, we attempt to prove that the games based on economic power between two countries determine the exchange rate. Based on this model, we suggest an exchange rate determination theory to better explain the changes in and the determination of exchange rates.

Assume that the desirable zones of exchange rate are I_1 and I_2 respectively for country 1 and 2, and $I_1 \cap I_2 = \varphi$. Let e_0 be the actual exchange rate.

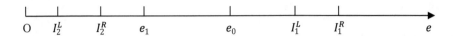

Figure 6.1 The exchange rate desirable zone and the current exchange rate e_0.

Figure 6.1 shows the situation that each country faces. Country 2 is in a disadvantageous position as shown in the figure. Define $l_1 = I_1^L - e_0$ and $l_2 = e_0 - I_2^R$, where I_1^L is the left-end point of I_1 and I_2^R is the right-end point of I_2. So l_1 and l_2 are the distance that the actual exchange rate deviates from the desirable zone. Larger l_1 and l_2 are harmful to the national interests of the countries. Being in a disadvantageous position, country 2 may request a change in the exchange rate, $\Delta l_2 = -\Delta l_1 \triangleq e_1 - e_0 \leq 0$, where e_1 is the target exchange rate of country 2. Such a change will increase country 2's utility but decrease the utility of country 1. In the following section, we employ utility functions to show that it is the economic power of each country that determines (1) whether country 2 will request a change in exchange rate, (2) the strategy that country 1 will choose to respond, (3) the degree of retaliation and counter-retaliation between two countries (4) the equilibrium strategies of the game. (3) and (4) are determined by both parties' economic power. Such an analysis demonstrates that the exchange rate is a significant variable in economic systems primarily determined in two phases. In phase one, countries, the state subjects involved in economic activities, play games based on their economic power, which is an important component in the determination of the actual exchange rate. That component is the change in both trends and goals that are dominated by government. In phase two, short-term fluctuations in the exchange rate are determined by the demand and supply in the exchange rate market, which realizes the actual exchange rate. This is the whole process of how exchange rates are determined.

A country's economic power and behavior choice

Just as being generally acknowledged, power here refers to the influence and control of a behavioral subject over other subjects by the possession of resources. Let $p^{(1)}$ be the economic power of country 1 and $p^{(2)}$ the economic power of country 2, then

$$p^{(1)} = p^{(1)} \left[t \binom{1}{2}, i \binom{1}{2}, s \binom{1}{2}, y^{(1)} \right] \tag{6.1}$$

$$p^{(2)} = p^{(2)} \left[t \binom{2}{1}, i \binom{2}{1}, s \binom{2}{1}, y^{(2)} \right] \tag{6.2}$$

where $t^{\left(\frac{1}{2}\right)}$ denotes country 2's exports to country 1 as a percentage of country 2's total exports, which reflects the degree of country 2's dependence on exports to country 1 and also shows country 1's influence and control over country 2, which is the economic power. Similarly, $t^{\left(\frac{2}{1}\right)}$ is the economic power that country 2 imposes on country 1, which is the asymmetric dependence between two countries mentioned in section "The essence of financial goods pricing determination." i and s denote investment and technology respectively. Similar to t, $i^{\left(\frac{1}{2}\right)}$, $s^{\left(\frac{1}{2}\right)}$ and $i^{\left(\frac{2}{1}\right)}$, $s^{\left(\frac{2}{1}\right)}$ represent degree of dependence on investment and technology between the two countries respectively. $y^{(1)}$ and $y^{(2)}$ stand for the total output or national income of country 1 and country 2, respectively. The above variables all reflect the economic power of a country. Obviously, $p^{(1)} \geq 0$ and $p^{(2)} \geq 0$; moreover, for each $k = 1, 2, j = 1, 2$, and $k \neq j$, partial derivatives of $p^{(k)}$ with respect to $t^{\left(\frac{k}{j}\right)}$, $i^{\left(\frac{k}{j}\right)}$, $s^{\left(\frac{k}{j}\right)}$, and $y^{(k)}$ are greater than 0. In the long run, Δl_1 and Δl_2, the changes in the exchange rate will have impacts on $p^{(1)}$ and $p^{(2)}$. However, considering that the two sides of games will make choice of strategies based on their economic power at the initial moment, and for the convenience of analysis, we assume that $p^{(1)}$ and $p^{(2)}$ depend on each variable only at the initial moment[8] and are not related to Δl.

Let r_2 stand for the retaliation of country 2 while r_1 the counter-retaliation of country 1, and η $(0 \leq \eta \leq 1)$ the degree of how country 1 satisfies country 2's requests. Based on the previous discussion, r_2 and r_1 should be functions of $p^{(1)}$, $p^{(2)}$, and η. Specifically, when $\eta = 1$, that is, country 1 fully satisfies the requests of country 2, country 2 will not retaliate; hence $r_2 = 0$. When $\eta = 0$, country 1 does not satisfy the requests at all, then country 2 will take the maximum level of retaliation based on its economic power. In this scenario, define $r_2 = p^{(2)}$. When $0 < \eta < 1$, country 1 satisfies partly the requests, then the degree of country 2's retaliation will decrease as η increases, satisfying the law of marginal diminishing. This law implies that the $r_2 - \eta$ curve is convex towards the origin. Therefore, we assume:

$$r_2 = \phi(\eta) p^{(2)} \tag{6.3}$$

$\phi(\eta)$ has the following properties: $0 \leq \eta \leq 1$, $0 \leq \phi(\eta) \leq 1$, $\phi(0) = 1, \phi(1) = 0$; and $\phi'(\eta) < 0, \phi''(\eta) > 0$. In other words, $\phi(\eta)$ is a monotonically decreasing convex function. As shown in Figure 6.2, the horizontal axis is for η and the vertical axis for r_2, while the unit of the vertical axis could be taken as $p^{(2)}$. Obviously, r_2 and $p^{(2)}$ are positively correlated, that is to say, country with

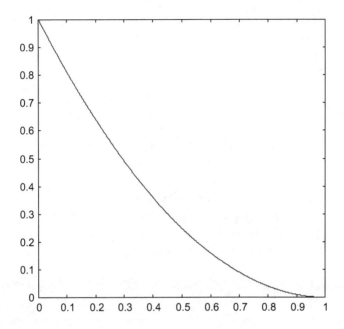

Figure 6.2 The $r_2 - \eta$ curve.

more economic power has stronger retaliation ability. This is consistent with economic reality.

Assume that the counter-retaliation of country 1 has the same magnitude[9] as the retaliation of country 2, so being affected by r_2 and ultimately determined by η, r_1 has a similar function to that of r_2. Curve $r_1 - \eta$ is also similar to curve $r_2 - \eta$, which yields,

$$r_1 = \phi(\eta) p^{(1)} = \phi(\eta) p^{(1)}, 0 \le \eta \le 1 \tag{6.4}$$

For exchange rate movements, the possible change in utility for each side depends on three components.

1 Exchange rate changes bring utility improvement via t, the trade variable, and w, the employment variable. Giavazzi and Pagano (1988) argue that the government's goal is to maximize social welfare. Hence, the economic variables of major concern include profits in the export sector and the unemployment rate. Therefore, these are the first components in the utility of a country, which implies that exchange rate movements will improve trade and employment. Let t_1 stand for the trade variable of country 1 and t_2 stand for the trade variable of country 2, it follows that $dt_k / dl_k < 0$ ($k = 1,2$). That is to say, the trade variables are decreasing

monotonically with l_1 and l_2. In addition, we use w_1 to denote the employment of country 1 while w_2 the employment of country 2, and also have $dw_k / dl_k < 0$ ($k = 1,2$). That is to say, the employment variables are decreasing monotonically with l_1 and l_2. Hence, we assume

$$u_1^{(1)} = \alpha_1 t_1 (l_1) + \beta_1 w_1 (l_1) \tag{6.5}$$
$$u_1^{(2)} = \alpha_2 t_2 (l_2) + \beta_2 w_2 (l_2) \tag{6.6}$$

Here, $u_1^{(1)}$ and $u_1^{(2)}$ denote the first components of country 1 and 2, respectively. They are functions of l through t and w. Coefficients α_1, β_1, α_2, and β_2 are greater than 0, which shows the relative importance of economic factors like trade and employment to country 1 and country 2. There may be the difference in the importance since each country has its own national value orientation. According to the above analysis, $u_1^{(1)}$ and $u_1^{(2)}$ are decreasing monotonically with l_1 and l_2.

2   The two countries can improve their utility via retaliation. Although retaliation practices will result in large utility loss to the other country, they may not bring the same amount of utility improvement.[10] If this is the case, the player with a stronger position in the game will have the impulse to infinitely resort to retaliation for more benefits, which is inconsistent with economic reality. In fact, if there are disputes and conflicts in the real economy, the parties involved will choose a deterrence strategy rather than a real retaliation and counter-retaliation to protect their own interests, particularly between the major powerful economies. The reason is that a country's retaliation can result in loss to the other countries but may lead to counter-retaliation from those countries. This could cause more utility loss to the country than its initial utility improvement. To characterize this economic reality, we define a parameter ε ($0 < \varepsilon < 1$) in the model to show that the utility improvement by retaliation is less than the utility loss of the opponents. To facilitate the analysis, we assume the two countries have the same ε; combining (6.3) and (6.4) we get

$$u_2^{(1)} = \varepsilon \phi (\eta) p^{(1)} \tag{6.7}$$
$$u_2^{(2)} = \varepsilon \phi (\eta) p^{(2)} \tag{6.8}$$

where $u_2^{(1)}$ and $u_2^{(2)}$ are the second component of the country1 and country 2's utility, respectively.

3   A country's utility will reduce if it there is counter-retaliation. As mentioned above, the decrease in utility caused by counter-retaliation

is greater than the increase in utility resulting from retaliation. These properties can be described by assuming

$$u_3^{(1)} = -\phi(\eta) p^{(2)} \tag{6.9}$$

$$u_3^{(2)} = -\phi(\eta) p^{(1)} \tag{6.10}$$

where $u_3^{(1)}$ and $u_3^{(2)}$ are the third component of the utility of country 1 and country 2, respectively, which are the reduction in utility caused by counter-retaliation. The reason for choosing -1 as the coefficient is that $|-1| > \varepsilon$ shows that the fall in utility caused by counter-retaliation is greater than the increase in utility resulted from retaliation.

In these components of a country's utility, the first component depends on l, while the others depend on η. However, it shall be clear from the following analysis about the game strategy that the value of η is determined by the contrast of economic power between the two countries. That is, the actual exchange rate is determined by the games of economic power, not other variables. So we obtain utility functions for the countries, using equations from (6.5) to (6.10),

$$u^{(1)} = u_1^{(1)} + u_2^{(1)} + u_3^{(1)} = \alpha_1 t_1 (l_1) + \beta_1 w_1 (l_1) + \varepsilon\phi(\eta) p^{(1)} - \phi(\eta) p^{(2)} \tag{6.11}$$

$$u^{(2)} = u_1^{(2)} + u_2^{(2)} + u_3^{(2)} = \alpha_2 t_2 (l_2) + \beta_2 w_2 (l_2) + \varepsilon\phi(\eta) p^{(2)} - \phi(\eta) p^{(1)} \tag{6.12}$$

Game strategy and its determinants

From (6.5) and (6.6), it follows,

$$du_1^{(1)} / dl_1 = \alpha_1 \times dt_1 (l_1) / dl_1 + \beta_1 \times dw_1 (l_1) / dl_1 \triangleq C_1 \tag{6.13}$$

$$du_2^{(2)} / dl_2 = \alpha_2 \times dt_2 (l_2) / dl_2 + \beta_2 \times dw_2 (l_2) / dl_2 \triangleq C_2 \tag{6.14}$$

Given the above assumptions, dt_1 / dl_1, dt_2 / dl_2, dw_1 / dl_1, $dw_2 / dl_2 < 0$, and α_1, β_1, α_2, $\beta_2 > 0$, so C_1, $C_2 < 0$. Since $du_1^{(i)} = C_i \Delta l_i$, $(i = 1,2)$, then the utility improvement for both countries resulted from changes in u_1 can be shown as $C_i \Delta l_i$ when the exchange rate changes; while the utility changes resulted from u_2 and u_3 depend on η, $p^{(1)}$, and $p^{(2)}$. The total utility change consists of these three parts.

Using the utility function (6.11) and (6.12), and combining (6.13) and (6.14), we list the possible game strategies for each player and the corresponding utility changes in each scenario in Table 6.1. The scenarios are referred to from top to end as the 1st to 8th scenarios hereafter. In fact, when η equals 0, the 6th, 7th, and 8th scenario are equivalent to the 2nd, 3rd, and 4th ones. The 8th scenario is equivalent to the 5th one when η equals 1. In order to facilitate analysis, we give the sign of utility change and the condition for it, $p^{(2)} > p^{(1)}$. In the table, this game is divided into four stages, denoted by I, II, III, and IV.

Table 6.1 Strategies and utility changes for both countries

I	II	III	IV	The utility change of country 1	The utility change of country 2
Country 2 doesn't request				0	0
Country 2 requests	Country 1 doesn't change $\eta=0$	Country 2 doesn't retaliate		0	0
		Country 2 Retaliate	Country 1 doesn't counter-retaliate	$-p^{(2)} < 0$	$\varepsilon p^{(2)} > 0$
			Country 1 counter-retaliate	$-p^{(2)} + \varepsilon p^{(1)} < 0$	$\varepsilon p^{(2)} - p^{(1)}$ $\left(when\ \frac{p^{(2)}}{p^{(1)}} > \frac{1}{\varepsilon},\ the\ payoff\ is\ "+",\ otherwise\ it\ is\ "-" \right)$
	Country 1 changes $\eta=1$			$C_1\Delta l_1 < 0$	$C_2\Delta l_2 > 0$
	Country 1 changes $0 < \eta < 1$	Country 2 doesn't retaliate		$C_1\eta\Delta l_1 < 0$	$C_2\eta\Delta l_2 > 0$
		Country 2 Retaliates	Country 1	$C_1\eta\Delta l_1 - \varphi(\eta)p^{(2)} < 0$	$C_2\eta\Delta l_2 + \varepsilon\varphi(\eta)p^{(2)} > 0$
			Country 1 counter-retaliate	$C_1\eta\Delta l_1 - \varphi(\eta)p^{(2)} + \varepsilon\varphi(\eta)p^{(1)} < 0$	$C_2\eta\Delta l_2 + \varepsilon\varphi(\eta)p^{(2)} - \varphi(\eta)p^{(1)}$ when $\varepsilon p^{(2)} - p^{(1)} > -\dfrac{C_2\eta\Delta l_2}{\varphi(\eta)}$, the payoff is "+", otherwise it is "-"

In stage I and III, country 2 chooses strategy, while in stage II and IV, country 1 makes the choice. These strategies in Table 6.1 are actually labeled as eight scenarios. To be more specific, in stage I, country 2 decides whether or not to raise a request to country 1 on the exchange rate. If it does, following the previous discussions and notation, then $\Delta l_2 = -\Delta l_1 \triangleq e_1 - e_0 \leq 0$. In stage II, country 1 will react to the request[11] given by country 2. Country 1 has a strategy set of $\eta \Delta l_2 \ (0 \leq \eta \leq 1)$. $\eta = 0, \eta = 1$, and $0 < \eta < 1$ represent, that country 1 ignores the request completely, that country 1 fully satisfies the request, and that country 1 only partly satisfies the request, respectively. In stage III, in view of the result in stage II, country 2 will decide to retaliate or not. If it retaliates, the degree of retaliation will be dependent on the value of η that country 1 chooses in stage II. Finally in stage IV, country 1 will decide how to respond to country 2's decision. It will counter-retaliate if country 2 retaliates in stage III;[12] otherwise, the game is over.

Based on the game process, strategies, and the analysis of the corresponding utility changes, we will discuss in detail the four stages with the help of Table 6.1. Our conclusion shows that the contrast of the players' economic power $p^{(i)}$ $(i = 1,2)$ not only affects the choice of strategies in four stages, but also determines the ultimate equilibrium strategy.

1   Stage I. If country 2 is at a disadvantageous position, it may take the strategy of not asking for a change in exchange rate, or request $\Delta l_2 < 0$. Specifically, (i) suppose that the relation of economic power between country 1 and 2 is $p^{(2)} < p^{(1)}$, then the equilibrium solution to the game is either the 1st or 2nd scenario, that is to say, either country 2 doesn't request any change in exchange rate or even if it does, country 1 doesn't accept such request. Country 1 will not make any move in stage II because its utility will decrease in the 3rd, 5th, 6th, and 7th scenario. In the 4th scenario, the condition for both countries to have positive utility changes are $\dfrac{p^{(2)}}{p^{(1)}} < \varepsilon$ and $\dfrac{p^{(2)}}{p^{(1)}} > \dfrac{1}{\varepsilon}$, but because $0 < \varepsilon < 1$, the conditions cannot be satisfied simultaneously; hence, scenario 4 can't be the equilibrium. Neither can scenario 8 be the solution because country 2 will choose scenario 6 instead of 8 in stage III since such a choice will improve the utility[13] when $p^{(2)} < p^{(1)}$. However, in scenario 6, the utility of country 1 decreases so it will not choose this scenario in stage II. In conclusion, the player with small economic power doesn't have ability to change the situation at present stage, unless there is a change in the contrast of power with development. (ii) Suppose that the relation of economic power between country 1 and 2 is $p^{(2)} > p^{(1)}$, then country 2 must choose $\Delta l_2 < 0$. This is because country 2 will gain non-negative utility change in scenario 2, 3, 5, 6, and 7. In scenario 4 and 8, country 2 may have negative utility change,[14] but it can choose other strategies in stage III to avoid these two scenarios. In conclusion, the player with

larger economic power has a stronger position in the game, and enjoys an advantage in the distribution of international economic interests.

2 Stage IV.[15] No matter what kind of strategy was chosen in stage II, country 1 must counter-retaliate if country 2 retaliates in stage III, because counter-retaliation increases the utility of country 1 while reduces the utility of country 2. So scenarios 3 and 7 are not the equilibrium solutions.

3 Stage III. Country 2 will decide whether to retaliate against country 1 or not, which in turn depends on the extent to which country 1 satisfies the request on an exchange rate change by country 2 in stage II.[16] Here, scenarios 2, 4, 6 and 8 are analyzed.[17] (i) Suppose first that country 1 completely rejects the request of country 2 in stage II, $\eta = 0$, then either scenario 2 or 4 occurs. Which of them happens depends on the contrast of economic power between the two countries. In scenario 4, when $\dfrac{p^{(2)}}{p^{(1)}} > \dfrac{1}{\varepsilon}$, country 2 has the payoff $\varepsilon p^{(2)} - p^{(1)} > 0$, so country 2 will retaliate. Then, scenario 4 is the equilibrium. Otherwise, scenario 2 is the equilibrium when $\dfrac{p^{(2)}}{p^{(1)}} < \dfrac{1}{\varepsilon}$. The economic interpretations are: the greater the economic power that country 2 has relative to country 1, it is more likely for country 2 to choose tougher strategy, namely, retaliation; however, country 2 will not be courageous enough to provoke if the two countries have the same economic power. Furthermore, when ε is small, that is, the utility improvement by retaliation is small, the relative power $\dfrac{p^{(2)}}{p^{(1)}}$ should become large if country 2 wants to take tough strategy. That is consistent with reality. (ii) Suppose next that country 1 partly satisfies the request of country 2 in stage II, $0 < \eta < 1$. Similar to the analysis above, we need to make a choice between scenario 6 and 8, which requires a comparison between the utility improvements of country 2 in the two scenarios. That is to say, we need to tell whether $\varepsilon \Phi(\eta) p^{(2)} - \Phi(\eta) p^{(1)} > 0$ or $\varepsilon \Phi(\eta) p^{(2)} - \Phi(\eta) p^{(1)} < 0$. After dropping $\phi(\eta)$, it can be shown that the result here is similar to the preceding one. That is, country 2's decision on whether to retaliate or not rests on whether $\dfrac{p^{(2)}}{p^{(1)}} > \dfrac{1}{\varepsilon}$ or not, and the result and economic interpretations are also the same as those in the preceding analysis. As for what strategy country 2 chooses, it relies on the strategy country 1 takes in stage II and the contrast of economic power between the two countries.

4 Stage II. For country 1, its strategy in scenario 2 dominates over that in scenario 4, and that in scenario 6 is dominant over that in scenario 8. Whether scenario 2 or 6 becomes the equilibrium solution depends on the relation between $p^{(1)}$ and $p^{(2)}$. For country 2, as long as $\dfrac{p^{(2)}}{p^{(1)}} > \dfrac{1}{\varepsilon}$, its

utility improvement in scenarios 4 and 8 is greater than that in scenarios 2 and 6; and hence, scenarios 4 and 8 will be the equilibrium solutions. According to the analysis of stage IV, scenarios 3 and 7 can't be the equilibrium. Scenario 5 is a situation in which country 1 completely satisfies the request of country 2. This is the worst scenario for country 1. The analysis so far states that the contrast of economic power between two countries determines what strategy country 1 chooses in stage II when country 2 requests a change in exchange rate. When $1 < \dfrac{p^{(2)}}{p^{(1)}} < \dfrac{1}{\varepsilon}$, country 1 will either reject or partly satisfy the request. That is, $\eta \geq 0$ is enough, not necessarily $\eta = 1$. In this case, though country 2's request is not satisfied, its utility will decrease if it retaliates. Therefore, scenarios 2 and 6 are equilibrium solutions, and the optimal solution is scenario 2 for country 1. When $\dfrac{p^{(2)}}{p^{(1)}} > \dfrac{1}{\varepsilon}$, the equilibrium solution is among scenario 4, 5, and 8. It requires a comparison of utility loss of country 1 to find the solution. In fact, scenarios 4 and 5 are special cases of scenario 8, that is, $\eta = 0$ and $\eta = 1$; therefore, we only need to discuss the relationship between utility change and η, but we set now $0 \leq \eta \leq 1$.

Let

$$H \triangleq C_1 \eta \Delta l_1 - \phi(\eta) p^{(2)} + \varepsilon \phi(\eta) p^{(1)} \tag{6.15}$$

The first-order condition for maximizing H is

$$\frac{\partial H}{\partial \eta} = C_1 \Delta l_1 - \phi'(\eta) p^{(2)} + \varepsilon \phi'(\eta) p^{(1)} = 0 \tag{6.16}$$

It follows that $\phi'(\eta) = C_1 \Delta l_1 / \left(p^{(2)} - \varepsilon p^{(1)} \right)$. Let $\psi()$ be the inverse function of $\phi'()$; hence

$$\eta^* = \psi \left[C_1 \Delta l_1 / \left(p^{(2)} - \varepsilon p^{(1)} \right) \right] \tag{6.17}$$

The second-order condition is

$$\partial^2 H / \partial \eta^2 = -\phi''(\eta) p^{(2)} + \varepsilon \phi''(\eta) p^{(1)} = -\phi''(\eta) \left[p^{(2)} - \varepsilon p^{(1)} \right] \tag{6.18}$$

Since $p^{(2)} > p^{(1)} > 0, 0 < \varepsilon < 1,$ and $\phi''(\eta) > 0,$ consequently, $\partial^2 H / \partial \eta^2 < 0.$ The second-order condition has been satisfied.

Let's turn to η^*. Since $\phi''() > 0$, then, $\phi'()$ and $\psi()$ are monotonically increasing. Moreover, since $C_1 \langle 0, \Delta l_1 \rangle 0, p^{(2)} > p^{(1)} > 0,$ and $0 < \varepsilon < 1,$ then, $C_1 \Delta l_1 < 0$ and $p^{(2)} - \varepsilon p^{(1)} > 0.$ In addition, when Δl_1 is given, $C_1 \Delta l_1$ becomes constant. Therefore, the value of $p^{(2)} - \varepsilon p^{(1)}$ will be bigger when the gap of economic power between the two countries $\left(p^{(2)} - p^{(1)} \right)$ gets larger, so is the value of $C_1 \Delta l_1 / \left(p^{(2)} - \varepsilon p^{(1)} \right)$;[18] consequently, η^* gets larger. On the contrary, the smaller the $p^{(2)} - p^{(1)}$, the smaller the η^*. It can be inferred that if $C_1 \Delta l_1 / \left(p^{(2)} - \varepsilon p^{(1)} \right) \to 0^-$, then $\eta^* \to 1^-$, and if $C_1 \Delta l_1 / \left(p^{(2)} - \varepsilon p^{(1)} \right) \to -1^+$, then $\eta^* \to 0^+$. The implication of η^* to the country 1's choice of strategy in stage II is that country 1 should make a bigger change in exchange rate, a large η^*, to avoid utility reduction caused by country 2's retaliation if the two countries have large discrepancy in economic power. When such discrepancy is large enough, then scenario 5 will take place, that is, country 1 will completely satisfy the request of country 2 in stage II.

In summary, when $\dfrac{p^{(2)}}{p^{(1)}} < \dfrac{1}{\varepsilon}$, country 1 will choose either scenario 2 or 6, which means country 1 will not, or only partly, satisfy the request of country 2. When $\dfrac{p^{(2)}}{p^{(1)}} > \dfrac{1}{\varepsilon}$, country 1's optimal strategy in stage II will switch from scenario 4 to 8, then to 5 as the gap of economic power between the two countries broadens. So the relative economic power of two countries determines the optimal strategy of country 1 in stage II, and the equilibrium solution to the game experiences a convergence path from scenario $2 \to 6 \to 4 \to 8 \to 5$, with the increasing difference in economic power.

From the above analysis, we find the following. In an exchange rate game, country 2 who holds an initial disadvantage will request either an exchange rate change $\Delta l_2 < 0$ or no change at all in stage I, relying on its economic power relative to the other country. In stage II, country 1 must choose one out of three options, namely, whether to make change, whether to satisfy the request partly or completely. If country 1 decides to partly satisfy the request, it must decide the value of η. All of the above decisions depend on the relative economic power plus other parameters. In stages III and IV, the retaliation and counter-retaliation between the two countries depend on the relative economic power. In brief, in the modern open economy, international trade, investment, and technology dependence, even national income and output, are all important resources on which the economic power of a country depends. Countries play fierce games on the significant factor in the modern international economy-exchange rate, to pursuit of national interests. Our research shows that economic power is the foundation of the game; the greater the economic power, the more likely it is a country can obtain favorable outcomes from changes in the exchange rate and thus obtain greater international economic interests. That is, the actual exchange rate's influence on stakeholders is isomorphic to the contrast of economic power between stakeholders. Therefore, we argue that the game based on economic power determines exchange rate movements, and market demand

and supply are only important factors that affect exchange rate fluctuations in the short run. This view explains the debates and exchange rate games between countries in the medium and long run and exchange rate fluctuations in the short run.

By defining utility functions, describing the games, and analyzing the choice of strategies, we provide the optimal strategies and the equilibrium in every stage for the two countries. However, in an open economic environment, the interdependence of players is so strong that they tend to choose suboptimal strategies instead of optimal strategies to reach a compromise that balances the interests of both players when they are concerned with long-term economic development, such as the openness of the economy, trades, and their reputation.

Specifically, if the current exchange rate is favorable to country 1, country 1 will choose the suboptimal strategy (scenario 6) instead of scenario 2 when country 2 requests a change in the exchange rate even though the economic power of country 2 does not satisfy $\frac{p^{(2)}}{p^{(1)}} > \frac{1}{\varepsilon}$. This is so because in scenario 6, country 1 partly satisfies the request so that it can avoid a potential extreme strategy taken by country 2 and maintain relatively favorable external conditions for long-term economic development. Canzoneri and Henderson (1991) note that the players always achieve some degree of cooperation in their repeated strategy games unless a player believes that the game is coming to an end. For country 2, however, even if $\frac{p^{(2)}}{p^{(1)}} > \frac{1}{\varepsilon}$ holds, as long as country 1 satisfies most of the request, the two countries can reach a compromise. That is, country 2 chooses the strategy of scenario 6, which ends the game. This is so because the utility increase from $u_2^{(2)} + u_3^{(2)}$ may be far less than the utility increase from $u_1^{(2)}$.[19] Then, country 2 is satisfied with the improvement in the utility and will abandon scenario 8 where the improvement is infinitesimal. Therefore, scenario 6 becomes the equilibrium solution to the game.

Our analysis of the exchange rate is consistent with the reality of the modern international economy. In fact, in the modern world, powerful countries that rely on their economic power always demand an exorbitant price where exchange rates are concerned. For example, the United States requested a major significant appreciation of the RMB (Frankel, 2005). As part of negotiations and based on its economic power, China can make certain compromises rather than fully satisfy its opponent's request because part of the request may be a component of a game strategy and not a real concern of interests. Moreover, the United States may not be able to attain the optimal situation. So, if China partly satisfies US's request, the US could retaliate to improve current utility in theory. However, in reality, the US has rarely employed such strategy. Of course, the above analysis is not contradictory to the theoretical analysis of models. Because considering long-term economic development or repeated games, the suboptimal strategies of both sides may well be the optimal strategy in the long run.

The power to decide interest rates and market interest rate determination

Theories on interest rate determination and limitations

There are many theories on interest rate determination in economics research. Classical interest rate theories suggest that the interest rate is determined by savings and investment. Savings and investment are affected by real factors such as time preference, patience, waiting, and marginal products of capital (Böhm-Bawerk, 1890; Fisher, 1930; Marshall, 1961). Therefore, the classical theories are actually the real interest rate theories represented by Böhm-Bawerk, Fisher, and Marshall.

Keynesian liquidity preference theory argues that interest rates are determined by the relationship between demand and supply in money markets, where central banks determine money supply and people's preference for liquidity determines money demand (Keynes, 1937). Moreover, the preference for liquidity is affected by the degree of precautionary, speculative, and transaction motives. Robertson (1940) and Ohlin (1935) criticize Keynes' theory that the interest rate is determined by the quantity of money. They propose the loanable funds theory, which states that the interest rate is the price paid for the right to borrow or access loanable funds, and the equilibrium interest rate is determined by the demand and supply of funds. The supply comes mainly from personal and business savings, government budget surpluses, and loans from foreign countries while demand comes mainly from personal credit, business investment, government budget deficits, and borrowing from foreign countries.

Hicks (1989) argues that interest rate determination is related to both goods and money markets simultaneously. That is, the level of income and interest rate will be determined simultaneously if the two markets attain equilibrium simultaneously, that is, the investment-savings and liquidity preference-money supply (IS-LM) analysis. In addition, financial instruments of various types and terms have different interest rates, which gives rise to theories on the term structure of interest rates. The theories are so called because they show that for securities with the same risk as liquidity, the term structure determines their interest rates while the theory of interest rate risk argues that security interest rates are determined by default risks, liquidity, and taxation.

From the above analysis, we find that theories on interest rate determination differ because they assume various perspectives in the analysis of interest rates and their role. For example, interest rate determination is a price issue from a market perspective while interest rates are a policy instrument from the perspective of macroeconomic regulation and control. From the perspective of credit and information, interest rates are determined by liquidity and risk. The difference in theory is the difference in hypothesis in the model. Furthermore, the various hypotheses reflect the differences in people's recognition of the essence of the issue.

In fact, interest rates have the attribute of duality. On the one hand, as a price of money, interest rates are determined by the markets. On the other hand, as a policy instrument, the benchmark interest rate is determined by monetary authorities. Correspondingly, interest rate determination occurs on two levels: market and state. Interest rate determination at the state level is often manifested in adjustments to the benchmark interest rate by central banks; hence, indirectly affecting market interest rates for economic regulation. Interest rate determination at the market level is the focus of our next discussion.

The stated theories have a common limitation, which is they ignore the logical relationship between interest rate determination and interest distribution. Interest rate determination is the process of interest distribution while interest distribution is realized through games among economic agents. Marx (2004) argues that interests are the surplus value that loaning capitalists take away from entrepreneurial capitalists; moreover, this concept determines that interest rates cannot exceed the profit margin. Marx also notes that the value of interest rates depends on the proportion of total profit margins distributed among the loaner and the borrower. However, Marx does not address how the proportion is determined.

The fundamental purpose of economic activity is to maximize the interests gained through distribution. In the market, distribution is embodied in the proportion of the trade surplus among all parties involved. The manifestation of the proportions is the transaction price. The market interest rate is actually the transaction price of funds in the money market. Different market interest rates practically determine the difference in interests that each party obtains through the distribution. The mechanism of interest distribution emerges as a result of various power games. The determination of the market interest rate reflects the pursuit of economic interests by transaction agents based on their pricing power. The greater the pricing power, the more likely it is that an agent will gain favorable results in the determination process; consequently, the agent will obtain more interests. Market interest rates include the interest rates in both formal and informal financial markets (also called private financial markets). In the next section, we analyze the factors that influence the interest rate under different circumstances by establishing bargaining models for both lenders and borrowers.

Interest rate determination in formal financial markets

Koskela and Stenbacka (2000) note two ways to deal with determining loan interest rates under non-perfect-competitive market structures for the banking industry. One method is to believe that banks provide differentiated financial products and explain the determination under this framework. The other method is to adopt the bargaining model involving lenders and borrowers developed by Caminal and Mature (2006). In this model, the borrower's bargaining ability reflects the intensity of the competition in credit market. We assume that a bank provides differentiated financial products, and a firm is engaged in a risk investment project that requires K amount of funds. According to Cobb-Douglas production function, the firm's profits will be:

$$V(r) = AK^{\alpha}L^{1-\alpha} - wL - (1+r)K \triangleq \theta - (1+r)K \tag{6.19}$$

where K, L, and A represent capital, labor, and the level of technology, respectively; r and w stand for loan's rate and wage rate; α, and $1-\alpha \in [0,1]$ denote output elasticity with respect to capital and labor, respectively; where $\theta = AK^{\alpha}L^{1-\alpha} - wL$.

Profits of the bank is

$$U(r) = (1+r)K - K - cK = (r-c)K \tag{6.20}$$

where c represents the cost of banking services.

The bargaining model for the firm and the bank can be written as the following constrained optimization problem:

$$\left\{ \begin{array}{l} \underset{r \in S}{Max}\, U(r)^{\beta} V(r)^{1-\beta} \\ \text{s.t. } U(r) \geq 0, V(r) \geq 0 \end{array} \right. \tag{6.21}$$

β *and* $1-\beta$ denote, respectively, the bargaining ability of the bank and that of the firm. Taking (6.19) and (6.20) into (6.21) derives the equilibrium interest rate,

$$r = \beta\left(\frac{\theta}{K} - 1\right) + (1-\beta)c \tag{6.22}$$

Taking $\theta = AK^{\alpha}L^{1-\alpha} - wL$ into (6.22), it follows

$$r = \beta\left[A\left(\frac{K}{L}\right)^{\alpha-1} - w\left(\frac{K}{L}\right)^{-1} - 1\right] + (1-\beta)c \tag{6.23}$$

Some discussions on the equilibrium interest rate given by (6.23) is as follows:

1   Taking derivatives of (6.22) gives

$$\frac{\partial r}{\partial \beta} = \frac{\theta}{K} - 1 - c \tag{6.24}$$

Note that the social constraints[20]

$$S(r) = U(r) + V(r) = \theta - cK - K \tag{6.25}$$

Therefore, when $S(r) > 0$, $\dfrac{\partial r}{\partial \beta} = \dfrac{\theta}{K} - 1 - c > 0$, an increase in β will cause r to rise, whose economic interpretation is that the greater the bank's bargaining ability, the higher the loan's interest rate r will be.

2   An increase in c will cause r to rise, that is, the higher the costs of banking services, the greater its reservation utility in bargaining, thus, the higher the loan's interest rate r will be.

3   An increase in A will cause r to rise, that is, the faster the technology progress is, the higher and the more urgent the demand for capital from firms, which will reduce the firm's bargaining ability, then the higher the loan's interest rate r will be.

4   For labor-intensive firms, namely, $\dfrac{K}{L} < 1$, an increase in α will cause r to decline; while for capital-intensive firms, namely, $\dfrac{K}{L} > 1$, an increase in α will cause r to rise. The economic interpretation is that an increase in α means more capital input brings more output. If it is a labor-intensive firm, then, its demand for funds is not high; therefore, the increase in borrowing from banks means that banks can sell more funds. In order to stimulate demands, the price of funds—the loan interest rate r will fall. Similarly, for the capital-intensive firm, its demand for capital is high, so an increment in α results in increasing demands for funds. When fund supply stays unchanged, the price of funds— the loan interest rate, r, will rise accordingly.

5   An increase in w will cause r to fall; that is, if the firm pays higher labor wage rate, the greater the reservation utility it will have in the bargaining process. Hence, the firm will expect a lower interest rate on loans; otherwise, it won't invest, and there will be no borrower.

6   Rewrite (6.23) as

$$r = \beta \left(Ak^{\alpha - 1} - wk^{-1} - 1 \right) + (1 - \beta) c \tag{6.26}$$

where $k = \dfrac{K}{L}$ is the capital stock per worker. From (6.26), it follows,

$$\frac{\partial r}{\partial k} = \beta \left[(\alpha - 1) Ak^{\alpha - 2} + wk^{-2} \right] \tag{6.27}$$

The condition for (6.27) to be greater than 0 is,

$$k > \left(\frac{w}{(1 - \alpha) A} \right)^{\frac{1}{\alpha}} \tag{6.28}$$

According to equation (6.28), when $k > \left(\dfrac{w}{(1-\alpha)A} \right)^{\frac{1}{\alpha}}$, an increase in k will

cause r to rise; when $k < \left(\dfrac{w}{(1-\alpha)A} \right)^{\frac{1}{\alpha}}$ an increase in k will cause r to fall. The

economic interpretation is that $k > \left(\dfrac{w}{(1-\alpha)A} \right)^{\frac{1}{\alpha}}$ means the firm needs more

capital per worker in the production. So when k rises, the firm demands for

more capital, then interest rates r will rise. Similarly, when $k < \left(\dfrac{w}{(1-\alpha)A} \right)^{\frac{1}{\alpha}}$,

the firm needs less capital per worker; therefore, when k rises, the banks have to sell more funds, then the interest rate r will fall.

In summary, if the bank can offer differentiated financial products, the bargaining ability between the bank and the firm (mainly reflected in the degree of market competition in the banking sector), the firm's demand for funds, the urgency of the demand, and the type of firm (capital versus labor-intensive) can be considered the factors affecting the pricing power of the lender and the borrower. The above analysis shows that the equilibrium interest rate is affected by these factors, or in other words, determined by the pricing power that emerges from these factors. In addition, the bank's service costs and the firm's labor wages affect the reserved profits of both the lenders and the borrowers; therefore, service and labor costs affect the equilibrium interest rate.

If banks provide homogeneous financial products, according to Caminal and Mature's (1997) framework, the structure of the banking market will decide the borrower's bargaining ability; that is, banking competition in the market determines the pricing power of the bank and the borrower. We conclude that fierce competition in the banking sector will lead to lower loan interest rates according to the bargaining model. For deposits, we conclude that fierce competition in the banking sector leads to a higher interest rate for deposits.

Interest rate determination in informal financial markets

Informal finance includes deposits, loans, and other financial transactions. Atieno (2001) notes that informal finance refers to financial transactions such as deposits, loans, and private lending that are dissociated from the formal financial system and beyond the purview of national credit and the central bank. On the surface, the existence of informal finance can be explained by banks in the formal financial market that prefer to provide loans to state-owned or large enterprises while small and medium-sized enterprises (SMEs) and private companies find it difficult to obtain loans in the formal financial market. At the same time, SMEs find it difficult to obtain financing in the secondary market because they are not qualified for this market in most cases. Thus, SMEs resort to the informal financial markets to raise funds necessary for their projects despite the potential high interest rates of informal financial markets.

There are two explanations at the deep level for the cause of market segmentation.[21] One explanation is transaction cost theory while the other is financial repression theory found in research of Adams and Fitchett (1992) and Ghate (1992). In addition, interest rates are mainly determined by market mechanisms in the informal markets, but there are significant variations in interest rates—the lowest rates are close to zero while the highest rate could be a monthly interest rate of 5%.[22] Moreover, there is no universal reference, and interest rates are set on a case-by-case basis depending on the specific circumstances. Analyzing interest rate determination in the informal market, Wang and Li (2005) and Cheng (2006) conduct thorough and detailed research from the perspective of bargaining between lenders and borrowers under different assumptions. The authors discuss a number of related issues, such as the relationship between the interest rates in formal and informal financial markets, the impact of borrowers' own funds, project risks, loaner competition, the costs of concluding an interest rate transaction in the informal market, and the relationship between external manager rewards and interest rates. With different assumptions, the authors' conclusions are not the same. Wang and Li (2005) note that regional informal financial markets are not perfectly competitive since each party involved has some market power. Market power, in essence, is the extrinsic form of economic power in negotiations, that is, bargaining power or market pricing power that emerges from the borrower and the lender's resources. We combine the framework in the above two studies to provide an explanation of interest rate determination in informal financial markets from the perspective of economic power with the venture capital lending model.

First, we will show what factors affect interest rate determination and the games between loaners and borrowers. Assume there are m borrowers and n loaners in the informal financial market. All participants are risk neutral. Each borrower needs 1 unit of capital for his investment project and has z amount of own funds; therefore, he needs to borrow $1-z$. Returns[23] to the project is a random variable Θ, which varies between 0 and H ($H > 0$); the density function of Θ is $f_\Theta(\theta)$. When the project returns are $\Theta \in [0, (1-z)(1+r)]$, the loaner obtains Θ and the borrower receives 0; when $\Theta \in [(1-z)(1+r), H]$ the loaner obtains $(1-z)(1+r)$ and the borrower receives $\Theta - (1-z)(1+r)$, r represents interest rate.

Let U and V be the objective functions of the loaner and the borrower, respectively, namely, the difference between the utility function and the reservation utility. The utility function is expressed as the expected returns:

$E\pi_U$ and $E\pi_V$ denote the expected returns of the loaner and those of the borrower. According the above analysis, we get

$$E\pi_U = \int_0^{(1-z)(1+r)} \theta f_\Theta(\theta)d\theta + \int_{(1-z)(1+r)}^H (1-z)(1+r)f_\Theta(\theta)d\theta \qquad (6.29)$$

$$E\pi_V = \int_{(1-z)(1+r)}^H \left[\theta-(1-z)(1+r)\right]f_\Theta(\theta)d\theta \qquad (6.30)$$

B_U and B_V denote the reservation utility of the loaner and that of the borrower. ρ represents the interest rate of the formal financial market for the current period; then, the loaner's reservation utility should be

$$B_U =(1-z)(1+\rho) \qquad (6.31)$$

The borrower's utility should be

$$B_V = z(1+\rho) \qquad (6.32)$$

β and $1-\beta$ represent loaner's and borrower's relative bargaining power, namely, the power to set interest rate, respectively. Obviously, β is related to variables m, n, and z. Cheng (2006) finds that for the borrower, the term of loan t, urgency to borrow e, and the managing capability w, and the institutional risk v, all have influence on β, and

$$\beta_m > 0, \beta_n < 0, \beta_t > 0, \beta_e > 0, \beta_w < 0, \beta_v > 0^{24} \qquad (6.33)$$

In summary, the game model for debit and credit side in the informal financial markets can be written as the following constrained maximization problem,

$$\begin{cases} \underset{r\in S}{Max}(E\pi_U - B_U)^\beta(E\pi_V - B_V)^{1-\beta} \\ s.t.\ E\pi_U - B_U \geq 0 \\ \quad E\pi_V - B_V \geq 0 \end{cases} \qquad (6.34)$$

The first-order conditions yield the following equation,

$$\frac{1}{\beta} = 1 - \frac{\partial E\pi_U/\partial r}{\partial E\pi_V/\partial r} \times \frac{E\pi_V - B_V}{E\pi_U - B_U} \qquad (6.35)$$

The optimal interest rate r^* is determined by equation (6.35). From (6.29) and (6.30) it can be derived that,

$$
\begin{cases}
\partial E\pi_U/\partial r = (1-z)\displaystyle\int_{(1-z)(1+r)}^{H} f_\Theta(\theta)\,d\theta \\[4mm]
\partial E\pi_V/\partial r = -(1-z)\displaystyle\int_{(1-z)(1+r)}^{H} f_\Theta(\theta)\,d\theta
\end{cases}
\tag{6.36}
$$

Take (6.36) into (6.35), we get

$$
\frac{1}{\beta} = 1 + \frac{E\pi_V - B_V}{E\pi_U - B_U}
\tag{6.37}
$$

To analyze the impulse-response relationship between the power of setting interest rate, β, and the interest rate, r, denotes

$$
\Pi = E\pi_U - B_U, \quad \Sigma = E\pi_V - B_V
\tag{6.38}
$$

Then, it follows

$$
\partial\left(\frac{1}{\beta}\right)\Big/\partial r = \frac{\Sigma_r \times \Pi - \Sigma \times \Pi_r}{\Pi^2}
\tag{6.39}
$$

If we denote $\Delta = \Sigma_r \times \Pi - \Sigma \times \Pi_r$, then the $\dfrac{\partial\left(\frac{1}{\beta}\right)}{\partial r}$ has the same sign as Δ.

Taking (6.29) and (6.32) into Δ, with the consideration that the function to be integrated contains r as independent variable, the following equation can be obtained.

$$
\begin{aligned}
\Delta = (1+\rho)(1-z)\times &\int_{(1-z)(1+r)}^{H} f_\Theta(\theta)\,d\theta - (1-z)\times \int_{(1-z)(1+r)}^{H} f_\Theta(\theta)\,d\theta \\
\times &\left[\int_{0}^{(1-z)(1+r)} \theta f_\Theta(\theta)\,d\theta + \int_{(1-z)(1+r)}^{H} \theta f_\Theta(\theta)\,d\theta\right]
\end{aligned}
\tag{6.40}
$$

Notice that

$$
\int_{0}^{(1-z)(1+r)} \theta f_\Theta(\theta)\,d\theta + \int_{(1-z)(1+r)}^{H} \theta f_\Theta(\theta)\,d\theta = \int_{0}^{H} \theta f_\Theta(\theta)\,d\theta = E\Theta
\tag{6.41}
$$

where $E\Theta$ is the average value of Θ, the project's returns. Taking $E\Theta$ into Δ, we obtain the following equation,

$$\Delta = \Sigma_r \times \Pi - \Sigma \times \Pi_r = (1-z) \times \int_{(1-z)(1+r)}^{H} f_\Theta(\theta) d\theta \times (1+\rho - E\Theta) \tag{6.42}$$

Because $\dfrac{\partial \left(\dfrac{1}{\beta}\right)}{\partial r}$ has the same sign as Δ, we can use Δ to analyze the impulse response relationship between β, the power to set interest rates, and r, the interest rates. First, the borrower's own funds are less than the funds required by the project. Otherwise, the borrower does not need to borrow from the credit markets, so the factor $1-z > 0$. Second, $(1-z)(1+r) < H$ should hold, that is, the loan plus interests must be smaller than the possible maximum gains;[25] otherwise, the borrower will not carry out the project. At the same time, the density function $f_\Theta(\theta) \geq 0$, and $f_\Theta(\theta)$ is not equal to 0, so the factor $\displaystyle\int_{(1-z)(1+r)}^{H} f_\Theta(\theta) d\theta > 0$.

Finally, consider the factor $1 + \rho - E\Theta$. For the borrower, when determining whether to borrow money to carry out a project, he needs to estimate whether the project's expected average returns[26] will cover the sum of all the own funds, the opportunity costs, the loans, and the associated interests. Because the loan's rate in the informal financial market tends to be higher than that in the formal market, given that the borrower is risk neutral, in order to make the constrained optimization problem (6.34) meaningful, the condition of $E\Theta > z(1+\rho) + (1-z)(1+\rho) = 1 + \rho$[27] should be satisfied, that is, the factor $1 + \rho - E\Theta < 0$. Through all the above analyses, we get

$$(1-z) \times \int_{(1-z)(1+r)}^{H} f_\Theta(\theta) d\theta \times (1+\rho - E\Theta) < 0 \tag{6.43}$$

That is

$$\partial \left(\frac{1}{\beta}\right) / \partial r < 0 \tag{6.44}$$

From (6.44) we can get the following impulse response relationship, that is, an increase in r will cause $\dfrac{1}{\beta}$ to fall; hence, β rises; however, if β rises, r will rise. Its economic implication is just the core idea that we emphasize— the power to set interest rate has an impact on interest rate determination; moreover, the greater power the loaner has, the higher the lending rate will be and vice versa. Taking into account equation (6.33), we can derive the direct impacts of various factors that affect β on the interest rate. As the number of borrowers (m), the loan term (t), the emergency to get loans (e), and the system risk level (v) get larger, the lending rate will become higher; however, as the number of loaners (n), and the management ability of borrowers (w) get larger, the lending rate will become lower.

Although the model in this section does not include the central bank and other participants in the money market, as discussed in the previous sections, these economic agents use pricing power formed by the resources under their control to bargain with other agents and secure a favorable interest rate arrangement. In this process, the determinant of market interest rates is the same as the result of analysis in this section, that is, power formed by the resources at market participant's disposal. Therefore, there must be a balanced economic power structure to achieve a balanced distribution of social welfare among the economic agents.

Capital, information, and the determination of securities pricing

Re-thinking the equilibrium process of securities pricing

With respect to goods pricing, Marx (2004) states that price exists because goods contain the general social labor of human beings, which reflects their commercial and use value under the conditions of professional division and exchange. Menger (1990) states that commercial value is the foundation of exchange; if goods cannot bring utility to people, there is no value and, consequently, no price. The value of a financial product lies in both the ownership and the claim of surplus returns. However, in fact, this value is realized to a great extent by investor's buying and selling behavior and the equilibrium between demand and supply.[28] Therefore, the price of securities has an internal logical link with the demand-supply relation. Despite this, we do not believe that price is essentially determined by demand and supply. Furthermore, we must consider what factors affect demand and supply. In financial markets, although there are remarkable differences in risk preference, investment techniques, and financial management skills among investors, every investor participates in transactions and decides demand and supply with the goal of maximizing profits. That is, all investors are subjectively rational. Some investors, such as big traders, could influence other investors' subjective expectations on profit maximization using the resources in their control. Consequently, demand and supply in the market are affected objectively. Then, the transaction price of securities is affected or even determined by a proportion of investors. This phenomenon is frequently observed in reality. Therefore, the main reason why the explanation of the price mechanism by traditional models is challenged is the inconsistency between market and theoretical price. The theoretical price cannot explain the market price. Moreover, there is a lack of essential considerations regarding transaction manipulation, information asymmetry, and the factors affecting the trader's ability to bargain. Thus, our analysis starts with the most important resources in securities market: capital and information. Then, we show how these resources affect securities prices and explain the associated mechanism. Based on the analysis, we raise a novel theoretical proposition for the determination of securities prices to explain the problem in reality at a deeper level.

Market manipulation is an unavoidable issue for the study of securities price determination. Manipulative behavior refers to exerting market influence to obtain benefits from that influence. Practically speaking, as long as there is a wide gap in the quantity of capital or funds among traders or asymmetrical information, manipulation or influence is inevitable whether intentional or unintentional. Allen and Gale (1992) classify this influence into acts, information, and transaction manipulation. Acts and information manipulation are generally considered illegal, so they are strictly supervised. Transaction manipulation is the most difficult to eliminate or supervise because it simply uses trading strategies to stimulate other investors' expectations without any observable behavior to change the value of firms, such as dispersing false messages as part of "pump and dump" schemes.[29]

Studies on transaction manipulation and information asymmetry can be divided into two categories: theoretical and empirical. Theoretical studies build models of certain types of manipulation and discuss their feasibility and welfare impacts. For instance, De Long, Shleifer, Summers and Waldmann (1990) describe how informed traders use positive feedback from traders to control the market price and profits based on the information advantage. Zhang and Fang (2007) note that a necessary condition for transaction manipulation to realize profits is that positive feedback traders account for a fairly large proportion of the market, and the sheep-flock effect (also called herd behavior) is sufficiently large. Empirical studies conduct data mining to verify the existence of manipulation and search for prevention measures and supervision methods. For instance, Khwaja and Mian (2003) use data from the Pakistan stock market and confirm the existence of pump and dump schemes.

Since the influence of the informed and the big traders on trading prices exists, some researchers study institutional pricing strategies from the perspective of games among institutions and small and medium investors. For instance, Laffont and Maskin (1990) develop a game model to show the stock pricing strategy of risk neutral institutional investors. Based on this study, Xiao and Tian (2002) depict the pricing strategy of risk-averse institutions that have negative exponential utility functions. The studies all note that big traders use their capital and information advantage to influence the market price and seek interests, which is feasible in theory and exists in reality. However, these studies have limitations. The studies mainly focus on explaining the feasibility of the manipulation while ignoring the essence of the issue, which is that the purpose of manipulation is to distribute the trading surplus. Manipulation is realized through pricing power formed by the resources on hand, not others.[30] In other words, the existing literature focuses on the interpretation of superficial phenomena and on handling the technicalities while ignoring the analysis of the original problem, that is, the effects and impacts of the economic power structure on micro-economic behavior, the trading surplus, social welfare distribution, and market efficiency.

The essential purpose of engaging in economic activities is the pursuit of maximum interests. While interests are obtained through distribution, market transaction prices reflect the distribution relationship of the trading surplus between the demand and the supply side. Therefore, transaction prices determine the interest distribution among traders. The fundamental purpose of big traders is to maximize their own interests. So what do the big traders rely on to influence the transaction price? What is the mechanism?

We believe that the formation of interest distribution mechanisms results from various forms of power games. In the securities markets, the economic power of large traders is embodied in the influence on transaction prices. The influence is related to two factors: capital and information. Since there is a huge difference in capital between big traders and medium and small investors, they are not in perfect competition. In fact, the medium and small investors are the price takers. This finding can be interpreted in two ways. On the one hand, big traders unintentionally influence the price. However, due to the huge trading volume, their selling and buying behavior influences the medium and small investors' expectations regarding securities. Then, the price is affected by market demand and supply. For example, a common behavior is to follow the market maker. Although big traders do not intervene the price initiatively, their actions are perceived as making market by small investors who willingly follow the big traders, and then result in price change. Shi (2003) finds that the intentions of market makers is an important type of information that individual investors in securities market are greatly concerned with.

On the other hand, big traders influence the transaction price intentionally, which means they try to change market expectations using their enormous resources to hand. Big traders may even conspire and collude with each other. In this way, they can induce other investors to operate following their hints, and the stock price will change. Information superiority is embodied in the accuracy, availability, and promptness of information. Big traders can hire specialized personnel to conduct information collection and field research on industries of interest. However, medium and small investors typically do not have the time, energy, and resources for such work. Gu and Liu (2004) note that the proportion of investors who obtain information is correlated with the equilibrium price of assets. Moreover, the higher the proportion of investors with information, the lower the risk premium level for the whole market. Essentially, this implies that the higher the proportion, the more balanced trader's impact on price and the lower the likelihood that certain individual investors will influence the transaction price. Therefore, the possibility of price bubbles will be much lower. That is, information symmetry has significant influence on the transaction price as we have emphasized.

In summary, the influence and control that big traders have on the transaction price through their superior resources, such as capital and information, could be viewed as economic power—pricing power in securities markets. Depending on this power, big traders could influence or even completely change the expectations of the small and medium traders and then affect the demand and supply in the market. Ultimately, they could affect or even decide the transaction price. In other words, big traders can exert influence on the distribution of market trading surplus to obtain excess profits.

Impact of the quantity of capital on pricing strategy

In this section, we proved that the resource of capital is one of the essential factors that contributes to the influence on price. Specifically, we establish the theoretical model by describing the choice behavior of games in signal transmission to prove that the pricing strategy of big traders to affect securities pricing is influenced by capital endowments.

Construction of the model

We introduce the following notations: (1) $N = \{1,2\}$ is the set of players, where 1 denotes the big traders while 2 the medium and small traders. (2) $\Theta = \{\theta_0, \theta_1\}$ is the space of the types of big traders, where the type $\theta = \theta_1$ represents the traders with massive funds, as called "strong market makers" while $\theta = \theta_0$ "weak market makers." The medium and small traders know the probability distribution of θ is $p\{\theta = \theta_1\} = \alpha$, $p\{\theta = \theta_0\} = 1 - \alpha$, but have no knowledge of the value of θ. (3) $M = \{p_1, p_0\}$ is the action set of the big traders, in other worlds, the signal space. p_1 and p_0 stand for the deviation in market price and that in the cost respectively when the big traders are pricing, and we assume that $p_1 > p_0$.[31] (4) $A = \{a_0, a_1\}$ is the action space of medium and small traders, where a_0 denotes not buying while a_1 buying. (5) Some notes on the sequential order of the game, in the first stage, big traders choose signal $m(\theta) = p \in M$. According to the value of θ, in the second stage, medium and small traders make inference π_k, on the type of big traders θ, based on the observed signal p_k. Obviously we could set $\pi_k = p\{\theta = \theta_1 | m = p_k\}$, $k = 0, 1$. Here, let h be the expectation on the increase of the stock price when the big traders are perceived by the medium-sized and small traders as the strong market makers and l be the expectation when big traders are perceived as the weak market makers; and $h > l$. We also let c be the extra cost[32] that the weak makers will pay compared to the strong makers when the pricing strategy is p_1. (6) For any given θ_k, p_k, a_k $(k = 0, 1)$, the payoff functions of two players in the game are: (We use u to represent the payoff function of big traders while v that of the small traders.)

$$\begin{cases} u(\theta_1,p_k,a_0)=v(\theta_1,p_k,a_0)=u(\theta_0,p_0,a_0)=v(\theta_0,p_k,a_0)=0,k=0,1 \\ u(\theta_1,p_1,a_1)=p_1,v(\theta_1,p_1,a_1)=h-p_1,u(\theta_0,p_1,a_1)=p_1-c \\ v(\theta_0,p_1,a_1)=l-p_1,u(\theta_0,p_1,a_0)=-c,u(\theta_1,p_0,a_1)=p_0 \\ v(\theta_1,p_0,a_1)=h-p_0,u(\theta_0,p_0,a_1)=p_0,v(\theta_0,p_0,a_1)=l-p_0 \end{cases} \tag{6.45}$$

Brief description of solving the game[33]

(1) Solve for the concise Bayesian strategy in the sub game upon which medium and small traders make inference, that is to say, find the solution to $max \sum_{\theta\in\Theta} v(\theta,\ p,\ a)\,p(\theta|p)$. (2) Solving for the concise Bayesian strategy in the sub game upon which big traders make inference, that is to say, find the solution to $max\ u[\theta,\ p,\ a_\pi(p)]$. (3) Find the concise Bayesian equilibrium, that is, use the results of two previous steps to find the separating and the pooling equilibrium.

The equilibrium results and their economic interpretations

The game may have different states of equilibrium given the difference in objective conditions and expectations of players. We will provide economic interpretations of game equilibrium through the following analysis.

a   When the results are separating equilibria.

1 When $c>p_1-p_0$, $p_1<h$, $p_0<l$, the equilibrium is:

$$m(\theta)=\begin{cases} p_1, & \theta=\theta_1 \\ p_0, & \theta=\theta_0 \end{cases},\ \pi_1=1,\ \pi_0=0,\ a(p)\equiv a_1;$$

2 When $p_1\geq h$, $p_0\geq l$, the equilibrium is:

$$m(\theta)=\begin{cases} p_1, & \theta=\theta_1 \\ p_0, & \theta=\theta_0 \end{cases},\ \pi_1=1,\ \pi_0=0,\ a(p)\equiv a_0;$$

3 When $p_1<\min(c,h)$, $p_0\geq l$时, the equilibrium is:

$$m(\theta)=\begin{cases} p_1, & \theta=\theta_1 \\ p_0, & \theta=\theta_0 \end{cases},\ \pi_1=1,\ \pi_0=0,\ a(p)=\begin{cases} a_1, & p=p_1 \\ a_0, & p=p_0 \end{cases}.$$

With the above separating equilibria, we conclude that big traders with substantial capital tend to choose high price levels, whereas a small amount of capital comes with low price levels although the premise of equilibrium differs. However, substantial capital has a greater impact on market price but does not guarantee a positive correlation between the amount of capital and the price. This is so because big traders may not offer a high temporary price when choosing pricing strategy because they may focus on maximizing the long-term benefits. The aim of a high price in the model is to show that big traders could obtain more profits with a significant amount of capital.

b When the result is a pooling equilibrium.

The scenarios for a pooling equilibrium do not reveal the direct effects of the quantity of capital owned by manipulators on the pricing strategy. However, we particularly emphasize the implication of pricing behavior and economic rationality.

To be more specific: (1) When $c \le p_1 - p_0$, $\alpha > \dfrac{p_1 - l}{h - l}$, $p_0 < h$, $h > p_1 > l$, the pooling equilibrium is: $m(\theta) \equiv p_1$, $\pi_1 = \alpha$, $\pi_0 > \dfrac{p_0 - l}{h - l}$, $a(p) \equiv a_1$. Explanations are as follows: $\pi_1 = \alpha > \dfrac{p_1 - l}{h - l}$ shows that in the case of p_1, medium and small traders tend to make the inference that big traders are "strong market makers" and $h > p_1$. As a result, medium and small traders will decide to buy in. Besides, $c \le p_1 - p_0$, that is to say, in the case of "weak market makers" the cost of pulling up prices is less than the expected profits. Under such circumstance, the optimal choice of big traders is always the high price level in order to obtain more profits.

2 When $\alpha \le \dfrac{p_0 - l}{h - l}$, $p_0 \ge l$, $p_1 \ge l$, the pooling equilibrium is: $m(\theta) \equiv p_0$, $\pi_0 = \alpha$, $0 \le \pi_1 \le \dfrac{p_1 - l}{h - l}$, $a(p) \equiv a_0$. Explanations are as follows: $\pi_0 = \alpha \le \dfrac{p_0 - l}{h - l}$ and $0 \le \pi_1 \le \dfrac{p_1 - l}{h - l}$ show that medium and small traders tend to make the inference that big traders are "weak market makers" and $p_0 \ge l$, $p_1 \ge l$. Consequently, medium and small traders will always choose not buying in. In this situation, the optimal choice of big traders is always to price at a low level so as to avoid paying more cost for pulling up the price.

3 When $\alpha > \dfrac{p_0 - l}{h - l}$, $p_0 < h$, $p_1 \ge l$, the pooling equilibrium is: $m(\theta) \equiv p_0$, $\pi_0 = \alpha$, $0 \le \pi_1 \le \dfrac{p_1 - l}{h - l}$, $a_\pi(p) = \begin{cases} a_1, & p = p_0 \\ a_0, & p = p_1 \end{cases}$. Explanations are as follows: $\pi_0 = \alpha > \dfrac{p_0 - l}{h - l}$ shows that medium and small traders tend to make the inference that big traders are "strong market makers" if facing a low price[34] and $p_0 < h$. In this scenario, the medium and small traders will choose to buy in. However, $0 \le \pi_1 \le \dfrac{p_1 - l}{h - l}$, which implies that the medium and small traders will make the inference that the big traders are "weak market makers" when facing a higher price level,

and $p_1 \geq l$. Under this circumstance, the medium and small traders will choose not to buy in. In a word, the optimal choice of big traders always set price at low levels to ensure the profit.

4   When $c \leq p_1 < h$, $\alpha > \dfrac{p_1 - l}{h - l}$, $p_0 \geq l$, the pooling equilibrium is:

$$m(\theta) \equiv p_1, \quad \pi_1 = \alpha, \quad 0 \leq \pi_0 \leq \dfrac{p_0 - l}{h - l}, \quad a(p) = \begin{cases} a_1, & p = p_1 \\ a_0, & p = p_0 \end{cases}. \text{ The expla-}$$

nations are as follows: $\pi_1 = \alpha > \dfrac{p_1 - l}{h - l}$ shows that the medium and small traders tend to make the inference that the big traders are strong market makers when facing a high price level, and $p_1 < h$. In this case, the medium and small traders will choose to buy in. However, $0 \leq \pi_0 \leq \dfrac{p_0 - l}{h - l}$ shows that the medium and small traders tend to make the inference that the big traders are "weak market makers" when facing a low price level, and $p_0 \geq l$. In this case, they will choose not to buy in. Thus, the optimal choice of big traders is always pricing at a high level.

In summary, big traders use pricing decisions to maximize profit while medium and small traders speculate on the strength of big traders after observing their prices to obtain profits as free riders. Each party chooses its own optimal action based on the assumptions of their rival's actions. The equilibrium illustrates two points. First, although the market price can be affected by big traders, big traders are also restrained by the amount of capital in hand. In other words, the more capital they have, the easier it is for them to attain their target prices. Obviously, this statement can be applied to the scenario whereby the smaller the difference in resource endowments between traders (similar to the concept of intense competition in goods markets), the closer the market price is to the price of perfect competition. Second, small and medium traders have the right to choose to participate in trading or to exit the market in a vote-by-foot fashion. Consequently, big traders must consider factors such as the market expectations of medium and small traders and the market atmosphere when setting prices. That is, big traders must collect all information.

The influence of asymmetric information on prices

In this section, by analyzing the trader's investment behavior under information asymmetry, we develop a simple mathematical model of excess profits obtained through information superiority to confirm the effect of the trader's information asymmetry on securities prices.

Notation

(1) The given information is true and good news.[35] It occurs at time 0 and is announced at time t. $p(\tau)$ and $p^e(\tau)$ are the securities price and the expected price at $\tau \in [0, t]$, respectively; (2) the initial price of securities is normalized

to be $0;^{36}$ moreover, under this information, the expected price in is p; (3) let $x(\tau)$ be the number of traders who can obtain the information at time τ, and $\rho_i(\tau)$ be the degree of information concentration at time τ with $x(\tau)$ and $\rho_i(\tau)$ being negatively correlated.

Modeling and analysis

The model concept is that the earlier the traders obtain information, the more opportunity the investors have for arbitrage. Once the information is announced, all the market participants will receive the information. According to the above assumptions, investors will have the same expectation for the securities price. At this time, the price will go up rapidly to p, and the trader will not gain any benefit from this information. The detailed analysis is as follows:

The first step is to specify demand and supply functions. According to the rational expectation model of Grossman and Stiglitz (1980), under the assumption that investors are subjectively rational, it can be derived that the volume of trade is a linear function of the difference between the expected and the actual market price. Therefore, assume that the functions take the following forms:

The demand function, $Q_d(\tau) = \alpha_0 + \alpha_1 \left[p^e(\tau) - p(\tau) \right]$ (6.46)

The supply function, $Q_s(\tau) = \beta_0 - \beta_1 \left[p^e(\tau) - p(\tau) \right]$ (6.47)

where $\alpha_0, \alpha_1, \beta_0, \beta_1 > 0$.

The second is to analyze trader's behavior and determination of the market price. At time τ, the insider, the player who has the knowledge about the price before others, will buy in because of $p^e(\tau) - p(\tau) = p - p(\tau) > 0$. Suppose that the i-th insider will buy an amount of $\Delta s_i(\tau)$, then at time, the total impact of the good news on the demand and supply for securities is $\sum_{i=1}^{x(\tau)} \Delta s_i(\tau).^{37}$ The uninformed player will sell out because of $p^e(\tau) - p(\tau) = 0 - p(\tau) < 0$. Since the uninformed player believes that selling out will bring profits, we assume that the demand of informed player is met by the supply of the uninformed player, which means market clearing at the equilibrium of demand and supply.[38] Taking the impact into equation (6.47), notice that the expectation of the uninformed player is $P^e(\tau) = 0$, we can derive that:

$$p(\tau) = \frac{1}{\beta_1} \left[\sum_{i=1}^{x(\tau)} \Delta s_i(\tau) - \beta_0 \right]$$ (6.48)

The third is to analyze the profits. Define the arbitrage interval as $p - p(\tau)$, the insider buys in at the price of $p(\tau)$ at time τ, and sells out at the price of p at time t, and gains profits. Obviously, at time τ, the broader the arbitrage interval is and the more the insider buys in, the more profits he will obtain (or the more losses the uniformed player will incur). These are expressed as:

$$R = \int_0^t \left[p - p(\tau) \right] ds(\tau) \tag{6.49}$$

Finally, equation (6.48) embodies the transmission mechanism of information asymmetry's effect on price, which is:

Increases in $\rho_i(\tau) \Rightarrow$ Decreases in $x(\tau) \Rightarrow$ Decreases[39] in

$$\sum_{i=1}^{x(\tau)} \Delta s_i(\tau) \Rightarrow \text{Decreases in of } p(\tau) \tag{6.50}$$

Otherwise, the lower the degree of information concentration or the more balanced the information between traders, the closer the price will be towards the actual price and the lower the degree of the effect of the asymmetric information will be on price.

In summary, traders in the securities market will affect the price through the economic power that emerges from the capital and information resources they have to hand. The greater the resource advantage, the greater the possibility of obtaining more profits. In other words, resource distribution among investors results in economic power structure among the traders. The more balanced the capital and information, the more reciprocal the pricing power will be. Therefore, the lesser the likelihood that securities pricing will be manipulated and the lesser the likelihood of a higher risk premium and welfare loss for medium and small investors. Hence, the market will be more efficient. Because financial institutions and insurance companies possess enormous amounts of capital, accurate and timely information, and a professional investment analysis team, they have superiority over medium and small traders in terms of resources. Therefore, these institutions have greater influence on market securities pricing than small and medium traders. To some degree, we can consider big traders as price makers and small and medium traders as price takers who seek opportunities under unfavorable conditions.

The mathematical models in this section confirm the ideas and statements presented at the beginning of this chapter, that is, that securities pricing is essentially affected, even determined, by the quantity of resources owned by a trader. As Zhao and Zheng (2002) state, in a situation of information asymmetry, an institution can manipulate the listed company's fundamental information to affect the stock price to gain excess returns. In fact, information asymmetry between institutional investors is less severe than that between institutions and individual investors. Therefore, it is feasible to reduce market manipulation by developing institutional investors. This is what we have emphasized above. The more balanced the power structure, or resources among investors, the less likely it is that the market price will be manipulated.

Notes

1 People often refer to "microeconomics" as "price theory" for the reason.
2 The concept of trading surplus is introduced here to illustrate the gains and losses of economic agents in market transactions. The concept is analogous to that of consumer and producer surplus.
3 That is, the weak eats the strong, the survival of the fittest.
4 Some literature called institutions, bankers, etc., which have similar connotations from the perspective of subjective influence on transactions.
5 This is what we call the power structure among traders.
6 Because the specific exchange rate value is affected by the supply and demand factors in the foreign exchange market.
7 Krugman, the 2008 Nobel laureate in economics, once proposed the exchange rate target zone theory, and the concept of the ideal exchange area of exchange rate is logically different. The purpose mentioned here is to show that while a country can benefit by influencing the exchange rate, it is not therefore possible to determine the optimal exact exchange rate value. More likely, all parties have their own ideal exchange rate, as long as the real exchange rate falls into this range, then its interests can be guaranteed. For the theory of the exchange rate target area can be found at: Paul R. Krugman. Target Zones and Exchange Rate Dynamics .J.
8 Or within a short period of time after the initial moment.
9 Under normal circumstances, when economic disputes between States occur, such as trade issues, even in cases of retaliation and counter-retaliation, to a much the same degree, we have not yet seen a country resort to its full counter-retaliation after minor reprisals. Because in an open economy, this is not in its own interest, especially among the major economic powers, so we assume that the degree of retaliation and counter-retaliation is basically equivalent.
10 For example, restrictions on imports will help domestic products but technology blockade will not improve a country's utility.
11 If country 2 has exchange rate requirements in stage I.
12 This is so because country 1 will improve its utility by counter-retaliation.
13 Since $p^{(2)} < p^{(1)}$ and $0 < \varepsilon < 1$, it follows that $\varepsilon\varphi(\eta)p^{(2)} - \varphi(\eta)p^{(1)} < 0$, which states that for country 2, scenario 8 results in a smaller utility change than scenario 6.
14 It depends on the strength comparison of the two parties and the value of related parameters.
15 For the convenience of analysis, this stage is discussed before stage II and III.
16 If country 1 completely satisfies country 2's request, then the game is over, just as described in scenario 5.
17 Scenarios 3 and 7 have been excluded already. In scenario 5, country 1 fully satisfies the request; hence, country 2 will not retaliate. So this scenario is not discussed here.
18 Note that this fraction has a negative value, so the larger the denominator the bigger the value of this fraction.
19 Because ε is small.
20 The analysis here is from the perspective of welfare, i.e., the goal of government or regulatory body is to gain positive total profits in economic activities.
21 That is, formal financial market coexists with informal financial market.
22 Data comes from Cheng (2006).
23 The returns here are not net profits because input costs are included. So there is the reservation utility issue.
24 It's not difficult to understand these relations, or we can say these factors obviously have the impact on setting interest rates.
25 Because when the borrower makes investment with his own funds, there will be the opportunity costs.
26 Given the assumption that the borrower is risk neutral, then he will make decisions based on the expected average returns.

27 We don't include the signs because only the cost constraints are considered here. In fact, if the project operates, the borrower has to pay for the labor and the professional managers; therefore, under the assumption of risk neutrality, the expected average returns should exceed capital costs.

28 In our country, for example, due to the low dividend, a significant number of traders buy stocks not for long periods of time in order to achieve investment returns, but to buy and sell on the secondary market to earn spreads.

29 That is, first at the low level, then pull up the price, sell at the top to make a profit.

30 Imagine that even if objective conditions are very favorable, such as the presence of a large number of irrational traders in the market, without a large amount of capital cannot achieve a high level of returns.

31 To make the analysis simple, we assume that big traders manipulate market by "pump and dump" scheme. Although the stock manipulation takes a variety of forms in real market, but our aim here is just to explain that it is the control and influence of investors for market activities that decide the transaction price. So our simplification can be justified.

32 The explanation here is that the "strong banker" has a large amount of capital and can buy a large amount of chips at a low position (the so-called "acquisition" and "washing"), so when the "strong banker" manipulates the price of securities to a higher price will not encounter greater resistance. And "weak banker" due to insufficient funds, can not get enough chips at the low level, then when the price is manipulated to a higher price, it will encounter a large number of arbitrage traders' selling orders, in order to achieve the transaction price. At the target price, large traders must passively buy chips at a price higher than the base price. Relative to the profit value calculated by the difference between the target price and the base price, this can be regarded as an additional cost. For the convenience of analysis, we may consider c here is the cost averaged to the value per share.

33 For details of the solution, please see Weisheng Yu and Zhengai Piao, "*Game Theory and Its Application in the Economic Management*" [M], Tsinghua University Press, ,2005, pp. 103–109.

34 At first glance it seems not sensible, but it makes sense if we consider the facts that there are numerous traders and everyone has his own attitude. From the perspective of game theory, there are two possibilities. One is that medium and small traders believe the strong makers pretend to be weak so as to reduce the number of followers. The other one is that the medium and small traders believe the market makers are the weak type once higher price levels are observed.

35 Even if the information is false or bad news, our analysis will not be affected and the conclusions will still hold.

36 This is for notation convenience, which doesn't affect the analysis.

37 At a particular moment, the total demand and supply include normal demand and supply plus and the shocks brought by the information. It can be imagined that the traders who could get the information in advance are the big ones, such as institutions, who possess enormous amount of capital or securities. Their strategy is always to sell or buy gradually in order to prevent reduction in returns caused by excessive short-term shocks to the demand and supply of stocks, by the excessive impacts on the market atmosphere, and by the leaking of information. Therefore, the shocks to the demand and supply at a particular moment include the operation of the traders who know the information before this moment.

38 Except for extreme cases such as a universal expectation of positive prospects for the market, demand will exceed supply because the market participants are reluctant to sell. Our objective is to illustrate that the asymmetric information may influence of market price, so we just consider the more general cases.

39 This is also related to the resource endowment of the insider, but in general, because the number of insiders is small, the total impact of supply and demand will be smaller.

7 Price determination in labor market

According to the theory of labor economics, the labor market is where labor demand and supply interact. Moreover, the labor market reflects the economic relationships of these interactions. The market is a mechanism that allocates labor resources through two-way selection reflecting both demand and supply under the effect of the value law and the competition law. The labor market embodies an exchange relationship based on the employment of individuals. The labor market is composed of workers, employers, wages, and market organizers. Through labor, these agents influence the economy. Labor is a function that creates value reflecting the utility and capability of individuals. Labor has been an indispensable factor of economies since commodity production began. With the development of social production, labor has gradually become a more scarce resource, and the scarcity is reflected in the price of labor; that is, wages. The market pricing system for labor is based on labor exchange. Studies on labor demand and supply and the determination of fair pricing compose the main focus of labor market theories.

A review of labor market theories

As with normal commodity and factor markets, the labor market is a type of exchange relationship based on price. Wages represent the price of labor, and studies on wages have been conducted throughout the entire history of labor market development. In classical economic theory, Smith (1950) first addresses the division of labor in his analysis of the nature of wages and the influencing factors of wage differentials. The author analyzes demand and supply relations and wage changes, which form the basic theory framework for labor market research. Ricardo (1891) proposes the distribution theory of wage determination and argues that wages are determined by the cost of labor reproduction. Moreover, Ricardo analyzes wage change patterns. Say (1861) establishes the law of the labor market using the price theory of production cost as a foundation. He argues that the law of value is effective for goods, factor markets, and labor markets, and the law directs demand and supply toward equilibrium automatically. The law of value eliminates fluctuations in labor prices and ultimately attains full employment. Walras (1881) suggests marginal utility and marginal analysis based on classical economic theories. Jevons (1879) uses this method to analyze personal best choice behavior in labor markets and emphasizes that wage is determined by individual marginal productivity. Walras proposes the general equilibrium theory by investigating factors and including labor, capital, land, and goods markets. Marshall (1961) develops this theory further by adding the element of entrepreneurs' management capability to three production factors and applies the equilibrium analysis to establish a full system of income distribution theory following neoclassical economics.

Neoclassical economics suggests that the price formation of labor is similar to that of ordinary commodities. Wages are determined by differences in workers' abilities and by market demand and supply. The more capable the worker, the higher the labor efficiency, or the greater the extent to which labor supply exceeds demand and the higher the wage. However, the market is assumed to be perfectly competitive in neoclassical economics, which is in sharp contrast to the reality. Furthermore, labor market analyses are based on macro aggregates, which consider individual decision-making behavior to a lesser extent. In the real market, some heterogeneity exists in terms of the value of workers and their skills, but such differences in capability are obviously asymmetric with respect to wages. Equilibrium theory struggles to explain that workers receive different payment for the same job and unemployment coexists with high wages. Therefore, some scholars study labor markets from other perspectives.

Veblen (1934) and Commons (1936) are the first to study labor markets using institutional theory. The authors maintain that the labor market is imperfectly competitive and has institutional and social barriers in the flow of information and personnel, which emphasizes the role of trade unions, large enterprises, culture, customs, and other factors in wage determination. The authors also highlight the significance of economic power in the determination, which implies that wage theory is breaking through the category of things and adding human initiative. Stigler (1961) and McCall (1970) present the search theory of incomplete information. The authors argue that the information is incomplete in labor markets, and each individual in the market searches for information to find a better job and maximize their wage. Wages are proportional to information costs. Keynes (1937) uses macroeconomic aggregate analysis to study a non-full employment problem in labor markets, breaks through the theory that market mechanisms are effective unconditionally, and proposes the theoretical view that governments should intervene in the labor market. Since the onset of economic globalization and the emergence of the knowledge economy, labor market environmental factors have changed. New factors have been added to the wage formation mechanism that scholars have studied extensively, particularly in the fields of experimental economics and game theory. Some problems are discussed in depth, such as the wage formation process, the realization of equity and efficiency goals, and the effectiveness of resource allocation in the labor market.

As the price of labor, wage is similar in nature and function to any ordinary commodity. Wages are the recognition of labor's value and the willingness to trade on both the demand and supply side. Wages reflect the macro-situation of demand and supply, such as the quantity demanded and supplied, the related changes in the market, and some micro-information on the basic attributes of labor as a commodity. For example, efficiency of labor, ability to create value, and labor substitutability. More importantly, wages are the primary mode of wealth distribution, which is the main income source for many workers. Moreover, wages are a channel for the distribution of corporate profits and wealth adjustment. The reasonableness of a wage is related to individuals' expectations but also to the impact on social stability.

From the perspective of economic equity, a reasonable wage should be calculated based on the contribution that workers have invested in value creation through their efforts and realize under the competition principle of equal opportunity—the equal value exchange of the commodity of labor. Moreover, a reasonable wage should increase the incentive to work and labor efficiency by providing a fair trade. However, such a context of perfect competition does not exist in reality, and there is no auctioneer to ensure the fair distribution of interests in the market. The price mechanism of neoclassic economics does not take effect spontaneously. As a main form of interest distribution, salary formation is the result of negotiation between demand and supply. The macro price mechanism is actually the market reflection of the combined individual effect. Compared with the price formation mechanism of ordinary commodities, wage negotiation is more complicated. The result of negotiation depends on the resources owned by workers and on integrated economic power from all types of resources, which is embodied by the negotiation power of both the demand and supply side. Wages are simply the cooperative game solution attained through negotiations among firms and workers based on their resources.

According to Aoki's explanation (1984), this game solution is characterized by the power balance among the players and the internal effectiveness of firms. The power mentioned by Aoki is the economic power of negotiating participants and the influence of each individual on others based on their resources to hand. On the labor supply side, sources of power include the physical and mental capabilities of workers and the information, knowledge, and the material wealth they possess. On the labor demand side, power resources include the wages offered and a series of non-monetary resources, such as the firm's economic conditions, geographical location, management mode, development prospects, working environment, benefits, and interpersonal relationships.

Each of the resources could possibly provide realistic or long economic and non-economic benefits to the workers. The magnitude of power produced by these resources is related to their role in value creation, their scarcity, and the extent of their substitutability. The greater the role, the more scarce the resources and the more difficult to substitute; thus, the greater the power. That is, the greater the economic power of an entity, the more advantageous position it will assume in negotiations, and the more benefits it will obtain. Therefore, for the entire labor market, interest distribution is isomorphic to power; moreover, the power agent that affects interest distribution is not exogenous. Instead, the power agent is part of the market mechanism. Wages are the outcome of the strategy interactions among all players in the game.

Discussions on the distribution of firm benefits from the perspective of power have a long history in economic theory. Hobbes (1998) argues power is the current means to gain any obvious future benefits. Weber (2009) states power means that even if a person or persons are confronted with resistance from peers in their social activities, they will still have chances to realize the intended goals. Coase (2012) notes that frequent internal transactions in a firm are not controlled by price mechanisms but by power. However, power resources cover a wide range of sources, all of which have their respective attributes and lack references. Additionally, the effectiveness of exercising power, or the magnitude of negotiation power, is related to the quantity of resources possessed by the participants and the determination and will of the negotiators. When one party in the game is more willing to face public conflicts in the negotiation, the other party may be likely to make concessions (Aoki, Greif & Milgrom, 1984). Obviously, man's will is invisible. It is hard to measure and define the magnitude of power derived from will, which makes a discussion on the issue of distributing firm's interests and wage formation from the perspective of power difficult. Therefore, although, in theory, scholars have already recognized the importance of power, the analysis on the effect of power has been limited to only a description. In recent years, with the development of game theory, some scholars have attempted to explain how power affects both the employer and labor in games. The corresponding models have been established, which makes the analysis based on power an economic research paradigm. According to the main resources invested in value creation, we divide the labor market into three components—the ordinary labor market, the high-skilled labor market, and the executive labor market—and discuss the game process of wage formation from the perspective of power.

The ordinary labor market

The ordinary labor market is composed of ordinary workers who supply physical and mental skills. Therefore, the quantity of ordinary labor accounts for the majority of the total market. Studies on this market have been conducted in great depth and for a long time. In terms of resource formation, the requirement to form the physical and mental resources of ordinary labor is relatively low. As long as the existence of potential resource owners is guaranteed and certain social connections are provided, labor resources will form as individuals mature to a certain age. The formation of labor capability cannot be adjusted even through individual will. Put simply, individuals cannot refuse to grow up. Therefore, the formation of labor resources has certain natural attributes. Once they have acquired the capacity to work, individuals make a living by providing labor and participating in value creation for society. This is the law of social development and the fundamental reason that ordinary labor resources prevail.

Due to the sufficient supply of ordinary labor, the basic assumption in neoclassic economic theories is that ordinary labor markets are in perfect competition, which emphasizes the role of market mechanisms and market factors in determining wage levels and allocating labor resources. Although the theory concedes that labor markets have their own particular properties, such properties are still affected and strictly controlled by market competition. Moreover, the equilibrium analysis of commodity prices is still applicable to labor markets. Consequently, neoclassic economic theory maintains that it is the demand-supply relation of labor markets that determines the price of ordinary labor as a commodity. However, this does not happen in reality. Each worker is an individual capable of independent decisions. The labor resource that each individual relies on has a certain degree of homogeneity, but individuals cannot replace one another freely. Although a worker's cooperation with a firm is affected by the market supply of labor, the final decision to work is made by that worker. In the meantime, the resources that negotiations rely on include the physical condition of workers and the information, wealth, and other resources the worker has to hand. Labor contract agreements rely on all the resources owned by workers and the results of negotiations with capital owners. The negotiation process is based on power.

Ordinary labor wage determination

The premise of a labor market is that each worker is free and able to make rational decisions. Labor contracts are agreed upon through negotiations between employers and workers. Nash (1950) analyzes negotiation results from the perspective of utility and obtains the final Nash equilibrium solution. However, his research is also based on some premises. First, the result must be Pareto optimal. Second, if the interactions stipulated in the game are symmetrical, the payments should be the same for each player. Third, the negotiation result will not change with the linear transformation of the utility function of each party. Fourth, if the negotiation set changes but the preceding Nash result is still feasible and the reserved payoff remains the same, the negotiation result should remain unchanged.

Under such premises, we assume that the employer and workers reach an agreement and create the value equal to 1. Then, the wage of workers depends on the result of negotiations on the value distribution. If worker L obtains the share of x ($0 < x < 1$), firm F will obtain the share of $(1-x)$. Under this distribution structure, they will get the utility $v(x)$ and $V(1-x)$, respectively. The optimal distribution result that satisfies the above assumptions is that the multiple of the utility of the two parties, ω, is maximized, that is, $\omega = v(x)V(1-x)$, under Nash equilibrium. According to first-order conditions of maximization, it can be derived that:

$$\frac{v'(x)}{v(x)} = \frac{V'(1-x)}{V(1-x)} \tag{7.1}$$

Equation (7.1) shows that, if the two parties have the same utility function, they will share the created value equally. Otherwise, the party with more diminishing marginal utility will obtain smaller share.

However, the utility is just the negotiation participant's subjective psychological state when comparing their actual income with their expected income. Utility is a theoretical analysis on the distribution result, but it neglects the negotiation process. If there is a significant difference in resources belonging to the two parties in a negotiation, the judgment standards will also differ. The poor may obtain higher utility since little wealth can bring them satisfaction. On the other hand, the wealth must obtain more benefits to reach satisfaction. Therefore, the same utility level may come from different levels of interest distribution. Meanwhile, the two parties do not know the interest distribution result until the negotiation on wage reaches agreement. Hence, in the negotiation process, both parties do not know the distribution scheme for certain and only have an expectation for the negotiation results. Therefore, studies on wages based on utility lack a theoretical foundation. In fact, wages are the final result of negotiation between employers and workers. The negotiation process is composed of multiple rounds of bargains based on the negotiating power of each party. The magnitude of negotiating power is based on the resources owned by each party and is the extrinsic manifestation of the economic power of the negotiators. Consequently, discussing wage formation from the perspective of power is closer to social reality.

Assume that $P(Q, k)$ is the contract agreed upon as the result of firm F's negotiation with worker L. Q is the output of F with its value equal to $S(Q)$, and k worker's payoff. $S(Q)$ is a strictly increasing concave function of Q. F maximizes the surplus value, $V(Q, k) = S(Q) - k$, while L maximizes interests, $U(Q, k) = k - C(Q)$, where $C(Q)$ is total labor input of the worker for the output level of Q and is a strictly increasing convex function. According to the Nash bargaining theory, contract $P(Q, k)$ should make the Nash multiplication maximized, that is:

$$MaxN = (S(Q) - k)^\tau (k - C(Q))^{1-\tau} \tag{7.2}$$

where $S(Q) - k > 0, k - C(Q) > 0$, τ and $1-\tau$ represent the bargaining power of F and L respectively, that is, their economic power. From the first-order condition, $\frac{\partial N}{\partial Q} = 0, \frac{\partial N}{\partial k} = 0$, it follows that

$$\tau S(Q)(k-C(Q))=(1-\tau)C(Q)(S(Q)-k)$$
$$\tau(k-C(Q))=(1-\tau)(S(Q)-k)$$

Further calculation gives

$$k=(1-\tau)S(Q)+\tau C(Q)$$

If it is to maximize social welfare, $W=V(Q, k)+U(Q, k)=S(Q)-C(Q)$, then the difference in interest distribution between the firm and the worker is:

$$\delta(Q, k)=V(Q, k)-U(Q, k)=S(Q)+C(Q)-2k$$

It could be derived that: $\qquad \delta(Q, k)=(2\tau-1)W \qquad$ (7.3)

From equation (7.3), it can be seen that, when $\tau=1/2$, that is, the power of the firm equals that of the worker, interests are equally distributed. Here it could be concluded that power plays a key role in distributing the interests in production process.

However, the above argument does not consider bargaining costs and insists that negotiations never fail. In fact, negotiation delays do have costs. Both parties in the negotiation use their negotiating power to obtain more benefits adding to the other party's costs. At the same time, negotiations are often unable to reach agreement. Based on the Rubinstein model, Bowles (2009) assumes that both parties have reserved payoffs and analyzes the interest distribution problem. This model assumes that firm F and ordinary worker L share the newly created value of 1. V and v are the income of the firm and the worker, respectively. Z and z are the reserved payoffs of F and L when the negotiation fails; that is, the opportunity benefits. δ_F and δ_L are the time discount factors of the firm and the worker. If the firm bids first, the share of the newly created value of each party is given by

$$V=\frac{(1-\delta_L)(1-z)}{1-\delta_F\delta_L}+\frac{Z\delta_L(1-\delta_F)}{1-\delta_F\delta_L} \qquad (7.4)$$

$$v=1-V=\frac{(1-\delta_F)\delta_L(1-Z)}{1-\delta_F\delta_L}+\frac{z(1-\delta_L)}{1-\delta_F\delta_L} \qquad (7.5)$$

If exit costs are ignored, that is, assume $Z = z = 0$, (7.4) and (7.5) could be simplified to the Rubinstein's game model:

$$V=\frac{1-\delta_L}{1-\delta_F\delta_L} \qquad (7.6)$$

$$v=\frac{\delta_L(1-\delta_F)}{1-\delta_F\delta_L} \qquad (7.7)$$

Equations (7.4) and (7.5) show that the sequence of actions, discount factors, the reserved payoffs when negotiation fails, and the negotiation time of each round are all crucial factors affecting the final results. For the action sequence, whoever takes the first move will gain an advantage. The party that sets the final allocation scheme will realize more favorable benefits. The size of the advantage depends on the length of the negotiations. The time preference of any party will reduce its benefit. That is, if one party has infinite patience during the negotiation, that party will obtain more benefits, and the final result will be in accordance with their strategy. Moreover, the extent of the party's patience depends on their discount rate. The larger the discount rate, the greater the costs of delay. If the negotiation lasts too long, the costs will also increase. Hence, the party will prefer the current period and become less patient. All of the above lead to an unfavorable position. Additionally, the size of the reserved payoffs affects the interest allocations. Negotiation failure has less influence on the party with a high reserve payoff, and their opponent will transfer some interests to facilitate the negotiation. This shows that the greater the reserved payoffs, the more interests will be gained in the negotiation.

The analysis on the negotiation results show the role played by each party's resources in the negotiation and the primary cause of wage differences in the ordinary labor market. Based on negotiation cost and time preferences, we assume that capital-intensive or large-scale firms gain more capital input, C_F, at the beginning stage of production. If the discount rate (δ_F) is positive and the discount loss within the negotiation period T is $C_F\delta_F T$, when the capital and discount rate are fixed, the loss will increase as the period lengthens. If the agreement cannot be reached soon, or if the negotiation fails, the firm will incur significant loss. Therefore, generally, capital-intensive or large firms have longer time preferences and are willing to pay higher wages to attract qualified workers and to shorten the negotiation process. The wages of capital-intensive or large firms are typically higher than those of labor-intensive or small firms. From the perspective of worker's negotiation costs, if a worker's existing survival material is V_L, and the quantity of consumption per time unit is c_L, the negotiation time the worker can accept is $T_L=V_L/c_L$. The time depends on the worker's current wealth. When the worker has no resources at all, negotiation failure will affect their wage and survival. Consequently, negotiation patience does not depend on psychological preference but the quantity of survival resources. The worker with few survival resources will have less persistence in negotiation and less negotiating power. On the contrary, if the worker owns more survival resources and is in no hurry to reach agreement, the worker will seize the initiative in the negotiation process.

Considering social reality, the workers with fewer survival resources, such as migrant workers from rural areas and laid-off urban workers, have no ability to negotiate with firms because they lack material resources and the corresponding national social security. Therefore, such workers must accept lower wages proposed by firms. In ordinary labor markets, when workers have similar physical strength and mental capabilities, the current resources the workers have to hand become the most important determinant of wages. Those who lack resources have less negotiating power and have to accept lower market wages. Although demand and supply are in equilibrium overall in the labor market, the difference in wealth resources among individuals could lead to different results from wage negotiations. If there are no third-party restraints, the "Matthew effect" of wage distribution will be widespread in the ordinary labor market. In this case, the dual structure of wages will emerge eventually and persist in reality with a corresponding dual structure of resource allocation. When an ordinary worker possesses personal wealth and has no sense of crisis with respect to income, that worker's negotiating power increases correspondingly and they will request higher wages in negotiations. When actual wages cannot meet the expected levels, the worker would rather forgo the work than accept a lower wage. This negotiating power is the reason for the recent serious labor shortages in the developed coastal areas of China where ordinary workers have experienced low growth in wages.

The influence of collective wage negotiation by unions

The pursuit of own interests by agents emphasizes the social contradiction that characterizes conflicts between employers and workers. Although every worker can reach an agreement on labor with a firm based on their abilities and to obtain some return, individual workers are typically at a disadvantage because the labor resources on which ordinary laborers depend are strongly substitutable, and every worker has fewer resources than a firm. However, this imbalance of power can be changed to improve the benefits for workers by collective negotiation. Collective negotiation is the foundation of a labor union. From an economics perspective, the union is the outcome of labor relations, and its function is to adjust labor demand and supply through collective negotiations on the price of labor. In economics, union influence on price formation is analyzed based on the following assumption: union members have common interests and goals, and there is no conflict between collective action and individual goals. The goal of the union is to secure maximum payments and employment for members. The trade-off between payment and employment depends on the internal organization and the workers' preferences. Under this assumption, if the union understands the labor needs of the firm, and the firm retains the rights to hire and fire, the "right to management model" (Nickell & Andrews, 1983) and the "efficiency model" (McDonald & Solow, 1981) of collective negotiation with union participation reflect the effects of unions.

Right to management model

This model describes the situation that the firm decides the payment through negotiation with the labor union, as well as the amount of employment according to the payment. Suppose that there are N members in the union, and the members are homogenous. The union aims to maximize the total expected utilities of all members. The labor demand of firm, L, is less than the number of members in the union, N. In the decision of employment, the firm chooses the workers randomly. When it pays the wage of ω, the utility of the workers is $u(\omega)$. And the workers are all risk averse $(u' > 0, u'' < 0)$. $\bar{\omega}$ is the reserved wage, that is, the income level of the unemployed, such as unemployment insurance and government unemployment benefits. Assume the employment probability of any worker is $l = L / N$, then the expected utility function of the worker can be written as

$$U = lu(\omega) + (1-l)u(\bar{\omega}) \tag{7.8}$$

The aim of the firm is still profit maximization. When the payment is fixed, the profit function is $\Pi = R(L) - \omega L$, where R is the general income function of the firm $(R' > 0, R'' < 0)$. ωL is the labor cost. Profit maximization determines the labor demand, which is

$$L^d(\omega) = R'^{-1}(\omega)$$

Furthermore, suppose that the profit of the firm will be 0 if the negotiation fails. The members of the union obtain the unemployed utility level. If the negotiation ability of the union is denoted by τ $(0 < \tau < 1)$, the solution to the negotiation should be given by the following programming.

$$\Phi = \text{Max}[\Pi(\omega)]^{1-\tau}\left\{L^d(\omega)\left[u(\omega) - u(\bar{\omega})\right]\right\}^{\tau} \tag{7.9}$$
$$s.t. \ L^d(\omega) < N, \ \omega > \bar{\omega}$$

where $\Pi(\omega) \equiv R\left[L^d(\omega)\right] - \omega L^d(\omega)$. In the case of interior solution, according to the first-order conditions of maximum, it follows that,

$$\Phi' = \frac{\tau}{L^d(\omega)}\frac{dL^d(\omega)}{d\omega} + \frac{\tau u'(\omega)}{u(\omega) - u(\bar{\omega})} + \frac{(1-\tau)}{\Pi(\omega)}\frac{d\Pi(\omega)}{d\omega} = 0 \tag{7.10}$$

Suppose that $\varepsilon_\omega^L = -(\omega/L)(dL/d\omega)$ stands for the absolute elasticity of wage with respect to employment and $\varepsilon_\omega^\pi = -(\omega/\Pi)(d\Pi/d\omega)$ does for that of wage with respect to the profit. Generally, the two values depend on the payment of ω. The first-order condition can be written as

$$\Phi'(\omega, \bar{\omega}, \tau) \equiv -\tau\varepsilon_\omega^L - (1-\tau)\varepsilon_\omega^\pi + \frac{\tau\omega u'(\omega)}{u(\omega) - u(\bar{\omega})} = 0 \tag{7.11}$$

When $\Phi''_\omega < 0$, the second-order condition is satisfied. Besides, there is $\partial\omega/\partial x = -\Phi''_x/\Phi''_\omega$ for any exogenous variable x that affects the payment. Therefore, the sign of $\partial\omega/\partial x$ is same with the sign of Φ''_x because

$$\Phi''_\tau = -\varepsilon_\omega^L + \varepsilon_\omega^\pi + \frac{\omega u'(\omega)}{u(\omega) - u(\bar{\omega})} = \frac{\varepsilon_\omega^\pi}{\tau} > 0 \tag{7.12}$$

According to (7.12), the payment is an increasing function of the bargaining power of the union. The marginal product of labor equals to the payment. Employment decreases as τ increases dramatically. This implies that the increase in the power of the union improves the income of its members; however, it does not improve employment. Similarly, the payment is an increasing function of the income of the unemployed workers. If workers have other alternative jobs, their barging power will be stronger. If the social unemployment benefits or insurance is viewed as the income of the unemployed workers, the barging power will also be improved by a sound system of social welfare, which will improve the labor income of the whole society.

According to (7.11), it follows,

$$\frac{u(\omega)-u(\varpi)}{\omega u'(\omega)} = \frac{\tau}{\tau \varepsilon_\omega^L + (1-\tau)\varepsilon_\omega^\pi} = \mu \tag{7.13}$$

Variable μ shows the difference in utility between the employed and the unemployed members in labor union. Because $\tau > 0$, the utility of an employed member is higher than the unemployed member. Meanwhile, for the optimum solution of bargains, the difference in utility is greater as the bargaining power strengthens. And the difference is smaller with the increasing of the labor demand and the absolute elasticity of wage with respect to profits. If $\tau = 1$, then $\mu = 1/\varepsilon_\omega^L$. At this time, the union completely decides the result of the negotiation, which means, the difference in utility between the employed and the unemployed members depends only on the labor demand and the absolute elasticity of wage. On the contrary, when the barging power of the union is 0, the result of negotiation is only determined by the firm; moreover, there is no difference between the employed and the unemployed members in terms of benefits.

The efficiency model

The right-to-management model analyzes the influence of labor unions on payments only. The model shows that the enhanced bargaining power of the union increases workers' incomes; however, it does not improve employment. Sometimes, higher worker incomes come with reduced employment. Nevertheless, the result of a collective negotiation is realized in the payment agreement and the working hours, the work environment, and employment. If there are many components to the negotiation, enhanced bargaining power may be advantageous. Additionally, the efficiency model assumes that the members are homogeneous. In fact, labor unions are composed of members with different efficiencies. If the difference in efficiency is considered, and both payment and employment are facets of the negotiation, the result will differ from the model. The new model to solve will be then,

$$Max[R(L)-\omega L]^{1-\tau}[u(\omega)-u(\varpi)]^\tau L^\tau \tag{7.14}$$
$$s.t. \quad 0 \le L \le N, \, \omega \ge \varpi$$

The first-order conditions can be obtained by taking derivatives of (7.14) with respect to L and ω, respectively, according to the Nash criterion.

$$(1-\tau)\frac{R'(L)-\omega}{R(L)-\omega L}+\frac{\tau}{L}=0 \tag{7.15}$$

$$-(1-\tau)\frac{L}{R(L)-\omega L}+\tau\frac{u'(\omega)}{u(\omega)-u(\varpi)}=0 \tag{7.16}$$

According to (7.15) and (7.16), it follows,

$$\omega-R'(L)=\frac{u(\omega)-u(\varpi)}{u'(\omega)}>0 \tag{7.17}$$

Equation (7.17) traces the locus of all tangency points between the profit curve and the indifference curve. On the locus, the negotiations on payment and employment make a Pareto optimal contract. Taking the derivative of the equation gives

$$\frac{d\omega}{dL}=\frac{R''(L)u'(\omega)}{u''(\omega)\,[\omega-R'(L)]} \tag{7.18}$$

If the members of a labor union are all risk averse, $u''<0$, the slope of the contract curve is positive. Under this condition, both the payment and employment increase with bargaining power. This implies that the union will use any opportunity to avoid unemployment uncertainty and to increase wages. The result of negotiation leads to excessive employment. The marginal output is then lower than the wage. Although the workers receive additional benefits, their productivity does not improve. When $u''>0$, the workers are risk takers, and employment decreases with bargaining power. When the members of a labor union are risk neutral, $u''>0$, the negotiation model of wage and employment leads to an employment level where the marginal revenue equals the reserved wage.

Whether the right to management model or the efficiency model is used, both models prove that labor unions can raise the wages of union members, and the wage effect of the union on the members stems from the influence generated from collective behavior. However, the influence of labor unions on employment is not definite. If the negotiations are only concerned with wages, negotiations will reduce overall labor demand in society while increasing members' wages. If the goals of the negotiations are extensive and include wages, employment, welfare, and redundancy fees, the negotiations will be more favorable to all of the members. If there is excess supply in the labor market, the existence of unions will effectively remove the competition among workers. For non-union workers, if the union requests wage rates that are too high, the firm could hire non-union workers instead of the union members. This option restricts the potential for union abuse and balances the power on both parties to form a relatively fair interest distribution pattern.

However, if there is a labor shortage in the market, or there is a high level of unionization, a monopoly on labor supply will emerge giving greater negotiating power to the unions. Thus, striking becomes the major means of negotiating power. In the models above, a strike is a threat that never occurs. Both parties can still attain an outcome without experiencing a real strike. Ultimately, the two parties could reach an equilibrium strategy of interest distribution. When the two parties cannot use negotiation to solve the wage problem, striking becomes a credible threat. Strikes are never optimal because both parties incur losses. Additionally, strikes prevent workers from receiving wages, and the firm loses the ability to create value while bearing the interest cost of investment. For the labor union, its potential income loss is borne by the members, but the loss per worker is much less than that of the firm. Therefore, strikes have a greater impact on the firm. If the union threatens to strike and the firm cannot hire substitute workers at that time, the union will dominate the negotiations with significant potential benefits at the cost of the firm. This could result in final wage levels that exceed the actual contribution of workers. Then, the firm's interests cannot be secured. Therefore, in a market with a labor shortage, if the level of unionization is relatively high, how to restrain the union from abusing its power should be the concern of institution designers. The theoretical derivation confirms the role of the power mechanism in the determination of labor market prices, and real-world examples also verify our analysis results.

The experience of China Fuyao Glass Industry Group Company, Ltd. in its efforts to invest in and establish factories in the United States fully reflects the role of power in the process of profit distribution. In May 2014, China Fuyao Group invested and set up a factory in the United States. When the factory was operational, the American Automobile Workers Union (UAW) attempted to establish a branch in the factory. The UAW stimulated significant publicity, visited workers' families, encouraged local celebrities to write open letters, rallied outside the factory to lobby workers, collected employee signatures of those who agreed to form a union, and promised Fuyao's workers that joining unions allowed workers more favorable contracts with enterprises and rendered them less vulnerable to factory lay-offs. If employees had a factory dispute, they could negotiate with the company regarding their complaint with the Chinese company's management.

The establishment of a union would naturally increase the power of union members and the potential for benefits in the competition between the employer and employees. Additionally, the UAW had a hidden motive to expand its influence and increase membership income. The investor enterprise, on the other hand, was naturally reluctant to recognize the establishment of an American-style union organization within its own organization. Although the number of UAW members has dropped from more than 1.5 million to more than 500,000 today, it remains a powerful force in the games of interest played with enterprises. Once UAW branches are established within an enterprise, the future management of employees and the formulation of corporate wage policies are constrained. To this end, Fuyao Group first negotiated with UAW and agreed to pay US$700,000 in exchange for a suspension of its activities in the enterprise. The payment was a compromise and an effort to avert additional competition from the union by transferring benefits in the form of capital to the workers. However, the UAW did not cease lobbying activities, and Fuyao Group was forced to fight back.

The focus of competition between Fuyao and UAW was winning worker support. In the three-party game, all parties have certain power resources. UAW has a geographical and image advantage and strong bargaining power due to its large membership. The advertised concept is also the main reason that the UAW attracted workers, that is, to seek greater benefits for members through the power of the union. The union claims that its creation produces a more reasonable distribution mechanism and employees have increased moral and motivation, which eases the psychological burden of employees that join the union. Fuyao Group still held the capital advantage. However, the company hired a "labor consultant" at a high salary to disrupt the union's organizational activities in the factory. At the same time, the company increased the hourly wage of each worker by two dollars. During working hours, the company made reasonable use of US laws and broadcast anti-union promotional videos to workers, allowed managers to conduct individual talks with workers, and conducted ideological sessions for employees. Staff became confused, and there were some suggestive threats that workers would be fired if they supported the union.

Although workers are dismissed for no reason, workers can claim their rights through legal channels. However, legal proceedings typically take a long time. It is difficult for American workers to bear the cost of legal proceedings. The Rubinstein game model confirms that whoever persists in the game for a long time can obtain more benefits, so companies that pursue lawsuits obviously have an advantage. In the Fuyao Group case, the investor also explicitly told employees that once the company had formed a union, the investor could decide to withdraw its capital and the workers could lose their jobs. This was a severe and credible threat. For American workers who have been unemployed for a long time, this is the last thing they want to see. Therefore, although American workers who find themselves at odds with the employers and the unions appear to be vulnerable groups, their choices will determine the outcome of the game between the enterprise and the union.

In this contest of power, enterprises and unions also have some weaknesses. The weakness of the company in the Fuyao Group case is that Chinese management concepts and methods are unacceptable to American workers. For example, when there are too many orders, workers are required to work overtime, and employees are not given reasonable overtime compensation in accordance with legal regulations. There are major safety risks in working procedures and methods. Enterprises lack clear reward and punishment mechanisms, experience labor disputes, and employees have no way to sue. Thus, American employees considered the power distribution in the enterprise's hierarchical structure unreasonable, and that employees lack sufficient power. In particular, Fuyao Group invested in the United States, and the local government provided tens of millions of dollars in subsidies. Enterprises cannot say that they will withdraw their capital, which has become an important component of union lobbying.

However, the UAW has its own problems. Workers must pay membership dues to join the union. The higher the worker's income, the higher the membership dues. The power obtained by joining the union is costly, yet it is unknown whether the power obtained can bring stable benefits. The scandal of the UAW's high-level corruption became the breakthrough for the company's opposition to the union. The company has repeatedly emphasized to employees that the union depends on membership fees to survive. In the United States, with sound laws and regulations, labor disputes do not require the participation of labor unions and can be resolved by law.

At the same time, the company used the profits to fund a series of activities to build a corporate culture and increase employees' sense of belonging, such as providing free meals for outstanding employees, organizing employee appreciation activities, giving gifts to veterans, hosting sports games, initiating a networking event for employees and friends, and increasing hourly wages for two consecutive years. Employees developed positive expectations, and there was less psychological distance between employees and corporate managers.

In November 2017, more than 1,500 employees of the entire factory participated in a vote on whether to form a union. The final result was 441 votes in favor, 868 votes against, and 186 votes in dispute, but this did not affect the final result. The vote meant that the union turmoil had come to an end. Although the enterprise had the upper hand in this game of power, more than 400 votes in favor also indicated that the union still had the support of some employees. At the same time, the expansion of capital and the pursuit of cost and efficiency did not result in conflict between labor and management. New conflicts will occur among the three parties in the future, and the parties will still face new choices.

The highly skilled labor market

The formation of a highly skilled labor market

The subjects in the highly skilled labor market are individuals with professional knowledge and skills and who use those resources as major input factors in creating value. The objects in the highly skilled labor market are innovative high-tech firms. The emergence of this market is the outcome of technology development in society. Society has realized the value of technology. For example, Say (1836) notes that man's techniques and capabilities can improve production efficiency, but such capability is costly to acquire. Marshall (1961) believes that wisdom and capability are important production factors and the driving force for productivity improvement. Moreover, the requirement for capabilities will be higher with the development of production. However, in economics circles, studies on the skilled labor market received attention only after the rapid development of technology had a substantial impact on contemporary society. Some scholars note that economic development has already exceeded the growth of physical capital, and the traditional view of economics, the capital homogeneity assumption, can no longer explain the mystery of economic growth.

In the 1950s, Solow (1957), as the representative of economists, measures "growth residuals," which cannot be explained by the traditional theory of capital determination using the statistical data from 1909 to 1949. The results show that the contribution rate of technical progress to the economic growth rate is 87.5%. This implies that without increasing production inputs, technical progress changes the production function to realize the long-term balanced growth of an economy. Although Solow proves the effect of technical progress on economic growth, any application of technology cannot be separated from human participation. Whether it is the manufacturing of equipment or the operation of such equipment that can improve production efficiency, technical talent that masters unique skills are particularly in demand.

Based on previous studies, Schultz (1961) combines economic development with the role of individuals and studies the return rate on educational investment and the contribution of education to economic growth. The conclusion shows that labor is the most important among all resources, and those individuals with knowledge and skills are the determinants of economic growth. Schultz establishes human capital theory and suggests the concept of human capital. Furthermore, he argues that human capital is the resource owned by individuals themselves and takes the form of knowledge, skills, qualifications, experience, and working proficiency. The author also states that the formation of human capital is closely related to the input of education and that education and training are a type of investment that will generate benefits in the long run. In empirical studies on the rapid recovery and development of Western European countries after World War II, Schultz shows that it is more important to increase the investment in human capital than physical capital for economic growth from the macro perspective. For the same time period, Becker (1962) analyzes human capital from the micro perspective. The author gives a full explanation of the nature of human capital and its corresponding investment behavior by combining human capital with income distribution.

In the 1980s, Romer and Lucas (1988) suggest the endogenous economic growth theory based on knowledge and the high-and-new technology contribution to the economy. The authors take human capital as the endogenous variable that would affect economic development and hold that knowledge and technique, as human capital, are the most important factors, and the returns are higher than those of physical capital. Furthermore, investment in knowledge capital is a key factor of economic growth. Lack of human capital is a major cause of economic underdevelopment of a country or region. Sveiby (1997) extends the above theories. He accurately defines the skills and knowledge of employees as knowledge capital, and recognizes this capital as a type of intangible asset of any firm or organization and a core competence of a firm.

From the demand side perspective, highly skilled individuals play an important role in production and even become the dominant factor of commodity production. Particularly since the 1980s and the emergence of the knowledge economy, significant changes have occurred with respect to new materials and technology, and numerous high and new technology firms have promoted the development of the global economy. Without doubt, highly skilled talent has played a prominent role. Compared with ordinary workers, the work of skilled labor is characterized as intellectual, complex, creative, exploratory, independent, and continuous in nature. Knowledge resources have become the main production factor in the creation of value rather than physical resources. The vying for talented employees among firms causes skilled workers to request higher wages. Currently, it is less efficient to attract talent purely by increasing wages and welfare. Offering ownership shares of a technology firm or holding the claims on a firm's surplus are common strategies used to motivate highly skilled personnel.

Characteristics of a highly skilled labor market

As with the labor resources of ordinary workers, the accumulation of knowledge and techniques takes time. However, the labor resources of skilled workers have their own unique characteristics.

1   Scarcity. Knowledge and technique are not innate. On the contrary, these traits are acquired through continuous study. The process is not easy, and becoming a highly skilled employee requires certain characteristics, education investment, and a long period of learning. The development of such resources also requires the willingness of the individual, persistence, and perseverance. Not everyone can develop such characteristics. Meanwhile, time is limited, and capital stock does not have long-term cumulative properties. Therefore, those who can master substantial knowledge and skills account for only a small proportion of the total population, which implies that highly skilled individuals are scarce market resources.

2   Individual ownership. Individuals are the natural carriers of knowledge and skills. Knowledge and skills cannot play their roles without carriers; therefore, the ownership of knowledge and skills belongs only to workers.

Although highly skilled workers acquire knowledge and skills through study, there is a difference in the knowledge and skills that each person accumulates. The knowledge accumulated in the development process is extensive, and it is not possible for anyone to obtain all knowledge and skills. Each individual behavioral agent can only master knowledge in one area due to limited time and energy. Therefore, specialization in a specific area is the best description of highly skilled labor. Each skilled individual can only display technical expertise in a particular industry or field. Moreover, resource heterogeneity implies that it is not possible to compare different behavioral agents or for them to replace each other. Therefore, even if there are many highly skilled individuals in the market, there will not be enough competition, and a monopoly will be the inevitable consequence due to differences in resources.

3   Implicitness. Skilled labor differs from physical resources because it is intangible. In the market, only the effects of resource owners' behavior can be observed, but the quantity of and difference among the owners cannot be judged by observation. The implicitness of skilled labor resource creates blind spots when the demand side evaluates the resource. If they cannot prove the quality and quantity of the resources to hand, owners are unlikely to be acknowledged by their employers. Although educational level is often used as justification of a person's capability, this method is subjective. Therefore, individuals who recently attained degrees cannot receive higher wages nor share the surplus of a firm. Only through experience can the ability to efficiently create value be proved.

4   Cumulative in nature. The production and consumption of physical resources are two separate processes and both cause resources to decrease over time. However, the resource of highly skilled labor does not follow this pattern since the production and consumption of such resources are combined. Over time, the quantity of the resource is increasing as experience accumulates. For this reason, labor resources are continuously growing in the production process along with the corresponding power.

5   Difficult to measure. Skills and techniques cannot be separated from the production process. However, due to the characteristics of highly skilled labor, it is difficult to calculate to what extent labor affects production. The measurement of the contribution of highly skilled labor to production has always been a challenge for economic studies, and employers and workers cannot reach agreement on the contributions. Consequently, there is room for negotiation on the interest distribution between the two parties.

Human-capitalization of skills and its effects

Compared with ordinary labor, highly skilled individuals have a higher wage level and may also become directly involved in the distribution of corporate profits. Highly skilled workers may hold shares, with technology being the investment that forms skilled human capital and creates significantly higher income for highly skilled personnel compared to ordinary workers. Many scholars discuss the phenomenon from an investment point of view, such as Schultz's and Becker's human capital investment theory. The theory states that investment in human capital is the same as investment in physical capital and represents actual investment behavior. Investment in human capital has the general properties of investment, but the object of investment is no longer a subject but human. According to the theory, in the knowledge and technology accumulation process, knowledge acquirers pay higher input costs, so their returns should be higher than ordinary workers. The high yields are the long-term returns. Individual and household income distribution gaps in the market are mainly caused by the unfair gap in human capital investment. Fair investment in human capital can effectively reduce the imbalance of individual income in society. Increased investment in human capital can also change the ownership of factors and cause the owner of physical capital to have fewer benefits to promote the equalization of social distribution.

The formation of skilled human capital is dependent on monetary capital investment. Income analysis on the highly skilled labor market from the perspective of investment and returns verifies at the macro level that a higher level of human capital investment can bring higher incomes. At the micro level, however, there are still problems that are difficult to explain using investment theories. For example, the same amount of monetary capital investment cannot bring the same amount of benefits. In reality, people with the same level of education may have huge differences in benefits while many with a low level of education have a higher income than those with a higher level of education. The premise of the theory is that monetary capital investment can be fully transformed into technical capital. Thus, the analysis focuses on the education time while ignoring the impact of education quality. The same investment in education due to individual differences may produce different results. The capacity of value creation may have significant differences among those with the same level of education, and the same is true for human capital investment. Such micro level differences affect the credibility of human capital investment theories; moreover, investment is more than an individual behavior. If the investor is a state or firm, how to calculate and allocate future returns is a problem.

Labor payment negotiations only consider the situation in the current period. If we consider the determination of other factor prices, the analysis of economic theories on monetary and physical capital generally do not take into account the acquisition costs of these resources and channels and only calculate the present value. Böhm-Bawerk (1890) regards monetary capital as "stored labor" or "natural force stored in labor." However, this view has never been integrated into the analytical paradigm of mainstream economics. In fact, the key factors in determining wage negotiations are still the resources that workers have to hand, including knowledge, skills, and health, plus other economic and social resources that support workers.[1] This is the micro basis for the determination of skilled labor's compensation.

In traditional economic theories, capital refers to the factor that is entitled to the claim on a firm's residuals at the cost of taking risks. However, there is no clear delimitation as to what type of factors can become capital. This depends on the degree of power that the owners of the various factors have. The residual claim of capital is the conversion of capital owners' economic power into interests. Due to the scarcity of production factors and their role in value creation, which varies at different times in the market, the definition of capital is also changing as is the residual claim of the capital owners. From land in feudal society, currency in capitalist society, and then to knowledge and skills in the era of the knowledge economy, capital structure has been gradually changing. This suggests that the allocation of firm residuals is not a fixed institution in economic and social structure. Rather, the allocation of firm residuals is the behavioral relationship that is constantly adjusting with the changes in the role of resources and is the outcome of the game between the agents of resources involved in value creation. The adjustment of internal distribution in a firm reflects the isomorphism of power structure with the pattern of interest distribution. Technical human capitalization is only a reasonable and legitimate form of expression of skilled labor's shares in profits in the new structure of interest distribution and is the result of growth in the power of skilled labor.

Many scholars have discussed technical human capitalization from different perspectives. Fang (1997) argues that skilled human capital's share of the firm's residuals manifests in the contractual relationship of property rights whereby the owner of human capital is the true creator of wealth. The reason is that diversification and securitization trends in the form of non-human capital gradually create a weaker and indirect relationship with firms, which have increasingly become risk avoiders. On the other hand, the trends of exclusive use of human capital and establishing teams create enhanced and direct relationships between firms and the owners of human capital, and the firms are increasingly the true bearers of risks. These changes highlight the subjective will and effort of human capital. The willingness to share interests gradually increases with capital's contribution to growth in production while bargaining power and negotiation skills gradually mature leading to changes in the structure of interest distribution. Yang and Yang (2001) argues that the social nature of human capital creates limitations on human capital application, for example, it can be mortgaged and has risks. Therefore, it should have residual claimants rights. But the realization of the rights relies on the exclusive use of human capital and teamwork. In addition, human capital relies on strong interdependence among the related resources. Thus, it can improve bargaining power and ultimately affect the ownership arrangements of firms.

Lu (2009) takes into account the scarcity and substitutability of capital and introduces the concept of re-purchasing costs. The author converts power, a variable that is difficult to quantify, into the quantifiable variable of repurchase costs. He establishes a model based on power. This model assumes that factors include human and monetary capital, within a firm, their resource endowments are x_L and x_K, respectively, and all capital is put into production. Then cooperative production function is: $y = f(x_L, x_K) = \min(x_L, x_K)$. Commodity price is $P = 1$. The price of x_L and x_K are ω_L and ω_K respectively. The net revenues created by cooperation are represented by a constant of π, while money capital receives θ amount of the revenues and human capital receives $1-\theta$ amount of the revenues. Then in the case where both parties choose to cooperate, the gains for each party are,

$$\pi_{L1} = \omega_L x_L + (1-\theta)\pi \qquad (7.19)$$

$$\pi_{K1} = \omega_K x_K + \theta\pi \qquad (7.20)$$

If one party chooses not to co-operate in the negotiations, the other has to re-purchase the factors in market. Assume the cost to repurchase is ξ_i $(i = L, K)$. It follows from common sense that the higher the substitutability of factor i, the lower the repurchase costs. If the revenues created by new partnership are still π, and the new factors acquired from market do not have bargaining power, that is, the revenues in this scenario are wholly owned by the purchaser of the original firm, then, with the new partnership, the revenues are distributed between employers and employees in the original firm according to the following rules,

$$\pi_{L2} = \omega_L x_L + \pi - \xi_K x_K \qquad (7.21)$$

$$\pi_{K2} = \omega_K x_K + \pi - \xi_L x_L \qquad (7.22)$$

Obviously, only when $\pi_{L1} \geq \pi_{L2}$ and $\pi_{K1} \geq \pi_{K2}$, the two parties can maintain the existing cooperation. From the above equations, the conditions for cooperation can be derived for the two parties,

$$\theta \leq x_K \xi_K / \pi \qquad (7.23)$$

$$\text{and } \theta \geq 1 - \xi_L x_L / \pi \qquad (7.24)$$

According to (7.23) and (7.24), then

$$(\xi_L x_L + \xi_K x_K) - \pi \geq 0 \qquad (7.25)$$

This shows that when the increment in gains of both parties under the new partnership is less than the repurchase cost, they will make a contract. When the increment in gains for either party is greater than the repurchase cost, both parties will either be unable to reach an agreement or terminate the existing contract.

If the negotiating power of each party is viewed as a function of the repurchase cost ξ_K, that is,

$$\alpha = \gamma\xi_k; \ \beta = 1 - \gamma\xi_K$$

where α and β denote the bargaining power of human capital and monetary capital, respectively; and $\gamma > 0$ states that the bargaining power is proportional to the repurchase costs. When the bargains between monetary and human capital reach an equilibrium solution, according to equations (7.19–7.22), the ratio of the interest distribution between both parties is

$$\theta = argmax\left[(\pi_{L1} - \pi_{L2})^\alpha (\pi_{K1} - \pi_{K2})^\beta\right] \tag{7.26}$$

According to the first-order conditions for maximization, it follows, after some calculations, that,

$$\theta = \gamma\xi_K + \frac{\xi_K x_K (1 - \gamma\xi_K) - \gamma x_L \xi_K \xi_L}{\pi} \tag{7.27}$$

When the cost of outsourcing labor $\xi_L = 0$, the monetary capital has greater right to choose and its bargaining power increases accordingly. According to the cooperation condition for a firm $(\xi_L x_L + \xi_K x_K) - \pi \geq 0$, it follows that $\xi_K x_K = \pi$. From (7.27), it yields $\theta = 1$. The capital owners of the firm will possess all of the residuals and the firm is completely the labor-employed-by-capital type. On the contrary, when the capital's repurchase cost is $\xi_K = 0$, it follows that $\theta = 0$. The owners of labor factor in the firm will take all the residuals and the firm is completely labor-employed-by-labor type. When $\xi_L, \xi_K > 0$, factor owners' shares of the residuals are proportional to the repurchase costs of the corresponding factors in market.

This model shows that when we only consider factor re-purchase costs, the scarcity of factors determines the magnitude of the factor owner's power. The more scarce the resources, the higher the re-purchase costs. Consequently, the greater the economic power of the factor owner, the greater the gain in the share of the residuals from the negotiations. The extent of economic power ultimately determines the residual distribution structure. In fact, the factor owner's bargaining power is not determined by a single factor. The extent of bargaining power depends on the degree of market scarcity of the factor in hand, the size of the contribution of the factor to value creation, the exit costs of the factor, and extent of the risk the factor bears. In the preceding analysis, skilled human capital is a scarce resource. Moreover, with improved technical requirements and heterogeneity, the degree of scarcity exhibits an increasing trend.

However, monetary capital shows the opposite pattern. In the early stages of economic development, monetary capital is a scarce resource; hence, the repurchase cost is relatively high. With long-term economic development and monetary capital accumulation, money stock has increased remarkably. Currently, there is a significant amount of hot money worldwide seeking favorable investment opportunities. Monetary capital is no longer a scarce resource, and the cost of repurchase is gradually falling. If looking at the tangible nature of capital, the inseparability implies that human capital is free to exit a firm without any capital losses. This is not the case for non-human capital. Thus, it is a potential threat to non-human capital. Regarding the ability to create value, knowledge and technology play an increasingly important role. In some areas, firm production relies on technology and highly skilled personnel. The status and role of technical staff have become increasingly prominent in firms. In the IT industry, only the presence of human capital can ensure, increase, and expand the value of non-human capital. Additionally, to maintain long-term competitive advantage, IT companies must continue to innovate using knowledge and technology. The owners of skilled human capital have become the real creators of wealth.

Meanwhile, new technology-based companies are constantly emerging. The shortage of talent in the market causes new companies to increase their compensation to attract highly skilled technical staff, which results in opportunities to improve the market benefits. Previous analysis has shown that when opportunity gains increase, the benefits for technical staff rise, and the staff eventually become the holders of corporate residual claimants rights. Therefore, the mode of production is no longer the type of capital employing labor in traditional firms; rather, it is the skilled labor that employs capital. This inherent nature is embodied in the contractual relationship of a firm's property rights. The owners of human capital share the firm's residuals, which realizes their dream concerning the property rights of the firm and confirms the transfer of dominance from money owners to wealth creators in the formulation of principles for distributing firm wealth.

The senior management labor market

The emergence of the senior management labor market and related theories

Senior professional managers are workers with extensive management experience and skills. Their knowledge and skills are the main resources they exchange on the market. Senior managers are in charge of production and operation activities and assume the decision-making power of a firm.

Administrators have existed since the early foundations of human society. However, from an economics perspective, management personnel were not a major concern until the advent of large-scale socialized production. In classical firms, investors are both entrepreneurs and managers. Owners of capital receive all firm residuals. However, with the growth in monetary capital and investment scales, firm management has extended beyond the capabilities of investors. Moreover, business owners may relinquish complex management to enjoy life and, in so doing, rely on individuals with management capabilities to ensure the healthy functioning of the firm. Ownership and management have been diverging resulting in specialized professional management groups that gradually form the hierarchical institutions of modern business management. Initial cooperation is built on the relationship whereby physical capital employs managers with wages as the employment costs. With constant expansion in investment scale, business management has become more complex and specialized. The coordination of internal resources requires management expertise and personnel capabilities. The complexity of a senior managers' job also requires that they possess the ability to manage practical problems and the ability to innovate. Innovation capacity requires innate qualities, education, personal growth, and the accumulation of practical experience. Senior management personnel are trained through a "learning by doing" process based on their education. Without actual work experience, it is difficult to obtain the ability to solve complex problems. Thus, practical experience, judgment, and decision-making ability are what ordinary managers lack. However, differences in the management requirements of firms render management capabilities based on practical experience non-universal. Senior management personnel in different industries or different enterprises cannot completely substitute for one another. Consequently, senior management personnel are the scarcest resources in the factor market.

It is precisely the scarcity of senior management talent that causes employers to keep raising their compensation to attract such talent and to motivate managers. Thus, equity motivation for managers has emerged that enables managers to share the firm's residuals. High wages have become a feature of the senior management labor market. Issues concerning high wages, high consumption, and the residual claimants rights of senior management labor are addressed by the existing economic theories. Classical economics analyzes the pricing of management personnel from the perspectives of both paid personal costs and contributions from management capabilities. For example, Schumpeter (1939) states that innovation activities of senior management break the old equilibrium, which helps the firm obtain excess profits. Therefore, profit sharing should be used as the return for the work of senior management personnel. Marshall (1961) expresses a similar view, which is that corporate profits are the outcome of management personnel's efforts to operate a variety of tangible and intangible resources. Thus, profits as a return for management are justifiable. Some scholars discuss from the perspective of capital and incorporate high levels of human capability into capital. In the "*Wealth of Nations*," Smith (1950) notes that any useful ability that individuals acquire after birth is an important component of capital and that more benefits are the compensation for the costs that individuals spend to improve their skills. Schultz (1961) and Becker (1962) believe that the acquisition of management skills requires certain costs. Moreover, such costs have the same nature as monetary capital and, hence, are a type of capital investment and eventually become a production factor and form human capital. Thus, senior manager corporate profit sharing is one right of capital owners. Contemporary theories on firms investigate the compensation of senior management personnel from a broader perspective. The theories hold that such factors as the autonomous nature of behavior, the difficulty of supervision, information asymmetry, and environmental factors mean that it is not enough to analyze senior management personnel's compensation purely from the perspective of capital and income. Rather, the analysis should focus on rights. Alchian and Demsetz (1972) propose a principle for the internal arrangements of rights, which is that ownership should be linked to the input factors whose contribution is the most difficult to evaluate. In modern firms, given the difficulty in measuring the contribution and prominent role of senior managers in value creation, managers should own the firm. Greater benefits to senior managers become an inevitable result of such a mechanism for the power distribution structure. Coase's theory analyzes connotations of firms and markets from the perspective of transaction costs and states that firms come into being as a substitute for the price mechanism. Coase (1995) states that with the emergence of modern firms, senior management personnel participate in the corporate contract as an independent subject of property rights. A concluded contract is the decision of each party to enter into the contract that delineates the interest distribution within their own power based on their forecast of future earnings. It is a form by which each party realizes their rights and interests. The main content of the decision concerns the residual control and the residual claim. An effective business arrangement is the corresponding residual control and residual claim. The unity of owners and managers in traditional business results in the non-existence of the power game between the two types of rights, but ownership and management are separated in modern firms. This separation means that the residuals have different agents to pursue. Under normal circumstances, each agent of action is rational and will not give up the incentive to maximize their own interests. Business owners always want to pay the minimum employment costs while hoping that managers will do their best to obtain the entire residual claimant right. Managers with information superiority and control over the residuals will try to obtain maximum benefits at minimum management cost. It is this contradiction of interests that leads to the principal-agent problem. The existence of corporate contracts places constraints on the conduct of all parties and attempts to attain the equilibrium allocation of interests for all parties. However, the complexity and variability of the market environment, as well as incomplete information, mean that the contract is imperfect. There are always loopholes in the interest distribution stipulated in the contract. For instance, the degree of effort and the contribution of individual managers in the creation of values are difficult to define in the contract, which results in uncertainty in the distribution of residuals. How to determine a reasonable return for senior managers becomes critical theoretical research.

The determination of senior management compensation

According to the principle of fairness, the criteria for income distribution should be determined by production factor contributions. However, due to the complexity of modern production processes, the contributions are difficult to measure as is the role of management in value creation. Thus, it is more difficult to quantify, which makes how to determine reasonable compensation for a senior manager a challenging economic problem with no criteria. Traditional economic theories state that a company owner, as the investor, enjoys ownership, usage, disposal, and returns associated with the property while other members produce goods under the manager's supervision and receive corresponding incomes. However, the residual claimant right is not a sound theoretical concept. Moreover, the traditional mechanism with shareholder supremacy in residual income distribution is no longer a theorem for profit distribution in modern firm theories. We concede that the essence of the firm is teamwork and that every production factor plays a role in the residual creation. Therefore, all the factors involved in a firm's value creation, particularly the senior technical and senior management factors, have capital characteristics and become either skilled human capital or entrepreneur human capital. The subject of labor should include residual claimants rights. Therefore, it is reasonable that managers obtain the residuals. The problem to be addressed is how to reflect deserved shares in the residual distribution of a manager's compensation.

The existing principal-agent theory studies profit distribution between company owners and senior managers under the condition of asymmetric information and incomplete supervision. According to this theory, the nature of the principal-agent problem is a contractual relation in which both parties are rational in the economic sense and maximize their respective interests. When market information is complete and manager behavior can be supervised, both parties can reach the Pareto optimal of profit distribution. In this case, the agent receives a fixed income, and the principal keeps the firm's residual. When market information is incomplete, and there are uncertainties in the external market, the principal-agent contract cannot contain all future uncertainties, and supervision will incur costs. Hence, a fixed wage level is no longer feasible. In a market with incomplete information, if there is a positive correlation between a manager's efforts and firm profits, and if the manager is risk neutral, profit distribution can be Pareto optimal when the manager bears risks. This will motivate the manager, and the agent receives a fixed level of revenues. If the agent is risk averse, there must be a trade-off between motivation and risk. Whether the Pareto optimal level of effort can be realized depends on the mode of distribution stipulated by the contract provisions.

The objective of a company owner, as the principal, is to add value to their monetary capital through a manager's effective operations. Therefore, the principal always hopes to find a manager with rich management knowledge and skills at the lowest cost. However, a senior manager, as the agent, is also "economic man" who maximizes his interests to obtain higher compensation. The prerequisite for cooperation between both parties is a mutually satisfactory wage contract. Usually, the principal designs a compensation contract, $S(Q)$, based on the firm's expected output Q, to negotiate with the agent whose expected return is: $v = Q - S(Q)$. Whether the agent accepts this wage level or not is closely related to his opportunity income, ω, plus the action cost of $c(a)$ in management. The agent's expected revenue is $\eta = S(Q) - c(a)$. The mathematical model for the above problem is

$$
\max v = Q - s(Q)
$$
$$
s.t. S(Q) - c(a) \geq \omega \qquad (7.28)
$$

From the model, a reasonable wage should be associated with the firm's output performance. If the principal's expected utility is unchanged, the better the performance and the higher the manager's wage. However, Murphy (1985), Jenson (1987), and Gibbons and Murphy (1990) study market data and show that although a correlation exists between performance and wage, it is weak. This means that performance is only one factor used when the principal designs wages and is an example of what the agent considers the cost of their effort and the opportunity income. If $S(Q) < \omega + c(a)$, both parties will not enter into a contract. Only when $S(Q) \geq \omega + c(a)$ are the conditions met for the contract. However, the level of wage depends on the resources held at the time of negotiation, in the other words, the bargaining power of each party.

The resources that a principal relies on are monetary capital. Therefore, in an era of monetary capital scarcity, the more capital funds invested, the larger the output, the longer a firm's life, and the better the working environment and opportunities for future development. Thus, the company provides a better working environment and opportunities for growth. These conditions are attractive to a talented manager and ensure a dominant position for the principal in contract negotiations. However, capital investment is an explicit resource and open market information. The longer the negotiation, the greater the loss caused by the discount costs that invested funds incur; thus, in the era of abundant monetary capital, higher capital input would be a disadvantageous factor for the principal. The resources the manager has are management knowledge, skills, and social relations, which have the characteristics of being non-explicit, difficult to measure, and with no discount, just like technical resources. If only the discount cost is considered, the Rubinstein model in previous discussions is suitable to explain the formation of the principal-agent contract. A higher capital cost reduces the principal's patience for negotiation, and time preference leads to a contract that is unfavorable to the principal. Thus, the final contract gives the agent higher returns. High input levels will also bring high management costs. In negotiations, the manager will consider their own labor cost and, hence, require a higher wage from a large firm.

In a market economy, the size and scope of companies continues to expand, and the market environment becomes more complex. Consequently, management knowledge and skills play an increasing role in production.

A firm's profits depend on manager talent to a large extent. Because of this dependence of benefits on human skills, the demand for management talent increases significantly in a competitive market environment. Since senior managers must have sufficient practical experience and are specialized in one particular industry with a long period of growth, management has gradually become the scarcest market resource.

According to the principle of the importance of the production process, the scarcer the resource, the greater the bargaining power its owners have and the more profits they obtain. If a senior manager has extensive management experience and can prove strong management capabilities that will help the firm achieve its expected objectives, the manager can capitalize on their human resources, and it is the most rational choice to share the residuals. The capitalization of human resources changes the power structure in the firm, which then changes the profit allocation mode. The principal accepts the manager's requirement to share the residuals. Additionally, giving the manager a higher wage becomes an inevitable result of the alternate roles of the two resources in the production process.

However, the employment contract is only the establishment of the principal-agent relation. The interest distribution mode written into the contract is subject to change. The contract content must be adjusted through renegotiation in two cases; first, if the principal-agent relation has expired, and both parties intend to continue the cooperation but the resources that the negotiations depend on have changed. Second, although the principal-agent relation does not expire, the resources for negotiations that affect the power of both parties may have changed significantly; consequently, the requirement for profit sharing will change accordingly. If the benefit of one party in the renegotiation is greater than the penalty and renegotiation costs, the other party in the cooperation will have to accept the renegotiation. The sresources of senior managers have the feature of learning by doing with management skills strengthened through experience.

Suppose the agent's ability is a function of output, expressed as $G(Q)$, and there is a linear relation between the growth in a manager's capability and his working time; that is, $\Delta G(Q) = \tau t$. With firm expansion, the resources in the firm that the agent directly controls also increase, which leads to an increase of the manager's bargaining power. Assume that the manager has worked for some time of t, and the scale of the firm is K_t, then the manager's power can be expressed as $P_\tau = \beta(G(Q) + \tau t) + \gamma K_t$ where β and γ are the conversion coefficients of resource power. When the power of the manager increases, the wage request will be higher. Correspondingly, there are costs of C_s associated with replacing the agent, which is mainly due to two factors. First, when management capacity is a scarce resource, there is a search cost to find qualified agents. Second, it takes a new manager some time to become familiar with all production factors in the firm. During this period, output may decrease. The larger the firm, the longer it will take for the new manager to acclimatize to the post and the greater the production loss. This can be expressed as $C_s = C_f + \lambda K_t$, where λ is the cost conversion coefficient based on scale. If the agent presents a new contract requirement and requests the principal's acceptance, the requested wage increment should not exceed the loss associated with replacing the agent; that is,

$$\Delta V(p_\tau) = f\left(\beta(G(Q) + \tau t) + \gamma K_t\right) \leq C_f + \lambda K_t \tag{7.29}$$

Equation (7.29) reflects the relation between the growth in scale and the change in a manager's compensation.

Reson and Miller (1982) explain this relation with a simple hierarchy model, which holds that a firm is an organization controlled by multi-level hierarchies. Moreover, managers at a higher level have the functions of managing and improving the workers underneath them. A senior manager's job has an amplifying effect in a hierarchical organization. This effect increases with the company's scale. Thus, the larger the scale, the greater the role of senior managers in the final output. This amplifying effect increases the bargaining power of managers, which results in wage increases with growth in the company's scale. Murphy (1985), Shleifer and Vishny (1986), Gibbons and Murphy (1990), and Boschen and Smith (1995) confirm the cumulative effect of growth in company performance on wage adjustment, which is ten times larger than the current response. This positive relation between the resources held by senior managers and the wage is also proved by Kostiuk and Follmann (1989) using US compensation statistics from 1969 to 1981. Generally, the change in company scale is smaller than the change in performance. As the basis of wage negotiation, this fact is favorable to senior managers; therefore, the larger the scale, the higher the manager's compensation request.

Manager's incentives and compensation adjustment

The premise for the principal-agent relation is the separation of ownership from control, which implies that these two powers exert effects on the same interest object in different ways. Therefore, the factors to be considered in the design of manager compensation are how principals can extract the optimal level of hard work from the agent for maximum output through reasonable motivation.

If market information is complete, the above issues are easy to solve because the manager's action a can be observed, and the principal implements rewards or punishments according to the observed actions. If the manager takes the optimal action a^*, the principal will pay the optimal wage s^* based on the manager's actions. The manager receives a fixed wage, and the principal obtains the residuals. If the manager does not work hard, the principal will pay at the level of $s < s^*$. If s is small enough, the manager will not choose non-optimal action. However, if market information is incomplete, the problem will be complicated.

Assume that there is a positive linear correlation between the output and the manager's efforts, that is, $Q = a + \varepsilon$, where ε with zero mean and variance σ^2 denotes exogenous uncertainty. A greater σ^2 indicates a larger impact of exogenous uncertainty. Compensation contract and the output also show a linear correlation, i.e., $S(Q) = \omega_0 + \beta Q$, where ω_0 is a fixed wage decided by market, which is independent of manager's performance; and β is the manager's share of output based on his efforts, which describes the incentives given to the manager. The principal's expected utility is equal to expected income

$$Ev(Q - S(Q)) = E(Q - \omega_0 - \beta Q) = -\omega_0 + (1 - \beta)Q \qquad (7.30)$$

As a result, the manager's wage will be affected by his efforts. If his utility function is $U = -\exp\{-\rho[S(Q) - C(a)]\}$, where $\rho > 0$ denotes his degree of risk aversion (or the amount of information the principal masters) and $C(a)$ stands for the cost of the manager's efforts, when information is completely open, that is $\rho \to \infty$, the manager will not choose any risky behavior and be satisfied with the wage contract based on company's performance and individual efforts. Suppose the cost of manager' efforts can be measured and its function can be assumed as $C(a) = ba^2/2$ according to the assumption of strict convexity, where $b > 0$ denotes the cost coefficient of manager's efforts, the greater the value of b, the higher the cost and the lower manager's efforts. The manager's actual wage can be expressed as

$$\omega = s(Q) - c(a) = \omega_0 + \beta(a + \varepsilon) - ba^2/2 \qquad (7.31)$$

When the random variable ε is unknown, the manager can only make decisions based on the compensation rules proposed by the principal, and his expected utility can be expressed as follows, according to the manager's utility function,

$$EU = -\exp\{-\rho[\omega_0 + \beta a - C(a)]\} E[\exp(-\rho\beta\varepsilon)] \qquad (7.32)$$

Since ε is a normal distribution with zero mean and variance σ^2, random variable $[\exp(-\rho\beta\varepsilon)]$ has a log-normal distribution with mean $\exp(\rho^2\beta^2\sigma^2/2)$. If the reserved utility of the principal is $\bar{U}$, the premise for cooperation is $EU \geq \bar{U}$. Suppose $\bar{\omega} = -\ln(-\bar{U})/\rho$, the principal-agent relation holds if

$$\max Ev = -\omega_0 + (1 - \beta)\alpha$$
$$\text{s.t. } \omega_0 + \beta\alpha - \rho\beta^2\sigma^2/2 - b\alpha^2/2 \geq \bar{\omega} \qquad (7.33)$$

Solving the maximization of manager' expected utility means that the manager can obtain the outcome of his efforts, that is, $C'(a^*) = \beta$, or

$a^* = \beta / b$. According to first-order condition of optimization, equation (7.31) yields

$$\beta^* = \frac{1}{1 + \rho b \sigma^2} > 0 \tag{7.34}$$

Equation (7.34) shows that the share of residual distribution that the manager receives is related to the openness of information, the manager's efficiency, and the impact of exogenous uncertainty. Information is a valuable resource and a major factor that determines the power structure between the principal and agent. The amount of information the principal holds is important in allocating the firm's residuals. If the principal is completely uninformed ($\rho = 0$), the power and responsibilities of both parties are completely asymmetric. Hence, the result of an effective motivation is that the manager receives all the residuals. If the principal possesses almost all market information ($\rho \to \infty$), the power and responsibilities of both parties are symmetric, and the motivation based on the corporation's performance will become insignificant. In this case, the manager receives only a fixed wage corresponding to their efforts. When market information is incomplete ($\rho \in (0, \infty)$), the higher the efficiency of the manager (the lower is b), the larger the residual share that the manager will obtain, which suggests that an efficient agent is more likely to be attracted by the wage arrangement based on performance. Moreover, if the principal cannot identify the characteristics of the agent's behavior, the principal may increase the flexible component of the compensation package to attract a more effective manager or motivate the manager to strive to improve efficiency. However, if exogenous uncertainty in the market is significant—that is, a large variance of σ^2—the correlation between a manager's efforts and output becomes weak. If σ^2 goes to infinity, the output is completely controlled by external uncertainties, and the principal cannot tell the correlation between output and the manager's efforts. Thus, the motivation through benefit distribution no longer exists, and the manager's share in output based on his efforts, β, goes to zero.

The analysis above is the result of a static one-round game. Although it is possible to prove theoretically the reasonableness of the agent's wage design in the context of incomplete information, given incomplete information as the premise, it cannot guarantee that the variables of concern in the design are fully captured. The design is only based on the principal's *ex ante* estimation of future results. Thus, naturally, the design cannot verify whether the ultimate wage is reasonable. Because of incomplete information, profit maximization is difficult to guarantee through *ex ante* motivation. However, under normal circumstances, if the market management mechanism is perfect, the performance of a firm is public information in the market, and the *ex post* motivation will encourage the manager to work hard in the future if the performance and the manager's efforts are positively correlated. There are two ways to achieve *ex post* motivation. One way is a compensation design based on *ex ante* performance, and the other way is to give senior managers certain profit distribution options.

Compensation design based on the preceding period's performance

The condition for a compensation design based on the preceding period's performance is the existence of long-term cooperation between all parties that can be divided into more than one contract period. Moreover, the *ex post* information in the market is always complete. The result of cooperation in the preceding period is used as an information basis for the game in the following period. In this way, the deficiency of incomplete information in the current period can be solved effectively provided that both the principal and the agent have the right to choose whether to cooperate in the next period. Fama (1980) holds that time can solve the principal-agent incentive problem in reality. In a competitive market of management talent, the value of a manager depends on their past operating results, and only in the market can the manager prove their abilities and obtain greater benefits in the future. Therefore, even without explicit incentives, managers may work hard and strive to obtain a better reputation in the market. Fudenberg, Holmstrom and Milgrom (1990) prove that if the owner and manager maintain a long-term cooperative relation, and the owner has the power to terminate the contract in the next period, a series of short-term contracts can solve agency risk problems. If the management level is given, the owner can always discover it after the preceding contract period even in the case of incomplete information. Therefore, there is always a lag effect in wage determination. If cooperation can be divided into t periods, a manager's wage can be expressed as

$$\omega_1 = f\left(E(\theta_1)\right), \omega_i = f\left(E\left(\theta_i | \theta_{i-1}\right)\right) i = 2,3,......t \qquad (7.35)$$

That is, except for the initial wage of the manager, ω_1, which is determined by initial expected output $E(\theta_1)$, the wage in any other period is affected by the output performance in the preceding period. When the manager's current level of effort cannot be judged immediately, the current wage design based on the preceding period's output performance, θ_{i-1}, is the best solution to replace the principle of "distribution according to work." If the output of the corporation is only an increasing function of the level of a manager's efforts, it is rational for the manager to work hard in all periods before t due to future benefits concerns. Therefore, if the manager has a long time to work in the future and there is no discount on future benefits, their effort level will be high even if there is little explicit incentive. This may be one reason younger managers work harder even at a lower wage level.

However, the reputation effect of efforts decreases as the manager's working time shortens. In this case, the explicit incentive must be strengthened to attain the same incentive effect. Lazear (1979) proves that the wage for seniority based on the year of cooperation has such an incentive effect. Higher wages are an incentive for senior managers, but also a type of constraint in long-term contractual relations. Boschen and Smith's (1995) empirical study shows that the increase in a current period's performance will raise the wage of senior managers in the following four to five years. Only in period *t*, according to the principle of economic rationality, will the level of effort possibly decrease significantly because there is no longer any impact on the future.

Stock option incentives

Stock options are the right that the principal gives to the agent to buy an amount of equity at a certain price in the future. This is a management tool often used by corporations and a type of *ex post* incentive based on actions and consequences. Incentive plans includes factors such as expiration, option price, and the amount of the option. The specifications on these factors will affect the agent's future wage directly. Stock option incentives are the right given by the principal as a reward, which is a creative method of compensation in the sense that the agent benefits from growth in the corporation's future profits. The agent may choose to exercise or to give up this right. The key to the decision is the corporation's stock price at the moment when the agent can exercise the right. If the actual stock market price at that moment is higher than the strike price, the agent will exercise this right and obtain profits from the difference in price. Let the output Q be an increasing function of the manager's efforts, a; that is, $Q = F(a)$, and P is the strike price while n is the quantity of equity. Suppose the stock price P' in the future is closely related to production performance; that is, $P' = F(Q) = F(f(a))$, the manager's revenues in the future can be expressed as

$$V = n(P' - P) \qquad (7.36)$$

Stock option incentives mean that the firm's value is an important variable in the manager's income function. Hence, the manager will improve the performance of the firm spontaneously to obtain more benefits by converting the option into cash. Such incentives link executive benefits with their efforts and reflect a basic property right requirement from the senior management human capital. Moreover, stock options reduce incentive costs. There is greater flexibility in scheme design and the options overcome the defect of wage adjustments in the current period that become less of an incentive as the game span shortens. Stock options have been widely used by corporations to motivate executives in recent years.

The impacts of constraint mechanisms on manager compensation

Whether a contract-based salary that motivates in the current period through residual sharing, or performance and option incentives that consider the time and economic effects, the goal is to achieve the economic objectives of the principals. That is, growth in the company's performance in the context of paying executives fair compensation. However, market data on Chinese and overseas companies show that the income growth rate of executives is much higher than that of company performance. The pay for CEOs according to Standard & Poor's (S&P) 500 companies between 1992 and 2002 increased more than four times in real terms, which is much higher than the growth rate in company profits and the pay for ordinary employees in the same period. The overall returns of the S&P 500 companies fell 12% in 2001, but the pay for the top five executives increased by 27%. The same problem occurs in the Chinese market. Statistics show that the growth rate of executive compensation is much higher than that of listed company profits in China and, for some companies, the pay for executives increases rapidly each year in spite of negative growth in profits.

By studying the executive option incentives among US companies, Jensen and Murphy (1990) show that although stock option incentives are more effective than salaries and bonuses, they have still a weak correlation with corporation performance. Because corporations do not have a sound information mechanism, many executives manipulate financial data by modifying corporate financial data and exaggerating management activity to raise the corporate stock price to ensure personal returns on stock options during their tenure. Hence, financial scandals weaken corporate governance and cause significant loss to the corporation. So far, the incentive effect of benefits to executives has not met the principal's expected goals, and the principal-agent problem remains a problem that modern corporate management cannot solve.

The goal of higher pay for executives is to motivate them to work hard and to minimize the loophole of management staff to improve the company's performance. Higher pay increases the default costs of executives in the case of asymmetric information. However, if there are no constraint mechanisms, even the highest pay cannot prevent executives from using asymmetric information to seize corporate residuals. The root of the principal-agent problem lies in asymmetric information. Information is a power resource. Executives (the agents) have information advantages over the owners (the principals). The information difference causes power asymmetry. Since power is isomorphic with interest, executives with power will naturally fight for their own benefits. When there is no constraint on power reciprocity, executives may deviate from the owners' goals and increase their own interests at the cost of the owners. That is, under the condition of asymmetric information, the principal's expected utility can only be achieved if the agent realizes maximum expected utility when they choose action *a*, which is the principal's desired action. Only when the power and the responsibility are symmetric for the principal and the agent can the corporation achieve the optimal allocation of its resources and profit distribution between both parties according to their contributions. Therefore, the principal-agent problem cannot be solved simply by compensation incentives.

The premise for the existence of a senior management talent market is the separation of management from ownership. Given the separation, a contradiction occurs as the two powers simultaneously affect the same carrier. In theory, ownership and control are unified, but because of the imperfect contract from incomplete information, the owner has the control only in name while the manager has the control in a real sense. The manager with actual control has the right to make decisions on undefined residuals according to their preferences. If there are no constraints on the manager's actions, the manager's decisions would be arbitrary and based on self-interest. Executives with actual control over a company may use information vulnerability to obtain extra benefits other than those written in the contract.

Bebchuk, Fried and Walker (2005) studies this issue and proposes a compensation theory based on the power pattern of managers according to the ineffectiveness of performance-oriented compensation design. The theory holds that although the pay for executives is the result of market transactions, due to the difference in power between the two parties, the contract might seriously breach the fairness of market transactions. Moreover, executives tend to use their power to seek rents. The longer the executive holds their position, the more internal information the executive possesses and the greater their influence over compensation decisions. The executive might use their power to influence the decisions of the board of directors and to affect the appointment of independent directors. Additionally, the executive might also use their power to exclude uncooperative directors from the board or use the company resources to force or bribe independent directors to conspire with them in compensation design. This causes the design to deviate from the performance-based concept and makes high compensation an unreasonable but legal component of the contract. Hart and Moore (1999) offer a more direct statement on this. They state that in a world of incomplete contracts, the person who has the right over residual benefits may not necessarily have residual control, and the individual with residual control will eventually obtain the profits of a corporation. Therefore, realization of the right of residual benefits depends on residual control. The latter plays a more significant role in profit distribution.

Therefore, the key to solving the principal-agent dilemma is power adjustment for the two parties, which clarifies the power and responsibilities of each party and establishes a mechanism of constraints to ensure symmetry between power and responsibilities for both parties. While executives have information advantages, they cannot seek rents at will. Principals can hold corresponding power relying on the resources they control and to develop means of constraints.

First, the principal has the power to terminate the contract, which means the agent loses the control. Although the goal of executives is the return of benefits, such benefits are not merely reflected in the form of currency. The right to work or continue working is also a need since such a right provides them the opportunity to display individual talents and to show their "entrepreneurial style," a self-fulfilling need that also satisfies the desire for power to control others. Meanwhile, executives enjoy perks that satisfy material pursuits in addition to compensation. Long-term returns to executives also depend on individual reputation. Once the information on their breach is disclosed, and the contract is terminated, long-term loss in benefits caused by such reputation loss might be far more than the income from the breach. This is an effective way to balance current power asymmetry. Deterrent institutional arrangements can be developed via reasonable contract designs.

Second, there is an economic punishment mechanism based on *ex post* information. Although the principal cannot fully grasp information on the agent's actions in the current period, a reasonable assessment mechanism can always ensure the adequacy of *ex post* information. Therefore, in corporate governance, we should strengthen audits and the information disclosure mechanism to ensure complete market information. Hence, the necessary conditions are satisfied for "settling old accounts in the future." The existing theory has proven that a rational economic punishment can reduce contract breaches by the agent and protect the legitimate rights and interests of the principal.

Note

1 According to the New PalGrave: A Dictionary of Economics, human capital is defined as the stock of skills and production knowledge embodied in human beings.

8 Theoretical foundations and boundaries for government intervention

Market failure and economic power out of control

Economic power refers to the relative ability of an economic agent to control and influence other agents using the resources they hold. In market transactions, agents develop new market rules through long-term dynamic games, which reallocates economic resources.

Scope and manifestation of economic agent's power

The essence of economic power is the right to freely allocate economic resources. "Freely" is emphasized here because economic power is reflected by the agent's ability to control or influence the activities or behavior of others. The greater the agent's economic power, the greater their freedom in disposal behavior, such as handling resource (factor) exchanges. On the contrary, the smaller the power, the lower the economic status of the agent, the less right they will have to freely speak, and the weaker their relative bargaining power, which further reduces their freedom in market transactions.

In classical economic theories, markets are divided into goods and factor markets, where the economic power agents are firms and consumers, respectively. In the factor market, consumers exchange production factors for goods and gain consumer surplus. In the goods market, firms exchange products for factors and gain profits. In an ideal state, through the market mechanism of resource allocation, goods and factors can reach equilibrium whereby both sides are relatively satisfied. Although the market mechanism can make adjustments to economic activities at the micro level, it cannot effectively address macroeconomic issues. The market mechanism can strengthen market agents' utilitarian goals but cannot overcome the external diseconomy. Additionally, market mechanisms can achieve economic efficiency but cannot achieve the diversification of social goals. Intervention by the government in its role as general administrator and a special economic agent is particularly necessary.

As the arbiter of and a participant in economic activities, the government already influences the economy beyond the traditional conceptual thinking of "small government." With the development of the market economy, the degree of connections and constraints between firms increases, and monopoly power suppresses market efficiency. These dynamics suggest that the government should assume more responsibilities. Governments should conduct traditional general administrative functions and be accountable for economic growth, full employment, price stability, the balance of international payments, and fair social distribution. Although issues unresolved by markets may remain unresolved by the government also, it is normal for a government to participate in economic activities as both an administrative and economic agent.

Therefore, market agents include the firms and consumers described in traditional theories, and the government. The operation of the entire economic system is the result of interactions and dynamic games among the power of governments, firms, and consumers.

Consumers, firms, and government are all agents of economic power, but the sources of their economic power differ. The concept of government can be explained in both a broad and narrow sense. In a broad sense, the government includes power branches (the legislative), executive branches (law enforcement bodies), and judicatory branches (the judicial bodies). Government in the narrow sense refers to national administrative bodies including central and local government. In this book, the term government is applied in a narrow sense and as the concept of "big government" in a market economy. According to Yang (2003), the theoretical frameworks for the existence of government can be classified into the violence theory, contract theory, and evolution theory. Regardless of the theoretical framework, the existence of government corresponds to government power from the mandate of a political organization, and its basic functions and responsibilities are to provide public goods and promote social welfare. Based on this, government is linked to public interests.

In theory, public interests represent the interests of all members of society, which are represented by government interests. Thus, the power held by government stems from trust in and authorization given to a government organization composed of minorities in the society. The government, as an agent, uses its unique position of power to supply public goods by intervening coercively in the market economy through microeconomic agents. According to the concept of economic power, firms are economic power agents that derive their power from the scarce resources under their control. Such resources can be core products, production materials, or core technology and talent; even the core competence factors such as market share that can bring sustainable competitive advantages are likely to become a source of a firm's economic power. In market transactions, to obtain a stronger position, firms often form alliances (interest groups) to win dominance in the rights to negotiate and speak in the games played with government, other firms (groups), and consumers. Consumers as individual economic power agents and possessors of labor factors exchange labor for consumer goods in market transactions. Therefore, consumer's economic power stems from their own purchasing power or the quality of their own labor. As a group, consumers obtain their economic power through organizations. The power of an organized consumer group has always been greater than the sum of power of each individual. Compared to a single consumer, a consumer group can organize and leverage its economic power with respect to transactions to lift their economic position and status. In this way, consumers can provide a relatively high level of welfare.

Consumers, firms, and government have various sources of economic power, and the content and form of their power differs. Under the conditions of a modern market economy, government is representative of public interests. The government's basic functions are to maximize public interests and to correct market failures. In performing its functions, a government's direct involvement in economic activities falls into the category of economic power. For example, government becomes the demand side of the market through government procurement. A government can also be an important supplier in the market if it provides public goods by establishing state-owned firms, holding shares in firms, or if it develops infrastructure and high-tech products. However, governments often act as a socio-economic administrator that indirectly intervenes in economic activities. In performing its basic functions, a government's indirect intervention in economic activities falls under the category of executive power. For example, governments set up market rules, regulate market order, and increase transfer payments. Without administrative intervention in the market, a government's basic functions cannot be performed. Compared with advanced economies, the government in China is more tempted to intervene in economic activities using executive power. For example, the Chinese government once coerced the military forces to substitute their vehicles with First Auto-Work (FAW)'s "Jie Fang" trucks, which saved FAW from becoming insolvent. This is a typical example of a government's direct intervention into economic activities. Recently, the Chinese government offered a 4 trillion RMB investment plan to stimulate the economy, which is another example of direct intervention in economic activities using a government's economic power.

The economic power of firms stems from the use and possession of resources. The more resources a firm has, the greater its economic power through which the firm can gain more profits. This is because the greater the economic power of the firm, the stronger the firm's bargaining power when transacting with the government. Hence, the firm can be subject to favorable government policies. Similarly, when transacting with other firms, the firm with greater economic power can easily claim a dominant position. Even in consumer transactions, the products of a firm with greater economic power are more easily accepted by consumers due to factors such as branding and firms gain more profits consequently.

Consumers typically affect and control the distribution of labor through their own endowments. Consumer's economic power mainly includes the right to claim labor returns, the freedom to choose goods, and the right to social security. The right to claim labor returns means that consumers are free to choose how much labor they are willing to sell according to the labor market price for returns. The freedom to choose goods means that consumers have the right to choose whatever consumer goods they like to maximize their utility. The right to social security (also called the distribution right for returns on public goods) means that a consumer can influence the supply of government policies to obtain certain public goods. Those public goods will maintain a certain standard of living for the consumer and facilitate their advancement.

The root cause of market failure: economic power out of control

Market failure, in the context of microeconomics, refers to efficiency. For instance, the market becomes incompetent when there is negative externality, negative internality, a monopoly, or injustice. In addition, market failure sometimes manifests as macroeconomic fluctuations. Due to the blindness in demand and supply from incomplete information, it is easy to induce an imbalance of macroeconomic aggregates when there is excess demand or supply in the market.

First, we will take the case of a monopoly. Since value maximization is the goal of a firm, a firm can realize this goal through pricing. The ability of a firm to control prices relies on the degree of monopoly. Compared to small firms, large firms hold more human resources, technology, physical capital, and public relations, which help to establish stronger bargaining power in market negotiations. Hence, large firms gain more benefits from market competition. In some cases, large firms have significant influence in the setting up of market rules including pricing for the entire industry. With an increasing degree of monopoly, a firm will have greater ability to control prices and, therefore, can maximize its profits more easily. The ability to monopolize reflects the firm's economic power. With no or few restrictions, monopolistic firms inevitably use their economic power to realize their goals. Pricing aside, firms will use destructive means, such as deceit and threats, to seize exorbitant profits if their economic power is unrestricted. Such actions erode the interests of other economic agents.

Second, negative externality occurs when the activities of one economic agent result in the negative effects of another agent that cannot be reflected by transaction price mechanisms. For instance, when enterprises discharge pollutants without supervision, the firm will benefit but at the expense of the general public's health. Moreover, any individual victim is unable to legally challenge the firm. However, if the public forms a united organization that holds substantial influence and is authorized to negotiate with the firm, the firm would have to compensate the public for its loss. Unfortunately, public organization is difficult; in other words, the costs to organize are too high. Thus, firms discharge pollutants that threaten public safety and the natural environment.

Finally, with respect to fairness, fairness can be categorized as economic equity and social equity. Economic equity is the concept of equal opportunity.

Economic agents buy and sell goods of equal value as a form of exchange following competitive rules and under market order restraints. Each agent in the market realizes the distribution of interests through the exchange of goods while firms realize the distribution of income based on the factor contribution ratio. Therefore, economic equity has the same connotations as the pursuit of efficiency under market conditions. Without economic equity, there is no economic efficiency. Social equity is the concept that members of society have equal opportunities and rights, particularly the rights to subsistence and development because they reflect the fundamental pillars of social equity. The right to subsistence is the right to clothing, food, housing, security, transportation, and medical treatment. The right to development refers to the equal rights of education, employment, and migration. Without the basic rights to subsistence and development, it is impossible to enjoy other economic and political rights. Although it is the premise and guarantee for economic efficiency, economic equity is difficult to achieve no matter through equivalent exchange or allocation by contribution in reality because the power between economic agents is not reciprocal. Particularly when there is an excess supply of certain production factors, the income from these factors is often less than their contribution. However, due to differences in individuals' endowments and resources, equal opportunities cannot guarantee the equal distribution of wealth. The equivalent exchange and distribution by contribution will inevitably result in a gap between the rich and the poor. Moreover, this gap will be substantial if there is no outside intervention.

Theoretical foundations for executive power intervention in economic activities

Concerns with market failure can be traced back to the 1930s and the Keynesian revolution in economics. Roosevelt government's "New Deal" in 1933 was the beginning of western and modern government interventionism in economic activities using executive power. Market failure is a normal state in economic activities. Since failure is the necessary consequence of unfettered economic power, it follows that the solution to failure relies on the intervention plus coercion of executive power. This is determined by a government's role in economic activities.

The limitation of market's ability to adjust

Whether negative or positive, externalities result in the deviation of resource allocation from the Pareto optimal state. According to Coase's theory (1991), the root cause of externalities is both the ambiguity in defining property rights and positive transaction costs. Coase argues that externalities can be resolved directly through markets if the definition of property rights is clear without transaction costs. However, in reality, even if the definition is clear, market adjustments are sometimes incompetent because negotiations between individuals are too costly or information is incomplete. Moreover, property rights cannot be defined without government as a third party. The same is true for internalities. Internalities cause efficiency loss. When negative internality exists, the actual market trading volume is below the social optimal level, and the allocation of resources by the market will deviate from the Pareto optimal state. Therefore, government must intervene using its executive power.

In addition to externalities, monopolies, asymmetric information, and the supply of public goods are problems that the market cannot solve on its own. Any form of imperfect competition will shift the social output inward from the production frontier. For instance, when a monopoly firm raises prices leading to a reduction in output, or oligopolistic firms collude to reduce supply, the output of a certain product will be less than its efficiency level, which is detrimental to the economy efficiency. At this point, government intervention is necessary to solve the problem of low efficiency caused by imperfect competition. Moreover, resorting to the market to resolve the public goods supply will not help. Public goods have the properties of non-exhaustibility and non-rivalry; hence, they are special goods with strong positive externalities. Individuals enjoy the utilities brought by such externalities but are unwilling to pay for their consumption. Thus, every agent is inclined to free-ride, waiting for others to produce public goods. Therefore, public goods cannot be supplied by firms and individuals via market mechanisms, and the government must intervene to encourage production.

Additionally, the problem of incomplete information cannot be resolved through market adjustment. Complete information is a basic assumption in microeconomics; that is, every agent's decisions are based on the full information of all the parties involved in the transactions. In general cases, the price signal reflects, comprehensively, all types of dispersed information. Thus, economic agents only need to react to prices to make the resource allocation Pareto optimal. In reality, however, neither consumers nor producers have complete information required by the Pareto optimal state. Consequently, incomplete information occurs, also known as the phenomenon of information failure. Whether adverse selection or moral hazard, information failure is the distortion of market resource allocation caused by asymmetric information. Incomplete and asymmetric information are the intrinsic defects of the market and cannot be resolved solely by market forces. Government intervention by executive power is necessary.

Economic equity, which is of the greatest concern, is reflected in markets as the exchange of equal value. In firms, economic equity is reflected in distribution based on contributions. However, since the resources held by each economic agent are different in terms of importance, quantity, scarcity, and substitutability, non-reciprocal power structures emerge with different negotiation abilities. Because there is a difference in negotiating power and position, it is impossible for the market to realize economic equity by itself. For instance, labor compensation and the prices of agricultural products in developing countries are illustrative of this theory. For social equity based on initial distribution, this must be resolved by the government through secondary distribution. Ensuring social equity is a government's natural duty while firms and markets have no such responsibility or function.

Government regulations and adjustment controls

Because market mechanisms have various defects, governments implement necessary and moderate intervention as an objective request. Government behavior that can affect the behavior of economic agents is considered government intervention. In theory, government intervention uses executive means, such as laws, policies, and regulations, to coordinate market operations with the assistance of executive means to correct, improve, and compensate for the deficiencies in the market mechanism. Specifically, a government's executive power intervention into economic activities takes the ultimate form of regulations and macro-level adjustment and controls. Government regulation is direct or indirect restrictions on microeconomic agents through laws and regulations instituted by the government and characterized by legal coercion. In addition to government regulation, macro-level adjustment and controls are another way that a government's power affects the market economy.

Direct regulation

Direct regulation occurs when the government uses executive permission to directly regulate certain market behavior of economic agents (firms). Direct regulation has two categories: economic regulation and social regulation.

ECONOMIC REGULATION

First, economic regulation is reflected in government regulation concerning natural monopolies. The focus here is regulation on entry, exit, and prices. Economies of scale and sunk costs are the reasons that competition among firms producing the same product create enormous waste; therefore, it is necessary for governments to regulate market entry. If a naturally monopolistic firm exits from the industry, the social supply will be affected as will the national economy. Hence, governments regulate the exit of natural monopolies to guarantee that the firms approved to enter the market can assume the responsibility of social security. Furthermore, governments must balance business interests and social welfare. That is, governments must guarantee that naturally monopolistic firms continue their business operation while ensuring that their freedom in pricing does not sacrifice consumer's interests. Consequently, governments must regulate prices. Second, economic regulation occurs as government's correct asymmetric information in the market using its executive power. Asymmetric information creates adverse selection and moral hazards, which triggers a crisis in trust between both parties in the transactions and results in eventual welfare loss for the parties. Hence, resource allocation will not be Pareto optimal. However, it is not realistic for medium and small businesses to solve the problem of asymmetric information if they fully rely on market means. Thus, governments must intervene.

SOCIAL REGULATION

Another aspect of government direct regulation is to directly regulate negative externalities and the negative internalities of firms using executive power. Internalities refer to the returns and transaction costs that are not stated in contracts even though the transaction has occurred. For example, utility loss and physical injuries to consumers brought about due to product defects or quality problems, vocation-related disease, or accidents in the workplace are all negative internalities. Regulation includes restrictions on business activities; qualifications and standards associated with the environment, health, and security; and examination and identification of safety conditions in the workplace.

Government social regulation on negative externalities is mainly reflected by regulation on environmental pollution behavior, such as noise, pollution, or nuclear radiation. Thus, the regulation is toward environmental quality. If the environment is viewed as a resource, it is also scarce. In a market economy, the environment will be abused or polluted if there is no intervention, causing environmental problems such as desertification, greenhouse effects, and tragedy of public land. There are products that are not exchanged in market transactions, such as wastes discharged in production and the wastes that pollute air and water. In this respect, negative externalities cause loss in resource allocation efficiency, which is equal to the efficiency loss caused by environmental pollution. If the problem of negative externalities is solved, then environment pollution will be resolved, including the overuse of resources. Governments in different countries manage negative externalities in various ways. The means include direct regulation, such as permits, quotas, and standards, and indirect regulation, such as pollution fees and pollution rights transactions. Pollution rights transactions are also called tradable pollution permits. The basic concept is that the regulator provides firms with a certain amount of pollution permits based on the targeted total amount of pollution. The actual amount of pollution permitted for each firm is reallocated through the market mechanism. This mechanism, in essence, converts the permit into a type of good that has value. The price of the permit fluctuates with the market for regular goods and, hence, the market for the permits emerges.

Indirect regulation

The main objective of indirect regulation is to restrict acts of unfair competition. Through legislation, antitrust rules, and the countering of unfair competition, indirect regulation regulates economic agents to ensure normal economic market order.

ANTITRUST

The indirect regulation of government executive power on monopolies is realized through the creation and enforcing of antitrust laws. The laws represent related procedure and substantive laws used by a country to adjust monopolistic actions or other actions that restrain competition. Such laws are also called the "economic constitution." Antitrust laws maintain market competition to exploit market resource allocation functions. Because a government's direct regulation addresses natural monopolies, there can be confusion. We believe that indirect regulation is only concerned with antitrust legislation and the associated laws and rules while leaving natural monopoly under the jurisdiction of direct economic regulation. The reason for this belief is that antitrust laws are designed to prohibit artificial monopolies; however, natural monopolies are not artificial or the prohibited object of the laws. Inevitable monopolies are not prohibited but restricted by the laws.

ANTI- UNFAIR COMPETITION

Unfair competition refers to all acts that are not appropriate in market transactions including those based on deceit, false information, and the promise of gains in the fields of production, service, and circulation. Unfair competition disturbs the social economic order, efficiency, and fairness. Therefore, governments in many countries have legislated to prohibit and restrict acts of unfair competition.

On December 5, 1980, the 35th General Assembly of the United Nations passed the United Nations Multilaterally Equitable Principles and Rules for the Control of Restrictive Business Practices, which aims to control acts such as abuse of market dominance. The World Trade Organization is also committed to instituting international rules on competition through regulation by countries and international organizations. These rules are designed to encourage fair competition, repress vicious competition, and promote balanced economic and social development.

Macro-level adjustment and control

Government executive power intervention takes another important form, that is, adjustment and control of the economy at the macro level. Government macro-level adjustment and control is intervention through macro areas with an emphasis on aggregate adjustments and the balance of overall economic performance. Major macro-level adjustment and controls include fiscal, income, industry, and monetary policies. Any macro-level adjustment and control policy is government executive power intervention in economic activities. Moreover, although any new policy may appear to be determined directly by executive power, it is, in essence, a game between economic and executive power. Since any new policy is a type of redistribution of interests, a full account of the reactions and possible moves of every economic agent is necessary. In addition, government intervention is an objective request for healthy and stable economic development, and the incentive for the invention is initially driven by interests. The reason is that intervention will create rent-seeking opportunities and help the government gain economic interests and the economic foundations for a stable ruling position.

Case study of games between economic and executive power

Policies and rules are one type of interest redistribution mechanism as a consequence of games between interest groups. Hence, an imbalance in power allocation will inevitably lead to inequality in distribution. The economic power of economic agents is the premise and basis of their striving to achieve their own interests. The agents can obtain favorable policies only when they hold the power needed for policy games. The reduction of state-owned shares evident in China's stock market at the beginning of the 21st century illustrates how a mass of shareholders used their power to force the government to rescind unreasonable policies by voting by foot.

In 2001, China's Ministry of Finance issued a policy that reduced state-owned shares with the aim of supplementing the gap in the nation's social security fund accounts. In fact, investors knew that although the shares to be reduced were low cost for the government, they would be sold at market prices directly in the secondary market. This was considered government action to compete for interests with the general public, which enraged stock investors. The investors voted by foot, which caused a sharp decrease in the stock market to a bear market. On January 26, 2002, China Security Regulatory Commission (CSRC) released the phase report on the scheme to reduce state-owned shares. The core of this report was to reduce the shares via bidding based on the net assets. Meanwhile, the report emphasized that the scheme was simply a framework and was not operational. Even so, the stock market had a strong response to the report. On January 28, 2002, the stock market fell nearly 7%. Many stocks fell to the decline limit, and the index fell below 1,400 points in the Shanghai Stock Market. The total trading volume in the Shanghai and Shenzhen markets was 14 billion RMB, and the decline showed no signs of reversing. The shareholders of the circulated stocks did not accept the amendment to the scheme to reduce state-owned shares. The CSRC issued an urgent statement,

> when making plans to reduce state-owned shares, all related parties will listen to complaints, opinions, and requests from society, pursue a win-win situation, protect the interests of the vast number of investors, gain support from shareholders of the circulated shares, implement maturity plans steadily, and maintain growth through stable markets.

However, from the investor's perspective, CSRC had adopted a delaying tactic to ease the tension but was not determined to make a complete correction.

According to the theory of fair pricing, the price floors of the reduced shares should be decided by discussions with investors. However, the phase report stipulated that the floors be set by shareholders of non-circulated shares excluding all the shareholders of the circulated shares. The vast number of investors owned stocks but had no right to speak and was in a passive and subordinate position. This fact obviously violates the principles of capital markets, which include the principle of equal obligations and rights and the symmetry principle of fairness, justice, and openness. The majority of listed state-owned firms in China had lowered their costs to only a dozen cents per share from their initial face value of 1 yuan RMB. The reason was the practice of allotment and bonus shares plus dividends awarded year after year. Even if net assets are used as a reference to reduce state-held shares, the shares would obtain net gains of five to ten times, exorbitant profits indeed. But with this treatment, investors would lose. Therefore, such schemes *per se* are a direct plunder of the medium and small investors. Investors with no right to speak had to vote by foot. On June 24, 2002, the State Council of China decided that except for firms seeking an overseas listing, Chinese listed firms in domestic stock markets should cease carrying out the stipulations to reduce state-held shares via stock markets in the Reduction of State-Owned Shares and Raising Social Security Fund Management Interim Measures, and there would be no more specific measures to implement such policies.

Up to this point, the vast number of medium and small investors collectively voted by foot with high costs for the termination of the reduction of the state-held shares policy. Within the span of one year, the vast number of medium and small investors became engaged in the power games of the policy using the right to vote. The reduction of state-held shares was the result of power games among several interest groups including the government, investors, and securities traders. The problem was that medium and small investors did not have the right to speak or the right to vote, which caused them to vote by foot. Although their actions affected the policy, it was at the cost of selling stocks at prices lower than the purchase costs. Such consequences did not benefit any party in the games. Therefore, the event verified that in the competition for interests and power games, power reciprocity affects the fairness of policies and is the key to the realization of Pareto optimal.

Power games among consumers, firms, and government based on externalities

Representations of the externality game model

Scholars have applied varying definitions for externalities according to the objectives. Here, the definition follows that in Mas-Colell, Whinston, and Green (1995). That is, with two economic agents, if agent A's action directly affects agent B's utility, agent A is said to have externalities on agent B. Economic power is defined as an agent's ability to control or influence other agents through the resources held by that agent. By comparing the two definitions, we note that the essence of externality is one economic agent exerting economic power on another agent through some kind of carrier. If agent A's action raises agent B's utility, agent A has positive externalities on B. If agent A's action lowers agent B's utility, A has negative externalities on B. Since the issue of positive externalities is similar to that of negative externalities, we formulate the discussions using only negative externalities as the setting. In our scenario, there are two economic agents: consumer and producer. Outputs of the producer include q amount of final goods, plus E amount of additional things inevitable in the production that can be viewed as the carrier of externalities or of the power between the consumer and the producer. The larger the value of E, the more power the producer has over the consumer. Let the consumer have a quasi-linear utility function, $U(q, E) = q + u(E) = q - D(E)$, the price is set to 1, $D(E) = -u(E)$ is a cost function of the consumer with regard to E. It is strictly increasing on E, and strictly convex, that is, $D'(E) > 0$, $D''(E) > 0$. The consumer chooses q to maximize his utilities under constraints.

$$\begin{cases} \max U(q, E) = q - D(E) \\ \quad s.t. \quad pq \leq W \end{cases}$$

The optimization gives the consumer's indirect utility function, $v(E) = \dfrac{W}{p} - D(E)$. Since $p = 1$, $v(E) = W - D(E)$. To focus on externalities, we use $v(E) = W - D(E)$ to describe consumer's utility. Here, $W = \dfrac{W}{p}$ represents initial wealth W of the consumer.

The indirect profit function of the producer is $\pi(E) = \max\limits_{q}(pq - c(q, E))$, where $c(q, E)$ is the production costs, and $\pi(E)$ is strictly convex on E. Given an externality level $E = \bar{E}$, when $E < \bar{E}$, $\pi(E)$ is strictly increasing and when $E > \bar{E}$, $\pi(E)$ is strictly decreasing. $\pi(E)$ reaches maximum at $E = \bar{E}$. Assume the production externalities are meaningful within a certain range, that is, $\pi(E) > D(E)$ when $E < \bar{E}$.

Economic efficiency of externalities and the relationship between power and responsibility

When there are externalities or non-reciprocal power between participants, what is the efficient externality level? To reach this level, consider the social welfare function,

$$S(E) = v(E) + \pi(E) = W + \pi(E) - D(E)$$

In solving for the maximization problem, the optimal level for the whole society is E^*, which is determined by the first-order condition $\pi'(E) = D'(E)$.
$\pi'(E)$ is the increment of returns for the whole society if the externality
level increases by one additional unit, and measures the returns to economic
power to the social planners (e.g., environment conservation departments
in government). $D'(E)$ is the increment of loss for the whole society if the
externality level increases by one additional unit, and measures the costs of
responsibility to the planners. The equation $\pi'(E) = D'(E)$ depicts the symmetry between planner's power and responsibility.

Corollary 1: Assigning power and responsibilities to the same planner, when
the power and the responsibility are reciprocal, the externality level E^* is
optimal for the whole society.

The first theorem of welfare economics tells us that the economic state
under conditions of perfect competition is Pareto optimal. When there are
externalities in a competitive market, will the economic efficiency still be
Pareto optimal? In this scenario, the externality level E^c is derived from
the profit maximization, $\max_{E} \pi(E)$, and satisfies the first-order condition,
$\pi'(E) = 0$. Since $\pi'(E^c) = 0 < D'(E^*) = \pi'(E^*)$, and given $\pi'(E)$ is strictly
decreasing, it follows that $E^c > E^*$; therefore, there are more negative externalities in the competitive market. In such a market, the producer has the
right to generate externalities without constraints. A reduction in market
efficiency will be due to non-reciprocity of power between consumers and
producers together with an asymmetric relation between the power and responsibility of the producer.

Corollary 2: In a competitive market with externalities, the non-reciprocity
between economic agents and the asymmetry of power between power and
responsibilities for the same agent causes a reduction in market efficiency.

The existence of externalities makes the first theorem of welfare economics invalid; hence, it becomes the excuse for government control and
regulation. The British economist Pigou was the first to suggest the idea to
levy taxes on pollution. In the "Economies of Welfare," the author suggests
that taxes should be levied on those who pollute according to the damage
caused by the pollution and be used to make up the gap between private
and social costs and equal the two costs. Such taxes are called Pigou taxes
(Pigou, 1951). We depict Pigou's thoughts with a two-stage dynamic game
model.

Participants in the model are government and producer. Government
sets the tax rate for externalities, τ, and subsidizes consumers with the
revenues from this tax. The firm chooses the externality level of E. For a
given τ and E, consumer's utility is defined as $U(E, \tau) = W - D(E) + \tau E$.
And the producer's profits are given by $\Pi(E, \tau) = \pi(E) - \tau E$. The utility of

government is $S(E, \tau)=U(E, \tau)+\pi(E, \tau)=W+\pi(E)-D(E)$. This game has two stages. In the first stage, government gives tax rate τ; in the second, the producer chooses the externality level after he observes τ. Backwards induction technique can be used to solve for a condensed Nash equilibrium in the sub-game of this dynamic game. In the second stage, the producer observes tax rate τ and chooses E to maximize $\Pi(E, \tau)$. For any given τ, the maximization problem will be $\max_E \Pi(E, \tau)=\pi(E)-\tau E$. From the first-order condition $\dfrac{\partial \pi(E, \tau)}{\partial E}=0$, we can derive the optimal reaction function (implicit) $\tau = \pi'(E)$ of the producer regarding τ.

In the first stage, government has knowledge of the producer's reaction function and chooses the tax rate $\tau = D'(E)$. The externality level of E^* given by $\pi'(E)=D'(E)$ is social optimal. The Pigou tax is a kind of adjustment and control policy that satisfies time consistency. Compared to the competitive market with externalities, there is an additional item, the responsibility item of τE, in the producer's profit function in the Pigou tax model. The tax rate τ can be explained as a responsibility coefficient. The policy stipulates $\tau = D'(E)$, that is, for each unit of externalities produced, the producer is required to compensate the associated social loss of $D'(E)$ so as to offset the benefits obtained from the pollution, $\pi'(E)$. In the model, games between government and producer result in the symmetry between power and responsibility; and hence, the efficiency state is obtained in this economy.

Corollary 3: Under the condition that government has externality cost information $D'(E)$, it is possible to reach the Pareto optimal by adjusting and controlling the economy through tax policy $\tau = D'(E)$.

Unlike Pigou, Coase (1960) holds a different view that there is no justification for producers to bear the responsibility for externalities. As noted by Coase in the "The Problem of Social Cost," it is necessary to know whether a business is responsible for damage caused. Without the establishment of this initial delimitation of power of each party involved, there can be no transactions to transfer and recombine such power. However, the ultimate result is independent of the legal position if the pricing system is assumed to work without cost. Coase offers some thoughts for solving the externality problem with a market transaction approach. That is, the problem can be solved by market transactions for externalities but under the premise that the rights of externalities are clearly defined. Particularly, when the transaction costs are zero, it is possible to reach an efficient level of externalities through bargaining between economic agents. Coase raised the idea of exchanging externalities through markets, the premise for such transactions, and the conditions for obtaining optimal externality levels.

However, he was, from the perspective of exchanging power through markets, seeking solutions to the efficiency problem caused by externalities and had no concern for the problems of interest distribution caused by differing initial definitions of power, transaction mechanisms, and agent's ability to negotiate. We address interest distribution with the model of exchanging externality power.

Transaction model of externalities

After the externalities of economic agents are defined initially, which is normally done by the government, they can be traded either in markets or between the representatives of interest groups organized by regulators. The form of the model depends on the comparison between transaction costs in markets and regulation costs.

THE MODEL WHEREBY THE CONSUMER HAS INITIAL POWER OF EXTERNALITIES

Assume that consumer has the power of not being harmed by externalities; the producer must compensate the consumer at the cost of t amount of transfer payment. The consumer has a utility function of $U(E, t) = W - D(E) + t$, while the producer has a profit function of $\Pi(E, t) = \pi(E) - t$. If there is no transaction of the power of externalities between the consumer and the producer, then $t = 0$ and $E = \underline{E}$, where $\underline{E}$ is level of externality for the consumer to maintain his basic consumption when economic agents cannot trade the power. The consumer's reserved utility will be $\bar{U} = W - D(\underline{E})$ and the producer's reserved profit will be $\underline{\Pi} = \pi(\underline{E})$.

Under the condition whereby the consumer has initial power of externalities, we discuss three mechanisms of externality transactions: transactions where consumers have the right to propose regarding externalities, transactions where producers have the right to propose, and transactions where both parties bargain.

Model 1: Transactions where consumer has the right to propose

Assume the consumer has the right to propose the externality level of E and the transfer payment of t, the producer has the right to accept or reject. Model 1 can be viewed as a model of externality contracts, or a special bargaining model with the negotiation power held fully by the consumer. Given the producer's participation condition, $\Pi(E, t) \geq \underline{\Pi}$ or $\pi(t) - t \geq \underline{\Pi}$, the consumer's action is to choose E and t so as to maximize $U(E, t)$. This problem is formalized as $\begin{cases} \max\limits_{(E,\,t)} U(E,\,t) = w - D(E) + t \\ \quad s.t. \quad \pi(E) - t \geq \Pi \end{cases}$. The optimal transfer

payment satisfies, which says the producer gives the rest of profits to the consumer as compensation after deducting the reserved profits of Π from the total profits. Substituting this into the utility function gives the unconstrained optimization form of $\max\limits_{E} U(E) = w - \Pi + \pi(E) - D(E)$.

From the first-order condition $\dfrac{dU(E)}{dE} = 0$, it follows that $\pi'(E) = D'(E)$ and $E = E^*$. Transfer payment is $t^{(1)} = \pi(E^*) - \Pi$. This shows that the producer exchanges for the externality power of E^* with his transfer payment $t^{(1)}$ plus the power constraint under participation condition on the consumer. Transfer payment internalizes externality problem into consumer's decision issue regarding externalities. From the above-unconstrained optimization problem, $\pi(E)$ can be viewed as the returns to consumer's power. At E^*, consumer has symmetry between power and responsibility, which leads consequently to Pareto optimal for the economy. The interest distributions for the consumer and the producer are $U^{(1)} = U\left(E^*,\ t^{(1)}\right) + t^{(1)} = S(E^*) - \Pi$ and $\Pi^{(1)} = \Pi$ respectively. The producer retains only profit Π while the rest of social welfare $S(E^*) - \Pi$ goes all to the consumer. Note that $S(E^*) > \underline{S}$ implies $U^{(1)} > \bar{U}$. So $\left(U^{(1)},\ \Pi^{(1)}\right)$ is Pareto improvement for $\left(\bar{U},\ \Pi\right)$. However, the gap in $\left(U^{(1)},\ \Pi^{(1)}\right)$ is larger than that in $\left(\bar{U},\ \Pi\right)$.

Model 2: Transactions where producers have the right to propose

Assume that the producer has the right to propose the externality level of E and the amount of transfer payment, and the consumer has the right to accept or reject. Model 2 can be regarded as a contract problem or a bargaining model with the negotiation power held fully by the producer. Given the consumer's participation condition, $U(E,\,t) \geq \bar{U}$ or $W - D(E) + t \geq \bar{U}$, the producer's action is to choose E and t so as to maximize profits. This problem is formalized as

$$\begin{cases} \max\limits_{(E,\,t)} \Pi(E,\,t) = \pi(E) - t \\ \\ s.t. \quad W - D(E) + t \geq \bar{U} \end{cases}$$

The optimal amount of transfer payment is $t = D(E) - D(\underline{E})$, which shows that when the producer has the right to propose regarding E, t, the optimal transfer payment is the compensation to the consumer's externality costs (after deducting $D(\underline{E})$). Substituting this into the unconstrained optimization problem, then,

$$\max_{E} \Pi(E) = \pi(E) - D(E) + D(\underline{E}) = S(E) - \bar{U}$$

Through transfer payment, the externality problem is internalized into the producer's decision problem and externality costs are passed on to the producer, too. Note that the producer's objective function differs from social welfare function, $S(E)$, only in one constant term. Thus, the level of externality a producer chooses, $E = E^*$, is also optimal for the whole society. At E^*, producer has symmetry between power and responsibility. The optimal transfer payment is $t^{(2)} = D(E^*) - D(\underline{E})$. Obviously, $t^{(2)} < t^{(1)}$, the corresponding interest distribution is, $U^{(2)} = \bar{U}$, $\Pi^{(2)} = S(E^*) - \bar{U}$. Producer's right to propose makes the consumer retain only the reserved utility, $\bar{U}$, and takes the rest of social welfare. Similarly, the distribution $\left(U^{(2)}, \Pi^{(2)}\right)$ is Pareto improvement to $(\bar{U}, \underline{\Pi})$, but $\left(U^{(2)}, \Pi^{(2)}\right)$ has a gap larger than $(\bar{U}, \underline{\Pi})$.

Model 3: Transactions where the consumer and producer bargain

As mentioned, with the comparison of market transaction costs and government regulation of fees, the transactions of externality power can be completed between consumers and producers through bargains among economic agents in markets and negotiations organized by regulators between representatives of interest groups. In the latter case, the regulator is in a position to make rules and control the negotiation results. The corresponding policies depend on the results of the negotiations. Therefore, policies are the result of competition for interests and the power games between economic agents. Since making the game rules and controlling the game results reflect the regulator's preferences and code of conduct, it is reasonable to assume that the Nash bargain axiom is satisfied. Further, due to the non-cooperative bargaining results by Rubinstein, when the bargaining time of participants is sufficiently small, it can be approximated by the Nash bargain. Therefore, we use the asymmetric Nash bargain solution to depict the transactions of externalities between the consumer and producer.

Let $\tau \in (0,1)$ be the relative negotiation ability of consumer, and $1-\tau$ be that of producer. Negotiation ability is the extrinsic form of economic power of the agents and affects the interest distribution among them. The Nash negotiation solution, (E^*, t^*), is given by the following optimization problem.

$$\max_{(E,\, t)} N = \left(U(E, t) - \bar{U}\right)^{\tau} \left(\Pi(E, t) - \underline{\Pi}\right)^{1-\tau}$$
$$= \left(t - D(E) + D(\underline{E})\right)^{\tau} \left(\pi(E) - t - \underline{\Pi}\right)^{1-\tau}$$

First-order conditions are $\dfrac{\partial N}{\partial t}=0, \dfrac{\partial N}{\partial E}=0$. From $\dfrac{\partial N}{\partial t}=0$, it follows that the optimal transfer payment satisfies $t=\tau\left(\pi(E)-\underline{\Pi}\right)+(1-\tau)\left(D(E)-D(\underline{E})\right)$. The producer's transfer payment to the consumer is neither $\left(\pi(E)-\underline{\Pi}\right)$, the profit after deducting $\underline{\Pi}$, nor $D(E)-D(\underline{E})$, the compensation for the consumer's externality loss. It is a value in between these two. From $\dfrac{\partial N}{\partial E}=0$, it follows $(1-\tau)\left(t-D(E)+D(\underline{E})\right)\pi'(E)=\tau\left(\pi(E)-t-\underline{\Pi}\right)D'(E)$. Substituting the expression of t into this gives $\pi'(E)=D'(E)$; consequently, $E=E^*$. To analyze the relationship between power and responsibility, we substitute t into $U(E,t)$ and $\Pi(E,t)$. Then we obtain,

$$U(E,t)=W-\left(\tau\underline{\Pi}+(1-\tau)D(\underline{E})+\tau\left(\pi(E)-D(E)\right)\right)$$
$$\Pi(E,t)=\tau\underline{\Pi}+(1-\tau)D(\underline{E})+(1-\tau)\left(\pi(E)-D(E)\right)$$

This shows that in the case of bargains, consumer and producer share both the costs and the returns that resulted from the externality level of E. The consumer shares a proportion of τ while the producer shares $1-\tau$. They jointly decide the externality level, $E=E^*$, which makes the relationship between power and responsibility symmetric for both consumer and producer. Besides, the economy is Pareto optimal.

At $E=E^*$, the amount of transfer payment to the consumer from the producer is $t^{(3)}=\tau\left(\pi(E^*)-\underline{\Pi}\right)+(1-\tau)\left[D(E^*)-D(\underline{E})\right]=\tau t^{(1)}+(1-\tau)t^{(2)}$. Obviously, $t^{(2)}<t^{(3)}<t^{(1)}$, the corresponding distributions of interests are

$$U^{(3)}=\tau\left(S'(E^*)-\underline{\Pi}\right)+(1-\tau)\bar{U}$$
$$\Pi^{(3)}=\tau\underline{\Pi}+(1-\tau)\left[S(E')-\bar{U}\right]$$

The distribution of $\left(U^{(3)},\Pi^{(3)}\right)$ is Pareto improvement to the initial distribution $\left(\bar{U},\underline{\Pi}\right)$ but with an increased income gap.

Notice that $\dfrac{dU^{(3)}}{d\tau}=S(E^*)-S(\underline{E})>0$; therefore, $U^{(3)}$ is increasing in τ and for any $\tau\in(0,1)$, $U^{(1)}>U^{(3)}>U^{(2)}$. $\dfrac{d\Pi^{(3)}}{d\tau}=S(\underline{E})-S(E^*)<0$; hence, $\Pi^{(3)}$ is increasing in $1-\tau$ and $\Pi^{(2)}>\Pi^{(3)}>\Pi^{(1)}$. That is to say, the agents will obtain more interests through bargains as their negotiation ability increases.

In order to compare the income gaps under the above three transaction mechanisms, it is necessary to make certain assumption on $S(E^*)$, which is $2\underline{\Pi}<S(E^*)<2\bar{U}$ where $U^{(1)}>\Pi^{(1)}$, $U^{(2)}>\Pi^{(2)}$; consequently, $\left(\Pi^{(1)},U^{(1)}\right)\supset\left(\Pi^{(3)},U^{(3)}\right)\supset\left(\Pi^{(2)},U^{(2)}\right)\supset\left(\underline{\Pi},\bar{U}\right)$. The order for these models is model 1, model 3, and model 2, with model 1 having the largest income gap and model 2 the smallest. Model 2 has both economic efficiency and small income gap.

The model where the producer has initial power of externalities

Assume that the producer has the power of externalities, the consumer must "bribe" with the transfer payment t to reduce the externality level so as to avoid the harms from externalities. The consumer's utility is $U(E, t) = W - D(\underline{E}) - t$, while the producers profit function is $\Pi(E, t) = \pi(\underline{E}) + t$. When there is no trade of externalities between the two parties, $t = 0$, $E = \bar{E}$. The producer keeps the reserved profits of $\bar{\Pi} = \pi(\bar{E})$ and the consumer's utility is $\underline{U} = W - D(\bar{E})$. Compared with the scenario where the consumer has the power of externalities, the producer has now more reserved profits, $\bar{\Pi} > \underline{\Pi}$. The consumer has less reserved utility, $\underline{U} < \bar{U}$. Corresponding to model 1, 2, and 3, we established model 4, 5, and 6 and then solved them. The results are summarized in Table 8.1.

Under the condition that producer has the initial power of externalities— in the transactions where consumer has the right to propose regarding externalities—producer obtains the reserved profits of $\bar{\Pi}$ and consumer takes the rest of total profits. In the transactions where producer has the right to propose, consumer obtains the reserved utility of $\underline{U}$ while producer takes the rest of total social welfare. In these two scenarios, the externality problem is internalized as consumer's or producer's decision problem regarding the externalities through the transfer payment from consumer to producer.

Bargains result in consumer and producer sharing both returns on and loss of externality level of E with their respective proportions of τ and $1 - \tau$. They jointly decide $E = E^*$, which leads to the symmetry between power and responsibility for both of them and to Pareto optimal for the economy. Distributions of $\left(U^{(4)}, \Pi^{(4)}\right)$, $\left(U^{(5)}, \Pi^{(5)}\right)$, $\left(U^{(6)}, \Pi^{(6)}\right)$ are all Pareto

Table 8.1 Models with producer having initial power of externalities

Model	Externality level & transfer payment	Interest distribution
4 Consumer has the right to propose	$E = E^*$, $t^{(4)} = \bar{\Pi} - \pi(E^*)$	$U^{(4)} = S(E^*) - \bar{\Pi}$, $\Pi^{(4)} = \bar{\Pi}$
5 Producer has the right to propose	$E = E^*$, $t^{(5)} = D(\bar{E}) - D(E^*)$	$U^{(5)} = \underline{U}$, $\Pi^{(5)} = S(E^*) - \underline{U}$
6 Bargains	$E = E^*$, $t^{(6)} = \tau t^{(4)} + (1-\tau)t^{(5)}$	$U^{(6)} = \tau U^{(4)} + (1-\tau)U^{(5)}$
		$\Pi^{(6)} = \tau \Pi^{(4)} + (1-\tau)\Pi^{(5)}$

improvements to $(\underline{U}, \overline{\Pi})$, but the income gaps are all larger than the initial situations.

$$\frac{dU^{(6)}}{d\tau} = S(E^*) - S(\overline{E}) > 0, \frac{d\Pi^{(6)}}{d\tau} = S(\overline{E}) - S(E^*) < 0$$

Therefore, $U^{(6)}$ is increasing in τ and $\Pi^{(6)}$ is increasing in $1-\tau$. For any $\tau \in (0,1)$, $\Pi^{(5)} > \Pi^{(6)} > \Pi^{(4)}$, $U^{(4)} < U^{(6)} < U^{(5)}$. That is, economic agents benefit more from the increase in negotiation power.

To compare the income gaps in these three mechanisms, we need to make an assumption on $S(E^*)$, that is, $2\underline{U} < S(E^*) < 2\overline{\Pi}$. Under this assumption, $\Pi^{(4)} > U^{(4)}$, $\Pi^{(5)} > U^{(5)}$; hence, $(U^{(5)}, \Pi^{(5)}) \supset (U^{(6)}, \Pi^{(6)}) \supset (U^{(4)}, \Pi^{(4)}) \supset (\underline{U}, \overline{\Pi})$. The mechanisms represented by model 4, 5, and 6 are ordered as model 5, 6, and 4, with model 5 having the largest income gap and model 4 the smallest. Model 4 is both efficient and small in income gap.

To see the impacts of initial distribution of power on the interest distribution under different transaction approaches, let's compare model 1 with 4, 2 with 5, and 3 with 6. It is not difficult to see that $U^{(1)} > U^{(4)}$, $U^{(2)} > U^{(5)}$, $U^{(3)} > U^{(6)}$, $\Pi^{(1)} < \Pi^{(4)}$, $\Pi^{(2)} < \Pi^{(5)}$, and $\Pi^{(3)} < \Pi^{(6)}$. This shows that when the transaction approach is the same, the agent with initial power of externalities obtains more interests after the transaction. If agents have the same bargaining power, that is, symmetry of power across economic agents, they will have the same income distribution.

We summarize the main conclusions for externality transactions. Regardless of how the initial power is distributed, if excluding regulation and transaction costs, six approaches to transactions all obtain the efficient externality level. Moreover, while improving economic efficiency, the transaction of externality level also increases the spread of initial income distribution. Assigning the right to propose to those agents who do not have the initial power of externalities will obtain the efficient level of externalities and, under certain conditions, narrow the gap in interest distribution. The magnitude of agents' bargaining power determines the magnitude of interests after transactions. If power is symmetric across agents, income distribution will be equal.

Traditional studies on externalities illustrate that if there is externality, it is impossible to reach the efficient state for an economy even in a competitive market. Failure of the invisible hand leads to efforts in resorting to the visible hand, that is, government adjustment and control. The Pigou tax is an outstanding work from these efforts. Coase theorem lays out the logic and the conditions for reaching an optimal economic state through the utilization of trading externalities, which is that initial property rights must be clearly defined, and transaction costs must be zero. However, such conditions are impossible to meet in reality. Similarly, in a case where regulation incurs costs, government regulation will not help to reach the optimal state. Therefore, whether the government or markets are relied on to solve the low efficiency problem caused by externalities is really determined by the size of the transaction and government regulation costs. However, from the perspective of power games between economic agents, the essence of the externality problem is an issue of economic agents using power. Symmetry between the power and responsibility of the decision maker on externalities can realize the economic optimal state. Reciprocity of power for the agents can realize equality in income distribution. Therefore, to solve the externality problem reasonably, it must be guaranteed that power and responsibility are symmetric for the same agent and power is reciprocal across agents. Only then can a pattern of equal interest distribution exist across agents.

Theoretical boundaries for the intervention of government executive power

Market adjustment mechanisms and government intervention have been controversial subjects in economics. Market adjustment, given the market environment, refers to firms' operational behavior, for example, making independent and rational decisions on production, investment, and sales based on market mechanisms. Market adjustment also refers to consumer behavior, such as making independent and rational decisions on the supply of human capital and choice of consumption. Government intervention is defined as the use of administrative and economic power to decide the investment and production of public goods and the use of anti-trust and regulations to maintain competition in the market. In fact, the market is a mechanism by which economic resources carry out free allocation. Whether government, firms, or individuals, economic resources exert influence on market transaction behaviors with their own power. Such influence is realized through power games between economic agents.

According to public choice theory, human society is divided into two markets: economic and political. Power agents in the economic market are consumers and firms, and the objects of transactions are private goods. In the political market, the participants are the voters, government officials, and interest groups. Voters and interest groups represent the market demand side while government officials who are the suppliers and the objects of transactions are public goods. Through democratic voting, people choose the legal institutions, policies, politicians, and public goods that can bring the best interests for them. In the economic research framework of the power paradigm, the government, as an agent, participates in economic activities in the pure sense in the economic market. As the power agent supplying public goods, the government *per se* is still the feature of rationality, which is a strong assumption of economic man. This is the basis of the theoretical boundaries for government power discussed in this section.

The influence of government executive power on the boundaries of firms' economic power

Coase believes that when it is cheaper to produce something than buy it from the market, firms emerge. By establishing an organization and assigning to it the power to allocate resources, some market costs could be reduced. Considering that a business organization can obtain production factors at lower prices than the market mechanism it replaces, entrepreneurs inevitably lower costs to accomplish their duties. This is because if they cannot succeed with a venture, the organization could always return to the open market at any time. Thus, Coase concludes that the scale boundary for the existence of a firm is that the marginal cost of its internal trading is equal to the marginal cost of trading in the market.

First, the government is directly involved in market transactions through its participation in state-owned firms or activities, such as investment in public utilities. Such government actions can directly facilitate improvements in the so-called hardware environment for market transactions. Consequently, improvements are possible to reduce market transaction costs. Relative to low market transaction costs, firms reduce their scale to lower internal transaction costs, which means that direct government involvement in the market to provide public goods can lead to marginal contraction of business scale. However, the government corrects market failures using the executive power it holds and balances income distribution among the interest groups through the mandatory transfer of wealth. All these improve market performance. Therefore, government executive power can reduce market transaction costs. Through direct and indirect effective market intervention, the government reduces market transaction costs so that firms do not have the momentum to strengthen their economic power by expanding their scale border.

Second, government power may cause firms to continuously expand their scale to resist the impact of the government's strong power. In some cases, in supplying public goods, a government may not consider public interests and be more concerned with increasing its wealth. Here, government intervention in the economy, executive power, corruption, and rent-seeking behavior occurs due to a lack of supervision or excessive use of discretion in regulation. Market transaction costs will increase sharply, and it is safe to say that the improper expansion of government power raises market transaction costs, which keeps business internal transaction costs relatively low. Therefore, it becomes an option for firms to enhance their economic power through the expansion of scale boundaries.

It follows from the above analysis on the content of agents' economic power that the amount of resources a firm possesses determines the magnitude of its economic power and reflects the scale boundary. Therefore, the scale boundary reflects economic power. A large-scale firm has stronger bargaining power and influence in market transactions. Government power may cause changes in the scale boundary in different directions; however, whatever changes occur, as long as government power can lower market transaction costs with intervention, it will reduce the scale of the firm. On the contrary, if government power cannot lower the transaction costs through intervention, it is bound to stimulate firms to continuously enhance their own economic power to offset the erosion in their own interests from government power. In reality, with continuous expansion in scale boundaries, the economic power of firms is also growing continuously, which enhances the firms' monopoly position. Such cases often occur in fields or industries that are over-protected by government power or where government power cannot be exerted effectively. For example, this is the case for some state-owned firms that rely on executive power to maintain a monopoly and some private firms that rely on breaching laws and regulations to expand rapidly.

If internal transaction costs are less than the market costs, the scale of firms will expand as a consequence. Firms will possess more resources, and their economic power will increase further. In the absence of external constraints, expansion of the economic power boundary will tend to be more obscure, which will inevitably result in relatively smaller influence from the other power agents in the economic system. Thus, firms with more power will have sufficient bargaining power and the right to speak. Ultimately, this is likely to lead to a monopoly and market inefficiencies. However, firms' economic power expands without limitations. When such expansion causes continuous inefficiency, other economic agents, including consumers and other firms, exert pressure on the government and request that the government restrain firms' economic power expansion, correct market failures, and improve government efficiency.

Nash equilibrium of power games between consumers and firms with government participation

Through intervention using executive power, the government can provide welfare favorable to certain economic agents and realize the mandatory transfer of wealth. The desirable power boundary is the maximization of the government's own interests through intervention policies. In the process of achieving this objective, the government faces the impact of economic power from various interest groups. The entire process of reaching equilibrium is full of dynamic economic power games between interest groups.

Assume that there are two economic power agents, 1 and 2, standing for firms and consumers respectively. They can improve their level of welfare by influencing government decisions. The economic power of the firm and the consumer can be characterized as their influence on government. So let P_1 and P_2 be the representations of such influence. However, the firm can exert influence on government decisions via the power in its hands so as to obtain relatively more transfer of wealth, $\tilde{E} = \tilde{E}(P_1, P_2)$. Obviously, $\dfrac{\partial E}{\partial P_1} > 0$

and $\dfrac{\partial E}{\partial P_2} < 0$. The greater the influence of the firm on government decisions, the more the wealth transfer it can obtain, but considering that costs must be paid for such transfer, the net benefit function of its power can be expressed as $E(P_1, P_2) = \tilde{E}(P_1, P_2) - C_E(P_1)$. Then, it's easy to get $\dfrac{\partial E}{\partial P_2} < 0$, and $\dfrac{\partial C_E}{\partial P_1} > 0$, and the magnitude of $E = (P_1, P_2)$ depends on the transferred wealth obtained by the firm via power and its internal organization costs. Compared with the consumer, the more the relative influence it has on government, the higher the costs it has to pay. Rational choice process always requires that the firm should measure the benefits from the government as well as the costs paid. As long as the expected final result $\partial E / \partial P_1 > 0$, it will take actions to influence government to make decisions favorable to it.

Similarly, the consumer makes use of the power he holds to exert influence on government decisions, so as to obtain relatively more wealth transfer $\tilde{I} = \tilde{I}(P_1, P_2)$, here $\dfrac{\partial \tilde{I}}{\partial P_2} > 0, \dfrac{\partial \tilde{I}}{\partial P_1} < 0$. Considering cost factors, the net benefit function of the consumer power can be expressed as: $I(P_1, P_2) = \tilde{I}(P_2, P_1) - C_I(P_2)$, $\dfrac{\partial I}{\partial P_1} < 0, \dfrac{\partial C_I}{\partial P_2} > 0$. Note that the rational choice of consumers is completely consistent with that of the firm. That is, as long as $\partial I / \partial P_1 > 0$, the consumer will exert influence on government to obtain benefits. Under such cost and benefit conditions, the firm and the consumer will play power games in order to obtain net benefit. In the static with full information, the game model is expressed as $G = N, S_1, S_2, u_1, u_2$, where $N = \{1,2\}$ and $S_1 = S_2 = [0, \infty]$ are the strategy sets for the firm and the consumer. $P_i \in S_i$ represents the economic power of the consumer and the firm, $i = 1, 2, u_1 = E(P_1, P_2), u_2 = I(P_1, P_2)$.

First-order conditions of the model are, $\dfrac{\partial E(P_1, P_2)}{\partial P_1} = 0, \dfrac{\partial I(P_1, P_2)}{\partial P_2} = 0$.

Based on this, the respective reaction functions can be derived. For any P_2 chosen by the consumer, the reaction function of the firm is $P_1 = R_1(P_2)$; for any P_1 chosen by the firm, the reaction function of the consumer is $P_2 = R_2(P_1)$. The Nash equilibrium of the power games between the firm and the consumer is the intersection of the above reaction curves, $\left(P_1^*, P_2^*\right)$. Under these conditions, both the firm and the consumer have no incentive to move away from $\left(P_1^*, P_2^*\right)$. This is because in order to obtain more profits, the firm will choose P_1^*,[1] which is its optimal choice under the expectation of consumer choosing P_2^*; however, if the firm does not choose P_1^*, it will inevitably lose the game, and this will eventually result in that government decides to supply policies favorable to the consumer. In the same vein, when expecting the firm choice being P_1^*, the consumer will choose P_2^*, also an optimal choice for him. If he chooses an arbitrary $P_2 \neq P_2^*$, the firm can always get the supply of favorable policies from government by choosing P_1^*. The realization of equilibrium in such power games is shown in Figure 8.1:

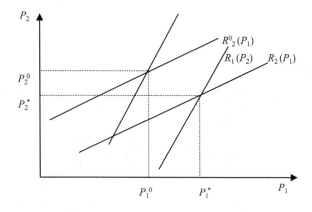

Figure 8.1 Nash equilibrium in the games of economic power.

For firms and consumers in the market, even if the Nash equilibrium, (P_1^*, P_2^*), exists in the power games of economic agents, it may not be the Pareto equilibrium under the condition of optimal resource allocation. In such games between consumers and firms, to obtain more transfers of government interests, each agent will inevitably compete with others and attempt to win favorable government decisions, resorting to the power they have in hand, and using all means at their disposal. However, such power games could lead to Pareto invalidity. As mentioned in the theoretical analysis, the agents in market transactions include consumers, firms, and government. Government involvement in economic activities does not solely reflect voter preferences for political support. In reality, governments play different roles in economic activities. As an agent, economic man both seeks self-interest and is an arbiter who regulates the market order. In other words, the government is a dual agent with both economic and executive power, which undoubtedly makes the games even more complex between every power agent in the whole economic system.

In addition, the power games between consumers and firms lead to inefficient resource allocation. This is because there are conflicts in the common interests between different power agents, which prevents the producer collusion in the Cournot model from emerging. However, the power game does not imply that there is no room for Pareto improvement. If the government has full information and often makes correct and effective decisions, it is highly possible that the games between consumers and firms have a positive effect under the guided objective set by government. That is, in market competition, firms seek greater economic power by providing high-tech and high-quality products. At the same time, consumers strive to improve their own quality and obtain more rights to benefits and consumption choices rather than a situation where firms become monopolies in goods markets and consumers monopolize consumption markets. Thus, the deadweight loss of economic resources declines along with the loss in social welfare. At this point, the games between the agents will gradually approach the Pareto equilibrium in the entire economic system.

Executive power boundaries

Resources allocation is determined by the power games among all agents of economic power. In theory, the games are a process that is usually divided into two stages, although there is no clear demarcation between the two stages in reality. The first stage starts with the market economy. At this stage, the market mechanism dominates the power games. Based on their economic power, consumers, firms, and government choose different strategies in different rounds when playing power games to maximize their own interests. At this point, the maximization objective of the government as an agent is to accumulate wealth instead of political capital. However, with the repeated games between power agents, the original equilibria are constantly interrupted. When markets fail, the government's maximization objectives change. The objectives may switch from that of rational economic man participating in economic transactions to how to win greater political prestige to dissolve the pressure caused by a series of social problems as a result of market failure. Here, agent power games enter the second stage. At this stage, the game rules have changed, and the entire process shifts from the economic to the political market. This is because the government uses the executive power in hand to intervene in the economy. Hence, the government has changed from a participant in the economic system to an arbitrator or policy supplier. Through intervention, the government completes the transfer of wealth. To gain favorable policies, consumers and firms use the power they hold to exert pressure on the government through various expression mechanisms of interest. In this state, according to Stigler's assumptions, firms and government are rational men seeking to maximize their own interests. The government's objective is to maximize political interests. That is, to achieve a new balance of interests among different agents of power via executive power to realize the effective[2] transfer of wealth and to secure greater political prestige. This can be demonstrated by model (8.1) as follows:[3]

$$max_p M = M(p, \pi)$$
$$s.t \ \pi = f(p, c), \ c = c(Q) \tag{8.1}$$

Where M is the object of government, p, π, c, and Q stand for price, profit, cost, and output respectively. The government objective M is based on their price and profit control over firms. $M'_p < 0$ states that as price goes up, consumers' discontents will result in a decline in the political interests of government. $M'_\pi > 0$ states that as profit goes up, firms' supports will result in a rise in the political interests of government. In such a state of conflicts government will balance the request for interests from consumers with that from firms, with an attempt to find the level of government power intervention (i.e., power boundary) when political interests are at maximum. Under the above constraints, we can find the solution to model (8.1). According to the Lagrangian equation $L = M(p, \pi) + \lambda(\pi - f(p, c))$, the solution can be derived as,

$$-\frac{M'_p}{f'_p} = M'_\pi = -\lambda \tag{8.2}$$

This implies that when consumers and firms exert influence on government with economic power, the boundary condition for the government's executive power to intervene in the economy is that the marginal political revenues based on business profits equal the marginal rate of profit substitution for the consumer surplus. Once the boundary of the executive power deviates from this equilibrium, it will favor firms, relax regulations causing higher prices, and stimulate consumer discontent. If the boundary favors consumers, it will enhance market control and punishment causing a decline in business profits, which stimulates firms' discontent. Therefore, the optimal regulation policy is a certain type of economic power equilibrium between consumers and firms. Such optimal policy choices are shown in Figure 8.2.

M_1 and M_2 are indifference curves of the government objectives, and $M_2 > M_1$. In order to maximize the objectives, government always tries to obtain relatively low prices and high profits through intervention of administrative power. This ends up at the equilibrium, point $o(P_o^*, \pi_o^*)$.

It is easy to find the equilibrium for the intervention of government's economic power in Figure 8.2, but in reality, the location of this equilibrium is the result of long-term dynamic games between economic power agents. The best policy choice of government's administrative power intervention represents the theoretical boundary of such intervention into economic activities.

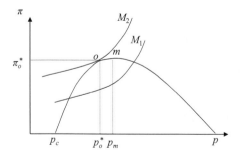

Figure 8.2 Optimal policy choice of government administrative intervention on economy.

Case study: the effects of government regulation

On October 15th, 2006, the Ministry of Commerce of China promulgated the order of Measures for the Administration of Fair Dealing of Retailers and Suppliers. An important component of this order was restrictions on slotting allowances, which are fees paid to retailers by suppliers who want to either enter goods into retailing or maintain advantageous shelf placement. There were concerns with the measures. The first was whether the order could be carried out in full, and the second was the impact it would have on the behavior of retailers and suppliers and the welfare of consumers. A systematic understanding of the sources and the effects of the allowances is required to address these concerns.

Shaffer (1991) argues that slotting allowances are the outcome of retailers' market power. The author develops a model incorporating a perfectly competitive manufacturing industry and a retail duopoly and proves that the allowances raise retail prices and increase profits of both suppliers and retailers. This finding implies that the market power of retailers benefits both retailers and supplies, but consumers pay higher prices. The reason is that in Shaffer's model, suppliers have the advantage of Stackleberg leadership, and the allowances have become an instrument used by suppliers to control retailers.

Charging allowances are indeed the manifestation of a retailer's market power. However, the major effect is influencing the interest distribution between retailers and suppliers. That is, in providing goods and services to consumers, suppliers and retailers have a cooperative production relationship. The returns to such cooperation are the total channel profits, which are the retail prices after subtracting production costs. How much of the total channel profits either side can obtain is determined by the contrast in power between the two sides. Interest distribution of channel profits can be fulfilled via the transaction prices between retailers and suppliers, such as factory price and wholesale price. However, such prices are probably unable to reflect the contrast precisely or in a timely way. As a result, the allowances become an adjusting mechanism that influences transaction prices to guarantee the interest distribution is consistent with the power comparison. This chapter constructs a model for a perfectly competitive manufacturing industry and a differentiated retail duopoly and uses the model to analyze the impact of the allowances on retail prices, sales volumes, consumer welfare, and to conjecture the outcome of government restriction on the allowances.

Basic assumptions for theoretical analysis

Assuming the whole industry is composed of competitive manufacturers and two retailers. Marginal costs are constant c for all manufacturers whose transaction prices, being w[4] for all, are determined by the overall demand and supply relations for the whole industry. The difference between retailers is reflected by that between coverage rates. Let the overall market size be 1 (see Figure 8.3), and retailer 1's coverage rate be $n_1 (0 < n_1 \leq 1)$, and retailer 2's coverage rate be $n_2 (0 < n_2 \leq 1)$. There is no blank area in the market, which means, $1 \leq n_1 + n_2 \leq 2$. $n_1 + n_2 - 1$ is a sub-market of the two competing retailers, the magnitude of which reflects the intensity of their competition. The larger the $n_1 + n_2 - 1$, the more intense the competition is.

Each retailer adopts a unified price strategy[5] within his own business region (n_1 is retailer 1's region while n_2 is retailer 2's). We use the following demand functions to depict the relationship between retailer's prices and sales.

$$q_1 = \left(1 - n_2 + \frac{n_1 + n_2 - 1}{2}\right)\left[1 - \frac{p_1}{s} + \frac{\gamma}{(1-\gamma)s}(p_2 - p_1)\right] \qquad (8.3)$$

$$q_2 = \left(1 - n_1 + \frac{n_1 + n_2 - 1}{2}\right)\left[1 - \frac{p_2}{s} + \frac{\gamma}{(1-\gamma)s}(p_1 - p_2)\right] \qquad (8.4)$$

These functions are based on Shubik-Levitan horizontal differentiation duopoly model. q_1 and q_2 denote sales of retailer 1 and those of retailer 2, respectively; p_1 and p_2 represent their retail prices; s is the function value of products (relative to the channel service value) and is determined by manufacturers. The larger the s, the smaller the price elasticity of demand will be. $\frac{\gamma}{1-\gamma}$ represents the competition intensity between the two retailers, where $\gamma = n_1 + n_2 - 1$. When $n_1 + n_2 = 1$, there will be no competition, $\frac{\gamma}{1-\gamma} = 0$, and the demand functions reduce to the Tirole demand functions of monopolistic firms. Sales of each retailer is only determined by his own retail price, and the retailer sets price based on monopoly market. When $n_1 = n_2 = 1$, $\frac{\gamma}{1-\gamma} \to \infty$, the two retailers compete with each other for the whole market (which has the capacity of 1). As long as p_1 and p_2 has infinitesimal difference, the two will have big difference in sales, which will cause the equilibrium price equal to purchasing costs.

The games are set up as follows. As the premise, the manufacturers have signed contracts with both retailers with the factory price being w for both of them. This price will not change within a certain period (e.g., one year).

In stage one, both retailers seek to maximize their profits based on the given factory price, w, and at the same time, set their retail prices, p_1 and p_2, respectively.

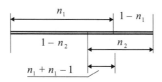

Figure 8.3 Distribution of retail markets.

In stage two, since the factory price is given, when the retail prices that resulted from competition are relatively low, their profits will be relatively low and could not guarantee the shares of total channel profits. As a means of adjustment, they will decide how much slotting allowance to charge manufacturers based on the magnitude of their power.

Government believes that retailers' charging the allowances with coercion is an action that falls into the category of abuse of advantageous position; therefore, it should be regulated. As exogenous variable, Φ is given as the intensity of government restriction. If $\Phi = 0$, there will be no restrictions. If $\Phi = 1$, there will be full restrictions. The actual amount of the allowances that retailers can obtain is affected by Φ.

Solution to the game model

The above process is a two-stage simultaneous-move dynamic game model. Backward induction is used to solve it.

HOW RETAILERS DETERMINE THE AMOUNT OF THE ALLOWANCE

Assume that retail 1's retail price is p_1 and his sales are denoted by q_1, then he and the manufacturers create jointly the channel profits of $(p_1-c)q_1$. If the factory price w is the only way of profit distribution, then profits that each side receives are $(p_1-w)q_1$ and $(w-c)q_1$, respectively. The higher the w, the more shares the manufacturer will get. As mentioned above, $(p_1-w)q_1$ and $(w-c)q_1$ do not reflect accurately the power comparison between retailer 1 and the manufactures. Therefore, retailer 1 will charge f_1 amount of the allowances to guarantee his profit shares[6] that are based on his power, that is,

$$(p_1-w)q_1 + f_1 = \delta_{r1}(p_1-c)q_1 \tag{8.5}$$
$$(w-c)q_1 - f_1 = \delta_{m1}(p_1-c)q_1 \tag{8.6}$$

where δ_{r1} represents retailer 1's power relative to the manufacturers; and δ_{m1} represents manufacturers' power relative to retailer 1.

Power of retailers mainly comes from the number of consumers they cover while for manufacturers it comes from function values of their products or in other words, the quality. Because the number of consumers and the function values cannot be compared directly, here we compare the power of retailers with that of manufacturers using their investment that aims to obtain the related power. Assume that retailer 1's investment is 1 unit[7] on the stores needed to cover 1 unit of consumers, then his coverage of n_1 amount of consumers will imply that his total investment is n_1. The function value of manufacturers' products is assumed to be s, which can be interpreted as the highest price that a typical consumer is willing to pay for one unit of the products. So, the function value is clearly measurable. Under these premises, assume that manufacturers make 1 unit of investment, such as fees spent on R&D, transformation of equipment, and upgrading equipment, to obtain 1 unit of function value. Then, to get s amount of function value requires total investment to be the amount of s. Therefore, the power index of retailer 1 relative to the manufacturers will be $\delta_{r1} = \dfrac{n_1}{s+n_1}$ after normalization. While the index of manufacturers relative to retailer 1 will be $\delta_{m1} = \dfrac{s}{s+n_1} = 1-\delta_{r1}$, after normalization. It follows from (8.5)

$$f_1 = \left[\delta_{r1}(p_1-c)-(p_1-w)\right]q_1 \tag{8.7}$$

The above equation states that the slotting allowances retailer 1 charges are equal to the difference between the profits he deserves due to his power and those calculated based on factory prices. This reflects the assumption made in this chapter that the allowances are adjustment mechanism of profit distribution.[8]

Similarly, retailer 2 charges the following amount of allowances,

$$f_2 = \left[\delta_{r2}(p_2-c)-(p_2-w)\right]q_2 \tag{8.8}$$

Given that the allowances are not disclosed, our models do not consider the case where the decisions of both retailers can affect each other.

Government puts restrictions on charging the allowances by announcing that certain categories of fees are not legal. As more and more types of fees fall into the illegal categories, the actual amount of allowances retailers receive will become less. Therefore, corresponding to the degree of government restriction, Φ, the actual allowances the retailers can collect will be $(1-\Phi)f_1$ and $(1-\Phi)f_2$, respectively.

RETAILING PRICE GAMES BETWEEN THE RETAILERS

Each retailer is able to forecast the function of allowances he will receive; therefore, the profit functions of the retailers to make price decisions are as follows,

$$\pi_{r1} = (p_1-w)q_1+(1-\Phi)f_1 \tag{8.9}$$
$$\pi_{r2} = (p_2-w)q_2+(1-\Phi)f_2 \tag{8.10}$$

Assume the conjectural variation of one retailer on the other's price is zero— the Bertrand competition case—then the equilibrium retail prices are,

$$p_1^* = \frac{c+(1-\gamma)s}{2-\gamma}+\frac{w-c}{4-\gamma^2}\left(\frac{2\Phi}{\delta_{r1}+\Phi\delta_{m1}}+\frac{\gamma\Phi}{\delta_{r2}+\Phi\delta_{m2}}\right) \tag{8.11}$$

$$p_2^* = \frac{c+(1-\gamma)s}{2-\gamma} + \frac{w-c}{4-\gamma^2}\left(\frac{2\Phi}{\delta_{r2}+\Phi\delta_{m2}} + \frac{\gamma\Phi}{\delta_{r1}+\Phi\delta_{m1}}\right) \quad (8.12)$$

These prices yield a set of equilibrium values, including

$$q_i^* = q_i\left(p_1^*, p_2^*\right) \; (i=1,2) \quad\quad (8.13)$$

$$f_i^* = f_i\left(p_i^*, q_i^*\right) \; (i=1,2) \quad\quad (8.14)$$

$$\pi_{ri}^* = \pi_{ri}\left(p_i^*, q_i^*, f_i^*\right) \; (i=1,2) \quad\quad (8.15)$$

Manufacturers' profits are equal to the total channel profits minus retail profits, which is,

$$\pi_{mi}^* = \left(p_i^* - c\right)q_i^* - \pi_{ri}^* \; (i=1,2) \quad\quad (8.16)$$

where π_{m1}^* represents the profits that arise from manufacturers' cooperation with retailer 1 and π_{m2}^* represents the profits that resulted from manufacturers' cooperation with retailer 2.

IMPLICATIONS OF THE EQUILIBRIUM RESULTS AND SOME ILLUSTRATIONS

For equations from (8.11) to (8.13), let $\Phi = 0$, we can derive the retail prices and sales without the allowances (see Table 8.2 for this case). As n_1 and n_2 get larger, equilibrium retail prices p_1^* and p_2^* become smaller. This states that since the expansion of their networks lead to more overlapping markets for the retailers, competition has become more and more intense between them; hence, the prices are inevitably decreasing when they are the only means of such competition. For any individual retailer, its sales grow with the expansion of its channels and at same time are offset by the channel expansion of its opponent. However, the overall retail sales $q_1^* + q_2^*$ grow with $n_1 + n_2$.

Figure 8.4 shows the increasing trend of the retail price index for major household electrical appliance and the decreasing sales trend for appliances since household electrical appliance retailers began.

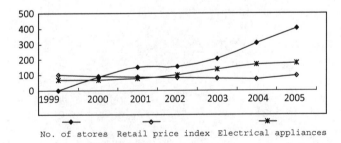

Figure 8.4 Trends in retail price indices and sales as the number of stores changes.

Our model states that retailer network expansion causes the retail price to fall but, at the same time, the expansion enhances manufacturers' relative power. As a result, he can charge slotting allowances to make up for the loss due the fall in price. Based on equations (8.11), (8.13), and (8.14), Figure 8.5 simulates the trend in the profits generated by prime operation (PPO) $\left(p_1^* - w\right)q_1^*$, the revenue from the allowances f_1^*, and the total profits π_{r1}^* (the sum of the first two) as n_1 increases while holding other factors constant. With expansion in the retailer's channel, profits from the margins between the purchase and selling price (PMP) are decreasing and even incur losses while the revenues from the allowances grow steadily, which guarantees growth in total profits. Figure 8.6 plots the correlation between the changes in profit composition and the growth in the number of stores for Gome since 2001, which yields results close to those in Figure 8.5.

The evidence shows that to contend with retailers' power derived from market coverage, manufacturers choose the function values of products, that is, continuously bringing in new products to substitute old ones. Each round of new product launches will raise the price coordinate to a higher level. It is clear from this remark that manufacturers regard function values as long-term means of competition or, in other words, the source of power. In the long run, the game between retailers and suppliers is the contest for power.

There are many cases illustrating the close relationship between slotting allowances and the power contrast between retailers and suppliers. According-ing to the *International Business* report, retailers of different sizes charge different slotting allowances for the same product from the same supplier. For dairy products, large-scale supermarkets charge a rate of 3.39% on av-erage as allowances while food supermarkets charge 1.96% on average, and convenience shops charge 1.23% on average. From the supplier's perspec-tive, the rate varies with the influence of brands. The more influential the

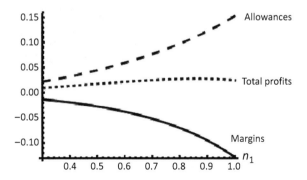

Figure 8.5 Channel expansion and changes in profit for retailers.

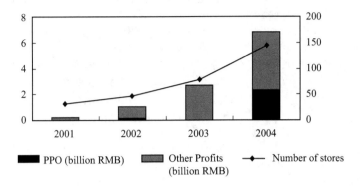

Figure 8.6 Trend of profit composition for Gome.

brand, the less the supermarkets will charge as allowances. The opposite holds if the brand is less influential. This shows that the power contrast between retailers and suppliers is the major determinant of the magnitude of the allowances.

ANALYSIS ABOUT THE EFFECTS OF REGULATIONS ON THE SLOTTING
ALLOWANCES

First, let's analyze the welfare effects of the allowances on consumers and the results of government intervention. For (8.9) to (8.11), let $\Phi = 0$ and $\Phi = 1$, the following table (Table 8.2) presents the equilibrium retail prices and sales in two scenarios, that is, the allowances are either permitted or prohibited.

Note that $s > w > c > 0$,[9] it is apparent that the retail price in the scenario where the allowances are permitted ($\Phi = 0$) is less than that in the other scenario ($\Phi = 1$). As for the equilibrium sales, the former ($\Phi = 0$) is greater than the latter ($\Phi = 1$). This indicates that the allowances have the effect of raising consumers' welfare, or in other words, government intervention reduces the welfare. We can explore further the nature of the allowances and the results of government intervention by analyzing the causes to the above results.

When $\Phi = 0$, $\pi_{r1} = \delta_{r1}(p_1 - c)q_1$ and $\pi_{r2} = \delta_{r2}(p_2 - c)q_2$. The ratio of each retailer's profits to total channel profits is deterministic, denoted by δ_{r1} and δ_{r2} respectively. The two retailers will maximize their own profits via maximizing the total profits in each channel, $(p_1 - c)q_1$ and $(p_2 - c)q_2$ respectively. This is equivalent to price competition based on manufacturer's costs c; therefore, it will result in low equilibrium prices and high level of equilibrium sales volume. If $\Phi = 1$, then $\pi_{r1} = \delta_{r1}(p_1 - w)q_1$ and $\pi_{r2} = \delta_{r2}(p_2 - w)q_2$. This is equivalent to price competition based on retailer's buying costs w; therefore, as long as $w > c$, it will result in high equilibrium prices and low level of equilibrium sales volume.

Table 8.2 Effects of government intervention on equilibrium

	No government intervention $(\Phi = 0)$	With government intervention $(\Phi = 1)$
p_1^*	$s - \dfrac{s-c}{3-n_1-n_2}$	$s - \dfrac{s-w}{3-n_1-n_2}$
p_2^*	$s - \dfrac{s-c}{3-n_1-n_2}$	$s - \dfrac{s-w}{3-n_1-n_2}$
q_1^*	$\dfrac{(1+n_1-n_2)(s-c)}{2(3-n_1-n_2)s}$	$\dfrac{(1+n_1-n_2)(s-w)}{2(3-n_1-n_2)s}$
q_2^*	$\dfrac{(1+n_2-n_1)(s-c)}{2(3-n_1-n_2)s}$	$\dfrac{(1+n_2-n_1)(s-w)}{2(3-n_1-n_2)s}$
$q_1^* + q_2^*$	$\dfrac{s-c}{(3-n_1-n_2)s}$	$\dfrac{s-w}{(3-n_1-n_2)s}$

Furthermore, when $\Phi = 0$ and $n_1 = n_2 = 1$, that is, there are the allowances and the retailers compete with each other in the entire market, then $p_1^* = p_2^* = c$, that is, retail price equals manufacturer's costs, and both retailers and manufacturers have zero economic profits. When $\Phi = 1$ and $n_1 = n_2 = 1$, that is, no slotting allowances but the retailers compete with each other in the entire market, then $p_1^* = p_2^* = w$, that is, retail price equals manufacturer's factory price, and the pressure of competition in retail market is blocked by factory price.

In summary, as a mechanism to adjust interests, we argue that slotting allowances effect pressure transmission. If allowances are permitted, competition pressure will be passed from retailers to manufacturers. Consequently, there will be low retail prices, high sales volumes, and an increase in consumer welfare. However, if allowances are prohibited, the pressure will not be passed to manufacturers in the current game period,[10] and retailers will set their retail prices based only on the given factory prices. Thus, the retail prices will be high, and sales levels will be low. Therefore, government regulation on the allowances results in a sluggish market mechanism.

We now investigate the effects of government intervention on the profits of both retailers and suppliers. The allowances transfer some of the channel profits to retailers from manufacturers, which increases retailer profits but reduces those of manufacturers. However, it is a mistake to simply think that restrictions on allowances will surely increase manufacturer profits. As mentioned above, government intervention has the direct effect of lowering the allowance, reducing sales, and raising prices. Changes in the allowance will only lead to the transfer of profits among channel members and will not affect total channel profits. However, the other two effects will affect total profits.

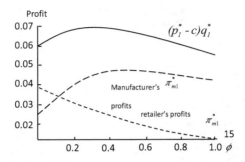

Figure 8.7 Manufacturer's profits and retailer's profits change with φ.

Figure 8.7 simulates the tendency of total channel profits of retailer 1 and manufacturers as well as that of each party's profits when φ increases. When government intervention is at a low level, the effect of rising retail prices dominates, and total channel profits increase. When the intervention exceeds certain limits, the effect of falling sales dominates, and total profits reduce. Hence, there is an optimal level of government intervention. When government intervention is at a low level, the benefits manufacturers obtain from the reduction in the allowances exceed the loss from the reduction in sales. Consequently, the profits increase. For retailers, the positive effect that intervention has on profits is increased prices while the negative effects include a reduction in the allowances and sales. The joint effect of both the negative and positive sides is that profits continue to decrease with φ. Note that changes in the parameters in the simulation only affect the location of the highest value of total channel profits, not the above pattern.

Finally, let's look at the impacts of government invention on the long-term decisions for both retailers and suppliers. The premise for above analysis is that s, n_1 and n_2 are given, which is equivalent to say that firms are playing games in a short-term. However, s, n_1 and n_2 are changing in the long-run; therefore, to analyze government intervention's impacts on them, it is necessary to add another phase of games where they are the decision variables. Because the process of finding the solution is quite complicated, we adopt the simulation approach to explore this issue. The first aspect is how government intervention affects the decision of manufacturers on product quality. Taking the corresponding equilibrium values into (8.16) gives the expression of π^*_{m1}, which is expressed by n_1, n_2, s, w, c, and Φ. Assume π^*_{m1} is fixed, Figure 8.8 shows the iso-profit curves with s being the vertical axis and Φ being the horizontal axis. For any given π^*_{m1}, that is on the same iso-profit curve, when $\Phi > 0$, the corresponding values of s, such as point B_1 and B_2, are smaller than that of s when $\Phi = 0$, such as point A. This states that if the degree of government intervention is not equal to zero, then there exists the condition for the manufacturers to obtain profits even at low quality. This means that the intervention weakens the incentive of manufacturers to improve quality. The shape of iso-profit curves are affected by parameters such as n_1, n_2, w, and c. By changing the values of these parameters, we find that the pattern of Φ's impact on s is stable.

The second aspect is how government intervention affects the decision of retailers on market coverage. Take retailer 1 for example, taking the corresponding equilibrium values into (8.15) gives the expression of π_{r1}^*, which is expressed by n_1, n_2, s, w, c, and Φ. Assume that π_{r1}^* is fixed, Figure 8.9 shows the iso-profit curves with n_1 being the vertical axis and Φ being the horizontal axis. For any given π_{r1}^*, that is on the same iso-profit curve, when $\Phi > 0$, the corresponding values of n_1, such as point B_1 and B_2, are greater than that of n_1 when $\Phi = 0$, such as point A. This states that if the degree of government intervention is not equal to zero, retailer 1 must expand its market coverage so that he can guarantee his profits not falling. That is, government intervention gives him the incentive to further expand his sales

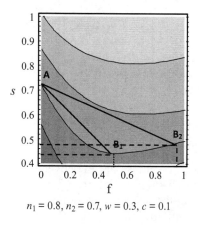

$n_1 = 0.8, n_2 = 0.7, w = 0.3, c = 0.1$

Figure 8.8 Iso-profit curves for manufacturers.

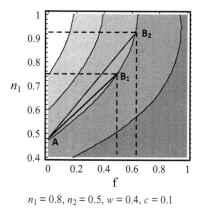

$n_1 = 0.8, n_2 = 0.5, w = 0.4, c = 0.1$

Figure 8.9 Iso-profit curves for retailers.

network. In Figure 8.9, the shape of iso-profit curves is affected by parameters such as n_2, w, s, and c. By changing the values of these parameters, we find that the pattern of Φ's impact on n_1 is stable.

Summary analysis

In providing goods and services to consumers, retailers and manufacturers have a cooperative relationship. Returns to such cooperation are the remaining part of income from sales after subtracting production costs. The distribution of the returns is positively related to the market power of each side. The market power of retailers comes from their market coverage while that of manufacturers comes from the functional values of the products. Both factory prices and the slotting allowances are forms of distribution. When the former is unable to reflect sensitively the contrast in power between retailers and manufacturers, the allowances emerge as an adjustment mechanism whose effect is to ensure the distribution of channel profits consistent with the contrast in power. The allowances pass the pressure of competition from retailers to manufacturers resulting in low retail prices and larger sales quantities, which raises consumer welfare. Government restrictions on the allowances will break the transmission of the pressure and cause the market mechanism to become sluggish. The restrictions will also reduce retailers' profits but not necessarily increase manufacturers' profits. In the long run, the restrictions will weaken manufacturers' incentives to improve product quality and motivate retailers to further expand their retail network.

Of course, this does not imply that the government should disregard the disorder in the retail and supply relationship. In some areas of China, particularly areas with highly developed commerce, the disorder has resulted in an imbalance between retail and supply. If interventions are abandoned solely because of the possible loss of consumer welfare, the economic disorder and social problems caused by the imbalance will ultimately reduce consumer welfare. However, there are many options regarding the form of government intervention.

The aggravation of conflicts between retailers and suppliers is directly caused by the imbalance in interest distribution. Hence, it is a natural solution to correct such an imbalance by charging slotting allowances. However, such logic reflects a planned economy mindset that has existed in China for a long time. Essentially, the mindset is that government should directly intervene in economic activities. We have discussed the consequences of intervention. Moreover, the order of Measures for the Administration of Fair Dealing of Retailers and Suppliers has a number of difficulties in practice. First, there is substantial ambiguity regarding the definition of slotting allowances. Second, to supervise frequent business activities requires a spectacular amount of administration costs. Third, if a retailer breaches the order by charging allowances, suppliers may not have the courage to accuse the retailer of wrongdoing because they are going to lose a distribution channel if they end their relationship with the retailer.

Essentially, an imbalance in interest distribution between retailers and suppliers is the consequence of a power imbalance. The power imbalance must first be corrected before adjusting the interest imbalance. The retailer's power must be restricted. This power comes from many sources, including consumer fidelity, market coverage, and own brands. Given current business development in China, market coverage is undoubtedly the most important resource of retailers and the most powerful way for retailers to keep suppliers under control. By scientifically designing the layout of commercial networks and strictly enforcing the layout to administrate business access, the government restrains the phenomenon of repeatedly setting up similar shops in the same area and the current disorder in competition. In France, commercial development and urban commercial plans are set up by the Commercial Urban Planning County Commissions (CDUC) after seeking opinions from all circles of society. Any license or permit for retail operations with 300 square meters is granted in accordance with the two outlines. International experience has shown that in planning commercial networks, a full investigation of public opinion is an effective measure to prevent excessive competition and to ensure consumers have sufficient choice. Second, it is necessary to enhance the power of suppliers. Power comes mainly from brand image, consumer recognition, and product quality. Compared to developed countries, the suppliers in China have the following characteristics: there are numerous suppliers in the market, and each is small in scale. Few are large suppliers who can contend with retailers, P&G is one exception, and they easily fall prey to retailer manipulation and an increasingly limited number of distribution channels. In addition, although the manufacturing industry in China has grown rapidly, there are still few brands and products that acquire consumer trust. Suppliers are, therefore, highly dependent on retail terminals. Therefore, in the long run, considering the enhancement of suppliers' power, the right choice is to encourage manufacturers to conduct independent innovation, cultivate brands, encourage large comprehensive traders, and to develop trade associations for medium and small suppliers.

Notes

1 The level of P_1 that a firm chooses is constrained by costs and the amount of resources used; hence, for the firm, it is not the more the better case in choosing the influence on government. Instead, it is a rational decision process.
2 This refers to the Pareto improved positive sum game process.
3 This book interprets Peizman's model of government regulation from the perspective of economic power paradigm.
4 It is not sensible to assume that all manufacturers have the same factory price if buyers have market power, but our model here allows retailers to reflect their magnitude of power by charging ex-post slotting allowances. So the assumption of a unified factory price is only to represent the fact that the factory price does not reflect differentiated power of different retailers.

5 Based on the above assumption, there seems to be two types of submarkets, namely, the duopoly submarket, n_1+n_2-1, and the monopoly submarkets $\tau = \alpha \times R$ (for retailer 1) and $\alpha = (a_1,a_2,....,a_n)$ (for retailer 2). Each retailer will set a monopolist price and a competitive one. Obviously, a unified price does not make sense. However, in fact, the unified price in this chapter is merely a synthetic price that reflects the degree of monopoly vs. competition. The benefit of such treatment is to simplify the question to make it easy to handle. As long as we guarantee that when $n_1+n_2=1$ both sides set monopolist prices and when $n_1 = n_2 = 1$, they set competitive prices, and the result of analysis will not be affected.

6 This assumption can be derived from theories. That is, if retailer and supplier bargain infinitely to split the profits at the discount rate based on their own power (see Rubinstein, 1982), then the result derived will be very close to ours here.

7 Of course, we can assume it to be λ units; as long as λ is constant, the choice of this parameter will not affect the conclusions of our analysis.

8 One possible scenario is $p_1 - w > \delta_{r1}(p_1 - c)$. In this case, f_1 is negative, that is, manufacturers are charging retailers the allowances. This represents the situation where retailers have small power and the factory prices are low. The franchise fees could be the case in point. However, in our discussion, we only consider the scenario where f_1 is positive. Consequently, we assume that the factory prices are high enough to guarantee positive slotting allowances.

9 s stands for the highest price that consumers are willing to accept, that is, the reserved price; therefore, w will not exceed s, and w will not be smaller than c.

10 In the next period of operation, retailers will reduce their purchases from suppliers, thereby ai reducing.

9   Economic power structure and the optimal allocation of production factors

As stated in previous chapters, we believe that the basic objective of people's economic activities is to maximize interests, but these interests depend on distribution since economic activities have group features. The formation of interest distribution mechanisms is the result of various power games. The pattern of power determines the pattern of distribution; distribution and power systems are isomorphic. Whether the distribution is fair will affect the input level and the efficiency of production factors. To achieve optimal allocation and full utilization of resources so that social interests and welfare can be optimized, it is necessary to ensure power equivalence among different economic agents at the same hierarchy level. At the same time, power and responsibility must be symmetric for the same economic agent. We use the idea of game theory and demonstrate the above viewpoints through a series of mathematical derivation.

Economic power and factor allocation

Economic power is defined as influence and control over other economic agents and stems from the resources the dominant agent holds. Bargaining power is one extrinsic form of economic power in the process of negotiation; hence, it is also called negotiation power. The optimal allocation of resources is a widely used definition whereby resources or production factors are applied where they can generate maximum economic value. This idea can be expressed as follows:

Given firm i's production function $Q_i = Q_i(X_1, X_2, ...X_m)$, $i = 1, 2,...n$, and the corresponding production value $G_i = p_i Q_i(X_1, X_2,....X_m)$, where p_i stands for the price for good i; therefore, optimal allocation of factors means,

$$\frac{\partial G_1}{\partial X_1} = \frac{\partial G_2}{\partial X_1} = ... = \frac{\partial G_n}{\partial X_1}$$

$$\frac{\partial G_1}{\partial X_2} = \frac{\partial G_2}{\partial X_2} = ... = \frac{\partial G_n}{\partial X_2}$$

$$\frac{\partial G_1}{\partial X_m} = \frac{\partial G_2}{\partial X_m} = ... = \frac{\partial G_n}{\partial X_m}$$

Hence,

$$p_1 \frac{\partial Q_1}{\partial X_1} = p_2 \frac{\partial Q_2}{\partial X_1} = \ldots\ldots = p_n \frac{\partial Q_n}{\partial X_1}$$

$$p_1 \frac{\partial Q_1}{\partial X_2} = p_2 \frac{\partial Q_2}{\partial X_2} = \ldots\ldots = p_n \frac{\partial Q_n}{\partial X_2}$$

$$p_1 \frac{\partial Q_1}{\partial X_m} = p_2 \frac{\partial Q_2}{\partial X_m} = \ldots\ldots = p_n \frac{\partial Q_n}{\partial X_m}$$

In the context of market economy, factor allocation is purely a spontaneous behavior of firms while they normally maximize profits in the short run. Therefore, each firm purchases factors in factor markets and sells products in goods markets. Based on the actual situation in market, we set up the following assumptions:

1   Firm $i\,(i=1,2,\ldots n)$ sells its products in goods market at the price p_i, and purchases factors X_k at the price $W_{ki} = W_k(R_i)$, where R_i is firm i's negotiation power in the process of purchasing factors, which is also the economic power.

2   Firm i realizes internal optimization, there will be the corresponding maximum output for any input combinations, which means production function $Q_i = Q_i(X_1, X_2, \ldots X_m)$ exists.

3   Factor markets are clear, that is, $X_{11}+X_{12}+\ldots+X_{1n} = \overline{X}_1$; $X_{21}+X_{22}+\ldots+X_{2n} = \overline{X}_2$; $\ldots\ldots$; $X_{m1}+X_{m2}+\ldots+X_{mn} = \overline{X}_m$; $\overline{X}_k$ is the total amount of X_k supplied, $k=1,2,\ldots,m$. Given above settings, firm i's optimal problem can be expressed as,

$$\max \pi_i = p_i Q_i (X_1,\cdots,X_m) - W_1(R_i) X_1 - W_2(R_i)$$
$$X_2 - \cdots - W_k(R_i) X_k - \cdots - W_m(R_i) X_m$$

The first-order condition for the optimal objective to be satisfied is $\dfrac{\partial \pi_i}{\partial X_k} = 0$, which gives,

$$p_i \frac{\partial Q_i}{\partial X_k} = W_k(R_i), \; i=1,2\ldots.n \;\; k=1,2,\ldots.m$$

Similarly, for firm j $(j=1, 2,\ldots n \;\; j \neq i)$, its first-order condition is,

$$p_j \frac{\partial Q_j}{\partial X_k} = W_k(R_j) \; j=1,2,\ldots n, \;\; k=1,2,\ldots m$$

Hence, as long as $W_k(R_i) = W_k(R_j)$, it must follow,

$$p_i \frac{\partial Q_i}{\partial X_k} = p_j \frac{\partial Q_j}{\partial X_k} \tag{9.1}$$

that is, the optimal allocation can be reached.

In the equation $W_k(R_i) = W_k(R_j)$, R_i and R_j stand for firm i's and firm j's bargaining capability which is the negotiation power in purchasing factor X_k, respectively. The negotiation power is actually influence and control over others by agents with the resources they possess including brands, capital, information, reputation, and scale as a type of extrinsic form of economic power. Therefore, as long as firms i and j have equal economic power, $R_i = R_j$ (9.1) holds. Under the above three assumptions, if and only if every firm participating in economic activities has the same economic power, optimal allocation of factors can be achieved.

In the current market structure: monopoly, monopolistic competition, oligopoly, and perfect competition. Only in perfectly competitive markets can the optimal allocation of resources, also called production factors, be achieved. This is so because only in perfect competition can factor markets be clear and full information be available with numerous buyers and sellers, undifferentiated products, and free entry into and exit from markets. In summary, only in a perfectly competitive market can all economic agents have the same amount of economic resources and equal influence, that is, equal economic power.

The symmetry between power and responsibility and economic efficiency

In the above analysis, there is one basic assumption or premise, which is to assume that a given amount of inputs will yield maximum outputs (otherwise, the function will not be single valued and, hence, will not be a function in the general sense). However, in real economic activities, it is not always true. Then how can economic efficiency be maximized? We argue that the fundamental approach to achieve this objective is to ensure that power and responsibility are symmetric for every economic agent, which we discuss in the following sections.

Economic power and economic interest distribution

Let (q,t) be the contract that economic agents A and B reached after bargaining, q is the output brought out by B's inputs, and t is the transfer payment by A to B for B's inputs, which is B's reward. The value of output q is $s(q)$. Since agent A is the representative of all other factors, $s(q)$ belongs to A. $s(q)$ is strictly increasing in q and strictly concave. Because of the rationality assumption of participants, A's pursuit is to maximize the residual, $V(q, t) = s(q) - t$, while what B's pursuit is to maximize the interests, $U(q,t) = t - c(q)$, where $c(q)$ is B's total inputs; the responsibility he must take to obtain interests t and $c(q)$ is strictly increasing and strictly convex.

Because contract (q, t) is the result of bargaining between A and B, according to Nash bargaining theory, (q, t) should ensure the Nash product is maximized, that is,

$$\max_{(q,t)} N = (s(q)-t)^\tau (t-c(q))^{1-\tau}$$

where τ and $1-\tau$ represent the bargaining capability of A and B respectively, which is their economic power. The magnitude of economic power is determined by the importance and scarcity as well as substitutability of the production factors. To guarantee the question is sensible, let $s(q) - t > 0$, $t-c(q) > 0$. The first-order condition means $\dfrac{\partial N}{\partial q} = 0$ and $\dfrac{\partial N}{\partial t} = 0$, then

$$\tau s'(q)(t-c(q)) = (1-\tau)c'(q)(s(q)-t)$$
$$\tau(t-c(q)) = (1-\tau)(s(q)-t) \tag{9.2}$$

To ensure the contract is executable, it is necessary to get a third party involved, which is normally government administrative agencies. The third party will punish participants for any violation since its pursuit is the maximization of social welfare $W = V(q,t)+U(q,t) = s(q)-c(q)$. The interest distribution gap between A and B is $V(q,t)-U(q,t) = s(q)+c(q)-2t$, and from (9.2) we know transfer payment is

$$t = (1-\tau)s(q)+\tau c(q)$$

Hence,

$$V(q,t)-U(q,t) = (2\tau-1)W \tag{9.3}$$

From (9.3) we know, if $\tau < 1/2$, B has stronger bargaining power which is the external manifestation of economic power than A, then B can obtain more interests. If $\tau > 1/2$, A has stronger bargaining power which is the external manifestation of economic power than B, then A can obtain more interests. If $\tau = 1/2$, A and B have equal economic power, both have the same amount of economic interests in this activity.

Economic efficiency and symmetry between manager's power and responsibility for the principal

If the principal (investor) offers a contract (q,t) to the agent (manager), where q is the output that the agent has to complete, t is the corresponding returns. For the agent, the value for q is $s(q)$, the principal shall possess the whole $s(q)$, by owning production materials. However, due to asymmetric information, the principal actually gets only $\rho s(q)$, where $\rho \in [0,1]$ is the extent to which the principal has the information. If $\rho=1$, the principal knows everything, which means perfect symmetry of information; if $\rho=0$, then he knows nothing at all.

$s(q)$ is strictly increasing in q and strictly concave; therefore, $s'(q)>0$ and $s''(q)<0$ are satisfied. The principal's aim of offering contract (q,t) is to seek for maximizing the residual $v(q,t)=\rho s(q)-t$. The agent must pay $c(q)$ as the costs necessary for producing outputs q, where $c(q)$ is strictly increasing in q and strictly convex. R is the agent's opportunity returns or the reserved interests; furthermore, there must be the explicit net returns for the agent, $U(q,t)=t-c(q)\geq R$; otherwise, the agent would not accept the contract (q,t), even though the actual net returns may be $\bar{U}(q,t)=t+(1-\rho)s(q)-c(q)$.

To guarantee contract (q,t) is executed, related government administrative agencies are necessary to be involved in as the third party. The government's objective is to maximize the social welfare,

$$W=V(q,t)+U(q,t)=s(q)-c(q) \tag{9.4}$$

Obviously, the first-order condition for such maximization is $s'(q)=c'(q)$.

In the games of making contracts between agents and principals, principals must pursue their objectives under the conditions recognized by agents so as to facilitate the transaction, that is, contract (q,t) is the solution to the following optimization problem,

$$\begin{cases} \max V(q,t)=\rho s(q)-t \\ s.t\ \ t-c(q)\geq R \end{cases}$$

Since $v(q,t)$ increases as t decreases, (q,t) should satisfy $t=c(q)+R$. After substituting it into the objective function, we get the unconstrained optimization problem,

$$\max V(q,t)=\rho s(q)-c(q)-R \tag{9.5}$$

whose first-order condition is $\rho s'(q)=c'(q)$. We have known that the first-order condition to satisfy maximum social welfare is $s'(q)=c'(q)$; therefore, to ensure the optimal solutions to formula (9.5) are also those to formula (9.4), $\rho=1$ must hold. When $\rho=1$,

$$\bar{U}(q,t)=t+(1-\rho)s(q)-c(q)=t-c(q)=U(q,t) \tag{9.6}$$

Formula (9.6) shows that when the principal is fully informed, the agent has to take the necessary responsibilities (the costs) as stipulated in the contract and receive the corresponding returns, that is, interests and responsibility are symmetric. As we have shown, how much economic power he has determines how much economic interests he obtains. Therefore, the symmetry between interests and responsibility is essentially that between power and responsibility. So the symmetry between power and responsibility is the necessary and sufficient condition to get the same optimal solutions to both formula (9.5) and (9.4). Let the optimal solutions be $q = q^*$ and $t = t^*$, because $W^* = V(q^*, t^*) + U(q^*, t^*)$, the maximum social welfare W^* is completely distributed to the participants; hence, the allocation (q^*, t^*) is Pareto optimal.

Thus, we have proved that as long as power and responsibility are symmetric, the economic allocation will be Pareto optimal.

Economic efficiency and symmetry between manager's power and responsibility for the team

Suppose the economic activity involves 1 principal and a team of n agents. The principal offers a contract (q, t) that the team is expected to produce q, with t being the transfer payment by the principal to the team and $s(q)$ being the value of q. Due to owning production materials, the principal obtains $s(q)$. $s(q)$ is strictly increasing in q and strictly concave. Hence, $s'(q) > 0, s''(q) < 0$ are satisfied, that is, marginal value $s'(q)$ is strictly diminishing. From the rationality assumption about participants, the principal offers the contract (q, t) so as to maximize the residual $V(q, t) = s(q) - t$.

Suppose the team has a fixed cost of 0, and marginal cost c, then the total production costs will be cq, and the returns for the team are $t - cq$. Each of the n team members has his reserved returns (the opportunity returns), denoted as $R_1, R_2, ..., R_n$, which are given exogenously based on the agent's basic or fundamental rights and also called reserved interests.

After n agents agree unanimously to accept contract (q, t), they soon start the games of how to obtain each one's share of the transfer payment t, denoted as $r_1, r_2, ..., r_n$, $(r_i \in [(0,1)])$, and how to share the total costs cq, denoted as $d_1, d_2, ..., d_n$, $(d_i \in [0,1])$. The net returns of n agents are

$$U_i = r_i t - d_i cq, i = 1, 2, ..., n$$

Under the conditions that $r_1 + r_2 + ... + r_n \leq 1$ and $d_1 + d_2 + ... + d_n \geq 1$, the strategy combination $((r_1, d_1), (r_2, d_2), ..., (r_n, d_n))$ of n agents, satisfying $r_1 + r_2 + ... + r_n = 1$ and $d_1 + d_2 + ... + d_n = 1$, is Nash equilibrium. In the games among n agents, $r_i \in (0,1)$ is the agent $i(=1,2,...,n)$'s claim on the transfer payment while $d_i \in [0,1]$ is agent i's responsibility to the team. As proved previously, power and interests are symmetric, that is, the obtained interests depends on the magnitude of power behind as the support. Consequently, the games at this phase can be called the game of power and responsibility within the team.

If the contract (q,t) offered by the principal and the Nash equilibrium r_i and $d_i(i=1,2,...,n)$ in the games of power and responsibility satisfy the individual rationality or participation conditions for n agents,

$$U_i = r_i t - d_i cq \geq R_i i = 1,2,...n$$

then the team of agents accepts (q,t) ; otherwise, rejects the contract. Such games between principals and agents are called the game of contract-making.

In the games of power and responsibility, if $r_i = d_i$, there exists reciprocity between agent $i(=1,2,...,n)$'s power and responsibility; otherwise, distortion between power and responsibility appears. Especially, if $r_i > d_i$, agent i has excess interests; if $r_i < d_i$, agent i has insufficient interests. The ratio of agent i's reserved returns R_i to the right to claim for transfer payment r_i is R_i / r_i, which is the relative reserved returns. Reserved return is the bargaining capital between the agent and the principal, and is also one type of resources to form economic power. The greater the reserved returns, the stronger the economic power, and hence, the agent is more able to obtain transfer payments.

To show that contract (q,t) is operative or the principal's commitment is credible, it is necessary to get a third party involved. The third party will punish the participants for their misbehavior because its objective is to maximize the social welfare,

$$W = V + \sum_{i=1}^{n} U_i = s(q) - cq$$

Obviously, the output q^* corresponding to maximum social welfare should satisfy the first-order condition, $s'(q^*)=c$. When $q=q^*$, social welfare reaches its maximum, $W^* = s(q^*) - cq^*$.

In a realistic setting, the third party is normally the government administrative agencies. In the mechanism design theory, the designer creates a mechanism in the form of a set of game rules to implement the social choice objective through equilibrium of the game. Using such theories to study economy of power has quite promising prospects.

Economic allocation under the symmetry between power and responsibility

Suppose there is symmetry between power and responsibility for every agent in the team, that is, the equilibrium of the game satisfies $r_i = d_i, i = 1,2,...,n$. The contract offered by the principal should maximize residuals $V(q,t) = s(q) - t$, given the agent participation condition. Rewrite the agent i's participation condition $r_i t - d_i cq \geq R_i$ as

$$t \geq cq + = \frac{R_i}{r_i}, i = 1,2,...,n.$$

Let agent K be the person who has the maximum relative reserved returns,

$$\max_{i=1,2,...,n} \{\frac{R_i}{r_i}\} = \frac{R_k}{r_k}.$$

It is obvious that if k's participation condition holds, the conditions of the rest of the agents must also hold. Therefore, the principal needs to consider only agent k's participation condition when offering contract (q,t). Thus, contract (q,t) is the solution to the following optimality problem,

$$\begin{cases} \max_{(q,t)} V(q,t) = s(q) - t \\ s.t.\ t \geq cq + \dfrac{R_k}{r_k} \end{cases}$$

$V(q,t)$ increases as t decreases. Hence, (q,t) should satisfy $t = cq + \dfrac{R_k}{r_k}$. Substituting it into the objective function gives the unconstrained form,

$$\max_q V = s(q) - cq - \frac{R_k}{r_k}$$

whose optimal solution is q^* that satisfies the first-order condition of maximizing social welfare, $s'(q^*) = c$. This value makes W reach the maximum, that is, $W^* = s(q^*) - cq^*$, and the corresponding transfer payment is $t^* = cq^* + \dfrac{R_k}{r_k}$. Here, $r_k = 1 - \displaystyle\sum_{i \neq k} r_i$; therefore, smaller r_k brings greater $r_i (i \neq k)$; the larger t^*, the smaller the $V(q^*, t^*)$ is.

Under contract (q^*, t^*), the principal and agent will get their own returns, respectively, defined as,

$$V^* = s(q^*) - cq^* - \frac{R_k}{r_k}, U_i^* = \frac{r_i}{r_k} R_k, i = 1, 2, ..., n$$

Contract (q^*, t^*) gives reserved returns to the agent who has the relative reserve returns, $\dfrac{R_k}{r_k}$, and increases the returns for the rest of the agents. With

$$W^* = V^* + \sum_{i-1}^{n} U_i^*,$$ the maximal social welfare is completely distributed to the participants, and the economic allocation (q^*, t^*) is Pareto optimal. Hence, we have demonstrated that whatever the value is for agent's reserved returns $R_i \ (i = 1, 2, ..., n)$, when the information is complete, the economic allocation will be Pareto optimal as long as every agent gets their power and responsibility symmetric.

From the perspective of economic efficiency and equity, Pareto optimal is reasonable, but it may not be able to meet the request of participants for social equity in income distribution. Huge gaps may exist in income distribution across the agent team members. If agent's power can be reciprocal, that is, $r_1 = d_1 = r_2 = d_2 = \ldots = r_n = d_n = \dfrac{1}{n}$, then the income distribution within the team is equal, namely, $U_1^* = U_n^* = \ldots = U_n^* = R_k$.

Economic allocation under distortion of the relationship between power and responsibility

Information economics does not consider the issue of power. Consequently, this stream of theory implicitly assumes that the participants have symmetric power with respect to responsibility. Information economics argues that under complete information, the contract offered by the principal is social optimal. In this section, we show that if there is distortion between an agent's power and responsibility, this conclusion no longer holds.

Consider a firm, where agent 1 is the manager and agents $2,3,\ldots,n$ are the employees. Agent 1 has great private benefits of control but does not pay the corresponding costs or take the responsibility. Therefore, the contract offered by the principal can be obtained from solving the following problem,

$$
\begin{cases}
\max_{(q,t)} V(q,t) = s(q) - t \\
s.t. \quad U_1 = r_1 t - d_1 cq \geq R_1 \\
\qquad U_2 = r_2 t - d_2 cq \geq R_2 \\
\qquad \vdots \\
\qquad U_n = r_n t - d_n cq \geq R_n
\end{cases}
$$

Suppose the employees have reciprocal power, $r_i = r_2, d_i = d_2, R_i = R_2$, $i = 1,2,\ldots,n$, then only two conditions are to be considered to solve the above optimality problem,

$$U_1 = r_1 t - d_1 cq \geq R_1$$
$$U_2 = r_2 t - d_2 cq \geq R_2$$

These can be rewritten as

$$t \geq \zeta_1 cq + \frac{R_1}{r_1}, \quad t \geq \zeta_2 cq + \frac{R_2}{r_2}$$

where $\zeta_1 \overset{\Delta}{=} \dfrac{d_1}{r_1}, \zeta_2 \overset{\Delta}{=} \dfrac{d_2}{r_2}$. The setting of this problem makes it reasonable to assume that: $r_1 > d_1, \dfrac{R_1}{r_1} < \dfrac{R_2}{r_2}$; consequently, $\zeta_1 < 1$. Because $\zeta_1 = \dfrac{d_1}{r_1} = \dfrac{1-(n-1)d_2}{1-(n-1)r_2}$, then

$d_2 > r_2$; therefore, $\zeta_2 > 1$. $\zeta_1 < 1$ means agent 1 (the manager) has distorted relationship between power and responsibility characterized by excessive interests. $\zeta_2 > 1$ means agent 2 (the employee) has distorted relationship between power and responsibility characterized by insufficient interests. Agent 1's distortion of power and responsibility with excessive interests can result in agent 2's distortion of power and responsibility with insufficient interests. Thus, we can ignore the first participation condition and simplify the principal's contract problem to the following optimal problem,

$$\begin{cases} \max\limits_{(q,t)} V(q,t) = s(q,t) - t \\ s.t.\ t \geq \zeta_2 cq + \dfrac{R_2}{r_2} \end{cases}$$

(q,t) should satisfy $t = \zeta_2 cq + \dfrac{R_2}{r_2}$, which can be substituted into the objective function to get the following unrestricted optimal problem,

$$\max\limits_{q} V = s(q) - \zeta_2 cq - \dfrac{R_2}{r_2}$$

The optimal solution is q^N, which satisfies the first-order condition, $s'(q^N) = \zeta_2 c$, and then it will determine $q^N = q(\zeta_2)$ and the corresponding transfer payment $t^N = \zeta_2 cq^N + \dfrac{R_2}{r_2}$. Thus, we obtain the contract (q^N, t^N) with agent 1 having excessive interests and agent 2 having insufficient interests. The contract possesses the following six properties that reflect the impact of distortion in the relationship between power and responsibility on the economy.

a　Since $s'(q^N) = \zeta_2 c > c = s'(q^*)$, and s' is strictly decreasing, then $q^N < q^*$, that is, the distortion of relationship between power and responsibility reduces outputs.

b　Note that $q^N = q(\zeta_2)$ derives from the first-order condition: $s'(q) = \zeta_2 c = 0$, then from the implicit function derivation method, we can obtain $q'(\zeta_2) = \dfrac{c}{s''} < 0$, which means the larger the extent of insufficient interests caused by the distortion, the fewer the outputs.

c　Since $s(q)$ is strictly concave, $s(q^N) - s(q^*) < s'(q^*)(q^N - q^*)$ holds. The gap between W^N, the social welfare under the distorted contract, and the maximum social welfare is

$$W^N - W^* = s(q^N) - cq^N - (s(q^*) - cq^*) = s(q^N) - s(q^*) - c(q^N - q^*)$$
$$< s'(q^*)(q^N - q^*) - c(q^N - q^*) = (q^N - q^*)(s'(q^*) - c) = 0$$

Hence, $W^N < W^*$, that is, contract (q^N, t^N) lowers social welfare.

d Since $W(\zeta_2) = s(q(\zeta_2)) - cq(\zeta_2)$, then

$$W'(\zeta_2) = s'(q(\zeta_2))q'(\zeta_2) - cq'(\zeta_2) = q'(\zeta_2)(s'(q(\zeta_2)) - c) = q'(\zeta_2)(\zeta_2 c - c) < 0$$

Under the distorted contract, social welfare $W^N = W^N(\zeta_2)$ is strictly decreasing in ζ_2, that is, the greater the extent of insufficient interests caused by the distortion, the lower the social welfare level is.

e Under contract (q^N, t^N), the principal is able to obtain the returns of

$$V^N = s(q^N) - t^N = s(q^N) - \zeta_2 cq^N - \frac{R_2}{r_2}$$

and agent 1 is able to obtain the returns of

$$U_1^N = r_1(t^N - \zeta_1 cq^N) = r_1\left((\zeta_2 - \zeta_1)cq^N + \frac{R_2}{r_2}\right) = \frac{r_1 - d_1}{1 - r_1}cq^N + \frac{r_1}{r_2}R_2$$

while other agents can get $U_2^N = U_3^N = \ldots = U_n^N = R_2$. If we require the agent team to yield outputs at q^*, and continue to hold the returns to principal and agent 1 unchanged as V^N and U_1^N, then the returns for the other agents are

$$W^* - V^N - U_1^N = W^* - W^N + (n-1)U_2^N > (n-1)U_2^N$$

Since it's possible to increase these agents' returns, the allocation is not Pareto optimal under the distorted contract (q^N, t^N)

f Against the same background, if there is symmetry between power and responsibility, then the income distribution within the team will be

$$U_1^* = \frac{r_1}{r_2}R_2, U_2^* = U_3^* = \ldots = U_n^* = R_2$$

while under contract (q^N, t^N), the income distribution within the team is

$$U_1^N = \frac{r_1 - d_1}{1 - r_1}cq^N + \frac{r_1}{r_2}R_2, U_2^N = U_3^N = \ldots U_n^N = R_2$$

Obviously, the income gap is expanded. Moreover, the greater the r_1 and the smaller the d_1, the bigger such a gap will be. That is, the distorted contract (q^N, t^N) makes the distribution gap within the team wider.

To summarize, we find that an effective way to realize Pareto improvement so that the income distribution gap can be narrowed is to increase the employee's economic power and bargaining power with the executives. However, this strategy relies on the power of the whole group. Any individual employee is not at the same hierarchy level as the executive; therefore, an individual alone is incapable of asserting influence. That is why developed countries establish trade unions and associations.

Power reciprocity and market clearing

The optimal allocation of resources makes one assumption or premise, which is market clearing or the full utilization of resources. Guo (1984) expounds with a full Keynesian model that goods, labor, and money markets must be in equilibrium at the same time to realize the full utilization of all economic resources. A simple version of the full Keynesian model is composed of the following sets of equations:

1   Expenditure sector (goods markets)

$$\frac{C}{P} = \frac{a}{P} + b\frac{Y}{P}$$

$$\frac{I}{P} = \frac{V_0}{P} - \frac{V_1}{P}i$$

$$\frac{Y}{P} = \frac{C+I}{P}$$

2   Money sector (money markets)

$$\frac{L}{P} = L\left(i, \frac{Y}{P}\right)$$

$$\frac{M}{P} = \frac{M_0}{P}$$

3   Production sector (labor markets)

$$\frac{Y}{P} = f(N)\left(f'(N) > 0, f''(N) < 0\right)$$

$$\frac{W}{P} = f'(N)$$

$$N = h\left(\frac{W}{P}\right)$$

In this model, Y is national income, C is consumption, I is investment, i is interest rate, P is price level, L is money demand, M is money supply, N is the number of labor, W is the wage, α, V_0, and M_0 are all constants while b and V_1 are coefficients.

Except taking price factors into consideration and making real variables represented by the relationship between nominal variables, goods and money markets are the same as described by the IS-LM model. The production sector is set up based on the classical economic theories.

The equilibrium condition for goods markets (the expenditure sector) is real savings equal to real investment, that is,

$$\frac{Y-C}{P} = \frac{I}{P}$$

or,

$$\frac{Y}{P} = \frac{\dfrac{a}{P} + \dfrac{V_0}{P} - \dfrac{V_1}{P}i}{1-b}$$

This is the IS equation derived from real outputs, which is called the $\dfrac{IS}{P}$ curve or expenditure curve. From the $\dfrac{IS}{P}$ equation, it follows that whether to add price factors will not affect the nature of the equation since P is a common variable and can be cancelled out.

The equilibrium condition for money markets is real money demand equal to real money supply, that is,

$$L\left(i, \frac{Y}{P}\right) = \frac{M_0}{P}$$

This is the LM equation derived from equating real money demand to real money supply, which is called the $\dfrac{LM}{P}$ curve or money curve. It states that real money demand is a function of interest rate and real income but real money supply decreases as price level rises. Hence, in money markets, an increase in price level will reduce the real money supply, and push the $\dfrac{LM}{P}$ curve upwards. Thus, the intersection between $\dfrac{IS}{P}$ and $\dfrac{LM}{P}$ curves will yield more than one equilibrium point; it will generate a series of equilibrium points according to different price levels.

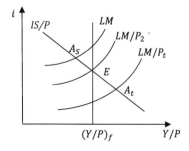

Figure 9.1 Simultaneous equilibrium in three sectors.

Therefore, once the price factor is introduced, the original IS-LM model can determine neither the equilibrium income and interest rate nor the corresponding price level. This is because there are three variables with only two equilibrium equations. To solve the problem, the production sector (the labor markets) is introduced to Keynesian model as the one set up in the classical economics. The equilibrium condition for labor markets is to produce with full employment level and to ensure the income level is equal to that of full employment, that is to say,

$$\frac{Y}{P} = f(N_f) = \left(\frac{Y}{P}\right)_f,$$

where $\left(\dfrac{Y}{P}\right)_f$ is called the output line of full employment or maximum output line (see Figure 9.1). The equilibrium national income, interest rate, and price level are obtained at the intersection point of these three curves, E. Consequently, there is only one price level that guarantees expenditure sector (goods markets), money sector (money markets), and production sector (labor markets) all at equilibrium.

In the production sector (labor markets), $\dfrac{Y}{P} = f(N)$ implies that output is an increasing function of labor N but marginal product is decreasing. $\dfrac{W}{P} = f'(N)$ states that the real wage is equal to marginal productivity of labor and that firms can obtain maximum profits only when this condition is satisfied. Because marginal productivity of labor decreases with the increase in employment, along with this, the real wages that firms are willing to pay will decrease. Thus, the labor demand curve is downward sloping. $N = h\left(\dfrac{W}{P}\right)$ states that labor supply is a function of real wages. The labor supply curve is upward sloping. The intersection between labor demand and supply curves is the point of full employment, corresponding to point N_f. It is clear that the state of full employment can be reached only when $\dfrac{W}{P} = f'(N) = N$, that is the real wage is equal to marginal product.

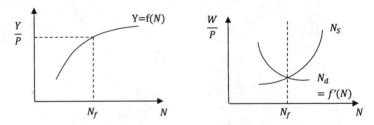

Figure 9.2 Labor demand and supply equilibrium.

With the same reasoning, it follows that whether in goods or money markets, the condition for market equilibrium—that is, full utilization of resources—is necessary for a firm to maximize profits. As long as it has not maximized its profits, the firm will continue to change the input level of factors. Hence, the market will be in disequilibrium. The conditions for this maximization problem are that the firm's marginal revenue is equal to marginal costs, interest rates are equal to the marginal products for the money factor, and prices are equal to the marginal contribution to the firm for material factors.

As we have proven, in order to equal the contribution and return for any production factor or resource, it is necessary that the power formed by various resources in addition to the direct contribution must be reciprocal across different agents. Furthermore, the set-up of a perfect Keynesian model implicitly assumes full information, no monopoly, and no government intervention. However, information, monopoly, and government attitude are all the resources that form economic power. The equalization nature of these resources is also the necessary condition for power reciprocity. In summary, it is necessary that the power formed by various resources in addition to the direct contribution must be reciprocal across different agents to fully utilize various resources or, in other words, the production factors.

10 Institutional change with power as the underlying logic

From barter to money circulation, and from the flow of goods to the transfer of ownership and property rights, the object of economic studies has changed. The object is no longer the production of wealth but the distribution of interests, that is, the economic relations between people. In this context, we study the influence of power on institutional change. New institutional economics applies the cost-benefit analysis approach of the neoclassical economics paradigm to the analysis of institutions based on the concept of transaction costs and explores the decisive role of institutions in economic development. However, many of the issues pertaining to institutional change are still unclear. Institutions are the rules and constraints of interaction among members of society.[1] Moreover, different institutions generate different economic consequences. What are the rules for institutional change? North (1981) classifies institutional change into primary and secondary changes. He argues that changes in relative prices and preferences provide the incentive for institutional change and that primary institutional changes provide the environment and rules for secondary changes. However, the mechanisms of primary institutional changes are not clear. In his later studies, North (1990) emphasizes the interactions between formal and informal rules. The author believes that formal rules can be manipulated and controlled by groups or individuals while informal rules are central to societal operations. However, how it works and the specific mode of its evolutions are not clear.

Government is the only mandatory provider of institutions and is an agent of interests under the existing institutional framework. Then, how does a society avoid falling into a state of opportunism, and how do we define the boundaries of government behavior? North's paradox of state only explains the positive and negative impacts of government on economic growth and property rights definition. The paradox notes that the state should be ultimately responsible for the efficiency of property rights structure (North, 1981). Lin (1994) develops the model of induced institutional change and mandatory institutional change. However, the motivations and conditions for the implementation of mandatory changes are not clear. Endogenous political institutions theory of the public choice school is aligned entirely with efficiency criteria. The theory gives the majority voting rules for participating in the establishment of laws and constitutions through economic analysis of costs and benefits (Aghion, Alesina, & Trebbi, 2004; Buchanan & Tullock, 1962). This approach ignores the motives of political and bureaucratic groups and admits that institutions are efficient evolutions themselves, which conflicts with North's state paradox. In fact, this is an inevitable result when the concept of transaction costs is used to analyze institutional change. North gradually abandons the methodology in his later studies. The author argues that institutional change is not necessarily effective, and the effectiveness of institutions is related to the adaptability and continuous adjustment of informal rules (North, 1990).

Institutions are the rules for the trading behavior of economic agents and provide all economic agents with common expectations and knowledge. Therefore, institutions are usually continuous and stable but do change over time. North (1990) notes that institutional change is a complex process. Moreover, a typical transition mode is gradual rather than intermittent. Aoki, Greif and Milgrom (2001) notes that institutional changes occur when there is an institutional crisis.

This chapter analyzes the formation and process of institutional change from the perspective of power while explaining the motivation structure of institutional change and the efficiency of the change, including the role of government in the change process. The power logic model of institutions shows that the changes and persistence of institutions are the equilibrium outcomes whereby institutions and power are compatible. The model is not complete if only institutional change or persistence is emphasized. The two attributes of institutions are different components of the same dynamic equilibrium framework.

The nature of institutions

If our goal is to study the formation and change of institutions, we must delimit the connotations and extension of institutions. To define a concept is usually to adopt an enumeration or functional approach. Abstract characterization can be used in mathematical models; however, in addition to clarifying the connotation, the role of defining institutions is more an exercise in identifying the nature of institutions.

The basic connotations: constraints

Institutions have broad connotations, from convention to traditions and even customs and culture. With the wide application of game theory methods in institutional analysis, there are different definitions of institutions. Because of different research directions and logic, the definition varies. According to the elements of the game, there are three broad definitions: institutions as participants in the game, game rules, and equilibrium strategies.

In North's studies, institution usually refers to organizations such as government, universities, foundations, and trade unions (Ménard, 2008). The use of the term institution and organization in English stems from the significant impact of Coase's transaction cost theory on the explanation of enterprise contracts. Firm contracts, or the rules of conduct within an organization and the power configuration, can be considered institutions. If a society and a state are also considered organizations, a reasonable explanation of state and social economic institutions can be derived through a micro corporate-level analysis.

North (1981) suggests that the institution is the rules of a game. He categorizes rules into formal and informal rules. Formal rules are specified before the game while new rules are the results of bargains between political organizations. As the institutions, the rules of the game are studied mainly from two aspects. First, some literature studies the results of the game under conditions of different institutional rules in order to compare institutional efficiency (Gardner & Ostrom, 1991). Second, according to the revelation principle, some studies consider the incentive compatibility and information constraints and design effective institutional rules under conditions of incomplete information, particularly for enterprise system such as the GHM theory. In fact, because North (1990) regards institutions as the rules of the game and causes the problem of circular argument on institutions, that is, where institutions come from and under what conditions did the participants of the meta-game form the rules of politics and state institutions.

The application of game theory to institutional study leads to a situation where it is natural to regard the institution as a game equilibrium. This stems from the equilibrium analysis of institution games pioneered by Schotter, who argues that institutions are created by the process of maximization by socio-economic individuals (Schotter, 2008). Although no one regards social institutions as the purpose of production, they emerge naturally in economic agent's cooperation and negotiation and are exactly the same as Smith's study of the economic process. Economic studies use the starting point of individual rationality maximization. Evolutionary game theory, which relaxes the assumption of complete individual rationality, studies the formation and equilibrium properties of institutions through the selection, learning, and mutation process (Weibull, 1997).

Recent game theory studies regard institutions as the community of both equilibrium and rules of games (Aoki et al., 2001; Greif & Laitin, 2004; Sugden, 1989; Young, 1998). These studies[2] argue that the institution is a self-sustaining system of common beliefs that determine how games will proceed. In essence, the institution is a condensed characterization of the significant and fixed feature of the equilibrium game path. On the one hand, each participant relies on condensed information to choose their own rules of action in different scenarios. On the other hand, all participants form their own action rules based on their subjective perceptions. The ultimate result is that institutions will form if participants have a sustainable belief concerning the action rules of others. Apparently, the institution is the action rule at the surface level, but it is actually the equilibrium belief that all participants share, that is, the outcome of the game. Rules and results confirm and strengthen each other, which constitutes a self-sustaining system.

In fact, whether the institution is viewed as rules or equilibrium, it is analyzed from the perspective of a third-party who is outside the game, which requires perfect individual rationality and perfect collective rationality. Subjective game theory emphasizes the cognitive ability of economic agents and relaxes the requirement of individual rationality in the research of the endogenous institution. After accumulating knowledge on the objective environment in the game, participants form their own subjective game model. The common subjective game model as common knowledge reduces the uncertainty that every participant has when predicting their rival's behavior. Under the common knowledge environment, the certainty connection between rules and the results of actions increase. Such common belief[3] and knowledge are endogenized in the subjective game model. From the perspective of a transaction agent, institutions can provide expectations on rival behavior or the behavior of other economic agents. Meanwhile, institutions also include the agent's own strategies. In other words, the most basic connotations of institutions are constraints, which can be punitive or motivating. Constraints can be coercive externally or self-enforcing.

The basic attribute of institutions: distribution

Institutional theory attaches significant importance to the role of institutions in economics realms. North (1990) integrates institutions into the main variables of economic growth, which is determined by the attributes of institutions. Commons (1936) regards the institution as a feasible mutual relationship that comes from conflicts of interest among economic agents. Such a relationship is a guarantee from rules to realize the anticipation of the future. Alchian and Demsetz (1972) directly defines institutions from the perspective of functions and states that in the context of trade, the institution helps people form expectations that can be reasonably controlled. Hayek (2013) argues that institutions that reduce ignorance and uncertainty through social contact define the connotation of institutions from the aspect of functions. Unfortunately, institution theories always ignore, whether deliberately or not, the attribute of distribution. This attribute determines that the institution must be restrictive. If there is no distribution of interests, naturally, there is no need to restrict participant's behavior. It is participant's behavior that codetermines the future cooperative income and the distribution of individuals' interests. Therefore, institutions must restrict participant's behavior.

In essence, the institution is a contract of distribution. Since the social division of labor or, from intertemporal transactions, the transaction price (the negotiation mechanism of the transaction) has been the most important content of institutions. From the moment the institution emerges, it has the attributes of constraint, motivation, or distribution. Otherwise, the institution would not be observed. Whether the institution has punitive restraint or self-enforcing constraints, participants must choose their own actions in the existing set of strategies. Moreover, the institutional framework gives the expectation that others also choose strategies from the set. These are all required by the income distribution that is expected in the framework. As mentioned, enterprise contracts, market contracts, and public policies are ways to distribute benefits. Contracts and policies determine the efficiency of resource allocation or the efficiency of institutions. Simply, the efficiency of institutions stems from the efficiency of distribution.

The above logic comes from Simondede. In the development of economic theories, production and wealth are given high priority. Simondede (1977) argues that classical political economics make a mistake when they take wealth as the research object and completely ignore individuals in the theoretical research. Unlimited expansion of production in a capitalist society coupled with the unreasonable distribution system leaves wealth in the hands of only a few while workers have insufficient income. This state of affairs causes the market to shrink and destroys the balance of production and consumption. Therefore, an economic crisis characterized by excessive production inevitably occurs. Obviously, Simondede's theory of distribution has significance in times when Keynesian consumption theory is spreading rapidly. The logic of economic research determines that the ultimate goal of the research must be economic efficiency and income distribution.

In addition, sustaining trading agent's expectations regarding rivals and preventing opportunistic behavior and moral hazard in transactions depends on the establishment of institutions. The emergence of institutions requires that trading agents must abide by these institutions, which necessarily involves the stability of institutions. In the context of existing institutions, transactions can be completed and can continue. Therefore, the property of the institutions should be stability, which can be called the persistence of institutions. If the institutions keep changing, they cannot participate with expectations for the behavior of other agents. Consequently, these are not institutions. The distribution attribute of institutions shows that when the endowment structure of resources changes for an agent, inevitably there will be requests to re-sign or modify the existing institutions. Within the institutional framework, through effort and investment, individual benefits increase accordingly. However, as the fundamental income distribution mechanism, if more and rapid increases in income are expected, changes to institutions become a good choice. Therefore, revolution must be the attribute of institutions.

Acemoglu, Cantoni, Johnson and Robinson (2011) sketch out a research framework for endogenous institutions based on political power (including economic power). In this framework, the power of different groups is the major factor in institutional change. The distribution of political power determines economic institutions, resource allocation, and economic growth. For exogenous institutional change, the change in power structure caused by radical change could bring effective institutions. Unfortunately, this framework tells only half the story of institutional change since it cannot explain the persistence of institutions in the process of change. After all, a stable institution can provide the expected behavior of rivals in the long-term process in transactions for an economic agent.

Categories of institutional changes: efficiency standards

The studies on institutional change categorize the changes. The changes are typically categorized by hierarchy and level, but categorizing changes by efficiency better explains the nature of institutional changes. Institutional changes are typically considered to be efficient, such as in North's study that applies cost-benefit analysis and Lin's study that focuses on induced institutional changes (North, 1990; Lin, 1994). Additionally, the subjective game model holds the same view, which is that only when participants receive motivation for a new benefit from constant trial and error, or through innovation, will common knowledge and beliefs of a subjective game change. However, this is apparently not realistic because new institutions may be ineffective and the old ineffective institutions may continue to exist. Categorizing institutions by efficiency works in theory, but in reality, institutional changes are mixed depending on the type of change. Of course, such theoretical categorization is necessary because it allows us to analyze the connotations, extension, and mechanisms of institutional changes under the framework of contract negotiations.

Institutional changes can be categorized as productive and distributive changes if the mechanism of their effects on economic growth is analyzed at the micro level and by incorporating government coercive public policy into the changes. The productive changes can achieve potential economic interests while the distributive changes can influence the established structure of the interest distribution. The general situation is that there are cooperative income and redistribution of interest in the process of institutional change. Schotter's study on customs and routines is based on certain games of the prisoner's dilemma. He notes that repeated social games may lead to certain rules of conduct to avoid the adoption of non-Pareto optimal equilibrium strategies (Schotter & Yale, 1981). Obviously, for the institution with the distribution attribute, the author ignores the institutional arrangements with Hicks efficiency improvements not to mention the arrangements that are entirely redistribution of interests.

Earlier comparisons of the points of view between power and efficiency portray the non-efficiency characteristics of institutional evolution. From the view of transaction costs, institutional arrangement is a mechanism that reduces transaction costs, a type of Pareto improvement. From the perspective of power, the evolution of institutions is not necessarily efficient. Nelson and Winter (1982), representing evolutionary economics, study business routines and find that business management routines are Pareto sub-optimal. Sugden (1989) argues that if the institutional arrangement is the result of a deliberate choice by collective rationality, the evolution of institutions will be efficient while the inefficient customs and routines will no longer exist. In fact, considering the distribution attribute of the existing institution, even if there is collective rational choice, different interest groups will have different motivations toward the institutional arrangement.

Using efficiency criterion, institutional changes can be placed in three categories. First, the changes are Pareto efficiency improvements. Because of exogenous factors including technological innovations, re-delimitation of property rights, and impacts of new interest groups and international trade, co-operation between economic agents can improve economic efficiency through new institutions, which will ultimately benefit all economic interest groups. Such institutional changes are common as the emergence of all new portfolios of production technology and new corporate organization structure are institutional changes with Pareto efficiency improvements. The most typical change is the emergence of the modern business organization structure. Because of management progress, advances in technology, and reductions in transport costs, the institutions of classical capitalist managers are gradually being replaced. The principal-agent theory suggests that the interests of investors are seized by managers. However, the coexistence of two types of institutions shows that both investors and managers benefit from the emergence of modern business institutions. Another example is China's economic reform. In the 30 years of reform and opening-up, the interests of the whole nation have improved. Therefore, all the citizens accept the changes.

Second, institutional changes are Hicks' efficiency improvements. This type of institutional change improves overall efficiency and brings enormous benefits for some interest groups but will jeopardize the interests of other groups. Therefore, the new institutions will be resisted to a certain degree. If the production effects of public policies, income compensation plans, and other supporting institutions are taken into account, such changes will be natural. Keynesian consumption policy is one typical policy adopted by modern governments. In terms of social utility, the policy increases national wealth, and the expansionary policy results in economic growth for the whole country, but it also increases the distribution gap of social wealth among different classes and the burden society places on the environment and resources (Hick, 1989). The current Chinese economic reforms, particularly the reform of political institutions, represent institutional change of this nature because the reform narrows the income gap and reduces rent-seeking space for administrative power. These are among a series of key issues concerning interest distribution. Therefore, the reform process has experienced impediments from some interest groups and will encounter more obstacles in the future.

Third, institutional change is completely inefficient. In the process of institutional change, some interest groups obtain interests while others incur losses. Moreover, the increase in social welfare is less than the reduction. From a moral point of view, such institutional changes are a waste of resources, or even exploitation of interests. The most typical example is that industrial policies often swing from one extreme to the other as a result of different political parties' efforts to compensate the interest groups. From an efficiency point of view, social resources are used for institutional change and crowd out production resources.

The first two types of institutional change can be called productive institutional change and pure distributive institutional change. The latter type should be avoided, which requires that the institution used to restrain social production and investment should have a certain degree of stability. As mentioned, transaction costs should increase with basic political institutional change. There is another issue: If the basic political institutions are ineffective, it will be impossible to yield more effective political institutions in the case of high transaction costs. According to endogenous transaction cost theory, stable institutions bring high transaction costs, but they reduce rent-seeking investment (Yang, 1998).

Therefore, democracy may make the rent-seeking behavior of interest groups institutional, but it will encourage the activities of private entrepreneurs. That is, high exogenous transaction costs limit the endogenous transaction costs produced by rent-seeking behavior. As a result, there is a need to maintain a balance between endogenous and exogenous transaction costs to guarantee the stability of political institutions on the one hand and to leave some space for the evolution of political institutions on the other. However, this is actually a pseudo-problem because there are no individuals or groups that have complete rationality and strive to maximize social welfare. Even if there is an organization that has such a goal, the organizational behavior may be consistent with social welfare maximization while the behavior of group members is, inevitably, self-interest.

Equilibrium of power games and the endogeneity of institutions

Institutions have been the object of study since the emergence of the old institutional economics. However, institutions also draw attention from mainstream economics due to contributions from new institutional economics whose starting point is Coase's concept of transaction costs. Nevertheless, the analysis of institution theory based on Pareto efficiency criterion and transaction costs create a dilemma for coercive institutional change.

The paradox of state and transaction costs

The underlying logic of transaction costs is the cost-benefit analysis of traditional economics or, in other words, contracts and institutions are studies in normative economics. In North's theory, two cornerstones are the theory of state and the theory of property rights. Property rights structure can reduce transaction costs while the delimitation of the structure is dependent on the state and government. Whether the state can delimit and ensure an effective property rights structure typically depends on the interactions between the state ruler's desire and the producers' attempts to reduce transaction costs.

On the one hand, if the state provides clear and effective property rights, social production will increase, and long-term national tax revenue will increase and stabilize. On the other hand, if the state provides an obscure property rights structure, the rulers will obtain short-term rents. Therefore, the overall goals of state and government are contradictory to those of some rulers; that is, the state is the crucial driving force of economic growth and the root of economic recession.

The state paradox results from the foundation of property rights theory; that is, the concept of transaction costs does not have the attribute of interest distribution. This is illustrated by the Coase theorem. The theorem uses the classic case where factory emissions pollute the laundry that local residents hang out to dry (Gao, 1994). No matter which side the definition of property rights protects, free market transactions will yield the most efficient outcome. If there are transaction costs, the efficient economic outcome may not be achieved. However, the definition of property rights affects efficiency and the benefits of each party in the transaction. If the law assigns the right of emissions to the factory, since there are no transaction costs, five households will reach an agreement to install dust collectors on the factory chimneys. The installation costs 150 yuan. Assuming that the bargaining ability of each household is the same, each household bears 30 yuan in costs while the factory bears no cost. If the law assigns the right to not experience pollution from the factory to residents, the factory will have to install a dust collector in the absence of transaction costs. The installation cost of 150 yuan is completely borne by the factory while the residents bear no cost. Apparently, the different legal provisions or different definitions of property rights bring different benefits to economic agents. Therefore, Posner (1983) states that legislative bodies have a powerful wealth redistribution tool.

If the existence of transaction costs is considered, the result will be obvious. Regardless of the final settlement on the pollution, as long as government assigns the residents the right to not experience factory pollution, the residents will bear neither the pollution nor the cost of dealing with the emissions. If the government assigns emission rights to the factory, the factory does not have to incur the cost of treating the emissions. The structure of the ultimate plan, and whether the result is effective, depends on the transaction costs—that is, the transaction costs compared to the benefits under different settlements. However, what is certain is that whether it is the residents or the factory that wins, it is more sensible to lobby parliament for a favorable definition of property rights than to compare the social efficiency under different solutions. Individual and collective rationality can yield consistent results under certain mechanisms (either market economy or political), but in the absence of effective political and economic institutions, the two types of rationality conflict. Particularly concerning the formation of an effective institution, collective rationality must give way to individual rationality.

The obscureness of the concept of transaction costs lies in the fact that the concept is static. From a static point of view, it is not meaningful to study transactions. This is akin to treating transactions as instantaneous in mainstream economics. Transaction costs in such instantaneous processes are only natural loss. Hence, the transaction will still attain the Pareto optimal solution. Transaction cost theories can be placed in three categories according to time and space: *ex ante*, *ex post*, and *ex ante* with *ex post* theories. *Ex ante* transaction costs are costs incurred before the business organization is established, including information, negotiation, and contract costs. *Ex post* transaction costs refer to the internal costs of business associated with motivation and transactions, such as costs related to the definition and control of property rights, supervision and management costs, and the costs of changes in institutional structure.

Transaction costs can be also categorized as endogenous and exogenous transaction costs. It is a general belief that they are alternatives. The reason why this chapter does not use such a classification is that compared to *ex ante* and *ex post* transaction costs, costs incurred from signing a contract can be called in-process transaction costs because this concept helps to analyze the possible effects of transaction costs on institutional change. From a static perspective, in-process transaction costs are costs for both parties in the transaction. From a dynamic perspective, transaction costs brought about by the emergence of new institutions are likely to occur after signing a contract. The institutional change itself faces different connotations of transaction costs. If the institution is stable, there are no in-process transaction costs. Only when the institution is undergoing a change will in-process costs occur. At a superficial level, in the dynamic process of signing a contract, the in-process transaction costs result from discontent on both parties regarding the transaction or cooperation with the contract, even objections against it. In fact, the cause lies in the objection to the holders of vested interests. Of course, such objection may come from a third party because the high transaction costs under the old institution may be the income of some economic agents. For example, exogenous transportation and bargaining costs are the income of transportation and communications companies while endogenous costs, such as shirking and speculation, are the rental income of economic agents who possess information superiority. Other examples include the income of lawyers, which comes from trade disputes among economic agents, and the income of entrepreneurs, which comes from incomplete competition and information asymmetry in the market economy. If institutional change causes some economic agents to lose market share, although this change improves the economic efficiency of the whole society, organizational structure changes that reduce transaction costs will inevitably face opposition from holders of the vested interests under existing institutions. Simply using the concept of efficiency and transaction costs is neither necessary nor capable of explaining institutional changes (Palermo, 2000).

In addition, the logic of improving efficiency only through the comparison of transaction costs ignores the income difference under different institutions. Yang (1998) notes that new classical economics studies first the comparison of different types of labor division (i.e., different corner solutions), and then variables such as price and efficiency in the labor division institutions. Hence, whether comparing the efficiency under different economic institutions or studying the evolution from one type of institution to another, it is necessary to consider the impact of new institutions on income compared to three factors: (1) the impact of the *ex ante* transaction costs brought about by the old institutions; (2) the *ex post* transaction costs brought about by the new institutions; and (3) the in-process transaction costs occurring in the transformation from the old to the new institutions.

Therefore, considering the impact of institutions on the final income distribution of the economic agents in cooperation and transactions as well as the *ex ante*, *ex post*, and in-process transaction costs, analyzing the efficiency of institutional change from the perspective of collective rationality causes the theory to depart from reality.

First, in the reasoning of taking transaction costs as a standard to define the structure of property rights, it would be better to directly gain a favorable definition of property rights instead of comparing transaction costs and the efficiency of the corresponding results. Similar to the conflict between individual rationality and collective rationality in the prisoner's dilemma problem, it is better for an agent to directly modify the rules of the game to be in their favor instead of selecting the most favorable solution under the given rules.

Second, with respect to institutional change, determining the efficiency of institutions by a simple comparison of the transaction costs under different institutions ignores the in-process transaction costs caused by changes to the proportion of economic agents' benefit distribution. Thus, taking the transaction costs into the analysis of institutional change creates a dilemma. If transaction costs are too high, for example, and there is obstruction from the groups with vested interests and the free-rider problem of collective action, new and more effective institutional innovation is unlikely to emerge. If transaction costs are too low, however, incredible commitments will inspire more interest groups to place productive resources into the reforms of distribution institutions (Acemoglu, 2005; Greif & Laitin, 2004; Qian, 1994;). Consequently, this will reduce social production and economic efficiency. Therefore, using transaction costs and Pareto efficiency criteria to study institutional change is one-sided and has inherent conflicts. The state paradox is precisely such a conflict.

Endogeneity of institutions and exogenous characteristics of power

We have not distinguished between the concepts of institutional change, evolution, and revolution, but these terms do not have the same connotation. The reason we use them interchangeably is that the boundary between endogeneity and exogeneity has been ambiguous until now. This book integrates two types of logic in the study of the relationship between power and institutions and, hence, clarifies the scope of study regarding the endogeneity of institutions.

Institutional economists are concerned with the impacts of institutions on agent's behavior and economic efficiency, but each researcher chooses their own research path and associated logic. Schott (2008) divides institutional studies into two categories. One is rational design resulting from Commons's collective action while the other is organic evolution from Menger's individual rationality. Menger (1990) regards institutions as the result of interactions between numerous self-interest behaviors of economic agents. Hayek's research follows this path. However, Hayek (1984) believes that it is not just institutions but the entire economic order that is spontaneous based on individual rationality interactions. Although spontaneous evolution of institutions is the result of individual rationality games between stakeholders, it has subtleties that individual rationality cannot detect. A variety of customs, routines, and rules will eventually become the institutions of society and state through evolution. The application of game theory in economics develops jointly with the study of the endogeneity of institutions. Efforts in this direction are well demonstrated by the studies on informal firm rules by Nelson and Winter (Nelson & Winter, 1982), the game model of institutional evolution by Sargent, and the application of evolutionary game theory to comparative institutional analysis by Aoki (Aoki et al., 2001). Commons (1936) does not deny the institutional evolution of customs and routines, but he emphasizes that intentional collective rationality exists behind the formation of institutions. North (1981) believes that the institution is a set of rules, law procedures, and moral norms for behavior. A comparison of these two types of logic shows that the analysis of institutional exogeneity emphasizes the collective and instrumental rationality of the institution.

The main difference between old and new institutional economics lies elsewhere. Representatives of old institutional economics, such as Veblen and Mitchell, are concerned with the evolution of non-artificially designed institutions (Veblen, 1934). After North's (1990) initial work, he begins to pay attention to the influence of informal rules, such as ideologies on formal rules and their interactive relationship. The reality is that many institutions are derived from social development, including economic and political institutions. Therefore, there must be endogenous institutions. However, completely ignoring rationally designed institutions is not sensible. For example, the transition from the planned economic system of socialist countries to market-oriented systems can be considered a designed process of institutional change. Endogenous institutional evolution itself has mutual influence and is correlated with external conditions. The evolution of local institutions is inevitably part of the overall behavioral environment of institutions.

Even among endogenous institution theories, scholars have different views.[4] One view argues that institutional endogeneity has nothing to do with collective rationality and differs from individual rational expectations (Hayek, 2013). Another view believes that as long as the institution does not have a priori existence, it is the optimal choice under collective rationality given the existing environment and social structure. Then, the institution is endogenous. For example, Greif and Laitin (2004) focuses on institutionalizing informal rules and organizational incentives. Fors and Olsson (2007) considers the trade-off that the aristocracy class must make between resource rents and company earnings to select the degree of constraints of property rights. From this point of view, the transformation from a planned to market economy is endogenous.

When comparing the logic in endogenous studies with that of exogenous studies as well as various endogenous views, there is one commonality. That is, under institutional rules, economic agents pursue their own interests whether from individual rationality or from collective rationality. Taking into account the constraints of institutional and organizational incentives on collective actions, it is not objective to completely ignore collective rationality in the formation of institutions. Therefore, institution endogeneity is not the criterion for the existence of collective rationality. Certainly, prior existence of institutions cannot be used as the criterion for distinguishing between endogenous and exogenous institutions. Institutional reference between different governments is an endogenous process of development from nothing for imitators. This book takes institutions as the endogenous variable. By analyzing the distribution of economic, political, and social power among different economic agents, we provide a research framework for the formation and change process of institutions. Based on this framework, we analyze the efficiency of institutions. If only institutions *per se* are considered without addressing the influencing factors of institutions, there is one aspect that cannot be avoided, that is, the vertical classification of institutions. North's basic institutions provide a game framework, or a set of strategies among economic agents, in the cooperation and transaction process (North, 1990). Aoki's approach embeds institutional change into the existing institutional environment (Aoki et al., 2001). Lin's approach places induced institutional change on top of coercive institutional change (Lin, 1994). Even Hayek (2013)'s spontaneous social order can be categorized into two types. The first is as an action structure for the numerous participants in the interactive network to commission and comply with the rules, and the second is an existing rule system. The evolution of an action structure occurs under the clearly discernible environment of rules (namely, the rule system) while the evolution of an existing rule system occurs in the environment without rules and can only be explained by culture and ethics. Thus, to study the rules of institutional change, a more original concept than institution is required, which is a highly suitable method to interpret the formation, changes, efficiency, and characteristics of institutions with respect to the concept of power.

In addition to the resources that economic agents already have, both formal and informal institutions endow agents with certain power. Therefore, institutions must be compared to power in terms of their origins. The power perspective has innate superiority in the study of institutional change, which is determined by the exogenous attributes of power. The exogenous attributes of power originate from within the institution and are endowed externally or even imposed. On the one hand, the power of modern society comes more from socio-economic and political institutions, but the most basic source of power is violence, which is prior to the formation of institutions, that is, interpersonal relationships and cooperation. In other words, there are no institutions in Hobbes jungle, but there is power. On the other hand, even if there are no derived resources (institutions, organizations), power can still be derived from other resources, particularly the meta-resource. Therefore, power comes before institutions. Although Hayek (2013) argues that institutions are spontaneous in their interactions among people, real institution that is considered to be effective results from the development of some obvious principles that are spontaneous and experience disagreement resistance. Disagreement resistance refers to the challenge that economic agents may use against institutions when their interests are damaged in the formation of institutions and during institutional change. To facilitate the study, we simplify the environment for the formation of institutions and the institutional changes to the power environment. For the influence of the institutional environment, under related or complementary causes, we use the power structure among agents to reflect the influence.

The formation of institutions: solidification of the distribution structure

Currently, there are four main approaches to explaining why countries differ in their institutions: the incidental institution perspective, the ideology perspective, the effective institution perspective, and the social conflict perspective. Since economics is the science of choice, the four perspectives are ordered in terms of their emphasis on the role of choice. The incidental perspective does not recognize the rational choice of economic agents and considers economic and political institutions as by-products or unintended consequences of historical events. The ideology perspective only admits the preferences in choosing desired institutions by political groups and suggests that the difference in economic systems between countries is due to differences in ideology. The effective perspective extends the subject of choice to different social groups and agents and emphasizes that social groups choose the most efficient economic system for society. The social conflicts perspective is an extension of the effective perspective on the concept of transaction costs. The social conflict perspective argues that the choice of economic institution is the result of conflict between the agent who controls the country and other interest groups.

According to the above analysis, the premises on the formation of institutions are as follows. First, the formation is endogenous, but it is also affected by artificial designs. The final results of the formation may be consistent with collective rationality, but they are different from the expectations because collective rationality is recognized by all related agents. Hence, there is no way that a single agent can completely dominate institutional design. Second, the agent that affects the formation can be a person or an interest group. Therefore, collective rationality cannot be fully denied. The reason is that the existing organizational motivation will ensure that collective action is possible, and it is not realistic to start with complete individualist rationality of economics. Third, institutions are related to the behavior constraints on all economic agents, both individuals and interest groups, in the future. More importantly, the institutions dictate the strategic behavior of the set of players. Consequently, the institutions have the properties of distribution and motivation.

To avoid the circular arguments of institutions, it is necessary to have an exogenous factor—power—that affects the formation of institutions. The existing institution provides a power environment only for the current participants. The distribution of economic power can also affect political power while political power determines the future political institution that will determine, in turn, the future economic institution. So, it is safe to say that the institution is the solidification of the distribution structure between interest groups, which reflects the current power structure and also affects future economic performance. The reason is that power is temporary while institutions are stable. Thus, power structure has the inherent requirement of being institutionalized. Analogous to Marx's statement, the institution is the superstructure determined by the economic basis. The economic basis is the power structure. Power comes from the current formal institution on the one hand; on the other hand, it comes from other resource endowments that economic agents possess. With the accumulation of social production, power structure is changing, but institutions are constant within a certain

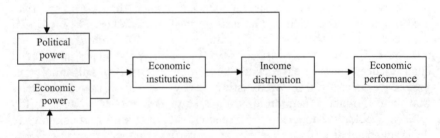

Figure 10.1 The process of institution formation.

period. As for the relationship between power and institutions, we consider that power has a decisive role in institutions while institutions play an influential role in power (Marx, 2004).

This model in this chapter, compared with the recent subjective and evolutionary game models, is more effective in explaining the characteristics of institutions from three aspects. First, the infinite reasoning of institutions is diverted to the social structure inherited from history and not to the environment of the original game. However, we admit that as long as the institution is considered the rule of the game, and games between economic agents are used, the problem of circular arguments cannot be avoided. Therefore, we explain how the original social structure and the institution are formed. The studies on the power and institution relationship completely avoid this problem. Institutions as the characteristic of power structure only affect the economic agent's future power, but power structure exists already, even in the jungle.

Second, as a synthesis of shared belief and game equilibrium, the institution is a variety of equilibrium solutions under different social, economic, and political factors. This also explains both the correlation and complementarity properties of institutions. Moreover, these models also explain why local imitation and transplantation of institutions often struggle to succeed. The reason is that institutions and informal rules in other areas affect the implementation of the new institution. Under the model established in this chapter, the collective rationality of interest groups is believed to affect the formation of an institution. Therefore, in different natural and social environments, different initial values naturally result in different paths of formation and evolution for the future institution. The model itself does not converge.

Third, the formation of institutions and institutional change are completely endogenous, which represents the greatest explanatory power of this model. The existing models often attribute institutional change to extrinsic environmental changes and exogenous shocks because changes in the external environment lead to suspicions by participants on the shared belief, who begin to look for new action rules based on information collection, learning, and experiments. Subsequently, new rules evolve.

However, the common sense in philosophy tells us that external factors can be effective only through internal factors. Therefore, even extrinsic environmental factors and exogenous shocks do not necessarily result in institutional change; rather, they may actually strengthen the current institutional structure. Of course, our model does not deny that the exogenous environment and shocks will affect the structure of power among the interest groups and lead to institutional change. For example, production technology progress and the reduction of earth's resources will lead to new relations of production, and new interest groups and organizations will gradually emerge that will change the power structure of the current society. Consequently, there will be new institutions.

Moreover, the institution model of equilibrium power games emphasizes the distribution attribute of institutions, which is more reasonable in explaining the boundary between endogenous and exogenous institutions. In addition to saving information costs and restraining individuals, institutions, as endogenous game rules, show that gains and losses in the income of participants are determined simultaneously. That is, institutions are not only the rules of games, but they provide incentives to motivate participants into action. Therefore, in the game process, collecting information, learning experiences, trial and errors, predicting rivals' actions, and forming shared beliefs are means of pursuing benefits. However, under the existing rules, the pursuit of production benefits yields much less than the pursuit of benefits from modifying the institutions. Therefore, it is not reasonable to regard the institutions as a by-product in the process of choosing individual behavior rules and strategies. However, regarding institutions completely as the product of human design is also biased. As stated by the spontaneous order theory of the Austria school, understanding current institutions is impossible. The operations of these institutions emerge spontaneously from interactions among millions of people and include sophisticated mechanisms that individuals do not understand. Although individual rationality affects only the distribution of wealth in a certain period, the efficiency of resource allocation that it brings may be inconsistent with expectations.

The basic attributes of institutions determine that the distribution structure of institutions corresponds to the power structure of economic agents. The motive of institutional change will inevitably emerge from the request for interests by the new power holders due to the fact that the existing interest distribution structure no longer matches the current power structure of economic agents. To institutionalize the distribution mechanism is the inherent requirement of economic agents when pursuing their interests while the benefit distribution brought by power structure is temporary. Such distribution is to some extent coercive, but its authority is far less than that of formal institutions. However, the possession of power may be only temporary (Acemoglu, 2005), but once institutions are established, even if there is no corresponding power support, they can also exist and restrain related groups and individuals. The process to institutionalize and make explicit the distribution mechanism may be spontaneous, such as the development of enterprise organization structure. It may also be coercive, such as the construction of property rights systems. The process of the institutionalization of the distribution mechanism will gradually penetrate social, cultural, moral, ethical, ideological, and value aspects in addition to the form of formal institutions. This is why institutions can still be effective after losing the corresponding support of power.

The change in power structure: unification of persistence and transformation of institutions

Institutional change is a violent process of reform of interest distribution and organization structure. Unless it is a Pareto improvement, the change will inevitably face strong resistance from the groups and societal class whose interests suffer. Even if the change is a Pareto improvement, it faces high transaction costs due to bargaining on the proportions of distribution. From the vertical classification of institutions, a low-level institutional change is Pareto improvement brought by new organization and a new incentive structure, in most cases, in an environment where basic institutions are not changing. For political institutions, if the income distribution commitment under the new institutions is credible, Hicks efficiency improvements in institutional change may also be successfully achieved. Of course, this depends on whether the new basic institutions are self-fulfilling. Completely inefficient institutional changes are typically mid-level institutional reforms. For instance, reconfiguration of the value chain brought by industrial policies faces objections causing the institution to be even more inefficient and leading to deterioration in income distribution. Nevertheless, institutions will change periodically, and the Pareto efficiency criterion is not the necessary condition in the process of institutional change.

For the power system, the structure is different for institutions, and power is always changing. The association between power and economic benefits results in the gradual accumulation of change in the allocation structure of resources, and the power structure adjusts accordingly. Thus, even without any external factors, changes in the power structure drive the evolution of institutions. Therefore, the power paradigm of institutional change conducts research from two aspects: First, even in the absence of exogenous parameters or changes in circumstances, when the cumulative energy of change in the power structure is large enough, the institution will also change. Economic performance and income distribution make it inevitable that resource endowments are changing at any moment across economic agents while the direction of the changes is closely related to the current political and economic institutions. Second, if the exogenous parameters or environmental change is large enough, particularly when new power agents emerge, institutions will change to reflect the new power structure. Changes in the structure of power come from an economy's own resource accumulation, but more from changes and shocks in the external environment. Usually, such external factors include changes in production techniques that lead to the emergence of a new economic class, which breaks down the existing social power structure. There may be mutations of power structure inside society caused by foreign invasion, or trade competition and resource rivalry may result in volatility in resource prices due to globalization, which triggers changes in the power structure within a country.

The disturbance to institutions from changes in power structure precisely reflects the durability and path-dependent characteristics of institutions. In the traditional institutional game model, the stability of institutions arises from the costs incurred in institution changes that exceed the corresponding benefits; or, stability results from path dependence caused by adaptive expectations and scale effects. In the evolution game model of institutions, stability is the nature of institutions since institutions are the equilibrium consequence after withstanding a number of exogenous shocks and remaining stable. However, with respect to power, system stabilization stems from the self-reinforcing aspect of power. In all social aspects, including ideology and values at the top level, institutions reflect and reinforce the current power structure as a solidified allocation mechanism. As long as the change in the power structure is acceptable within the scope of the current institution, the institution is stable.

After being recognized by the participants, the institution has inherent stability and durability. The institution will not respond immediately to small and continuous change in the power structure between economic agents. Since institutional structure is identical to the initial resource endowment structure, if the initial resource structure is given, income distribution will continuously accumulate in the same proportion. The social wealth distribution structure between economic agents is stable, but accumulation in wealth will result in a more serious problem of an income distribution gap. Consequently, the power structure will experience a qualitative change within a certain period. In other words, the institution is consistent with the social power structure configuration at the moment of formation. Thereafter, the power structure begins to deviate from the institutional structure. When the conflict between the power structure and the institutional structure reaches a certain level—that is, when the threshold of power deviation the original institution can bear—the new institution will emerge.

Changes in environmental and external factors, particularly the income gap caused by intrinsic resource allocation, will gradually change the power structure between interest groups and between social strata. The continuous and small changes in the power structure will not immediately change the existing institutions of distribution and production. Once the institution is established, it has the durability and stability to penetrate other areas. On the one hand, culture is the rational and effective influence on the current institution and impacts the subjective awareness of economic agents. On the other hand, there is a certain complementarity and correlation between different organizational structures under the current institution. Even if there is disagreement on the current institutions of distribution and production, any behavior that goes beyond the individual conduct strategy set will lead to loss of interests. More importantly, past behavior, culture, and organizational structure affect the values. The easiest and optimal incentive strategy will continue to strengthen its adaptability under the current institutional framework. Therefore, the possibility that the old mode will experience a qualitative change is reduced. In fact, if the power structure changes do not reach a certain degree, changes to the existing set of rules of conduct will not yield more incentives; or, the expected benefits from changing the current institution will be insufficient to cover the costs of such reforms. Therefore, institutional innovation is inevitably limited.

The analysis of institutions based on the power structure shows that institutional change must be the unification of persistence and transformation. The persistence is determined by the attribute of institution constraints while the transformation is caused by the attribute of distribution. Institutional changes imply changes to the power structure with the aim of pursuing a distribution structure that matches the current power structure. A stable structure of institutions implies continuous accumulation of wealth distribution as well as changes in the power structure, which will eventually lead to changes in the institutions. Persistence and transformation are the intrinsic characteristics of institutions. They appear to be contradictory at a glance, but they are essentially unified.

A model of economic institutional change

Although an institution is, in essence, a mechanism for the distribution of benefits, institutions at different levels have different means to affect the distribution of benefits. Economic institutions may appear as direct stipulation as to how cooperative benefits are allocated (such as enterprise contracts and minimum wage laws). Institutions may also appear as the redistribution of income among different groups (such as tax institutions and public expenditure policies). The institutions may be embodied in delimitation on the control of different groups over economic resources, which affects the negotiating power when they reach a cooperation agreement and, ultimately, the distribution of the benefits of cooperation (such as delimitation of property rights or granting a monopoly position). In contrast, the impact of political institutions is more disguised because the political institutions typically only stipulate who has the right to choose the economic institution. However, it can be inferred that granting different groups the right to choose economic institutions means, of course, a different distribution of interests. The investigation of the mechanism of institutional change becomes more complex as the level of institutions become complicated. Political institutions are more disguised than economic institutions, but government is increasingly involved in the institution with increased institutional level. How the political institution emerges, and what government objectives will inevitably shift our focus of research from economics toward political science, are beyond the scope of our study. To express the logic of institutional change, a feasible strategy is to focus on the determination of economic institutions. Since the determination cannot be separated from political institutions, political power, and government participation, our study includes the variables representing the political institution and political power and will make assumptions on government objectives.

Basic assumptions

Economic institutions

Assume that there are two groups, A and B, in the society and that they produce total output q in cooperation based on labor division. Following the conventions in literature, the economic institution is the share of A in q, denoted by δ (correspondingly, the share of B is $1-\delta$). Therefore, the absolute benefits for A is the amount of δq, while B receives the absolute benefits of $(1-\delta)q$. Such an approach, although simple, overlooks one important detail, that is, the economic institution is the income share of economic agents in the total output given the inputs of the agents and is not a simple ratio irrelevant to the input level. If the agent A's input is $R/2$ or $R/3$ in the cooperation and gain half of the total output ($\delta=0.5$) in both cases, then the same value of δ represents two completely different economic institutions.

For the sake of rigidity, we define the economic institution as a mapping of the income share from the resource inputs. Specifically, the functional form is as follows:

$$\delta(\theta, R, S) = \frac{\theta R}{\theta R + (1-\theta)S} \tag{10.1}$$

where δ is the share that A should receive according to the institution (accordingly, the share of B is $1-\delta$). R and S denote the amounts of inputs for the two groups. θ is the weight in calculating the shares of both groups, or in other words, it is the price of the resource put in by the agents. The assumption expressed by equation (10.1) is that when (R, S) changes, $(\delta, 1-\delta)$ also change accordingly. How to change depends on the size of θ. Given (R, S), the greater the θ, the larger the share that A obtains. The difference in economic institutions lies in θ. Under the condition that it is not misleading, θ can be called the economic institution.

Production function and economic power

Social production requires two factors: X and Y. The production function is $Q = TX^{\alpha}Y^{1-\alpha}$, where T is the level of technology while α and $1-\alpha$ are the output elasticities of X and Y, respectively, representing the relative importance of both factors in production. Economic agent A owns R amount of resources that can be used as X, while agent B has S amount of resources that can be used as Y. In the case where A and B cooperate in production, both agents make use of their own specialties. The total social output is

$$q = TR^{\alpha}S^{1-\alpha} \tag{10.2}$$

In the case where A and B do not cooperate, each party uses part of his resources to substitute the other party's resources so as to complete the production independently. Assume one unit of A's resources can replace λ_1 units of B's resources, while a unit of B's resources can replace λ_2 units of A's resources. Since such substitutions do not make use of the specialized function of each party's resources, so, $\lambda_1 < 1$, $\lambda_2 < 1$ that is, the substitution is not perfect. A large λ_1 with a small λ_2 means that it's easy for A's resources to replace B's resources but it is hard to replace A's resources with B's. In other words, A's resources are strongly irreplaceable, while B's resources are weakly irreplaceable.

Substitutability is closely related to the output elasticity of production $(\alpha, 1-\alpha)$. By calculating the substitution rate of X for Y based on the production function $Q = TX^{\alpha}Y^{1-\alpha}$, it gives that holding the level of output constant, one unit of X can replace the $\dfrac{\alpha Y}{(1-\alpha)X}$ units of Y. This shows that the substitutability of X on Y is positively related to the output elasticity α. Of course, such substitutability is also related to the specific values of X and Y. However, no matter what the values are, the factor with greater output elasticity has always a strong substitutability. For the convenience of analysis, let $\lambda_1 = \alpha$ and $\lambda_2 = 1-\alpha$. Given the rate of substitution, each party has also to decide what amount of resources to be used to replace the other party's resources, and what amount to be used for its original purpose. A logical assumption is that each side allocates resources to maximize total output under the constraint of resources. However, such decisions require that economic agents be fully aware of the level of output under various allocations, that is, a thorough knowledge of the production function. The reality is, however, that before the cooperation collapses, the two parties conduct joint production only at point (R,S); moreover, the social production technology is also adapted to the ratio of $R : S$. Therefore, once cooperation breaks down, their substitution goals return the $R : S$ input ratio before the breakdown. The model here assumes that A and B determine resource allocation according to the following rules: A's selection of r satisfies

$$\frac{R-r}{\alpha r} = \frac{R}{S} \tag{10.3}$$

where r is the amount of resource X that A decides to use as Y. B chooses s, satisfying

$$\frac{S-s}{(1-\alpha)s} = \frac{S}{R} \tag{10.4}$$

where s is the amount of resources of S that B decides to use as X. Solving (10.3) and (10.4) gives r and s. With the production function $Q = TX^{\alpha}Y^{1-\alpha}$, the output of each side under the non-cooperative scenario can be calculated, which is,

$$q_a = T(R-r)^{\alpha}(\alpha r)^{1-\alpha} = \frac{\alpha R}{\alpha R + S} TR^{\alpha}S^{1-\alpha} \tag{10.5}$$

$$q_b = T\left[(1-\alpha)s\right]^{\alpha}(S-s)^{1-\alpha} = \frac{(1-\alpha)S}{R+(1-\alpha)S} TR^{\alpha}S^{1-\alpha} \tag{10.6}$$

The fact that $\dfrac{\alpha R}{\alpha R+S}+\dfrac{(1-\alpha)S}{R+(1-\alpha)S}$ is less than 1 indicates that level of output under non-cooperation is less than that under cooperative production. This decreasing in the level of total output results in elements that do not completely replace in the production of non-cooperative situation. In the scenario of non-cooperative production, the independent level of output for each side is only equivalent to part of that in the cooperative production scenario, that is, $\dfrac{\alpha R}{\alpha R+S}$ and $\dfrac{(1-\alpha)S}{R+(1-\alpha)S}$. However, this proportion depends on the resource quantity $(R,\ S)$ of the economic agent and the importance of the resources $(\alpha,\ 1-\alpha)$ in production. The more the resources, the greater the importance will be in production; consequently, the higher the level of independent production will be. Define each party's economic power as the ratio of the output under non-cooperative to that under cooperative, that is, economic power of A is $E_a = \dfrac{\alpha R}{\alpha R+S}$ and that of B is $E_b \dfrac{(1-\alpha)S}{R+(1-\alpha)S}$. Such power is a comprehensive reflection of quantity and quality of the resources that an economic agent owns.

In addition, since E_a and E_b are defined based on the same set of variables $(R,\ S,\ a)$, the economic power of both parties is complementary. If one party is unsatisfied with the current economic institution $\delta(\theta,R,S)$, he can deter the other party by threatening to withdraw the cooperation. While the withdrawal of cooperation may result in losses for both parties, the party with stronger economic power will incur fewer losses than the other party, and may even obtain more income shares than in the current economic institution. Taking E_a and E_b into (10.5) and (10.6), it follows, $q_a = E_a q$, and $q_b = E_b q$.

Political power

Political power is the ability of interest groups to affect the choice of economic institution through their control over resources. Such resources may be the economic resources controlled by interest groups. For example, interest groups can use financial support as bargaining chips to exchange with the judiciary, the legislators, or the ruling persons. However, political power may be derived from the organization resources of interest groups. For example, when the economic situation for interest groups worsens, interest groups tend to organize themselves and exert pressure on government. The greater the number of interest groups, the more intricately linked they are, and the greater their organizational strength.

We denote the political power of group A and that of group B as jR and jS, respectively, based on economic resources, where R and S are the economic resources controlled by group A and B, j (>0) is the correlation coefficient between political power and economic resources. The greater the j, the stronger the correlation will be between political power and economic resources. Define the political power of group A and that of group B as f_aS/R and f_bR/S, respectively, where S/R and R/S represent the economic situations of the two interest groups, while f_a and f_b represent, respectively, the organizing capacity of the two interest groups. To sum up, the political power of group A and B can be expressed as $P_a = jR + f_aS/R$ and $P_b = jS + f_bR/S$. Parameters f_a and f_b, and the size of j depend on the political institution, and demographic and cultural characteristics.

Single-period game model of institutional changes

The initial state

A and B own economic resources R and S, respectively, and the current economic institution is θ, which is the result of the previous power game. The economic power of A and B are denoted, respectively, as E_a and E_b, while the political power for the two is denoted as $P_a = jR + f_aS/R$ and $P_b = jS + f_bR/S$. The normalized political power indicators are $\xi_a = P_a/(P_a + P_b)$ and $\xi_b = P_b/(P_a + P_b)$.

Game structure and payoff functions

In any economic institution, every interest group hopes that the institution will change in its favor, but such hope may not necessarily result in practical action. Only when a group feels that its political power is sufficient to influence government decisions will it raise the requirement to change the institution. Therefore, assume that when $\xi_a > \xi_b$, A requests an institutional change. When $\xi_a < \xi_b$, B requests an institutional change. When $\xi_a = \xi_b$, neither of them will request a change and government will not take the initiative to change the economic institution. Figure 10.2a and 10.2b depict the game structures when A or B requires to make an institutional change, respectively.

a   A requests a change $(\xi_a > \xi_b)$

If government decides to reform, the economic institution will move to $\theta + \Delta (0 < \theta + \Delta < 1)$ from θ. This will damage B's interests, so B will make a choice between obedience and resistance. When B chooses obedience, the two parties will invest all resources R and S to produce in collaboration. Social output is q according to the economic institution $\theta + \Delta$, the payoffs are $u_1 = \delta(\theta + \Delta)q$ and $v_1 = 1 - \delta(\theta + \Delta)q$ for the two parties, respectively. When B chooses resistance, B will not cooperate with A in production. A has to produce independently. The payoffs are $u_2 = q_a = E_aq$ and $v_2 = q_b = E_bq$ for the two parties, respectively.[5] q is always greater than $q_a + q_b$, which states that from the perspective of society as a whole, cooperation will produce more output than non-cooperation. However, when B chooses obedience or resistance, it does not consider the total social output; instead, it compares $v_1 = [1 - \delta(\theta + \Delta)]q$ with $v_2 = E_bq$. If

$\delta(\theta+\Delta)$ is big enough so as to make $v_1 < v_2$, then B will choose resistance, leading to low efficiency of social economic activities.

The government decision has dual goals: First, total social output should be maximized because this generates more tax revenues for the government. Second, the government should obtain political acknowledgment because this will allow the government to hold tax revenues over the long term. Defined government payment in the selection of a particular economic institution is the social outputs multiplied by the political power indicator of the policy supporters. When the government decides to change the economic institution from θ to $\theta+\Delta$, B is always discontented. Choosing obedience or resistance is a reaction due to the lack of alternatives and does not imply any difference in power stance. As long as government decides to reform, the political power of B is a threat to government. In contrast, A is the beneficiary of the institutional change. Whether B resists or not, the political power of A is always the force supportive of the reform. In addition, the reform is a social project, except for overcoming the political obstacles from the opposition; it also entails a certain amount of administrative costs. Assume that such costs account for a proportion of the total output, that is, ϕ. To summarize the above analysis, if a government chooses to reform, when B chooses obedience, the government payments are $g_1 = q\xi_a(1-\phi)$; when B chooses resistance, the payments are $g_2 = (q_a+q_b)\xi_a(1-\phi)$.[6]

If government decides not to reform, then the economic institution will remain unchanged at θ. This will cause the A's discontentment; therefore, it is A's turn to choose either obedience or resistance. When A chooses obedience, the two parties invest all resources of R and S to produce in cooperation. Social output will be $q = TR^\alpha S^{1-\alpha}$. Based on the economic institution, payoffs of A and B are $u_3 = \delta(\theta)q$ and $v_3 = [1-\delta(\theta)]q$, respectively, while the payoff to government is $g_3 = q\xi_b$. When A chooses resistance, it will not cooperate in production; hence, the payoffs are $u_4 = q_a$ and $v_4 = q_b$, respectively, to A and B, while the payoff to government is $g_4 = (q_a+q_b)\xi_b$.

b   B requests a change $(\xi_a < \xi_b)$

The structure of the game is the same as that of the previous scenario, but supporters of the reform switch their role with the opponents. Whether government makes reform or not yields results opposite to those in the previous scenario. We use similar method to construct the payoff functions for both sides under various strategic combinations, details of which are shown in Figure 10.2b.

Conditions for various institution equilibria

Since the game structure in Figure 10.2a is completely analogous to that in Figure 10.2b, we will focus on the equilibrium conditions for the games in Figure 10.2a in the following part.

In Figure 10.2a, there are four possible equilibrium paths in the figure, representing all possible games that the institutional change could result in when A requests a change. They are the result of strategy combinations of the players, and the objective in choosing strategies is to maximize the player's payoff. Therefore, conditions for the equilibrium paths can be obtained by comparing payoffs of players under different strategies. Table 10.1 lists all possible equilibrium conditions. The analysis of these conditions can explain the reasons for institutional changes.

a   B: If there is a reform, then obey; A: If there is not any reform, then obey $(v_1 \geq v_2, u_3 \geq u_4)$

Taking $u_3 = \delta(\theta)q$, $u_4 - E_a q$, $v_1 = [1 - \delta(\theta + \Delta)]q$, $v_2 = E_b q$ into $u_3 \geq u_4$ and $v_1 \geq v_2$, then rearrange and get

$$\delta(\theta) \geq E_a \tag{10.7}$$

$$1 - \delta(\theta + \Delta) \geq E_b \tag{10.8}$$

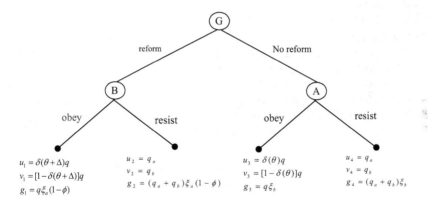

a) A requires reform

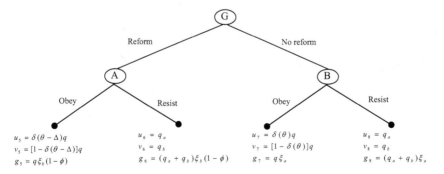

b) B requires reform

Figure 10.2 Institutional game with government participation.

The left-hand side of (10.7) and (10.8) is the income share of A and B calculated based on the target institution, while the right-hand side is the indicators of relative power. The indicators can be also viewed as the obtainable share based on the actual economic power, that is, the independent output if there is no cooperation. The two equations have the "≥" relationship, which shows that the share calculated based on the institution is in excess of that calculated based on economic power. If there is a reform in this scenario, then B obeys; if there is no reform, then A obeys. Rearranging (10.7) and (10.8), respectively, gives

$$\theta \geq \alpha / (1+\alpha) \tag{10.9}$$
$$\theta + \Delta \leq 1 / (2-\alpha) \tag{10.10}$$

Equation (10.9) shows that A's share before reform is not lower than a certain value. Equation (10.10) shows that A's share is not higher than a certain value after the reform. When the difference in the institution before and after reform is within a certain range $\left(\left[\alpha / (1+\alpha), 1 / (2-\alpha) \right] \right)$, then regardless of whether the government reforms, the two parties will adopt the strategy of obedience. Notice that $\alpha / (1+\alpha) \leq 1 / (2-\alpha)$ holds for any $\alpha \in [0,1]$, and the values at both parties of the inequality sign increase with α. This states that the change in distribution institutions before and after the reform is within an interval that is roughly consistent with the importance of the production. In other words, the institutions before and after the reform are consistent with economic contributions.

If both B and A take the same strategy of obedience when there is a reform and no reform, the social output is q. Then, government's decision on reform or not becomes irrelevant to efficiency. In both scenarios, the government's payoff function are g_1 (reform) and g_3 (not reform) respectively. If $g_1 > g_3$, the government chooses to reform; if $g_1 \leq g_3$, it

Table 10.1 Conditions for paths of an institutional change when A requests reform

B		A		Government			Strategy
Condition	Strategy	Condition	Strategy	Condition	Strategy	Equilibrium	mix
$v_1 \geq v_2$	Obey, if there is a reform	$u_3 \geq u_4$	Obey, if there is no reform	$g_1 > g_3$ $g_1 \leq g_3$	$\theta \to \theta + \Delta$ $\theta \to \theta$	1 3	1
$v_1 \geq v_2$	Obey, if there is a reform	$u_3 < u_4$	Resist, if there is no reform	$g_1 > g_4$ $g_1 \leq g_4$	$\theta \to \theta + \Delta$ $\theta \to \theta$	1 4	2
$v_1 < v_2$	Resist, if there is a reform	$u_3 \geq u_4$	Obey, if there is no reform	$g_2 > g_3$ $g_2 \leq g_3$	$\theta \to \theta + \Delta$ $\theta \to \theta$	2 3	3
$v_1 < v_2$	Resist, if there is a reform	$u_3 < u_4$	Resist, if there is no reform	$g_2 > g_4$ $g_2 \leq g_4$	$\theta \to \theta + \Delta$ $\theta \to \theta$	2 4	4

chooses to maintain θ unchanged. Taking $g_1 = q\xi_a(1-\phi)$ and $g_3 = q\xi_b$ into $g_1 > g_3$ and $g_1 \leq g_3$, we can get conditions for government reform and non-reform are

$$\frac{\xi_a - \xi_b}{\xi_a} > \phi \qquad (10.11)$$

$$\frac{\xi_a - \xi_b}{\xi_a} \leq \phi \qquad (10.12)$$

Equations (10.11) and (10.12) show, when the political power of A relative to B is large enough to overcome the costs of the institutional change, government changes the economic institution from θ to $\theta + \Delta$; otherwise, it keeps the institution unchanged at θ. The above analysis shows that when the economic power of either A or B is not strong enough to resist the coming reform, government's decision on whether to reform depends on the political power of A and B and the costs of the institutional change.

b   B: If there is a reform, then obey; A: If there is no reform, then resist $(v_1 \geq v_2, u_3 < u_4)$

From conditions $u_3 < u_4$ and $v_1 \geq v_2$ it can be derived that

$$\delta(\theta) < E_a \qquad (10.13)$$
$$1 - \delta(\theta + \Delta) \geq E_b \qquad (10.14)$$

Equation (10.13) shows that when the economic power of A guarantees to obtain more shares from non-cooperation than that under the institution of θ, A will resist if government chooses not to reform. Equation (10.14) shows that shares of B endowed by reformed institution θ exceed that by B's economic power, B will obey. Further simplification of (10.13) and (10.14) yields

$$\theta < \alpha / (a + \alpha) \qquad (10.15)$$
$$\theta + \Delta \leq 1 / (2 - \alpha) \qquad (10.16)$$

Equations (10.15) and (10.16) show that when the original institution is much unfavorable to A while quite favorable to B, and the institution after reform is still favorable to B, then the strategy mix will be that A will resist if government does not reform and B will obey if there is a reform. Government's policy choice depends on whether $g_1 > g_4$ or $g_1 \leq g_4$. Expanding the two inequalities gives the conditions for government making reform and not making reform, which are

$$\frac{q}{q_a + q_b} \xi_a(1-\phi) > \xi_b \qquad (10.17)$$

$$\frac{q}{q_a + q_b} \xi_a(1-\phi) \leq \xi_b \qquad (10.18)$$

The government will choose to reform when the political power of A is larger and the cost of reform is smaller, or when A's resistance will lead to great efficiency loss, $\dfrac{q}{q_a+q_b}$. Otherwise, it maintains θ unchanged, although A's resistance would lead to the reduction in the total social output.

c   B: If there is a reform, then resist; A: If there is no change, then obey $\left(v_1 < v_2,\ u_3 \geq u_4\right)$

From conditions $u_3 \geq u_4$ and $v_1 < v_2$, it can be derived that

$$\delta(\theta) \geq E_a \tag{10.19}$$
$$1-\delta(\theta+\Delta) < E_b \tag{10.20}$$

The economic power of B can ensure that his share under non-cooperation exceeds the share under the institution of $\theta+\Delta$ after the reform. If government reforms in this scenario, B will resist. The economic power of A is not strong enough to resist the current institution, if government does not reform, A will choose to obey. Further simplifying (10.19) and (10.20) gives

$$\theta \geq \alpha / (1+\alpha) \tag{10.21}$$
$$\theta+\Delta > 1 / (2-\alpha) \tag{10.22}$$

Equations (10.21) and (10.22) state that, the existing institution θ is not difficult for A to accept, while the new institution $\theta+\Delta$ makes B's share drop substantially. Then, the strategy mix will be that A chooses obedience if there is no reform and B chooses to resist if there is the reform. Under this combination of strategy, whether $g_2 > g_3$ or $g_2 \leq g_3$ determines whether government reforms or not. By expanding the two equations, conditions for government's making reform and not making reform are derived as follows,

$$\xi_a(1-\phi) > \frac{q}{q_a+q_b}\xi_b \tag{10.23}$$

$$\xi_a(1-\phi) \leq \frac{q}{q_a+q_b}\xi_b \tag{10.24}$$

When the political power of A is larger relative to B or the cost of reform is relatively small, or the loss in efficiency caused by B's resistance is relatively small, then the government will reform; otherwise, the institution will remain unchanged.

d   B: If there is the reform, then resist; A: If there is no reform, then resist $\left(v_1 < v_2,\ u_3 < u_4\right)$

For the government, this situation is a dilemma. From $u_3 < u_4$ and $v_1 < v_2$, it can be derived that

$$\theta < \alpha / (1+\alpha) \tag{10.25}$$
$$\theta+\Delta > 1 / (2-\alpha) \tag{10.26}$$

The existing institution θ is too unfavorable to A, but the new institution after reform, $\theta+\Delta$, makes the B's income share drop significantly, which is a scenario where the original economic institution cannot appease the economic power of A while the proposed reform is too radical. Taking into account that the alternative system in reality is not a continuum, it is possible for this situation to occur. Whether government reforms or not, it will inevitably lead to the loss in current social output. The government's choice depends on contrast of the political power between A and B, as well as the consideration of the cost of reform. Expanding $g_2 > g_4$ and $g_2 \le g_4$, and then making simplification, the conditions for government's making reform and not making reform are derived as follows,

$$\frac{\xi_a - \xi_b}{\xi_a} > \phi \tag{10.27}$$

$$\frac{\xi_a - \xi_b}{\xi_a} \le \phi \tag{10.28}$$

When the political power of A relative to B is enough to overcome the cost of reform, the government will reform. Otherwise, the institution will remain at θ unchanged.

The efficiency of institutional change

In the case of the strategy mix (1), regardless of whether the government reforms the current economic institution, it will not encounter resistance from the party whose interests are hurt. Institutions reform or not does not result in non-cooperative production. The reform does not cause changes in total social output. In the case of strategy mix (2), the reform can avoid the efficiency loss caused by A's resistance, so that institutional change is efficient. However, such efficient changes do not necessarily happen. If the political power of B is strong, the government will cease reform due to political resistance and prefer to accept the low economic output resulting from A's resistance. In the case of strategy mix (3), no reform can avoid the loss in efficiency caused by B's resistance. However, if the political power of A is strong, the government prefers to reform even if B resists. Such an institutional change is inefficient since it at least causes a reduction in the total social output in the current period. In the case of strategy mix (4), institutions reform or not will cause resistance from the party whose interests damage. The government chooses to reform because of the political pressures from A instead of concerns for economic efficiency. In fact, economic efficiency is low either before or after the reform.

The above comparison of the economic efficiency of instituting reform is just a short-term analysis. A reform that increases total social output in the short run may not increase the potential of economic growth in the long run. In the short run, social production declines due to resistance from

284 *Institutional change with power*

opponents, but the resistance may also be helpful to economic growth in the long run. The reason is that the amount of total output depends on the economic agent's investment incentives and on whether they have sufficient economic resources available for investment. Given the social production function $Q = TX^\alpha Y^{1-\alpha}$ and the total social economic resources E, it is possible to solve for the allocation of resources that maximizes Q. Let x be the amount of resources used as factor X, and accordingly the amount of resources used as factor Y is $y = E - x$. Solving the maximization problem $\underset{x}{Max} Tx^{\alpha}(E-x)^{1-\alpha}$ gives $x = \alpha E$, $y = (1-\alpha)E$. If they are just the quantity of resources of agent A and B, then the total social output is maximized in the case of cooperation in production. Take the strategy mix (2) of the above analysis as an example. Suppose $\alpha < 0.5$, that is, B should occupy more resources according to the principle of maximizing social output. If government changes the economic institution from $\delta(\theta) < 0.5$ to $\delta(\theta + \Delta) > 0.5$ in order to avoid the resistance from A, and changes repeat according to the ratio of $s_1(\theta + \Delta) = \dfrac{(\theta + \Delta) R_t}{(\theta + \Delta) R_t + (1 - \theta - \Delta) S_t}$ (where t is the sequence number of the game), then B's proportion of resources will become smaller and smaller. This seriously deviates from the resource ratio, $\delta(\theta) < 0.5$, required by the maximization of social output.

Broadly speaking, institutional change may be efficient in the short run because it avoids the reduction in output caused by the resistance against the original institution. However, institutional change may also be inefficient because the government makes a coercive change to gain political support regardless of the resistance from a certain group. The uncertainty of the efficiency of institutional change stems from the fact that the changes are driven by the power games between agents (economic agents and government) for their own interests and not by efficiency motives. In the games, both economic and political power are involved. The complex effects of various types of power lead to many possibilities regarding institutional change. The changes that are efficient in the short run may be inefficient in the long run while the changes that are inefficient in the short run may be efficient in the long run. Short-term effects may deviate from the long-term effects because social production requires factors to be allocated according to a specific proportion. However, in reality, resource allocation is the cumulative result of short-term institutional change. Institutional changes, from the perspective of the change process, do not occur with planning or foresight.

Multi-period recursion of the institutional change game model

Given the parameters of the game, namely, the political institutions j, f_a, and f_b, the cost of reform ϕ, the production technology T, the degree of resource contribution α, the extent of the reform Δ, and the initial state variables θ, R, and *S*, we can solve for the equilibrium institution in the current period and the total social output and benefits of each economic agent under this institution. However, based on the results of the current game, more interesting questions are the following: how will the institution and the corresponding economic operation change after another period of the game? What will the path of institutional change be with multi-period recursion? Is there a long-run stable economic institution? Finding the answers to these questions requires simple assumptions on the transition rules of state variables. Assume that at the beginning of next period,

$$\text{Institution: } \theta_{t+1} = \begin{cases} \theta_t \text{ equilibrium paths at period } t \text{ are } 3,4,7,8 \\ \theta_t + \varDelta \text{ equilibrium paths at period } t \text{ are } 1,2 \\ \theta_t - \varDelta \text{ equilibrium paths at period } t \text{ are } 5,6 \end{cases}$$

A's economic resources:

$$R_{t+1} = \begin{cases} q_{a,t} \text{ equilibrium paths at period } t \text{ are } 2,4,6,8 \\ \delta(\theta_t + \varDelta)q_t \text{ equilibrium path at period } t \text{ is } 1 \\ \delta(\theta_t - \varDelta)q_t \text{ equilibrium paths at period } t \text{ is } 5 \\ \delta(\theta_t)q_t \text{ equilibrium paths at period } t \text{ are } 3,7 \end{cases}$$

B's economic resources:

$$S_{t+1} = \begin{cases} q_{b,t} \text{ equilibrium paths at period } t \text{ are } 2,4,6,8 \\ [1-\delta(\theta_t + \varDelta)]q_t \text{ equilibrium path at period } t \text{ is } 1 \\ [1-\delta(\theta_t - \varDelta)]q_t \text{ equilibrium paths at period } t \text{ is } 5 \\ [1-\delta(\theta_t)]q_t \text{ equilibrium paths at period } t \text{ are } 3,7 \end{cases}$$

where equilibrium paths 1,2......8 are the eight paths of game decisions in Figure 10.2.

For the transition of the resource variables of A and B, we do not consider consumption. The reason for this treatment is that consumption is not a factor addressed in this book. In theory, we assume that the consumption of economic agents is a transformation of one economic resource into another. For example, education consumption creates human resources, and automobile consumption saves the resource of time. These new resources are still productive in the next period of economic activity.

Numerical simulation analysis of multi-period institutional changes

Convert those single-period institution game rules and inter-temporal state transition rules described above into computer program (Mathematica program), and give the parameters and the first period (*t*) values of state variable, then run the program to collect game outcomes by recursive calculation of every period and plot the game results against time, we can observe the changes with time of the economic institution θ, the social output $Q \in \{q, a_a + q_b\}$, the long-run output efficiency $\rho = Q / Q_{max}$,[7] the distribution proportion of social wealth $\lambda = \dfrac{R}{R+S}$, and the political power indexes ξ_a and ξ_b; moreover, the corresponding relations among different indexes in the same game period are also able to be observed. We also analyze the long-run efficiency and the characteristics of paths of institutional changes.

In the rest of this section, several graphs are plotted to illustrate the correspondence between the indexes and time t. The game starts at period $t = 1$. R_1, S_1, λ_1, $\xi_{a,1}$, $\xi_{b,1}$, $E_{a,1}$, and $E_{b,1}$ are given as the initial state values or the derived state indexes based on the initial states while θ_1, Q_1, and ρ_1 are the results of the game at the end of the first period. It should be noted that, before θ_1 is established by the game in period $t=1$, there may be an initial value θ different from θ_1. The initial value θ cannot be drawn in the graph because both θ and θ_1 appear in period $t = 1$; however, they are provided in the parameter list below the related figures. R_t, S_t, λ_t, $\xi_{a,t}$, $\xi_{b,t}$, $E_{a,t}$, and $E_{b,t}$ are the initial state values in period t and are the results of game at period $t - 1$; θt, Q_t, ρ_t are the game results of current period.

A typical process of resource—power—institutional change

In the economic model illustrated by Figure 10.3, the economic resources of A have a strong productivity ($\alpha = 0.6 > 1 - \alpha$), but the initial economic institution is unfavorable to A ($\theta = 0.4$); B gets the majority income from the co-operative production, resulting in a decreasing proportion of A in the social wealth stock (λ). Such a collective decline in economic status impels group A to organize and form the political power ($f_a S / R$) based on organizational resources. In period 5 and 6, government is forced by the political pressure of group A ($\xi_a > \xi_b$) to implement the institutional change ($\theta_5 = 0.5$, $\theta_6 = 0.6$). Since then, with the stable economic institution ($\theta = 0.6$), the wealth proportion of group A (λ) increases due to this favorable institution, which will not only help to enhance its economic power (E_a), but also enhance its political power (jR) based on economic resources. As a consequence, in period 13, the economic institution continues to change in a direction that is favorable to A. Such excessive inclination of economic institution decreases the wealth proportion of group B, ($1 - \lambda$), and seriously weakens B's economic power (E_b). However, its political power ($f_b R / S$) based on organizational resources tends to be strengthened and is ultimately reflected by the fact that ξ_b is significantly greater than ξ_a after period 15. Under the dominance of political power, the institutional change from period 15 begins to develop towards a direction that is favorable to B, despite that the economic power of A, (E_a), is significantly higher than that of B (E_b).

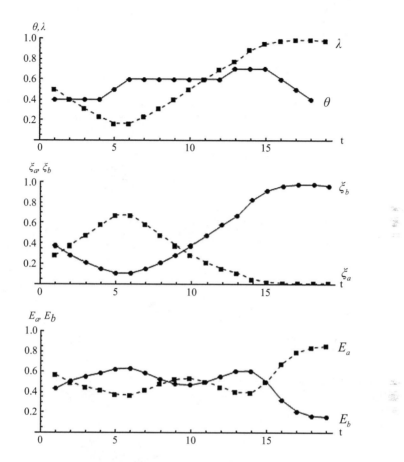

Figure 10.3 Numerical simulation of resource—power—institutional change.

Dependence of the paths of institutional change

The institutional change path in Figure 10.3 seems to be an endless recipro-
cating motion, which is actually a special case under particular settings of the
initial states and the parameters. Due to the difference in initial states (θ, R,
S), the political institution (j), the social and cultural factors (f_a, f_b), the change
cost (ϕ), and the difference in the possible range of change (Δ), economic institutional changes may have quite diversified paths. Figure 10.4 plots the paths
of institutional changes under three different initial settings of institution (the
initial values of θ are 0.3, 0.5, and 0.7, respectively). If we change the other initial
state variables and parameters, the paths will be more complex and diversified.

The efficiency of institutional change

Figure 10.5a and 10.5b show the change in the distribution effects of
wealth and output efficiency in the same process of institutional change.

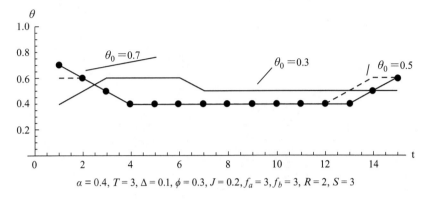

$\alpha = 0.4, \ T = 3, \ \Delta = 0.1, \ \phi = 0.3, \ J = 0.2, f_a = 3, f_b = 3, \ R = 2, \ S = 3$

Figure 10.4 Institutional change paths under different initial settings of institution.

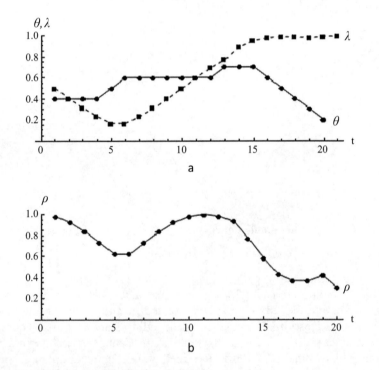

Figure 10.5 Efficiency of institutional change.

Institutional change is the result when we extend the period in Figure 10.3 to 20 periods. Before institutional change in periods 5 and 6, as the most productive group, A cannot possess the corresponding economic resources; hence, total social output is inefficient relative to the potential output. After the changes in periods 5 and 6, this inefficient allocation of resources is corrected, and the efficiency of social output (ρ) shows an upward trend. However, as the economic institution becomes more inclined to A ($\theta = 0.7$) in period 13, A holds most of the economic resources, and B has almost no resources to put into social production. Therefore, the efficiency of social output ρ begins to decline, and will not show a lagged upward tendency until period 19. Tracking the simulation processes shows that ρ appears to fall once again in period 20, which is caused by A's resistance to institutional change (non-cooperation) in the current period. This numerical simulation process at least proves that there are institutional changes that are beneficial to the efficiency of social production, but there are also changes that are unfavorable to efficiency. Moreover, whether institutional changes occur is not determined by the standard of efficiency. Rather, the driving force of change comes from the change in the power contrast caused by changes in the economic resources controlled by economic agents.

Notes

1 Connotation of institutions is very broad, at least in the views of Commons and Schott, customs and routines are both some forms of institutions, so their research also focuses on formation and evolution of informal institutions like customs and routines. The institutions here include the informal ones, too, but they refer mainly to the formal institutions.

2 In fact, the new institutional economics studies institutions with the method of game theory, but the focus varies from one research to another. Sugden and Young relax the rationality of economic agents by evolutionary game theory, while Greif uses repeated games. Therefore, they come up with different definitions of institutions. However, in Masahiko Aoki's view, to avoid circular reasoning of the institution, it is necessary to regard the institution both as rule and as equilibrium. He emphasizes that the formation of the common belief of economic agents, namely, his consideration of the rival's behavior and equilibrium outcome is certain simultaneously when game subjects made choice of the balanced strategy. In this sense, the institutions defined by Sugden and Greif play the same role as the common belief.

3 The mode of subjective game and Greif's endogenous institutions regard the commonality of knowledge or belief as the nature of institutions. This commonality helps predict the behavior of other players; hence, it reduces the uncertainty of behavior in the game; however, it plays an important role in equilibrium selection for multiple games and reduces the uncertainty. In other words, the endogenous theory of institutions argues that the most basic characteristic of the institution is to reduce uncertainty in the process of games. However, it is apparent that this is not the basic property of the institution.

4 This can be seen from the different classifications of the system. Lin Yifu divided the system into induced system changes and mandatory system changes. The former is endogenous and the latter is exogenously designed. Aoki divides the system into autonomous institutional changes and induced institutional changes; the former is endogenous and the latter is exogenous. Lin Yifu believes that the inducing factor of institutional change is efficiency, and Aoki Changyan believes that changes in government policies and laws have induced institutional changes.

5 In reality, if B chooses to be obedient, it may not invest all its resources S; while if chooses to resist, B may be cooperative to some extent, and make some

investment of its resources according to the magnitude of $\delta(\theta+\Delta)$. To simplify the analysis, the model here uses a dichotomy that B either completely co-operates or completely resists. Such treatment is capable of fully demonstrating the motivation function of institutions. Of course, the simplification loses some delicate results but this is the tradeoff that our analysis has to make.

6 Note that it is a relative indicator, so defining the government payment function does not ignore the influence of B's political power.

7 $Q_{max} = \underset{x,y}{Max} T x^{\alpha} y^{1-\alpha}$,   s.t. $x+y=R+S$ is maximum possible output under the assumption that social resources can be allocated arbitrarily, given the gross social resources R + S.

11 Conclusions and prospects of the research based on power paradigm

Conclusions of the research based on power paradigm

In the past 40 years of China's Economic Reform and open up, a series of institutional changes have made great achievements in China's economy attracting worldwide attention. Such as the reform of land contract responsibility system in Xiaogang Village of Anhui Province, the reform of modern enterprise system in state-owned enterprises, and the reform of decentralization system in central and local governments. The essence of these reforms is nothing more than the core content of "decentralization and interest concessions." However, when the reform of "decentralization and interest concessions" is not carried out systematically, in place and thoroughly, it will lead to the imbalance of interest distribution of different groups, which is reflected on the imbalance of rights between urban citizens and rural residents, interest groups and the civilian class, large monopoly enterprises and small or medium-sized private enterprises. These rights imbalances hinder economic restructuring and private wealth growth. From such economic realities, we gradually abstract the relationship between resources, power and economic interest distribution, and interpret Chinese economic changes in the past hundred years as the structural changes and games between economic power and political power. We also interpret the current economic reform as the process of redefining various power boundaries and cultivating market subjects, that is, the central government's power is decentralized and decomposed, and then interacts with the market's economic power in a complex process. We propose and believe that power is the decisive factor behind the existence and change of the institution. Based on the typical facts at home and abroad, we construct the power paradigm of economics research, take the concept of power as the main research unit, and analyze the role of power in the game field of market, enterprise, government.

The book has three features. First, the power paradigm we proposed has something in common with the Neoclassical Paradigm, Hayek Paradigm, and Marxism Paradigm. The power paradigm is special in that it can interpret and evaluate other theories, and can also supplement the theoretical blind spots of other paradigms. Therefore, the theory of this book can be used to explain not only the abstract market economy, but also the concrete history of economic operation and development. Second, we believe that the market economy is more than just the equilibrium between demand and supply; it also embodies the relationship between the demand side and the supply side and the distribution of the remaining benefits of the transaction. The change of market price is the focus of interest contention; it is the contest of power. Therefore, the real manipulation of the market is not the invisible hand of price, but the power. Third, the power paradigm of economic research can not only profoundly reveal what are the essential factors that determine economic activities, but also naturally solve the rupture between macro economy and micro economy, and the relationship between politics and economics.

Prospects of the research based on power paradigm

The scope of our research has shifted from the basic principles of economics to the basic principles of political economy, and the focus of our research has been extended over "prosperity" to "common prosperity," trying to clarify the relationship of political, economic, and social wealth distribution in the path of achieving common prosperity. If prosperity can be achieved mainly by market forces, it is absolutely impossible to achieve common prosperity without the government's leadership. For the government, in order to achieve this goal, it must keep pace with the times through institutional innovation: Power reciprocity needs to be shared among different economic agents at the same hierarchy level while making sure that power and responsibility are equivalent for each economic agent. This is the fundamental way to achieve common prosperity.

The current situation of wealth distribution and the predicament of common prosperity

In a long-term and overall sense, "prosperity" means the maximization of social wealth, which requires the joint efforts of all social members. Its effective incentive is to let the public realize "common prosperity." Therefore, in this sense, prosperity and common prosperity go hand in hand. But in the short term and in part, prosperity and common prosperity are really two different concepts, because prosperity often starts from some individuals first, and it is unlikely that everyone will move forward at the same time. In addition, the common prosperity we are talking about here is not equal prosperity. The history of China's economic development shows that egalitarianism "mess together" is really inefficient before social wealth and people's ideological consciousness are greatly improved. However, China's strategy of "Let some people get rich first" is fraught with real worries about the current rich-poor gaps.

The year 2020 is a decisive one for securing a victory in building a moderately prosperous society in all respects and the fight against poverty. It is also the concluding year of the 13th Five-Year Plan. After more than 40 years development of reform and opening up, the resident's income level in China has been significantly improved. The annual Real GDP per capita levels have crossed $10,000 in 2019, and the per capita disposable income has reached 30,000 yuan. On the road to achieving common prosperity, China has basically completed the stage victory of getting rid of poverty as a whole.

While the income level is rising, the significance of the rich-poor gaps cannot be ignored. The consideration of the rich-poor gaps can be carried out from two dimensions: one is the income gap, and the other is the wealth gap. From the perspective of income gap, according to the national resident income gap data released by the National Bureau of Statistics of China, the Gini coefficient of resident income has been fluctuating between 0.4 and 0.5 in the past decade, which can be said to be at a high level. Although it has declined by recent years, the decline is not significant. Chen, Wang and Zhou (2018) made a detailed analysis of the structure and causes of Chinese resident's income distribution, indicating that at present, the distribution of resident's income in China is pear shaped, and the proportion of low-income and middle-low-income groups is still large. Under the influence of the dual structure, the proportion of rural farmers in the low-income layer is high, and the income span of the high-income layer is large, which further widens the income gap of the whole society.

From the perspective of wealth gap, the problem of the rich-poor gaps is more prominent. According to the 2014 report on the development of Chinese people's livelihood released by the China Social Science Research Center of Peking University, the Gini coefficient of the wealth gap of Chinese residents has reached about 0.7 in 2012. Under the government's control measures, the income gap has slightly narrowed, but the wealth gap has not been improved. In mid-to-late October 2019, the Urban Households' assets and liabilities investigation research group of the Survey and Statistics Division of People's Bank of China carried out an investigation on the assets and liabilities of more than 30,000 urban households in 30 provinces (Autonomous regions and Municipalities directly under the central government). The data presented a complete and detailed picture of assets and liabilities of urban residents. The average total assets of urban households stood at 3.179 million yuan, where mainly real assets and housing account for nearly 70% and the distribution of assets is obviously differentiated. The average net worth of urban households was 2,890,000 yuan, which was more differentiated than that of assets. Compared with the United States, China's urban household wealth distribution is relatively balanced (the net assets of the top 1% of households in the United States account for 38.6% of the total net assets, while China's is 17.1%).

In recent years, the pace of deepening the reform of income distribution system has been accelerating. In February 2013, the State Council issued the circular of opinions on deepening the reform of income distribution system, which pointed out that

> To deepen the reform of the income distribution system, we should adhere to the common development and sharing of achievements. We should encourage people to seek prosperity through hard work, support entrepreneurship and innovation, and protect legitimate business operations. While constantly creating social wealth and enhancing comprehensive national strength, we should generally improve people's wealth. We should continue to focus on efficiency and fairness. Both primary distribution and redistribution should give consideration to efficiency and fairness. In primary distribution, we should pay attention to efficiency, create a level playing field for opportunities, and maintain the dominant position of labor income. In redistribution, we should pay more attention to fairness, improve the efficiency of public resource allocation, and narrow the income gap. We should adhere to market regulation and government control. We should give full play to the basic role of the market mechanism in the allocation of factors of production and the formation of prices, better leverage the role of the government in regulating income distribution, and standardize the order of income distribution, increase the income of low-income people, and adjust excessive income. Adhere to the positive and act according to one's ability. We should properly handle the relationship between reform and stable development, focus on solving the contradictions and problems that the people have highlighted, and highlight incremental reform to drive stock adjustments.

The reform of the income distribution system has promoted the change of the income structure of Chinese residents. From the perspective of income sources, residents' income is generally divided into wage income, operating income, property income, and transfer income. Wage income has always been the highest proportion of urban residents' income in China, accounting for about 70%. In the past decade, driven by the reform of income distribution system and the promotion of economic growth, the proportion of operating income and property income in residents' income has been increasing. In addition, the real estate market has been booming, and the channels of family wealth appreciation have been constantly expanding. With the increase in residents' income level, the family wealth level has also been rising rapidly, widening the gap between family wealth on the whole. At the same time, differences in the pace of regional development are also obvious. First-tier Cities[1] and Second-tier City[2] have become the core driving forces for economic development. The strength of traditional industries continues to grow, while the emerging Internet industry and financial services industry are also concentrated in these cities, further widening the wealth gap between regions. The value of real estate, such as house estate, has been rising all the way in the economically developed regions, which is in sharp contrast to the shrinking development trend of Third-tier City[3] and Fourth-tier City.[4] This sharp contrast contributes to the difference in household wealth between regions. There are also obvious differences in the structure and growth trend of household wealth between urban and rural residents. In 2018, the per capita property of urban and rural households was 292,920 yuan and 87,744 yuan, respectively. The per capita property of urban households was 3.34 times that of rural households, and the per capita property of Urban Households grew faster than that of rural households. Most of the houses in rural households were self-built houses, and the speed and price of circulation were significantly lower than that of urban areas.

The reality of economic development shows that the problem of family wealth gap is more complex and difficult to solve than the problem of income gap. Cai Fang, Zhang Che Wei et al. (2016) indicated that the key reason why the income gap in China is hard to narrow is that the redistribution lacks the role of regulating income distribution. Compare with the income gap, which mainly controls the flow process of new wealth, the regulation of wealth structures also involves multiple issues such as the change of stock wealth value and the transfer of intergenerational wealth. The superposition of these problems increases the difficulty of achieving common prosperity.

To resolve the contradiction between the development goal of common prosperity and the current rich-poor gaps, it is necessary to break through the limitation of the current research on income gap. The realization of common prosperity is not a single process of adjusting income, nor can it be achieved by pure economic activities. However, the difficulties in constructing an applicable framework, establishing relevant theories, and improving the system design in the problem of wealth distribution, as Thomas Piketty pointed out in his book "Redistribution of Wealth," is that "the complete analytical theory of wealth inequality has not made much progress." In the first chapter of "Capital in the Twenty-First Century," Piketty decomposed the dimension of wealth distribution; he believed that wealth distribution includes two dimensions: one is the "factor" distribution, and the other is "individual" distribution. Factor dimension is the reward that labor and capital get from the role of production factor in the overall, while individual dimension considers the inequality of labor income and capital income at the individual level. In particular, he stressed that these two dimensions are equally important, and only by analyzing them at the same time can we fully understand the distribution problem. Piketty's viewpoint pointed out the complexity of wealth distribution to some extent, but it does not fully reflect the extreme complexity.

In terms of purely economic research, the process of wealth distribution is basically consistent with Piketty's analysis. Wealth distribution is the result of systematic economic activities. There are not only the distribution of capital and labor factors in the overall dimension, but also the diversification of income sources in the individual dimension, as well as the flow of factors and wealth in the time and space dimension. From a broader perspective, common prosperity is not only to meet the income or wealth needs of the simple residents in consumption, but also to achieve multi-dimensional prosperity of the whole society through the realization of common prosperity. It is not only economic prosperity, but also spiritual prosperity. Only comprehensive prosperity can achieve a high level of civilization. Therefore, for the new research framework, it is necessary to reflect not only the attribute characteristics of local micro fields, but also the internal complex association structure of the society, and then further integrate and reflect the overall distribution structure and the impact on the macro-economy.

We believe that the power paradigm is very applicable to the study of wealth distribution. It can not only explain the micro formation basis of income gap and wealth gap in the resource level, but also study the mechanism of individual relationship on the change of income and wealth structure in the game analysis, and also analyze the wealth effect of economic and social institutional changes. The research logic of "resource, power, economic benefit distribution" proposed in this book can be extended to "resource, power, wealth distribution" in a broader scope, which opens a new research path for the theory of wealth distribution. Moreover, the power analysis of wealth distribution shows that the application of power paradigm in the future is not only limited to the research from the perspective of pure economics, but also the common paradigm of many social science researches, such as economics, politics, sociology, law, and so on.

The way to the common prosperity under the power paradigm

The creation of wealth requires the cooperation of human resources, material resources, technical resources, and organizational resources, so wealth creation must fully mobilize the enthusiasm of economic activities, especially those with productive contributions. Owning more returns is the intrinsic motivation for the subject to participate in economic activities. At this point, the motive of the participant to obtain more benefits will surpass the motive to create wealth. Therefore, some of the participants will obtain more wealth by relying on resource advantages, or even obtain more benefits by non-economic means. Obviously, creating more wealth to achieve wealth may not be able to achieve common prosperity. Social subjects with resource advantages will more actively strive for the channels to occupy wealth, or even open up new channels to occupy wealth, especially beyond economic means. For the non-economic means that affects the realization of common prosperity, we will discuss the following issues in the future research to find the fundamental way to common prosperity.

First, we will find out the impact of social organizations in wealth distribution. In the age of Internet, the number of social organizations and groups goes up exponentially, which are not only registered in the Civil Administration Department, but also set up by the people among neighbors, or in the wechat group on cell phones even they have never met each other before, or the alumni association of college, the vast majority of the establishment of a social organization is not for economic purposes, but they also play a role in the distribution of wealth. These organizations and groups link social subjects more closely together, and push the information transmission in a broad and high speed way. In organizations and groups, people share their successful experience of wealth creation, learn from each other's behaviors of wealth obtaining, and increase the power of wealth accumulation. Compared to the traditional organizational resources, the wealth effect of a social organization is more significant in the information age, and the wealth distribution mechanism by social organization expands from the social capital effect to network connection effect. In the power paradigm, the resources and power structure will change because of the abundance of social organization, and affect the wealth distribution and the wealth gap.

Second, we will focus on the influence of the social system on the distribution of wealth. The integrated development of economic and social integration is the general trend of future development, so it may lead to the results bias that researches ignore the influence of political system and social system in economic analysis. The distribution of wealth is the result of solving the conflict of interest by the power relationship among the social subjects, and the formulation and implementation of the political system and social system is the way for the social subjects to consolidate their interests. For example, under the multi-party competitive system, the ruling party is the social elite represent alternate for political resources advantage of the political system. And the ruling party will engage and reward his supporters for their political interests and economic interests, and the voter also will choose for their personal interests in the electoral system; so we can see that the political system has widely affected the wealth distribution. The market economy is the economic system highly fit with the rule of law society, for the core of the rule of law is highlight the equality in social governance, the market economy promote equality of competition in the market. The society with market economy and under the rules of law is more likely to form toward equality consistent social power structure, and avoid excessive wealth gathered in the distribution of wealth, and improve the effect of the regulation of wealth redistribution.

Third, we will look at the function orientation of the government and the influence of the exercise of power on the distribution of wealth. The economic system presents increasing complexity, which makes it impossible to achieve common prosperity by relying on the internal power of the economic system. Therefore, the government must play a leading role in the process of achieving common prosperity. From the perspective of government functions, the government should, however, take the economic function of mobilizing economic activity and play the neutral role of redistributing wealth. The redistribution bias by the government is necessary and does exist, seemingly contradictory with neutral redistribution responsibility. Actually we emphasize that neutral redistribution is about the government's own interests, should be under the supervision of the social forces and constraints, and must cut the interest relations with local groups. While redistribution bias is to balance the public interest, and the government need to improve the structure defects by effective redistribution. In general, it is necessary to achieve the equality of power among various subjects, including the government, and the symmetry of power and responsibility among the subjects of the same society; otherwise, the goal of common prosperity cannot be achieved.

Notes

1 First-tier Cities refer to the metropolises that play an important role in the national political, economic, and other social activities and have the leading role and the ability to radiate and drive. The first-tier cities in mainland China generally refer to Beijing, Shanghai, Guangzhou, and Shenzhen.
2 Second-tier Cities are generally provincial capitals, strong economic cities in the eastern region, or regional central cities in the economically developed regions in China.
3 Third-tier Cities are generally the economically developed cities in the eastern region, the provincial sub-central cities, regional central cities, or economically strong cities in the central region, and the provincial capital cities in the western region.
4 Four-tier Cities are mostly medium-sized cities with relatively common urban scale, economic and social development level, and traffic construction.

Afterword

This book is presided over by Professor Zhang Yishan; the main participants are (in order of surname strokes): Professor Yu Weisheng, Professor Wang Guangliang, Dr. Wang Fan, Associate Professor Kong Lingzhu, Associate Professor Liu Yuhong, Professor Liu Haiying, Professor Du Yushen, Dr. Du Jiao, Professor Xin Benlu, Dr. Gao Liyuan. In addition, Professor Jin Chengxiao and Professor Dong Zhiqing also participated in most of the discussions.

References

Acemoglu, D. (2003). Why not a political Coase theorem? Social conflict, commitment, and politics. *Journal of Comparative Economics, 31*(4), 620–652.

Acemoglu, D. (2005). Politics and economics in weak and strong states. *Journal of Monetary Economics, 52*(7), 1199–1226.

Acemoglu, D., Cantoni, D., Johnson, S., & Robinson, J. A. (2011). The consequences of radical reform: The French revolution. *American Economic Review, 101*(7), 3286–3307.

Acemoglu, D., Johnson, S., & Robinson, J. A. (2005). Institutions as a fundamental cause of long-run growth. *Handbook of Economic Growth, 1*, 385–472.

Acemoglu, D., & Robinson, J. A. (2000). Political losers as a barrier to economic development. *American Economic Review, 90*(2), 126–130.

Acemoglu, D., & Robinson, J. A. (2001). A theory of political transitions. *American Economic Review, 91*(4), 938–963.

Acemoglu, D., & Robinson, J. A. (2005). *Economic origins of dictatorship and democracy*: Cambridge University Press, New York.

Adams, D. W., & Fitchett, D. A. (1992). *Informal finance in low-income countries*, Westview Press, Boulder, CO.

Aghion, P., Alesina, A., & Trebbi, F. (2004). Endogenous political institutions. *The Quarterly Journal of Economics, 119*(2), 565–611.

Alchian, A. A., & Demsetz, H. (1972). Production, information costs, and economic organization. *The American Economic Review, 62*(5), 777–795.

Allen, F., & Gale, D. (1992). Stock-price manipulation. *The Review of Financial Studies, 5*(3), 503–529.

An, Y. (2007). Game-appreciation pressure's RMB exchange rate policy choice. *Journal of Northeast Normal University: Philosophy and Social Sciences, 1*, 47–51.

Aoki, M. (1984). *The co-operative game theory of the firm*. Oxford University Press, Oxford.

Aoki, M., Greif, A., & Milgrom, P. (2001). *Toward a comparative institutional analysis*. MIT Press, Cambridge.

Aquinas, T. (1997). *The political ideas of St. Thomas Aquinas*. Simon and Schuster, New York.

Atieno, R. (2001). Formal and informal institutions' lending policies and access to credit by small-scale enterprises in Kenya: An empirical assessment. *Nairobi: African Economic Research Consortium, 111*.

Balakrishnan, P., & Eliashberg, J. (1995). An analytical process model of two-party negotiations. *Management Science, 41*(2), 226–243.

Barker, E. (2012). *The political thought of Plato and Aristotle*. Courier Corporation, Massachusetts.

Bebchuk, L. A., Fried, J. M., & Walker, D. I. (2002). *Managerial power and rent extraction in the design of executive compensation*, Managerial power and rent extraction in the design of executive compensation (69)3.

Becker, G. S. (1962). Investment in human capital: A theoretical analysis. *Journal of Political Economy, 70*(5, Part 2), 9–49.

Böhm-Bawerk, E. V. (1890). *Capital and interest a critical history of economical theory*. Macmillan and Company, London.

Boschen, J. F., & Smith, K. (1995). You can pay me now and you can pay me later: The dynamic response of executive compensation to firm performance. *Journal of Business, 68*(4), 577–608.

Bowles, S. (2009). *Microeconomics: Behavior, institutions, and evolution*. Princeton University Press, Princeton, NJ.

Bowles, S., & Gintis, H. (1994). Power in economic theory. *The Elgar companion to radical political economy,(pp. 300–305), Edward Elgar pulishing limited*, UK.

Broz, J. L., & Frieden, J. A. (2001). The political economy of international monetary relations. *Annual Review of Political Science, 4*(1), 317–343.

Buchanan, J. M., & Tullock, G. (1962). *The calculus of consent* (Vol. 3). University of Michigan Press, Ann Arbor.

Caminal, R., & Matutes, C. (1997). Can Competition in the Credit Market be Excessive? *CEPR Discussion Papers, 1725.*

Canzoneri, M. B., & Henderson, D. W. (1991). *Monetary policy in interdependent economies: A game-theoretic approach*. MIT Press, Cambridge and London.

Chen, W. J. (2007). Exchange rate system selection of East Asian economies: Analysis based on game theory perspective. *Special Zone Economy, 5,* 86–87.

Chen, Z. S., Wang, X. Y., & Zhou, Y. B. (2018). Building up a socialist market economy with Chinese characteristics for a new era: The past and future of China's economic structural reform. *Comparative Economic & Social Systems, 4,* 24–41.

Cheng, K. (2006). Informal financial interest rate decision mechanism: An analysis of nash bargaining, basic symmetry of information. *Shanghai Economic Research, 5,* 37–45.

Clower, R. W. (1986). *Money and markets: Essays by Robert W. Clower*. Cambridge University Press, Cambridge.

Coase, R. (1937). The nature of the firm. *Economica, 4*(16), 386–405.

Coase, R. H. (1960). The problem of social cost. In *Classic papers in natural resource economics* (pp. 87–137): Springer, Palgrave Macmillan, London.

Coase, R. H. (1995). The nature of the firm. In *Essential readings in economics* (pp. 37–54): Springer, Palgrave, London.

Coase, R. H. (2012). *The firm, the market, and the law*. University of Chicago Press, Chicago.

Collins, N. R., & Preston, L. E. (1969). Price-cost margins and industry structure. *The Review of Economics Statistics, 51*(3), 271–286.

Commons, J. (1936). Institutional economics. *The American Economic Review, 26*(1), 237–249.

Commons, J. R. (1934). *Institutional economics: Its place in political economy*: Macmillan, New York.

Cui, Z. (2004). Lang Xianping wants China to build a "good" market economy [online] Availabe at http://www.ce.cn/new_hgjj/hgplun/more/200411/10/t20041110_2239783_1.shtml (10/11/2004 10:34)

Cyert, R. M., & March, J. G. (1963). A behavioral theory of the firm. *Englewood Cliffs, NJ, 2*(4), 169–187.

De Long, J. B., Shleifer, A., Summers, L. H., & Waldmann, R. J. (1990). Positive feedback investment strategies and destabilizing rational speculation. *The Journal of Finance, 45*(2), 379–395.

Dietrich, M. (1994). The economics of quasi-integration. *Review of Political Economy, 6*(1), 1–18.

Easton, D. (1965). *A framework for political analysis.* Prentice-Hall, Englewood Cliffs, NJ.

Engdahl, W. (2004). A century of war. *Anglo-American oil politics the new world order,* Pluto Press, UK.

Etzioni, A. (1974). *Political unification: A comparative study of leaders and forces.* Krieger Publishing Company, New York.

Fama, E. F. (1980). Agency problems and the theory of the firm. *Journal of Political Economy, 88*(2), 288–307.

Fang, Z. L. (1997). A trend: Human capital owners have corporate ownership. *Economic Research, 6*(10), 36–40.

Fisher, I. (1930). *Theory of interest: As determined by impatience to spend income and opportunity to invest it.* Augustusm Kelly Publishers, Clifton.

Fors, H. C., & Olsson, O. (2007). Endogenous institutional change after independence. *European Economic Review, 51*(8), 1896–1921.

Frankel, J. (2005). On the renminbi: The choice between adjustment under a fixed exchange rate and adjustment under a flexible rat*e*. Retrieved from National Bureau of Economic Research *working paper* No. 11274.

Friedman, M. (2009). *Capitalism and freedom*: University of Chicago Press, Chicago, IL.

Fudenberg, D., Holmstrom, B., & Milgrom, P. (1990). Short-term contracts and long-term agency relationships. *Journal of Economic Theory, 51*(1), 1–31.

Furubotn, E. G., & Pejovich, S. (1972). Property rights and economic theory: A survey of recent literature. *Journal of Economic Literature, 10*(4), 1137–1162.

Galbraith, J. K. (1983). The anatomy of power. *Challenge, 26*(3), 26–33.

Galbraith, J. K. (1992). Culture of contentment. *New Statesman and Society, 5,* 14–16.

Galbraith, J. K. (2001). *The essential galbraith*: HMH, Boston.

Galbraith, J. K. (2007). *The new industrial state*: Princeton University Press, Princeton, NJ.

Gale, D. (2000). *Strategic foundations of general equilibrium: Dynamic matching and bargaining games*: Cambridge University Press, Cambridge.

Gamson, W. A. (1968). *Power and discontent,* Dorsey Press, USA.

Gao, H. Y. (1994). 私有制，科斯定理和产权明晰化. 当代思潮(5), 10–16.

Gardner, R., & Ostrom, E. (1991). Rules and games. *Public Choice, 70*(2), 121–149.

Ghate, P. (1992). *Informal finance: Some findings from Asia*: Oxford University Press, Hong Kong.

Giavazzi, F., & Pagano, M. (1988). The advantage of tying one's hands: EMS discipline and central bank credibility. *European Economic Review, 32*(5), 1055–1075.

Gibbons, R., & Murphy, K. J. (1990). Relative performance evaluation for chief executive officers. *ILR Review, 43*(3), 30-S–51-S.

Goodhart, C. A. (1998). The two concepts of money: Implications for the analysis of optimal currency areas. *European Journal of Political Economy, 14*(3), 407–432.

Greenwald, B. C., & Stiglitz, J. E. (1986). Externalities in economies with imperfect information and incomplete markets. *The Quarterly Journal of Economics, 101*(2), 229–264.

Greif, A., & Laitin, D. D. (2004). A theory of endogenous institutional change. *American Political Science Review, 98*(4), 633–652.

Grossman, S. J., & Hart, O. D. (1986). The costs and benefits of ownership: A theory of vertical and lateral integration. *Journal of Political Economy, 94*(4), 691–719.

Grossman, S. J., & Stiglitz, J. E. (1980). On the impossibility of informationally efficient markets. *The American Economic Review, 70*(3), 393–408.

Gu, J., & Liu, J. Z. (2004). Information asymmetry and stock price changes. *Economic Research Journal, 2*, 106.

Guo, W. R. (1984). 總體經濟學: 三民书局.

Hart, O., & Moore, J. (1999). Foundations of incomplete contracts. *The Review of Economic Studies, 66*(1), 115–138.

Hay, D. A., Morris, D., & Morris, D. J. (1991). *Industrial economics and organization: Theory and evidence*: Oxford University Press, Oxford.

Hayek, F. A. (1945). The use of knowledge in society. *The American Economic Review, 35*(4), 519–530.

Hayek, F. A. (1984). *The essence of Hayek* (Vol. 301): Hoover Institution Press, Stanford, CA.

Hayek, F. A. (2013). *The constitution of liberty: The definitive edition* (Vol. 17): Routledge, London.

He, F., & Li, Z. Y. (2002). Political and economic analysis of exchange rate changes and exchange rate system reform. *World Economy and Politics, 11*, 26–31.

Hicks, J. R. (1989). A suggestion for simplifying the theory of money. In *General Equilibrium Models of Monetary Economies* (pp. 7–23): Elsevier, Amsterdam.

Hobbes, T. (1998). *Hobbes: On the citizen*: Cambridge University Press, Cambridge.

Hodgson, G. M. (1999). *Evolution and institutions*. Duke University Press, Durham, NC and London.

Jensen, M. C., & Murphy, K. J. (1990). CEO incentives: It's not how much you pay, but how. *Journal of Applied Corporate Finance, 22*(1), 64–76.

Jenson, J. (1987). Changing discourse, changing agendas: Political rights and reproductive policies in France. In Katzenstein and Mueller(Ed.), *The Women's Movements of the United States and Western Europe: Consciousness, Political Opportunity and Public Policy*, Temple University Press, USA.

Jevons, W. S. (1879). *The theory of political economy*: Macmillan, London.

Jiang, M., & Liu, X. (2007). The decision of RMB exchange rate from the game perspective. *China Opening Herald, 3*, 72–75.

Kaldor, N. (1985). *The scourge of monetarism*: Oxford University Press, Oxford and New York.

Keohane, R. O., & Nye Jr, J. S. (1973). Power and interdependence. *Survival, 15*(4), 158–165.

Keynes, J. M. (1937). The general theory of employment. *The Quarterly Journal of Economics, 51*(2), 209–223.

Khwaja, A. I., & Mian, A. (2003). Price manipulation and phantom markets—an in-depth exploration of a stock market. *Working Paper*, University of Chicago, Chicago.

Koskela, E., & Stenbacka, R. (2000). Is there a tradeoff between bank competition and financial fragility? *Journal of Banking Finance, 24*(12), 1853–1873.

Kostiuk, P. F., & Follmann, D. A. (1989). Learning curves, personal characteristics, and job performance. *Journal of Labor Economics, 7*(2), 129–146.

Laffont, J.-J., & Maskin, E. S. (1990). The efficient market hypothesis and insider trading on the stock market. *Journal of Political Economy, 98*(1), 70–93.

Lazear, E. P. (1979). Why is there mandatory retirement? *Journal of Political Economy, 87*(6), 1261–1284.

Li, F. C. (2003). Interest balance and game behavior in the choice of exchange rate system. *International Business Studies, 2*, 32–37.

Li, J. P. (1996). On the state of power analysis in political science research. *Tianjin Social Sciences, 3*, 22–25.

Li, Z. G., & Dong, L., W. (2005). Exchange rate decision in the frame of double-layer game——taking the Sino-US controversy over RMB exchange rate as an example. *Finance Teaching and Research, 6*, 2–6.

Lin, Y. F. (1994). Economic theory on institutional change: Induced change and mandatory change. *Property Rights and Institutional Changes, 12*.

Lu, Z. L. (2009). Distribution of power within the enterprise under the framework of cooperative game. *Economic Research Journal, 12*, 106–118.

Mahan, A. (1897). The Influence of Sea Power Upon History. *The Interest of America in Sea Power, Present*.

Malthus, T. R., Winch, D., & James, P. (1992). *Malthus: 'An Essay on the Principle of Population'*: Cambridge University Press, Cambridge.

Marshall, A. (1961). *Principles of economics: Text* (Vol. 1): Macmillan for the Royal Economic Society, London.

Marshall, A. (2009). *Principles of economics: Unabridged eighth edition*: Cosimo, Inc, New York.

Martin, W. J. (1988). *The information society*: Information Today Incorporated, USA.

Marx, K. (1911). *A contribution to the critique of political economy*: CH Kerr, Chicago.

Marx, K. (2004). *Capital: Volume I*: Penguin, London.

Mas-Colell, A., Whinston, M. D., & Green, J. R. (1995). *Microeconomic theory* (Vol. 1): Oxford University Press, New York.

McCall, J. J. (1970). Economics of information and job search. *The Quarterly Journal of Economics, 84*(1) 113–126.

McDonald, I. M., & Solow, R. M. (1981). Wage bargaining and employment. *The American Economic Review, 71*(5), 896–908.

Ménard, C. (2008). A new institutional approach to organization. In C. Ménard and M. Shirley (eds.), *Handbook of new institutional economics* (pp. 281–318): Springer, Boston and New York.

Menger, C. (1990). *Carl Menger and his legacy in economics* (Vol. 22): Duke University Press, Durham, NC.

Mincer, J. (1974). Schooling, experience, and earnings. Human behavior & social institutions no. 2: National Bureau of Economic Research, New York.

Murphy, K. J. (1985). Corporate performance and managerial remuneration: An empirical analysis. *Journal of Accounting Economics, 7*(1–3), 11–42.

Nash, J. F. (1950). Equilibrium points in n-person games. *Proceedings of the National Academy of Sciences, 36*(1), 48–49.

Nelson, R. R., & Winter, S. G. (1982). The Schumpeterian tradeoff revisited. *The American Economic Review, 72*(1), 114–132.

Nickell, S. J., & Andrews, M. (1983). Unions, real wages and employment in Britain 1951–79. *Oxford Economic Papers, 35*, 183–206.

North, D. C. (1981). *Structure and change in economic history*: Norton, New York and London.

North, D. C. (1990). *Institutions, institutional change, and economic performance.* Cambridge University Press, Cambridge and New York.

Nye Jr, J. (1995). The case for deep engagement. *Foreign Affairs, 74*(4), 90–102.

Nye Jr, J. S. (2004). *Soft power: The means to success in world politics*: Public Affairs, New York.

Ohlin, B. (1935). *Interregional and international trade*: Harvard University Press, Cambridge, MA.

Palermo, G. (2000). Economic power and the firm in new institutional economics: Two conflicting problems. *Journal of Economic Issues, 34*(3), 573–601.

Patinkin, D. (1984). *Anticipations of the general theory? And other essays on Keynes*: University of Chicago Press, Chicago, IL.

Pfeffer, J. (1981). *Power in organizations*: Ballinger Pub Co, Florida.

Pigou, A. C. (1951). Some aspects of welfare economics. *The American Economic Review, 41*(3), 287–302.

Posner, R. A. (1983). *The economics of justice*: Harvard University Press, Cambridge, MA.

Qian, Y. (1994). A theory of shortage in socialist economies based on the "Soft Budget Constraint". *The American Economic Review, 84*, 145–156.

Rajan, R. G., & Zingales, L. (1998). Power in a theory of the firm. *The Quarterly Journal of Economics, 113*(2), 387–432.

Ren, B. (2000). *Catastrophe theory-looking for another China*: BeAuthor Press, Middletown.

Ricardo, D. (1891). *Principles of political economy and taxation*: G. Bell and Sons, London.

Robertson, D. H. (1940). *Essays in monetary theory*: PS King & Son, Ltd, London.

Romer, P., & Lucas, R. (1988). On the mechanics of economics development. *Journal of Monetary Economics, 22*(1), 3–42.

Rubinstein, A. (1982). Perfect equilibrium in a bargaining model. *Econometrica: Journal of the Econometric Society, 50*, 97–109.

Russell, B. (2004). *Power: A new social analysis*: Psychology Press, Taylor & Francis Group, UK.

Samuels, W. J., & Schmid, A. A. (1997). The concept of cost in economics. *The economy as a process of valuation*: Edward Elgar Pub, Cheltenham, 208–298.

Say, J. B. (1816). *Catechism of political economy: Or, familiar conversations on the manner in which wealth is produced, distributed, and consumed in society*: Sherwood, Neely, and Jones, London.

Say, J. B. (1836). *A treatise on political economy: Or the production, distribution, and consumption of wealth*: Grigg & Elliot, Philadelphia.

Schmid, A. A. (2003). Discussion: Social capital as an important lever in economic development policy and private strategy. *American Journal of Agricultural Economics, 85*(3), 716–719.

Schotter, A. (2008). *The economic theory of social institutions.* Cambridge Books, Cambridge University Press, Cambridge.

Schotter, A. B., & Yale, M. (1981). Economic search: An experimental study. *Economic Inquiry, 19*(1), 1–25.

Schultz, T. W. (1961). Investment in human capital. *The American Economic Review, 51*(1), 1–17.

Schumpeter, J. A. (1939). *Business cycles* (Vol. 1): McGraw-Hill, New York.

Schwartz, A. J. (1987). *Financial stability and the federal safety net*: American Enterprise Institute for Public Policy Research, Washington.

Shaffer, G. (1991). Slotting Allowances and Resale Price Maintenance: A Comparison of Facilitating Practices. *The RAND Journal of Economics, 22*(1), 120–135.

Shi, K. (2003). 提高素质——个体投资者心理行为研究, 见: 成思危 (主编). 诊断与治疗: 揭示中国的股票市场. In: 北京: 经济科学出版社.

Shleifer, A., & Vishny, R. W. (1986). Large shareholders and corporate control. *Journal of Political Economy, 94*(3, Part 1), 461–488.

Simon, H. A. (1950). Administrative behavior. *The American Journal of Nursing, 50*(2), 46–47.

Simon, H. A. (1997). *Models of bounded rationality: Empirically grounded economic reason* (Vol. 3): MIT Press, Cambridge.

Simondede. (1977). *New principles of political economy*: Annual Edition of Commercial Press, Hongkong.

Smith, A. (1822). *The theory of moral sentiments* (Vol. 1): J. Richardson, London.

Smith, A. (1950). An inquiry into the nature and causes of the wealth of nations, (1776): Methuen, London.

Solow, R. M. (1957). Technical change and the aggregate production function. *The Review of Economics Statistics, 39*(3) 312–320.

Stigler, G. J. (1961). The economics of information. *Journal of Political Economy, 69*(3), 213–225.

Strange, S. (1995). Political economy and international relations. *International relations theory today*, 154–174, Pennsylvania State University Press, USA.

Sugden, R. (1989). Spontaneous order. *Journal of Economic Perspectives, 3*(4), 85–97.

Sun, G., & Deng, L. Y. (2005). The empirical analysis of purchasing power parity of RMB with parallel data unit root is used to judge the rationality of RMB exchange rate. *Research on Financial Issues, 10*, 36–44.

Sveiby, K. E. (1997). *The new organizational wealth: Managing & measuring knowledge-based assets*: Berrett-Koehler Publishers, San Francisco, CA.

Taylor, J. B. (1995). The monetary transmission mechanism: An empirical framework. *Journal of Economic Perspectives, 9*(4), 11–26.

Tirole, J. (1997). Formal and real authority in organizations. Paper presented at the *The Journal of Political Economy, 105*(1), 1–29.

Veblen, T. (1934). The theory of the leisure class: An economic study of institutions. 1899. The Modern Library, New York.

Walras, L. (1881). *Principe d'une théorie mathématique de l'échange: Correspondance entre: M. Jevons et M. Walras*: Impr. et Lithogr. Chappuis.

Wang, S. Q., & Shi, W. S. (2007). On exchange rate decision mechanism, fluctuation range and policy coordination. *Finance, Trade and Economics, 4*, 52–60.

Wang, W. S., & Wu, S. A. (2004). Review on the development of post-Marshall's price mechanism theory. *Economic Research Journal, 2*, 45–49.

Wang, Y. M., & Li, M. B. (2005). Informal financial market lending rate decision stake: A new framework for analysis. *Financial Research, 7*, 12–23.

Weber, M. (2009). *From Max Weber: Essays in sociology*: Routledge, London.

Wei, W. X. (2004). Dynamic game model and application of exchange rate strategy. *Statistical Research, 4*, 38–41.

Weibull, J. W. (1997). *What have we learned from evolutionary game theory so far?* Retrieved from https://www.econstor.eu/handle/10419/94851

Williamson, O. (1985). *The economic institutions of capitalism: Firms, markets, relational contracting.* The Free Press, New York.

Williamson, O. E. (1975). *Markets and hierarchies*: Free Press, New York, 2630.

Wrong, D. H. (1979). *Power: Its forms. Bases uses*: Harper and Row, New York.

Xiao, X. R., & Tian, C. Z. (2002). Institutional investors and retail investors in the stock market: An analysis of speculative game. *The Journal of World Economy, 5*, 62–68.

Yang, C., M. (2003). 转型经济中的宏观收入分配: 中国劳动社会保障出版社.

Yang, R. L., & Yang, Q. J. (2001). Specificity, exclusiveness and enterprise system. *Economic Research Journal, 3*(6), 3–11.

Yang, X., K. (1998). 经济学原理 (杨小凯).

Young, D. (2000). Firms' market power, endogenous preferences and the focus of competition policy. *Review of Political Economy, 12*(1), 73–87.

Young, H. P. (1998). Individual strategy and social structure: An evolutionary theory of institutions. Princeton University Press, Princeton, NJ. *Henrich: Cultural Transmission the Diffusion of Innovations, 1*(1), 0.8.

Yue, H. (2005). Game theory analysis of international exchange rate system selection. *Journal of East China Normal University: Philosophy and Social Sciences Edition, 37*(6), 105–112.

Zhang, Y. S., & Fang, Y. (2007). Model and policy analysis of dealer trading manipulation in China's stock market. *Management World, 23*(5), 40–48.

Zhang, W. (1996). The contractual nature of the enterprise. In *Enterprise system and market organization*: Beijing People's Press, Beijing.

Zhao, C. M., & Wang, H. M. (2005). Exchange rate game between the intergovernmental power: A study on the RMB exchange rate under the huge trade balance between China and the United States. *International Trade Issues, 1*, 018.

Zhao, D. M. (2005). Research on price discretization in e-commerce market. China Agricultural University, Beijing.

Zhao, T., & Zheng, Z. X. (2002). Information asymmetry and institutional manipulation: Game analysis of chinese stock market institutions and retail investors. *Economic Research Journal, 7*, 41–48.

Index